A HISTORY OF WESTERN PHILOSOPHY OF EDUCATION

VOLUME 5

A History of Western Philosophy of Education
General Editors: Megan Jane Laverty and David T. Hansen

Volume 1
A History of Western Philosophy of Education in Antiquity
Edited by Avi I. Mintz

Volume 2
A History of Western Philosophy of Education in the Middle Ages and Renaissance
Edited by Kevin Gary

Volume 3
A History of Western Philosophy of Education in the Age of Enlightenment
Edited by Tal Gilead

Volume 4
A History of Western Philosophy of Education in the Modern Era
Edited by Andrea R. English

Volume 5
A History of Western Philosophy of Education in the Contemporary Landscape
Edited by Anna Pagès

A HISTORY OF WESTERN PHILOSOPHY OF EDUCATION

IN THE CONTEMPORARY LANDSCAPE

VOLUME 5

Edited by Anna Pagès

BLOOMSBURY ACADEMIC
LONDON · NEW YORK · OXFORD · NEW DELHI · SYDNEY

BLOOMSBURY ACADEMIC
Bloomsbury Publishing Plc
50 Bedford Square, London, WC1B 3DP, UK
1385 Broadway, New York, NY 10018, USA
29 Earlsfort Terrace, Dublin 2, Ireland

BLOOMSBURY, BLOOMSBURY ACADEMIC and the Diana logo are
trademarks of Bloomsbury Publishing Plc

First published in Great Britain 2021

Copyright © Anna Pagès and contributors 2021

The Contributors have asserted their right under the Copyright, Designs
and Patents Act, 1988, to be identified as Author of this work.

For legal purposes the Acknowledgments on pp. xxiv & xxv constitute
an extension of this copyright page.

Cover design by Charlotte James
Cover image © Allan Grant/The LIFE Picture Collection via Getty Images

A catalogue record for this book is available from the British Library.

A catalog record for this book is available from the Library of Congress.

ISBN: HB: 978-1-3500-7457-6
         ePDF: 978-1-3500-7458-3
         eBook: 978-1-3500-7459-0
         Series: 978-1-3500-7466-8

Typeset by Integra Software Services Pvt. Ltd
Printed and bound in Great Britain

To find out more about our authors and books visit www.bloomsbury.com
and sign up for our newsletters.

CONTENTS

FIGURES

SERIES INTRODUCTION

MEGAN JANE LAVERTY AND DAVID T. HANSEN

A History of Western Philosophy of Education is a five-volume series that traces the development of philosophy of education through Western culture and history. It seeks to illuminate the philosophical origins of contemporary educational debates, policies, and practices. Focusing on philosophers who have theorized education and its implementation, the series constitutes a fresh, dynamic, and developing view of educational philosophy. It expands our educational possibilities by reinvigorating philosophy's vibrant critical tradition, connecting old and new perspectives, and identifying the continuity of critique and reconstruction.

AN UNBROKEN CONVERSATION

Education and philosophy of education are not historical constants, either as concepts or as practices. Their meaning and enactments transform across space and time. What education meant to a medieval monk differs from how a twentieth-century child-centered educator conceived it, and both differ from the understanding of an ancient Roman. However, the *questions* that reside at the heart of philosophy of education have a long-standing lineage. These questions can be traced at least as far back as Plato. In Plato's dialogues, ranging from the *Laches* and *Protagoras* to the *Meno* and *Republic*, Socrates asks: "Can you teach a person to be virtuous (i.e. good)?," "Which of us is truly a teacher of the souls of youth?," and "What is the relation between education and a just society?" In these questions, we see the meeting of philosophy and education: a fusion of the spirit of inquiry into fundamental issues of life characteristic of philosophy, with the necessity of education for human continuity, growth, and renewal. Plato thereby helps inaugurate an open-ended conversation that continues through the present day. It is a conversation, to cite Michael Oakeshott's (1989) poetic terms, "in which human beings forever seek to understand themselves" (p. 41). The terms and the idiom of this conversation may change over time, but the questions persist, and in a pressing way.

The value of participating in this historical conversation is that it allows today's students and professors to "disentangle [themselves], for a time, from the urgencies of the here and now" (Oakeshott 1989, p. 41). This practice positions everyone to engage with thinkers from the past as if they were sitting around the table with us today. We revisit their writings in order to learn from them and, in an important sense, with them, for each is an inquirer rather than a peddler of a dogma. To learn from, and with, the past is to have one's definition of and criteria for education challenged and potentially transformed, and in a highly distinctive and invaluable manner. While we do learn much from our contemporaries, we are typically too close to them in space and time to shake loose from their (and our) assumptions of what counts as "learning." Every generation of scholars, teachers, and students faces this "almost insurmountable difficulty," to borrow terms from John Dewey (1985, p. 154), of seeing beyond the end of its own nose. This predicament, too, is part of the long-standing conversation in philosophy of education: it calls for a dedicated effort to participate. The redeeming fact is that the conversation is always already at hand to assist us in facing the problems of a "presentist" myopia. The past can teach precisely because it stands outside current passions and fashions, even while helping us grasp how the latter came into being and why they grip current sensibilities.

None of the above implies the past has a "superior" voice, any more than does the present, a point to which we will return. The long-standing conversation at the juncture of philosophy and education has been a constant process of criticism of the past, but always in the very moment that the past challenges the present to become self-aware and self-critical of that which it most takes for granted. To learn from the past is to overcome its limitations, even while striving to overcome one's own.

Philosophy of education features what can be seen across all domains of philosophy: an erotic aspiration, as Andy German (2017) puts it, to look beyond its own tradition and find a way back to the beginning: to that existential moment, metaphorically speaking, when "the first question" about education was enunciated, so that we might pose it in our own terms in light of our own realities. The perennial yearning in philosophy to overcome its own tradition— even while depending upon it as an indispensable inheritance (like one's native language acquired as a child)—mirrors a deep, typically unspoken desire to grasp the unity behind the "bewildering variety of positions and doctrines" in the field (German 2017, p. 7). "Unity" does not mean unanimity in thought. It is a unity in eros. It represents a longing to find that existential place, named above, that is prior to the emergence, proliferation, and intensification of competing perspectives. "[T]he surest mark of philosophically inclined spirit," contends German, is to be "seized" by this eros (p. 7). The educator aspires to truly think, and to think truly, rather than to mimic others' thought. This desire means they must "find" their thought even as they "found," or ground, their distinctive voice in the conversation (see Cavell 1989). The return "to the beginning" in philosophy, which we will witness across the volumes in this series, constitutes what Iris Murdoch conceives of as "an abiding and not regrettable characteristic of the discipline" (1997, p. 299).

Contributors to this series do not examine ancient and modern philosophies of education in order to "improve" upon or "correct" them. Rather, they approach thinkers across the ages as our nonliving contemporaries, having recognized that they have something meaningful to say to us. Entering this conversation enables "another's thoughts to re-enact themselves in [our] own mind," thereby positioning us to understand ourselves afresh (Oakeshott 1989, p. 68). The educational questions first posed by Socrates and others burst upon each new generation of educators, inviting them to take hold of their educational inheritance and contribute to it in their own singular, irreproducible ways. Although each generation must answer the questions anew, they do not do so *de novo*, for the history of thought is a reservoir of responses waiting to be drawn upon and engaged.

This series invites readers into the history of the most important philosophical questions for education. This history comprises an unbroken, lively, and vivid conversation across time. In looking back over the history of Western philosophy of education, we bear witness to the continuity of the questions, and to the profound commitment our forebears brought to addressing them. We hope the series will help readers sustain this crucial commitment.

A FRESH CANON

Education is at the heart of the human experience. Philosophy of education is important because our values—that is, views on how we *should* live—do not emerge from nowhere. They must be cultivated or supported in individuals by means of education. As the process by which a society renews *and* improves itself, education is far more than social reproduction, and far less than total revolution. It is an elusive middle path constituted by love for the extraordinary endeavor of conceiving, and bringing to life, human possibilities.

From the beginning, canonical philosophers such as Plato, Aristotle, Jean-Jacques Rousseau, and John Dewey have addressed education. They have thought philosophically about education's aims and methods, the nature of learning and thinking, the character of knowledge, and the contributions of curriculum, pedagogy, and schooling to maturation. Philosophers' answers to these questions have defined key periods in the history of philosophy of education from antiquity, to the Renaissance and Enlightenment, and into the present.

Although studying the history of Western philosophy writ large can advance the understanding of philosophical problems in education, this series attends directly to philosophy's contribution to conceptions of education. It offers a fresh canon of educational philosophy rather than an overview of the philosophical canon per se (Mintz 2017). For this reason, readers will find that such prominent Western philosophers as Thomas Hobbes and Benedictus Spinoza, who wrote very little on education or whose work lacks explicit educational ramifications, will not be covered in detail. Instead, the contributors focus on those philosophers and educators who have theorized education and its practices, thereby identifying a dynamic and ever-changing canon of thinkers for philosophy of education. Individual thinkers or clusters of thinkers representing schools of thought—feminism, pragmatism, or phenomenology, for example—will be situated within the context of ongoing influences and intellectual relationships.

A "canon" in philosophy can be understood as a body of continuously consulted, respected texts that have stood the test of time. People turn to them across the generations not as a result of dogmatic adherence or for purposes of propaganda (though every text, once it leaves an author's hands, is subject to countless uses and abuses—consider, among other examples, Friedrich Nietzsche's oeuvre). Nor do people take them in hand because they necessarily subscribe to the thinkers' views. Agreement or disagreement, as such, is not the key issue, though it remains important depending on context. People read canonical works because they continue to provoke fresh thinking across space and time. As already touched on, they spark new lines of questioning and insight. Contemporary scholarship in any field, including in philosophy of education, is radically uncertain about which recent texts will endure. Current popularity does not necessarily predict longevity. At the same time, the canon in philosophy of education is ever-changing precisely because of new contemporary contributions, some of which spotlight hitherto neglected or forgotten writings, including by marginalized and excluded people in societies past and present. While many of these works will not themselves endure, in terms of a continued readership, they generate an ethos that makes it possible for others that will. This process is how a scholarly ethos functions, a dynamic which is equally true of the ethos in the arts. Shakespeare's plays are found on stages everywhere in the world today not because they are pure miracles of genius or because some authority has made it so. They emerged out of traditions of theatre that created an ethos for them to take hold of people's imaginations. Without that ethos, we today would likely have never heard of them. We illustrate this point in the next section with regards to what is often referred to as "progressive education."

THE HISTORICAL ORIGINS OF CONTEMPORARY PHILOSOPHY OF EDUCATION

Roughly speaking, progressive education represents a commitment to fuse values sometimes seen as in tension: genuine student autonomy, alongside a strong, democratic social spirit. The approach pivots around learning by doing. Rather than sitting passively in rows of seats in the classroom while educators "pour" knowledge into them, students should be engaged actively with inquiring, discussing, experimenting, exploring, and more. While the progressive education movement began in the United States with the reception of John Dewey's (1859–1952) philosophy of education, Aristotle (384–322 BCE) was one of its earliest precursors. He argued that individuals develop practical wisdom by engaging practically in wise activities rather than by studying theories of wisdom alone. The early modern thinker Michel de Montaigne (1533–92) deployed this Aristotelian insight to argue that education should aim not at filling students with information but rather at cultivating persons holistically from an intellectual, aesthetic, and ethical point of view. From his perspective, young people develop practical wisdom—qualities of tenacity, flexibility, and sound judgment in the face of difficulty—by interacting with a diverse range of social, cultural, and physical environments. Seventeenth- and eighteenth-century developments were also important. Jean-Jacques Rousseau (1712–78), an avid reader of Montaigne, Plato, and other forebears, highlighted the qualities of integrity, decisiveness, and consistency that would, in his view, liberate the student to act autonomously. Rousseau would have the student learn firsthand, through concrete experience as well as in developmentally appropriate ways, about the unpredictability of countless life events, the necessity of work, the values in friendship, family, and mutually dependent, supportive male–female relations such as marriage, and the responsibilities of citizenship.

Rousseau cautions traditional educators that their intense preoccupation with mature adulthood leads them to neglect the intervening and formative years. He argues that the core dispositions of humane adulthood, compassion and conscience, only develop if the individual fully experiences infancy, childhood, and adolescence. In his educational treatise, *Emile, or on Education* (1763), Rousseau-the-tutor attends closely to what Emile perceives, comprehends, needs, and desires, from birth through adolescence. Like Montaigne, Rousseau anticipates Dewey's thesis that the first step in educating children is to observe them in their most natural state. An important philosopher of education influenced by Rousseau's *Emile* was Johann Heinrich Pestalozzi (1746–1827). Pestalozzi founded several pioneering schools designed to educate the whole child. He promoted caring relationality rather than one-sided, top-down adult authority, as a model for the artful or well-lived life, including in his educational novel *Leonard and Gertrude* (1781). After visiting Pestalozzi's schools, Friedrich

Fröbel (1782–1852) developed his own progressive educational philosophy and practice. He established the first kindergarten (German for "children's garden" or "garden of children") in the world, which stressed the importance of play in the education of the young (and which is now a prominent feature of progressive classrooms).

In summary, while Dewey is the most renowned philosopher of progressive education, *A History of Western Philosophy of Education* clarifies the significance of his thought for contemporary educational theory by providing a rich account of its antecedents and shaping influences. The series identifies the key intellectual and pedagogical movements that inform progressive educational thought from antiquity, to the Renaissance and Enlightenment, and to the ethos created by Dewey and his contemporaries, among them Jane Addams (1860–1935), Elsie Ripley Clapp (1879–1965), William James (1842–1910), George Herbert Mead (1863–1931), Francis Parker (1837–1902), and Ella Flagg Young (1845–1918).

As with so many figures in the history of Western educational philosophy, Dewey's voice resonates with those of other thinkers. For example, there are unspoken resemblances between Dewey's and Paulo Freire's (1921–97) influential philosophy of education. Both argue that teachers, to quote Peter Roberts on Freire, Ira Shor, and bell hooks, "need to have an understanding of what they stand for: what they value and why. At the same time, both thinkers caution that teachers must avoid imposing their truths and their ideals on students. Teaching should, they suggest, foster a love of learning, respect for others, and a sense of community" (Roberts, volume five, p. 123). And as with Dewey, Freire's thought "is shaped by multiple intellectual traditions, including liberalism, Marxism, critical theory, existentialism, phenomenology, radical Catholicism, and postmodernism" (Roberts, volume five, p. 111). As with progressive education, Freire's critical pedagogy did not spring *de novo* on the scene, as our contributors to this series make plain.

The continuity found in the history of educational philosophy is also present in educational practice, albeit with constant reconstruction and reframing. For example, as long as humans have inhabited the earth, young people have gathered to listen and to learn from their elders. The ancient Athenians formalized this indispensable intergenerational encounter into what they called *paideia*. The term denotes a systematic pedagogical course of study and activity, involving the education of both mind and body, intended to prepare good citizens. This conception, as Oakeshott (1989) argues, was "passed on (with appropriate changes) from the schools of the Roman Empire to the cathedral, the collegiate, guild and grammar schools of medieval Christendom ... [It] informed the schools of renaissance Europe and ... survived in our own grammar and public schools and their equivalents in continental Europe" (p. 71). Throughout this history, children and adolescents, concerned parents, professional teachers, and in some cases school administrators and representatives of the church or state, have all had a vital presence. Their debates about a developmentally appropriate curriculum, what is in the best interests of children, the requisite training and expertise of teachers, and the role of national interests served to motivate, direct, energize, and in some cases thwart educational reform.

As emphasized, philosophers of education today do not scrutinize the history of educational thought for merely antiquarian purposes. On the contrary, they debate continuously their respective interpretations of past thought precisely because of its critical pertinence for forming sound theory and associated practices in our time. In the same breath, they engage one another in spirited dialogue about education's foundational concepts such as teaching, learning, and curriculum. Understanding and sustaining such debates is critical to the ongoing vitality of the field. As the philosopher W.B. Gallie (1968) argued, reasoned disagreements regarding essentially contested concepts underscore the unity of a field—a unity not of thought but based on a shared spirit of inquiry—and further its optimum development. Philosophers of education know that how they understand educational practice and the constituent concepts of education will be contested by others who perceive them differently, though not so differently that they cannot appreciate the criteria implicit in each other's understandings. In short, the more philosophers of education appreciate the merits of rival interpretations, the more they contribute to the quality and inclusivity of scholarly debate within the field.

A DYNAMIC AND CRITICAL TRADITION

What are "ideas"? Where do they come from? And what are "thinking," "inquiry," "study," and "criticism"? How do they arise? One way to respond to such questions is to ask: To what extent is philosophy, and by extension philosophy of education, a reflection of the particular culture in which it takes place? Is it largely an expression of the taken-for-granted assumptions and presuppositions of the surrounding culture, as might be said of the latter's other practices pertaining to family life, health, and politics? Or does philosophy generate a different relation with culture, not one of simply swimming in it but of stepping outside the stream in a spirit of criticism and open-ended inquiry? We see truth on all sides of the equation. A heartening development in the long conversation touched on here has been how, in recent decades, it has been steadily recognizing how philosophy itself, like its surrounding milieu, has been at times exclusionary and discriminatory, if not in intent then in consequence. Philosophers and schools of thought have not always acknowledged, much less responded to, realities of sexism, racism, adultism, speciesism, and other "isms" emergent in culture over the millennia.

We are moved by being participants in the intellectual-political-academic sea changes of our time, which have opened scholarship up to an expanding range of hitherto marginalized or uninvited voices, an array of whom will be heard across the volumes in this series. We picture this turn continuing, and suggest it promises an ever-widening, ever-deepening cosmopolitan ethos in the academy, in general, and in philosophy of education, in particular.

At the same time, with regards to the question about the origins of ideas, of thinking, of inquiry, and the like, it is well to remind ourselves that our thoughts can have reasons behind them, not causes, whether the latter be cast as cultural or genetic (Oakeshott 1989, p. 20). This truth is both epistemic and ethical. As Richard Eldridge (1997) poetically writes: "[M]y remembrance of my humanity and its expression or repudiation, is not something that happens in me; it is not the effect of mental or physical or social substance acting according to their fixed and given natures. It is something that I, animated through my life with others, do" (p. 290). The philosophers and intellectual movements featured in this series, and which have given the long conversation its texture and open-ended trajectory, are not reducible to expressions of the cultural assumptions prevalent in their respective eras. Quite on the contrary. In many cases, ranging from Plato, to Montaigne, to Karl Marx, to Dewey, and to Hannah Arendt, they have been among the most critical thinkers the world in its totality has ever seen: critical of society, critical of prejudice and moral blindness, critical of themselves. To spotlight one specific example among others, in Immanuel Kant's essay *Perpetual Peace*—a document that deeply informs the intellectual background to many peacemaking projects, including the creation of the United Nations—the author eclipsed his own prejudices in arguing against European imperialism and colonial exploitation. It bears adding that many thinkers in the long conversation have not even been "Western," at least in a narrow intellectual sense of the term. In many cases, ranging again from the likes of Plato through Ralph Waldo Emerson, they have been mindful of ideas from the world over, and have embraced this influence.

The central point in these remarks is that the history of Western philosophy, and specifically of philosophy of education, is not marked by a preset, linear progression, any more than it is marked by a single cultural, social, or political voice. People rediscover and reconstruct philosophy of education in each new encounter with the tradition, with each new retelling of how previous thought and present concerns intermingle. This five-volume series comes at a time when the horizons of Western philosophy of education are expanding to incorporate the insights of post-anthropocentric, postcolonial, and indigenous and Eastern philosophies. A vital starting point of these new and inspiring theoretical developments is to acknowledge misunderstandings and blind spots, across space and time, and then attempt to correct them. And yet, if we fail to examine closely the intellectual movements that have shaped these misunderstandings *and* fueled their transcendence, we risk narrowing our thinking, constraining our possibilities, and reducing our potential for improvement (Carr 2004; Mintz 2017; Ruitenberg 2010). Leading scholars of educational philosophy have demonstrated the significance of the history of philosophical debate for critically reviewing extant research fields and developing emergent ones.

Ultimately, this five-volume endeavor seeks to be a prize resource for students and scholars in education who perceive that the critical spirit of Western philosophy, including philosophy of education, remains a truly inspirational tradition. Our interest is in keeping the philosophical tradition vibrant so that it can continue to support the infusion of new voices, critiques, and reconstructions. This posture differs wholeheartedly from traditionalism. As a living tradition, Western philosophy of education has the "capacity to develop while still maintaining its identity and continuity" (Pelikan 1984, p. 58). It constitutes a dynamic, ever-changing constellation of pressing questions about teaching, learning, assessment, and more—including questions about how it has identified and posed questions in the past (Hansen 2001a, b). In contrast, intellectual traditionalism constitutes a reactionary, heels-dug-in attempt to resist any challenge to "the way things are."

PHILOSOPHY'S TWO TRADITIONS

We have spoken of "tradition," but philosophy can be viewed as a dynamic intertwining of two long-standing traditions that reach back to such pioneering figures as Socrates and Confucius. The first tradition is theoretical and conceptual. It distinguishes education from socialization, parenting from schooling, and civics from indoctrination. The second tradition is philosophy conceived as an art of living. It not only embodies the desire to be wise but strives to incorporate philosophy within such a life. In this light, the art of living has four interrelated components: a moral component (living ethically); a social and political component (commitments to inquiry and communication); a psychological or spiritual component (enjoying peace of mind and curbing egoistic passions); and an intellectual component (thinking carefully and critically about one's value-oriented vision of the world and one's place within it). The pedagogical methods or "spiritual exercises" intended to help people achieve such a life include intellectual training, contemplative practices, and somaesthetic activities (Gregory and Laverty 2010; Hansen 2011).

Living ethically involves engaging conceptions of human values as we seek to cultivate an awareness of how our own experiences are variously marked by compassion, selfishness, honesty, cruelty, and fairness. Ethical inquiry strengthens our capacities to think and feel carefully, to consider sound alternatives, and to self-correct problematic habits of belief and behavior. Moreover, arriving at the most reasonable judgment of an issue requires the free and open exchange of ideas. It calls upon the moral imagination as well as the virtues of intellectual humility and courage. The social and political component of the art of living requires individuals to be alive to the myriad ways that power operates in experience (racism, sexism, class oppression, etc.) and to forge and sustain practices of just interaction. The psychological or spiritual component involves working on the self to curb reactivity and recognizing the self's relation to sources of deeper meaning that inspire awe and reverence, such as nature, cultural or religious traditions, and works of art. The intellectual component of the art of living has been a central focus because it drives the criticism of its very constituents, and such criticism is itself part of the tradition.

Philosophy of education brings these two long-standing philosophical traditions—philosophy as the theorization of education and philosophy as a formative practice—into dialogue. Historical and contemporary philosophers who have theorized education in quite different ways nonetheless respect the Socratic imperative for wisdom-oriented education. In this spirit, contributors to the series examine the extent to which society and schools enhance or undermine personal and social transformation. They seek to revivify the two traditions today by refining them and demonstrating their relevance to practices of teaching, teacher education, curriculum development, and policy-making.

THEMES ACROSS THE VOLUMES AND CHAPTERS

Philosophers of education across space and time do not share a consensus as to the aims, nature, and means of education. Nonetheless, we judge it valuable to identify characteristics that, taken together, distinguish philosophy of education from other fields of philosophical endeavor. In view of the divergence of thought among philosophers and intellectual movements, the characteristics should be understood as "family resemblances"—to recall a well-known term coined by the philosopher Ludwig Wittgenstein (1889–1951)—rather than as airtight ideational compartments. These characteristics comprise the themes and key questions that are addressed across all five volumes.

Philosophical anthropology: What does it mean to be human? How are we to understand the relationship between the mind and body? Who should be educated? Is human maturation developmental or cyclical? What happens to our younger (past) selves? Is the child animal-like? Is childhood a form of life in its own right? Is philosophy native to children? What is the significance of our natality and mortality for education?

Ethics: What does it mean for humans to live well or, as the issue is often expressed, to flourish? How does education contribute to living well or to flourishing? What forms of teaching and curriculum might ensure for all an artful, meaningful life? What are the virtues of teaching and learning? How should teachers be expected to conduct themselves in and beyond the school? What ethical dilemmas are unique to schools and school leadership?

Social and political philosophy: What is justice and how should we teach it?

How do we educate for a more equitable and just society when the educators and educational institutions themselves belong to the very society that they seek to reform? Is the aim of citizenship education knowledge of government, nationalistic patriotism, or a commitment to the common good? How can we ensure an equitable distribution of educational opportunity? Should education be monitored by national standards and tests? What authority should the state have over education? What authority should teachers have over education? What are the rights of children and parents?

Epistemology: What constitutes an educational "experience"? What is knowledge?

Where does knowledge come from? Is knowledge innate or does it come from sense impressions of the external word? Is it found, discovered, or made? If it is constructed, is that construction individual or social? Should teaching strategies focus on drawing out what the learner already knows or pouring in what the learner does not know? How does the structure of knowledge relate to the structure and sequence of learning? How does knowledge impact individual and social formation? How might education teach us to distinguish between knowledge and wisdom? What is the nature of reason? Is reason procedural/ instrumental (i.e., distinct from the passions), or does it combine thinking with intuitive valuing capacities that are oriented to the real and the good?

Aesthetics: What are the felt qualities of experience and how can we learn to be mindful of the qualitative dimension of our lives? What is the role of beauty in human experience and education? How might education influence our fundamental sensibilities toward the world? How could education enhance our ability to be sensitive, responsive, aware, and concerned? How might individuals tell their life stories? What are the aesthetic qualities that make the good stories?

Pedagogy, schooling, and education: What is the ultimate aim of education? Is the aim of education to promote social order and assimilation or individual freedom? What is the role of institutions like school for generating such experiences? Should schooling focus on developing students' marketable skills or on their cultural and political awareness? What instructional methods are most appropriate, and how do we warrant them from an epistemic and ethical point of view? How shall we conceive teacher education? Should we think of teachers as state functionaries and/or as "elders" with a profound responsibility for educating children and youth?

Philosophy of Psychology and the Social Sciences: How should education be assessed? What does it mean to "measure" a human being's education? What are the strengths and limitations of social scientific research into education? What is the distinctive contribution of the arts and humanities? What are the degrees of freedom individuals, communities, and societies have to form and reform themselves?

CONCLUSION: AN OVERVIEW OF THE SERIES

A History of Western Philosophy of Education consists of five volumes, each devoted to an examination of canonical philosophers of education and schools of thought in a distinct period.

1. Antiquity (Ancient Greece to Early Christian) (500 BCE–500 CE)
2. The Medieval and Renaissance Period (500–1600)
3. The Age of Enlightenment (1600–1850)
4. The Modern Era (1850–1914)
5. The Contemporary Landscape (1914–present)

Each volume covers a recognizable period in the Western tradition because we want to contextualize emergent and abiding philosophical and educational ideas within a relevant historical and cultural context. To this end, we conclude Volume 1 and commence Volume 2 at 500 CE, which demarcates the fall of the Roman Empire and the beginning of the Middle Ages. In these two volumes, we see the emergence of the Sophists, Cynics, and Stoics, and their later eclipse by the rise of the Judeo-Christian tradition that would prove so definitive of later thought. We end Volume 2 and begin Volume 3 with the start of the seventeenth century given its inextricable association with the Enlightenment and its emergent embrace of science, human rights, and liberal democracy. We conclude Volume 4 and commence Volume 5 with 1914, the year that saw the beginning of the First World War. This conflagration, unprecedented in its destruction and magnitude, would generate the conditions for the Second World War and the Holocaust, as well as spur the creation of the United Nations and innumerable other movements to foster peace, social justice, improved health and nutrition, and expanded educational provision the world over.

While the dates that begin and end each volume serve to pivot us from one historical period to another—with each of these characterized by defining social, cultural, political, and economic events, unique and influential thinkers, and diverse schools of thought—they do not represent fixed, impermeable boundaries. The philosophical survey and analysis of education presented by this series transcends easy capture by historical dates. The discussion is wide-ranging and ever-dynamic, moving back and forth into the past and the future. The dates should be seen as porous membranes that allow for the easy flow of ideas across the different historical periods. Readers will see that the authors make connections between thinkers and lines of thought and practice from different eras, all of which shows the play of tradition across geographical and historical markers. While the volume dates are valuable to note, our focus in the series is on the thematic conversations that are woven throughout the history of Western philosophy of education.

Chapters in the series are intended to be useful both in a retrospective sense, helping readers grasp the importance of previous thinkers and movements, and in a prospective sense, pointing out areas of inquiry for scholars and students to pursue. Part of what makes this retrospective and prospective approach possible is that many of the contributing authors work to correct stereotypical readings of seminal thinkers in the tradition. They work hard to explain why it behooves us to resist and move beyond canned views about the past.

Readers will not find everything there is to know about Western philosophy of education in this series. While comprehensive in scope, the series does not attempt to be encyclopedic or exhaustive. Each volume comprises up to ten chapters and a wide-ranging introduction penned by the volume editor. With few exceptions, chapters were researched and written by professional philosophers of education. These philosophers of education were invited to draw upon, but not to repeat or rely on, their preexisting scholarly oeuvre. They were asked to reengage with a philosopher of education or school of educational philosophy that they knew well, in the spirit of contextualizing that thinker or school of thought in the broader sweep of educational history. Many took it as an occasion to ask new questions and read more broadly than they would have otherwise done. Some authors familiar with a given philosopher's educational corpus chose to read other texts, including memoirs, plays, novels, and letters. Others familiar with the oeuvre of a particular philosopher of education chose to read texts by the individual's contemporaries and critics. Still others familiar with one intellectual tradition choose to articulate it with another. Along the way, the contributors engaged in their own liberal learning as authors of the chapters—an experience not that dissimilar from our own, as general editors and readers of the chapters. We hope that future readers of the series will have a comparable experience. To study philosophy of education is to participate directly in one's own ongoing education.

SELECT BIBLIOGRAPHY

Bailey, Richard, Robin Barrow, David Carr, and Christine McCarthy (eds.) (2010), *The Sage Handbook of Philosophy of Education*, Los Angeles: Sage.

Biesta, Gert (2014), "Is Philosophy of Education a Historical Mistake? Connecting Philosophy and Education Differently," *Theory and Research in Education*, 12 (1): 65–76.

Carr, Wilfred (2004), "Philosophy and Education," *Journal of Philosophy of Education*, 38 (1): 55–73.

Cavell, Stanley (1989), "Finding As Founding," in Stanley Cavell, *This New Yet Unapproachable America: Lectures after Emerson after Wittgenstein*, 77–118, Albuquerque, NM: Living Batch Press.

Chambliss, Joseph James (1968), *The Origins of American Philosophy of Education: Its Development As a Distinct Discipline*, The Hague: Martinus Nijhoff.

Coetzee, J.M. and Arabella Kurtz (2015), *The Good Story: Exchanges on Truth, Fiction and Psychotherapy*, London: Penguin.

Curren, Randall R. (ed.) (2005), *A Companion to the Philosophy of Education*, Oxford: Wiley-Blackwell.

Curren, Randall R. (2018), "Education, History of Philosophy of," *Routledge Encyclopedia of Philosophy*, Taylor and Francis. https://doi.org/10.4324/9780415249126-N014-2.

Education," in John Dewey, *The Middle Works, 1899–1924*, Vol. 9: *Democracy and Education 1916*, ed. J.A. Boydston, Carbondale: Southern Illinois University Press.

Eby, F. and C.F. Arrowood (1940), *The History and Philosophy of Education: Ancient and Medieval*, Saddle River, NJ: Prentice.

Eldridge, Richard (1997), *Leading a Human Life: Wittgenstein, Intentionality, and Romanticism*, Chicago: University of Chicago Press.

Gallie, W.B. (1968), *Philosophy and the Historical Understanding*, New York: Schocken Books.

German, Andy (2017), "Philosophy and Its History: Six Pedagogical Reflections," *APA Newsletter on Teaching Philosophy*, 17 (1): 1–8.

Gregory, Maughn Rollins and Megan Jane Laverty (2010), "Philosophy, Education, and the Care of the Self," in "Philosophy, Education and the Care of the Self," special issue of *Thinking: The Journal of Philosophy for Children*, 19 (4): 2–9.

Hansen, David T. (2001a), "Teaching and the Sense of Tradition," in David T. Hansen, *Exploring the Moral Heart of Teaching: Toward a Teacher's Creed*, 114–36, New York: Teachers College Press.

Hansen, David T. (2001b), "Cultivating a Sense of Tradition in Teaching," in David T. Hansen, *Exploring the Moral Heart of Teaching: Toward a Teacher's Creed*, 137–56, New York: Teachers College Press.

Hansen, David T. (2011), *The Teacher and the World: A Study of Cosmopolitanism As Education*, London: Routledge.

Hayden, Matthew (2012), "What Do Philosophers of Education Do? An Empirical Study of Philosophy of Education Journals," *Studies in Philosophy and Education*, 31 (1): 1–27.

Higgins, Chris (2011), *The Good Life of Teaching: An Ethics of Professional Practice*, London: Wiley-Blackwell.

Horlacher, Rebekka (2004), "'Bildung': A Construction of History of Philosophy of Education," *Studies in Philosophy and Education*, 23 (5–6): 409–26.

Kaminsky, James S. (1988), "The First 600 Months of Philosophy of Education—1935–1985: A Deconstructionist History," *Educational Philosophy and Theory*, 18 (2): 42–9.

Meyer, A.D. (1965), *An Educational History of the Western World*, New York: McGraw-Hill.

Mintz, Avi (2017), "The Use and Abuse of the History of Educational Philosophy," in Natasha Levinson (ed.), *Philosophy of Education Society Yearbook 2016*, 406–13, Urbana, IL: Philosophy of Education Society.

Muir, James R. (1998), "The History of Educational Ideas and the Credibility of Philosophy of Education," *Educational Philosophy and Theory*, 30 (1): 7–26.

Murdoch, Iris (1997), "The Idea of Perfection," in Peter Conradi (ed.), *Existentialists and Mystics: Writings on Philosophy and Literature*, 299–336, London: Penguin.

Neiman, Susan (2014), *Why Grow Up? Subversive Thoughts for an Infantile Age*, New York: Farrar, Straus & Giroux.

Oakeshott, Michael (1989), *The Voice of Liberal Learning*, Indianapolis, IN: Liberty Fund.

Pelikan, Jaroslav (1984), *The Vindication of Tradition*, New Haven, CT: Yale University Press.

Roberts, Peter (2021), "A Philosophy of Hope: Paulo Freire and Critical Pedagogy," in Anna Pagès (ed.) *A History of Western Philosophy of Education in the Contemporary Landscape*, 107–28, London: Bloomsbury Publishing.

Rorty, Amélie Oksenberg (ed.) (1998), *Philosophers on Education: New Historical Perspectives*, London: Routledge.

Ruitenberg, Claudia (2010), *What Do Philosophers of Education Do? And How Do They Do It?*, Malden, MA: Wiley-Blackwell.

Siegel, Harvey (ed.) (2009), *The Oxford Handbook of Philosophy of Education*, Oxford: Oxford University Press.

Soltis, Jonas F. (ed.) (1981), *Philosophy of Education since the Mid-Century*, New York: Teachers College Press.

Standish, Paul (2007), "Rival Conceptions of Philosophy of Education," *Ethics and Education*, 2 (2): 159–71.

Titone, Connie (2007), "Pulling Back the Curtain: Relearning the History of Philosophy of Education," *Educational Studies*, 41 (2): 128–47.

GENERAL EDITORS'
ACKNOWLEDGMENTS

The General Editors wish to thank the individuals who worked so tirelessly and graciously on this series. We owe a significant debt to our dedicated and tenacious volume editors: Andrea English, Kevin Gary, Tal Gilead, Avi Mintz, and Anna Pagès. They undertook a Herculean effort without which this series would not have been possible. We thank the chapter authors in each volume for their scholarly commitment and their responsiveness to our editorial suggestions. We appreciate the artful editorial assistance of three doctoral students in our Program in Philosophy and Education at Teachers College: Buddy North, Kirsten Welch, and Ting Zhao. Our editor at Bloomsbury Publishing, Mark Richardson, and his always upbeat assistant, Kim Bown, provided the perfect slipstream for our many-sided endeavor. Before Kim Bown, Maria Giovanna Brauzzi offered patient guidance as we shifted to the Bloomsbury Content Management System. We also want to thank the many colleagues who provided support and guidance along the way. Family and friends were always there to lighten our spirits at the end of a long day. For us, the series evokes the many years we have spent together with students in our program reading and discussing the great texts in our field, moving toward our deepest inquiries, and participating in one of humanity's most compelling conversations.

VOLUME EDITORS'
ACKNOWLEDGMENTS

I am extremely thankful for the resolute and generous support of Megan Jane Laverty and David T. Hansen, without whom I would have not had the opportunity to engage in the thought-provoking project that is this volume. They were always available to share ideas and encouragement, always ready with advice on the important small things to consider while the volume was taking shape. They have also been the kindest and friendliest of companions on this journey. I also want to give my very special thanks to the authors in the volume: Chris Higgins, Lovisa Bergdhal and Elisabet Langmann, Christopher Martin, Peter Roberts, Robert H. Haworth, Maughn Rollins Gregory, Agata Bielik-Robson, Troy Richardson, and René V. Arcilla. They have succeeded in giving life to the volume, translating the making of contemporary philosophy of education into an innovative and interesting language and style, across many of the relevant and urgent questions the discipline faces today. From the very beginning, they have put their intellectual creativity at the service of a common understanding about what it means to write the history of contemporary philosophy of education. I also want to thank Maria G. Brauzzi from Bloomsbury for her patient guidance at the beginning of the project, and William A. Bromberg, my English tutor. I am very grateful to the Faculty of Education-Blanquerna (Ramon Llull University) for granting me a sabbatical leave that helped me to develop the project in the first semester of 2019–20.

TIMELINE

1859–1909	Francisco Ferrer, anarchist thinker and educator, founder of the Modern School, *Escuela Moderna,* in Barcelona, Spain (1901), which eventually spread internationally
1866–1912	Voltairine de Cleyre, anarchist and feminist writer and speaker
1869–1940	Emma Goldman, anarchist activist and writer; founded the anarchist journal *Mother Earth* in 1906
1883–1973	A.S. Neill, educational innovator; founded the Summerhill School in 1921; published *Summerhill: A Radical Approach to Child Rearing* (1960), later revised as *Summerhill School: A New View of Childhood* (1993)
1889–1976	Martin Heidegger, philosopher; published *Being and Time* (1927), *What is Called Thinking* (1954), and *Discourse on Thinking* (1959)
1891–1937	Antonio Gramsci, Marxist politician, thinker, and educator; wrote the *Prison Notebooks* in prison between 1929 and 1935, which were published in the 1950s and translated into English in the 1970s
1895–1975	Mikhail Bakhtin, philosopher and literacy theorist; published *Problems of Dostoevsky's Creative Art* (1929), later revised as *Problems of Dostoevsky's Poetics* (1963), and *Rabelais and His World* (1965)
1899–1977	Robert Maynard Hutchins, scholar and innovator in higher education; became President of the University of Chicago in

1929; published *The Higher Learning in America* (1936) and
Education for Freedom (1943)

1900–1976   Gilbert Ryle, philosopher; published *The Concept of Mind*
(1949)

1900–2002   Hans-Georg Gadamer, philosopher; published *Truth and
Method* (1960), *Philosophical Hermeneutics* (1976), and
Dialogue and Dialectic: Eight Hermeneutical Studies on Plato
(1980)

1901–1990   Michael Joseph Oakeshott, philosopher, political theorist,
and educator; published *On Human Conduct* (1975) and *The
Voice of Liberal Learning* (1989)

1902–2001   Mortimer J. Adler, educator; he and Robert Maynard
Hutchings created the Great Books Foundation in 1947;
published *How to Read a Book: The Art of Getting a Liberal
Education* (1940) and *The Paideia Proposal: An Educational
Manifesto* (1982)

1905–1990   Myles Horton, social activist and educator; founded the
Highlander Folk School with Don West and James A.
Dombrowski in 1932

1906–1975   Hannah Arendt, philosopher and political theorist; published
The Human Condition (1958), *Men in Dark Times* (1968),
and "The Crisis in Education" (1968)

1908–1986   Simone de Beauvoir, philosopher, novelist, and feminist;
published *The Second Sex* (1949)

1910   The Francisco Ferrer Association was formed in New York
City by American anarchists including Emma Goldman,
Alexander Berkman, Leonard Abbott, and Harry Kelly

1911–1972   Paul Goodman, writer, anarchist thinker, and educator;
published *The Present Moment in Education* (1969) and
New Reformation: Notes of a Neolithic Conservative
(1970)

1913–2008   Aimé Césaire, poet, writer, and de-colonialist activist; author
of *Discourse on Colonialism* (1950/1955) and numerous
works of poetry and theatre; he and Léopold Sédar Senghor
led the literary movement, *Négritude*, in Paris in the 1930s

1914–1918   First World War

1917–2014   Maxine Greene, philosopher, feminist, and social activist;
served as Philosopher-in-Residence of the Lincoln Center
Institute for the Arts in Education from 1976 to 2012;

	published *Teacher as Stranger: Educational Philosophy for the Modern Age* (1973) and *The Dialectic of Freedom* (1988)
1919–2011	Richard Stanley (R.S.) Peters, philosopher and educator; published *Education as Initiation* (1963), *Ethics and Education* (1966), and *The Logic of Education* (1970) with Paul Heywood Hirst
1920s	The Harlem Renaissance (then known as the "New Negro Movement") unfolded in Harlem, New York
1921–1997	Paulo Freire, philosopher, activist, and educator; first used his pedagogical methods to teach farmworkers and other laborers in the early 1960s; imprisoned in 1964 and then exiled from Brazil between 1964 and 1980; published *Pedagogy of the Oppressed* (1970) and *Education, the Practice of Freedom* (1976)
1923–2010	Matthew Lipman, educator; published *Harry Stottlemeier's Discovery* (1971); founded the Institute for the Advancement of Philosophy for Children (IAPC) at Montclair State College (now Montclair State University) in 1974
1923–2014	Israel Scheffler, philosopher and educational philosopher; published *Conditions of Knowledge: An Introduction to Epistemology and Education* (1965), *Reason and Teaching* (1973), *The Language of Education* (1983), and *On Human Potential: An Essay in the Philosophy of Education* (1985)
1924–2010	Colin Ward, anarchist thinker; published *Anarchy in Action* (1973), *Streetwork: The Exploding School* (1973) with Anthony Fyson, and *The Child in the City* (1978)
1925–1961	Frantz Fanon, psychiatrist, scholar, and revolutionist in de-colonization; published *Black Skin, White Masks* (1952), *A Dying Colonialism* (1959), and *The Wretched of the Earth* (1961)
1926–2002	Ivan Illich, philosopher, theologian, scholar in history, sociology, and education; founded the Centro de Investigaciones Culturales (later Centro Intercultural de Documentación, or CIDOC) in Cuernavaca, Mexico (1961); published *Deschooling Society* (1971) and *Tools for Conviviality* (1973)
1926–1984	Michel Foucault, philosopher, historian, and social theorist; became the head of the Philosophy Department at the newly

founded University of Paris VIII in 1968; published *The Order of Things: An Archaeology of the Human Sciences* (1966), *The Archaeology of Knowledge* (1969), *Discipline and Punish: The Birth of the Prison* (1975), and *The Hermeneutics of the Subject* (1982)

1927–   Paul Heywood Hirst, philosopher and educator; published *The Logic of Education* (1970), *Liberal Education and the Nature of Knowledge* (1973), and *Knowledge and the Curriculum* (1974)

1928–   E.D. Hirsch, literary critic and educator; founded The Core Knowledge Foundation in 1986; published *Validity in Interpretation* (1967), *Cultural Literacy: What Every American Needs to Know* (1987), and *The Schools We Need: And Why We Don't Have Them* (1996)

1929–   Nel Noddings, philosopher, educator, and feminist; published *Caring: A Feminine Approach to Ethics and Moral Education* (1984) and *The Challenge to Care in Schools: An Alternative Approach to Education* (1992)

1929–2011 Gareth Matthews, philosopher, specialized in philosophy for children; published *Philosophy and the Young Child* (1980) and *Dialogues with Children* (1984)

1929–   Jane Roland Martin, philosopher, educator, and feminist; published *Reclaiming a Conversation: The Ideal of the Educated Woman* (1985), *The Schoolhome: Rethinking Schools for Changing Families*. Cambridge (1992), and *Cultural Miseducation: In Search of a Democratic Solution* (2002)

1929   Great Depression, which spread worldwide in the 1930s

1930–2004 Jacques Derrida, philosopher; published *Voice and Phenomenon: Introduction to the Problem of the Sign in Husserl's Phenomenology* (1967), *Of Grammatology* (1967), *Writing and Difference* (1967), and *Specters of Marx* (1994)

1930–1992 Allan Bloom, philosopher and translator; published *The Closing of the American Mind: How Higher Education Has Failed Democracy and Impoverished the Souls of Today's Students* (1987); translated Plato's *Republic* (1968) and Rousseau's *Emile, or On Education* (1979)

1939–1945 Second World War

1940–	Jacques Rancière, philosopher; published *The Ignorant Schoolmaster: Five Lessons in Intellectual Emancipation* (1987) and *Hatred of Democracy* (2007)
1942–	Giorgio Agamben, philosopher and political theorist; published *Homo Sacer: Sovereign Power and Bare Life* (1995), *Remnants of Auschwitz: The Witness and the Archive* (1998), and *The Highest Poverty* (2011)
1942–2010	Ann Margaret Sharp, educator, specialized in philosophy for children
1945–	Ira Shor, educator; published *Critical Teaching and Everyday Life* (1980)
1946	Beginning of the "Cold War" pitting the Soviet Union against the United States
1947–	Martha Nussbaum, philosopher; published *Cultivating Humanity: A Classical Defense of Reform in Liberal Education* (1997), *Women and Human Development: The Capabilities Approach* (2000), and *Not for Profit: Why Democracy Needs the Humanities* (2010)
1950s	The American civil rights movement started and achieved its greatest legislative gains in the mid-1960s
1952–	bell hooks (pen name for Gloria Jean Watkins), feminist and social activist; published *Ain't I a Woman? Black Women and Feminism* (1981), *Feminist Theory: From Margin to Center* (1984), and *Teaching to Transgress: Education as the Practice of Freedom* (1994)
1956–	Judith Butler, philosopher and social theorist; published *Gender Trouble: Feminism and the Subversion of Identity* (1990) and *Giving an Account of Oneself* (2005)
1960s	The Free School Movement (or the New Schools or Alternative Schools Movement) began
1968	In May events in France broke out, with youth protests around the world
1985	The International Council for Philosophical Inquiry with Children (ICPIC) was established
1991	Collapse of the Soviet Union, which along with the Revolutions of 1989 marked the end of the Cold War
1994	The Zapatistas (the Zapatista Army of National Liberation) movement began in Mexico

Introduction

ANNA PAGÈS

> What man needs is not just the persistent posing of ultimate questions, but the sense of what is feasible, what is possible, what is correct, here and now.
>
> (Gadamer 2001)

THE ROLE OF METAPHORS IN CONTEMPORARY PHILOSOPHY OF EDUCATION

Throughout its history, education has faced a permanent contradiction: on the one hand, there is the duty of transmitting a cultural legacy, while, on the other hand, there is the opening up of the possibility for real novelty and transformation in life. This ongoing contradiction makes the practice of education always aware of cultivating tradition in very different ways, articulating the past with the various challenges of the present. As David T. Hansen pointed out referring to the sense of tradition in teaching: "Just as no two poets respond to tradition in identical ways, so no two teachers can duplicate each other's odyssey into the practice" (2001: 146). In this sense, in every practice and cultural setting, philosophy of education tries to respond to tradition from the present circumstances, defending itself against an overwhelming invasion of the immediate, the very often *urgent-right-now-just-do-it* view.

In this introductory chapter, I will use two different metaphors to address contemporary history of philosophy of education as it is presented in the volume. I shall highlight the philosophically productive notion of metaphor because it can shed light on infinite aspects of reality. Metaphors can become a starting point for a kind of thinking based on the impulse of imagination, as Hans-Georg Gadamer has pointed out: "the way we experience historical traditions, the way we experience the natural givenness of our existence and of our world, constitute a truly hermeneutic universe, in which we are not imprisoned, as if behind insurmountable barriers, but *to which we are open*" (2001: 315, emphasis added). In the case of philosophy of education in our time, the use of metaphors might allow us to escape from a foreclosed world, making it possible to reshape what we mean, today, by the word "contemporary" from a historical perspective. The strong point of a metaphor is precisely the possibility it offers to disclose innovative and nuanced meanings, in a "surplus of expressive achievement" (Blumenberg 2010: 35). By posing these metaphors, we seek to respond to an ongoing feeling of inadequacy generated by the permanent tension in history between what is supposed to remain and what is escaping in a blow, a tension that pervades, today, our experience of daily time. In this sense, the history of contemporary philosophy of education constitutes a reflective and speculative pursuit, a human attempt of giving sense to a huge bunch of little experiences in the middle of a rush, a misunderstanding, or even what Erich Heller (1958: 195) had called today's *great calamity* of not being sure how to look for truth.

I am using the term *an experiment with time* as a first metaphor. Is it possible to do an experiment with the flow of time, frustrated as we are by the ongoing feeling that time is constantly escaping from us? How could we define the historical contemporary side of time from this perspective? The writer Vladimir Nabokov and the philosopher Emmanuel Levinas will be our guides as we attempt to reflect upon this question. Both have referred to time as an awkward human experience, filled with paradoxes and contradictions. We will try to define the contemporary meaning of time using the notions of vigilance and sleep. In his insomniac dreams, Nabokov attempted to translate the unthinkable into literature. In a similar way, Levinas privileged the idea of sleep, conceived not literally but as a turning off of the will to control and possess versus the notion of vigilance as the will's dominance over living experience.

The second metaphor is the image of a *landscape*, as indicated in the title of the volume. The practice of contemplating a view from afar can offer some clues to show us the thinking in philosophy of education today and how we can slow down a bit to look and pay attention to the seen and the unseen. In a way, it consists of finding the right distance to contemplate a landscape, an issue that art critics have described very well. Indeed, when we examine a painting of a landscape, we often seek the detail we have missed, the subtle element escaping our notice at first glance. Similarly, a missing point can be philosophically interpreted as an as-yet unformulated question. In this sense, the history of philosophy of education can be cast as the narrative of how we, in the present, reformulate old questions, and how we engage in an uninterrupted process of recontextualizing what has come before, an endeavor that brings to light a steady stream of heretofore unnoticed meanings and unperceived and unexpected details of the past for the present landscape.

This volume is intended to give readers the opportunity to get inside another view of what might seem to be a series of always well-known questions in the history of philosophy of education. We hope that, in the light of a contemporary landscape, the reader can address these questions from a revealing and alternative perspective, thanks to the suggestive contributions of the authors in the volume.

AN EXPERIMENT WITH TIME

Insomniac dreams

On October 14, 1964, the writer Vladimir Nabokov started a private experiment, which consisted of writing down whatever he could rescue from his dreams. This activity can be described as rather odd, nocturnal, and intimate. Nabokov (2019) thought dreams were precognitive as well as related to the past. In other words, he believed that time's progress was a myth: that time was "not unidirectional but recursive: the reason we do not notice the backflow is that we are not paying attention. Dreamland is the best proving ground" (Nabokov 2019: 2).

Nabokov's intention was to recover the things he had not fully grasped when dreaming. The dream's event served as a bridge to writing, trying to give meaning to his personal story through what he called his chronic condition (insomnia). To him, this was a way to go through an experience of permanent exile. He was always out there, in the liminal, gray area of a deep forest, somewhere between being asleep and waking up.

Inspired by the work of J.E. Dunne, who in 1927 (the same year as Heidegger's *Time and Being*) published *An Experiment with Time*, Nabokov developed a way of thinking about time as a strange human feeling, relating past and future in a circular flow of images and narratives, ideas, preconceptions, universes of significance at play. In the end, the present is only a today by virtue of the sense we attribute to it. Time gets caught in webs of significance. Both Dunne and Nabokov believed that, in fact, our dreams tell us about the future, like the angel's voice speaking to the prophets. The present would then be no more than a fictional construction, the result of an awkward process of sewing together disparate remnants to unite past and future.

Nabokov's obsessive collection of dreams might be understood as an instance of magical thinking, a kind of delirious quest to control the flow of time. But it was probably something else: an attempt to build a certain living order in the midst of chaos. We can recognize here what John Keats called negative capability: "that is, when a man is capable of being in uncertainties,

FIGURE 0.1 Blue sky with white clouds nature background. *Source*: MarBom / iStock Photo.

mysteries, doubts, *without any irritable reaching* after fact and reason" (quoted in Barkhust and Fairfield 2016: 44, emphasis added). Without any irritable reaching: this is a key point to Nabokov, who was always struggling to organize the uncertainties that haunted him. To think might well be a failed attempt to maintain an impossible order.

John Dewey himself referred to a similar notion using the expression *idle thinking*, which he characterizes as follows:

> Daydreaming, building of castles in the air, *that loose flux of casual and disconnected material* that floats through our minds in relaxed moments are, in this random sense, thinking. More of our waking life than we should care to admit, even to ourselves, is likely to be whiled away in this inconsequential trifling with idle fancy and unsubstantial hope. (1997: 2)

Nabokov's obsessive transcription of his dreams allowed him to revel in a permanent state of daydreaming (such as Dewey referred to in the previous quote), his mind wandering among disconnected materials. This pleasure is shared by philosophy, an activity always in the middle ground between a negative capability and the challenge of doing something rational or regular, something that can eventually make sense.

Why are we beginning here with Nabokov's story? In my view, this approach, much like the ideas of negative capability or idle thinking, constitutes a provocative metaphor for the role of contemporary history of philosophy of education. It serves as a starting point for building a future on the foundations of the intellectual promises of the present. In this sense, rather than remaining stuck at an impasse, amidst the relativism and liquidity of postmodernity, we are striving to reread the philosophical tradition with a creative (or literary) attitude in our time: collecting the dreams of philosophy of education because we want to think them differently.

Contemporary philosophy of education brings together all the contradictions that we have inherited. In our time, any contemporary field of research will inevitably become a battleground between, on one hand, what Megan Jane Laverty and Maughn Rollins Gregory have called "the wealth-obsessed, violently unjust and ecologically doomed environment of late capitalism" (2017: 526), the context of postmodernity (moral relativism, segregation, homogenization, liquidity, and the collapse of absolute truth), and on the other hand, the hope for better times to come through an impulse for greater social justice, respect for minorities, emancipation, and pluralism. And so, experimenting with time can also be a thrilling contemporary adventure, like the personal journey of the main character in Thomas Mann's novel *The Magic Mountain*, Hans Castorp, who leaves his birthplace for the mountains of Davos Platz, where the persistence of reproduction and routine in the Berghof sanatorium makes him realize that life is, in the end, "strange to itself." Knowledge and time are coming together in the flow of historical events, however traumatic or liberating these may be.

Philosophers from St. Augustine to modern thinkers such as Kant, Kierkegaard, Nietzsche, Husserl, and Heidegger, among others, have placed the problem of time at the heart of philosophical debate. In this context, education has come to be one of the most confounding experiences of time. We are supposed to grow up while we receive an education, but what does it really mean to become an adult person searching for a purpose in life? Education constitutes a crucial experience of time, pointing out a feasible purpose in life to be discovered (and perhaps deconstructed) under the constant changing circumstances of our existence.

Jacques Derrida makes a clear distinction between the future and what he called "time-to-come" (Fr. *l'a-venir*). He writes that time-to-come represents a threshold that we are about to cross, a frontier between what we were and what we can become. Education itself can actually become this kind of threshold, but we, like Socrates hesitating on the doorstep of Agathon's house in *The Symposium*, so often find ourselves lingering on the verge, wondering if we are allowed to cross or if we are rather waiting a bit more. If the doorstep has been crossed, we reach what Gadamer, in his masterpiece *Truth and Method* (1960), called a hermeneutic insight, the possibility of reaching a new kind of acquaintance within ourselves. It is a very special knowledge of who we are and what we do, what we doubt and what we trust, as well as a deeper perspective on the things that make up our familiar little worlds. In this sense, a history of philosophy of education in the contemporary landscape becomes, through every contribution in this volume, a form of hermeneutic insight, an alternative awareness of what education has become today.

But let's go back to the previous point. What does it mean to approach contemporary philosophy of education, today, as an experiment with time? How could we describe it, borrowing from Nabokov's and Dunne's attempts to record forgotten dreams and salvage them from oblivion? What is the topic or the question that we have neglected or totally forgotten, in our task of reconceiving philosophy of education in our time? We can answer these questions by treating them like crumbs left behind, scraps that have fallen unnoticed from the table, left uncollected in a dark corner of the cupboard. Why did we fail to see them before? What about certain philosophical notions opening up new promising perspectives? Why did we fail to catch them? Perhaps we were too fascinated with other ossified forms of knowledge or with long taken-for-granted philosophical orientations, or obsessed by the onerous emphasis on accountability in education today. Contemporary philosophy of education should set itself a great challenge: to recast the past of the field of education with a freer, more buoyant sense of possibility. Our litany of long-standing concerns, issues such as evaluation, accountability, teaching and learning, equity and segregation, inclusion, methodology, and educational goals, could then be viewed from a different perspective. This is the most important task of the present volume.

In our time, we are also attempting to find other metaphors. Nietzsche's shadow helps us to discern the utter void in front of us, when he referred to the other gods we will invent after God's death (or murder, as it is written in Aphorism 125 of *The Gay Science*; Nietzsche 1974). We know the move would be to replace anxiety with civility, brutality with kindness, discontent with plenitude. We are aware of resisting the temptation to fill the gap with a mindless, conventional push for material "happiness" and physical satisfaction, gods whose worship has become generally accepted. To fight against this inclination, how can we fashion a distinctive metaphor for philosophy of education as an art of living? Perhaps, for example, we might start using some metaphors such as dispossession and despair in posing the problem of equity, denial in the topic of teaching critical thinking, misinterpretation as a clue to analyze the modern crisis in pedagogy, kindness rather than power as a pedagogical experience, the revelation of personhood and belonging instead of mere school inclusion. As such, philosophy of education constitutes a way to make present life more vivid and more intensely human, a path forward toward more sensitive and profound forms of civility. This movement toward the civilized side of present times lets us look out beyond the constraints of denial, in an attempt to understand the world's most veiled truths. In doing so, perhaps we will find that old questions lead us to uncover an unexpected wisdom for our time. As the French philosopher Olivier Réboul (1989) has put it, philosophy of education draws on questioning the experience of education in its utopian dimension. This utopia takes part in everyday life, though concealed in the tissue of its daily domestic vulnerability.

In this volume, the reader will discover different manifestations of this particular approach: each chapter offers a wholly innovative perspective on what could otherwise be thought of as typical subjects in the field. The contributors to the volume have recovered certain nuances, facets that were already present but whose theoretical implications had yet to be thoroughly examined.

In this sense, seen as an experiment with time, the history of philosophy of education in the contemporary landscape can be simply defined as a similar practice of waking up at dawn to write down a dream. Nabokov's problem was that he could never sleep, so in fact, he was trying to write about dreams he hardly ever had. Like him, in a task of patient and slow reconstruction, the past of philosophy of education can be continually recast from its present, with the discipline engaged in a spirited, ongoing narrative experience. This is what Gadamer has called the fusion of horizons, Michael Oakeshott the conversation of mankind, Dewey common understanding, and Jean-Jacques Rousseau the use of all the powers that bear witness to us of our own existence. All of these are different philosophical ways to put into words the fact that we are indeed persistently thinking under different styles. In this sense, and as Liam Gearon and Emma Williams have written, we should consider "the attempt to embolden philosophers of education sometimes to enter unknown territories or fields, to take risks at incursion, and though it may appear uncomfortable at times, to welcome intruders and apparent strangers who in the end may be more kindred in aims and outlook" (2018: 583).

The history of philosophy of education in the contemporary landscape works as an attempt to recover the forgotten details of historical experience. It means taking the risk of interrogating education from a philosophical view, searching for a small truth, opening up meanings in the daily flow of real educational practice, all the while withstanding the everyday pressure for better "outcomes" exerted by institutions whose view of education is often reduced to the concept of machinery or what Giorgio Agamben (2009) called apparatus.

In the face of these pressures, philosophy of education commits itself to the hard work of holding a perennial dialogue between a forgotten past and a vivid present, moving in the direction of what has yet to be said, thought, and made. But, as Nabokov did in his own way, this effort needs to be formalized, written down, put into words. It has to be sayable. We need a certain degree of narrative to map the territory. Without a doubt, every contribution included in this volume is an attempt to move this project forward: like Nabokov, we are working here inside an experiment with time.

Time can also be thought of as the point from where our consciousness emerges. The history of philosophy of education as an experiment with time can also reimagine a lost connection between seemingly irreconcilable perspectives: while recovering the past, we try to explain what occurred as a basis for thought-provoking questions. What is education? What is justice? Is thinking properly a question of language? Is it possible to give an alternative meaning to liberal education today? What are the consequences of despair and mortification in the endeavor of teaching? Can we address education as a promise of equity thanks to the rise of alternative and emancipatory voices? What will change if we include those voices in the scholarly approach to philosophy of education? To what extent can dispossession and guilt about the past be channeled into new commitments for young generations? What does it mean for a teacher to be a person? Is pluralism in education a task of translation?

Contemporary philosophy of education is definitely one of the future promises to be recovered from our forgotten dreams, or the dreams to come. If we want to succeed, it is necessary to understand our field from the inside, seeking out the spark that once escaped our notice, to reinvent, in a way, an original attitude. The original attitude of contemporary philosophy of education might well consist of a humble yet tenacious and never-ending human effort to unveil a truth. As an academic discipline, it is engaged in illuminating the essential core of education as a reflection of the desire to acquire something beyond mere knowledge of the world's empirical phenomena. This struggle represents a refusal to take the world for granted, a rejection of the idea that things just *are* the way they are. New questions will always emerge from the acute sense of what becoming human can mean. Such new perspectives are bound to appear among scholars and educators experiencing a wide variety of circumstances, among different people, places, cultures, and fragile settings, as the fruit of fears and hopes, limitations, and traumas. They reflect the struggle for a better life to live together, on a global level, in a cosmopolitan view of dialogue, tolerance, and conviviality. As David T. Hansen stated: "Cosmopolitanism means participating in pluralist change as an agent, as an actor, rather than remaining passive or merely reactive to events" (2011: 89).

In this sense, contemporary philosophy of education as an experiment with time constitutes an interpretive move, a path toward greater clarity of themes and ideas. It constitutes a concrete shift toward the same legacies that will continue to matter regarding the experience of thinking about education and its practice.

On the other hand, contemporary thought in philosophy of education has long been engaged in an intense conversation on the nature and the goals of education, struggling, at the same time, to recover forgotten themes, lesser-known authors, readings left out of the dominant history or the scholarly canon. Let's give an example of what we mean: without a doubt, Agamben has read Rousseau. But in light of our experiment with time, the questions would be: What passages might Agamben have neglected to explicitly set out in his work *History and Childhood*? What are the unspoken ideas that are nonetheless somehow present in the author's particular reading of Rousseau? We could formulate a similar question for every chapter, as the authors have all attempted to unearth what has been buried somewhere along the historical path between the readings and the readers. The historical philosophical canon has progressively weaved a lace curtain for education. Even a thing of beauty can sometimes obscure your view. This is the main reason why our essential endeavor, today, must be to lift the curtain so we can see clearly out the window and let the light in. This is what every chapter of this volume is trying to do: to describe how the readings, issues, and authors that make up the legacy of this field have worked to produce our idea of the contemporary as a challenge to think differently.

But there is still another movement to consider. Even if philosophy of education has been paying ever closer attention to its own history, the discipline never stops thinking anew about education as a human experience structured with the tissue of time. In this direction, contemporary philosophy of education tends to multiply toward a new polysemy a series of well-known notions: concepts such as freedom, reason and thinking, justice, equity, pluralism, otherness, consciousness, revolution, language, and emancipation. These words are to be redefined under the present circumstances, finding other practical settings for them. Avi Mintz develops this approach with a very provocative question, using the expression "encounters," when he asks: "What kind of encounters with the history of educational philosophy occur, and what kinds of encounters do we encourage?" (2018: 406).

We can say that every chapter of this volume represents a different encounter: between critical pedagogy and thinking, pluralism and education, liberal education, feminist philosophy of education, deconstruction, anarchism, philosophy for children, decolonization and education. Every chapter includes an encounter with a number of questions, authors, and readings, and with the philosophical task of looking closer at the past from the perplexity of our somewhat awkward present. Continuing with our initial metaphor, that of a bridge between sleep and wakefulness, how can we develop these encounters? Let's take a closer look at this question.

Withdrawing from vigilance

In his essay *Time and the Other* (1941), the French philosopher Emmanuel Levinas refers to the metaphor of vigilance and sleep. He establishes a difference between the notion of consciousness and that of existence. In what was a thrilling insight, he perpetrates a reversal of the usual approach to the notion of existence in the German and French philosophical tradition. He writes:

Insomnia is constituted by the consciousness that it will never finish—that is, there is no longer any way of *withdrawing from the vigilance* to which one is held. Vigilance without end ... It is always the same present or the same past that endures ... Here, time begins nowhere, nothing moves away or shades off ... But it is necessary to ask if vigilance defines consciousness or if consciousness is not indeed rather the possibility of *tearing itself away from vigilance*, if the proper meaning of consciousness does not consist in being a vigilance backed against a possibility of sleep, if the feat of the ego is not the power to leave the situation of impersonal vigilance. In fact, consciousness already participates in vigilance. But what characterizes it particularly is its always retaining the possibility of withdrawing "behind" to sleep. *Consciousness is the power to sleep.* (1941/1987: 49–51, emphases in original)

Levinas highlights the fact that, if we want to understand something, or to be aware of it, we must withdraw from it rather than try to possess it fully. "Awareness" here takes on the meaning not of waking up but of being able, at last, to fall asleep. What a strange metaphor for defining consciousness as an instant of vitality!

Levinas's intellectual move reflects a particular way of being alive and thinking about what living means. He introduces a specific view of the global dimension of existence beyond the characteristic features of Heideggerian existentialism. For Levinas, the key is to withdraw from an idea of knowledge based on the absolute control of the knowledgeable object. His perspective represents a dismissal of the idea that consciousness constitutes vigilance in and of itself. The alternate view of consciousness as the power to sleep refers to a rest, a sudden halt in the nonstop quest to apprehend reality or the others.

In the end, both Nabokov and Levinas considered time to be a combination of what has been recovered as a dream and what we can possibly imagine or even let go: the narrative terms of a rescued dream as a sort of an imagined and encountered future.

This volume can be considered as an experiment with time. It seems as if we are ending a story but, in fact, we are starting it all over again, looking outward toward a creative horizon, one that, as Virginia Woolf says in *To the Lighthouse*, is "full of matches struck unexpectedly in the dark" (1927: 33), since we embrace our ability to sleep and then to wake up. And after that, following Nabokov, we are trying to write our own dreams: defying and questioning the contemporary, postmodern view of the educational experience, undermining the currently dominant perspective that looks at everything through the prism of accountability, regulation, classification, and segregation.

Each of the contributions to the present volume bears witness, in its own clever way, to this preoccupied awareness in contemporary philosophy of education. The collection as a whole can serve as a flashpoint, one capable of illuminating a landscape, much as the dream collector Nabokov once attempted to do.

SCRUTINIZING A LANDSCAPE

Our second metaphor, as it is presented in the title, is that of a landscape. The word landscape calls to mind a long journey, one where we can stop to look around and rest, take a breather in the middle of a marvelous walk, enjoy the view. A landscape can also be a vista looked upon from afar. However, this kind of vantage point does not allow us to make out the small figures down in a valley or at the top of a mountain, because we are at a great distance. Even though they are so far away, we very frequently play the game of looking carefully at a landscape and trying to identify every small figure that we can make out. Focusing in on each of the little points, we try to guess: Is it a bird, a lamb, a tree, a hill? Look, it seems to be moving, no, it's a hawk, it's flying!

A landscape can also be something we look at in a painting. In that case, it's the opposite of a picturesque stopping point on a journey. We become quiet spectators. In this case, it is when we get too close that it becomes difficult to see what is really there, to take in the scene the painter wanted to represent. Other times, we miss the finer details, small enough to escape our notice if we don't pay attention, if we don't have the patience to stay there, gazing at the painting for a while. Patience and time are required to get a sense of the whole and its particularities, to detect the colors, the shapes, the artist's inspiration. In front of a painting, a suitable sense of distance is absolutely necessary for a proper look.

Something similar happens in contemporary philosophy of education. Like Nabokov lying in bed with his notebook on his knees, trying to find the words to rescue a dream, we can look carefully at the landscape by expanding our philosophical perspective. If we want to really remember the landscape (a real one or a painted one) it is necessary to discover with surprise the small detail that was forgotten or went unnoticed at first glance. As Daniel Arasse said of the act of looking at a painting, "On n'y voit rien" (We don't see anything there). Quoting Arasse, the French philosopher Jean-Claude Milner stated: "There is something that conceals what is to be seen" (2012: 17). He suggests searching for that which we cannot easily grasp at first glance to understand a painting from a particular detail. This is what a landscape architect will do when imagining the aesthetic of a new garden. There is a beginning under the form of an idea that fertilizes the project.

Let me ask readers to put on a brand new pair of glasses to look at what every chapter is saying about different aspects of philosophy of education, as if they were trying to make out the tiniest detail in the picture of a landscape.

Like a detective wielding a magnifying glass, or a landscape architect in search of inspiration, let's see what we can find in every chapter and in the volume as a whole: that which is not obvious but is nonetheless visible in a sort of purloined letter from Poe's story by that name.

Contemporary thought, especially that which emerges from the thinkers that Paul Ricoeur called the philosophers of suspicion (Nietzsche, Marx, Freud), has reversed our traditional idea of how to inhabit the world. We no longer think the same way as we did in modernity. This is not bad news in itself, as long as we analyze the challenges that go along with this reversal, such as the possibility of a broader sense of the unknown and of the human cosmopolitanism needed to cultivate a globalized commonality (not to be confused with homogeneity). But we can also adopt a different, freer kind of relationship with tradition. Alain Touraine (1997) describes present times using the expression de-modernization. He defines this notion as a process of disintegration that rips apart the seams that once joined together social life, individual projects, and economic activity. In the end, de-modernization is no more than a process of gradually expanding individualization, one that functions to exclude more and more people from the system.

In this context, contemporary philosophy of education can serve as a guide to analyze and try to reconstruct our experience of this disintegration. It can become what Blumenberg (2010) defined as a metaphorology of postmodern times. As I mentioned in the first paragraph of this Introduction, a metaphor can work as a philosophical model for interpreting reality. In the way we are using the term here, it becomes more than a pure rhetorical figure: it is a philosophical tool that allows us to go through multiple human experiences using figurative language as a way to reach a certain truth.

In the following paragraphs, we will describe some of the problems that underlie or cut across the chapters included in this volume. The attentive reader of the volume will also notice throughout these pages other hallmarks of a particular way of revisiting the philosophical tradition. The authors come mostly from English-speaking countries (Peter Roberts is from New Zealand; Christopher Martin from Canada; Chris Higgins, René V. Arcilla, Troy Richardson [Saponi/Tuscarora], Robert Haworth, and Maughn Rollins Gregory from the United States), except for the European women (Agata Bielik-Robson is Polish, Lovisa Bergdahl and Elisabet Langmann are from Sweden, and I am from Spain). I would say, though, that despite (or perhaps even because of) the mix of cultural, racial, and gender backgrounds, the chapters in this volume come together to form a coherent whole, underpinned by a common approach to the set of shared problems that we together have identified in contemporary philosophy of education. We all express similar worries when looking closer at the same problems today. Almost every chapter starts with a real situation in education: a manner of addressing common concerns, sparking in the reader a recognition of a similar voice or gesture. As the French philosopher Jean-Luc Nancy wrote:

> A contemporary is not always someone who lives at the same time, nor someone who speaks of overtly "current" questions. But it is someone in whom we recognize a voice or gesture which reaches us from a hitherto unknown but immediately familiar place, something which we discover we have been waiting for, or rather which has been waiting for us, something which was there, imminent. (1996: 107)

In the same direction, Agamben underlined the singular relationship that the contemporary entertains with a certain idea of a dissonant time:

> Contemporariness is, then, a singular relationship with one's own time, which adheres to it and, at the same time, keeps a distance from it. More precisely, it is that relationship with time that adheres to it, through a disjunction and an anachronism. (2009: 41)

This view of time as disjunction—in Hamlet's words, "The time is out of joint"—can be very productive. Time makes it impossible to acquire the proper sense of what is adequate. However, it affords us an opportunity to look carefully at a landscape, as anachronistic as it might appear to be. But the advantage of philosophy of education is that it allows us to free ourselves to move when we feel stuck in a sudden state of paralysis, following our artistic inquisitiveness toward the emergence of imaginative figures. In this sense, metaphors can guide us through an unknown landscape, perhaps through a dreamland that nobody has ever had the proper words to describe.

QUESTIONS AND CONTRIBUTIONS

Chris Higgins opens the volume with Chapter 1, "Education, Pluralism, and the Dynamics of Difference." Higgins makes clear the relevance of grasping the complexity of the issue of pluralism, moving right to the core of what we are so often reluctant to ask, to think, and for sure, to confront intellectually. Quite often, the focus when it comes to pluralism is narrowed to the particular question of how schooling must evolve to deal with problems of cultural difference. How can schools become more inclusive and fairer to redress historical exclusions and bias, and to cope with shifting demographics or prepare students for life in the global village? When we equate education with schooling and reduce pluralism to intergroup difference, something crucial gets lost: far from being a special problem of schooling, difference is the very catalyst of education in all of its forms. Higgins substantiates this claim, re-clearing the overgrown paths leading out into this wider territory so that we can think "more pluralistically about pluralism and more dynamically about education."

The first part of the chapter shows how we have been myopic about educational pluralism, while the rest presents four new paths, offering in each case an introduction through one thinker, to the way in which difference, in one of four great "classrooms" of informal education (the inner life, culture, language, history), provides the occasion for education in one of its richest and most dynamic forms. The thinkers chosen are Freud on the Struggle for Personhood; Oakeshott on the Conversation of Culture; Bakhtin on the Polyphony of Language; and Gadamer on the Encounter of Tradition.

Is philosophy of education a neutral act? How have women contributed to the development of philosophy of education from a historical standpoint? How is philosophy of education supposed to be written? In Chapter 2, "Feminism within Philosophy of Education," Lovisa Bergdahl and Elisabet Langmann describe feminism as an ongoing and living conversation between generations. They do so using the metaphor of the wave, so often used in feminist theory, and they adopt three main approaches (or topics of conversation): feminism as recovery, feminism as critique, and feminism as reconstruction.

What relevance, role, and meaning will categories such as "woman/girl" and "feminine/femininity" have in educational research in the future? Has the concept of "woman" run out of steam within feminist philosophy of education? As the authors address these issues, they take into account the inherent instability of the categories woman/girl and feminine/femininity in feminist theory. The chapter describes the three waves of feminism from a historical perspective: the first wave (1848–1949), the second wave (1949–90), and the third wave (1990–present). The metaphor of the wave serves as the chapter's conceptual framework. The chapter is addressing different aspects of the subject, such as women's and girls' equal access to education and public life, along with the question of "missing" works by women in the field of philosophy of education. The authors describe the work of the three second wave feminist "mothers" within feminist educational philosophy: Maxine Greene, Jane Roland Martin, and Nel Noddings.

The authors focus especially on relationality and epistemology as crucial topics to be interrogated in contemporary research in the field. These perspectives call into question the notion of the feminine as a Platonic essence. The chapter's conclusion stresses the importance of maintaining the bonds between different generations of feminists.

In Chapter 3, "Analytic Philosophy of Education," Christopher Martin delves into the question of language as a tool for thinking critically. This has historically been the main purpose of the analytic tradition in philosophy. Martin starts his reflection about critical thinking with the example of the generalized confusion between critical thinking and questioning authority. Thinking critically is not the same as being *critical*, in the sense of challenging all kinds of dominant beliefs and assumptions in a knee-jerk reaction. Instead, critical thinking means analyzing how words are being used: "terms such as 'indoctrination,' 'critical thinking,' and 'education' play an important role in educational thought and action. However, if these concepts are misconceived or misunderstood, our thoughts and actions are likely to be *mis*guided" (Martin, Chapter 3, this volume). Martin shows how we bear responsibility for how we use the very term critical thinking when we say that we are teaching children to think in this way: "If teachers operate on the assumption that 'critical thinking' is the same as 'questioning authority,' they will likely be missing something essential in their efforts to instill critical thinking in students." An important task of the philosopher of education is to map out the meaning of key terms and concepts within educational discourse.

The author offers a historical overview of the principal authors who have reflected upon the issue of critical thinking from the analytic tradition: the "London line" led by Paul Hirst (with his concept of forms of knowledge) and R.S. Peters (education as an initiation), and the work of Israel Scheffler from Harvard University (with his conceptual analysis of knowledge). Martin also analyzes two contemporary concepts in education: autonomy (from Dearden's work on personal autonomy) and indoctrination (with reference to Snook's idea of moral failure). The contribution does not shrink from the challenge of critically assessing the critical dimension of analytic philosophy of education and analyzing its possible contribution to future scholarship in this field (see Figure 0.2).

FIGURE 0.2 Large circular clouds (Altocumulus lenticularis duplicatus) in the sky.
Source: katatonia82 / iStock Photo.

In Chapter 4, "A Philosophy of Hope: Paulo Freire and Critical Pedagogy," Peter Roberts describes the movement of critical pedagogy as a multidisciplinary field of inquiry. This particular perspective is concerned with identifying, analyzing, and transforming oppressive structures, practices, and relations, based on a view of education as a political process. The crucial idea is that education can be a means for social change and a more just society. Roberts stresses the difference between critical thinking (as detailed in Chapter 3 on analytic philosophy) and critical pedagogy. The latter "implies a willingness to examine and engage not just texts, ideas, or arguments but also hierarchies of power and privilege in economic, political, and cultural systems and institutions." Critical pedagogy focuses not only on theorizing but also on resistance, and (in some cases) on revolution. Marx's Eleventh Thesis on Feuerbach, which says "Philosophers have hitherto only interpreted the world in various ways; the point is to change it," is an underlying inspiration for critical pedagogy as a philosophy of education.

In his chapter, Roberts points out the importance of context in teaching. The main questions a critical pedagogue might raise are, for instance: "What do I stand for, and why? With whom am I working? Under what circumstances?" Taking into account the diversity of authors in the philosophical tradition of critical pedagogy, Roberts focuses on the works of Paulo Freire, author of the classic text *Pedagogy of the Oppressed* (1972); Ira Shor, specifically the work *Critical Teaching and Everyday Life* (1980); and bell hooks (the nom de plume of Gloria Watkins). All of these writers struggle to sketch a radical, transgressive pedagogy and an anti-racist mode of education. To what extent can the endeavor of humanization, conscientization, and liberation through education in the social world be updated to face the present circumstances? Can *love* in education still be claimed as "a form of deep care and commitment"? Roberts writes: "Critical pedagogy prompts us to examine ourselves and the world in a fresh light." This is why, in his view, critical pedagogy is more needed than ever, especially if we conceive of hope not as an abstract virtue but as a kind of praxis, a strong commitment, at the very core of teaching and education, to changing and improving the world as we know it today.

In Chapter 5, "The Changing Landscapes of Anarchism and Education," Robert H. Haworth addresses problems of power, authority, and education from the historical record of experiences of anarchist education. Anarchist education encompasses a series of values such as cooperation and mutual existence beyond the state and authoritative practices. The chapter describes the essential disposition of men and women who thought of freedom as a possible reality in the field of educational practice. The author presents and discusses some of the philosophical developments in anarchism and education during the nineteenth and twentieth centuries. The chapter also explores the philosophical foundations for an anarchist critique of state-driven teaching and learning practices, based on Ivan Illich's *Deschooling Society*, an essential critique of school's institutional effects, as well as on the work of Paul Goodman. The radical postures of the anarchist historical approach call to mind the question of the political meaning in education. They provide arguments for a deeply critical perspective on contemporary education, marketplace values, and privatization in general. The chapter also considers some contemporary philosophical shifts and plausible ways to continue having conversations and creating anarchist learning spaces now and in the future. Haworth's chapter will help the reader realize the extent to which anarchism represents an acute critique of the present postcapitalist structures that perpetuate different sorts of injustice and new forms of human slavery under the guise of accountability and constant monitoring of performance.

"Philosophy for Children and Children's Philosophical Thinking" is the title of Chapter 6 by Maughn Rollins Gregory. The title reveals the distinctive approach of this contribution. Gregory reviews the evolution of today's concept of philosophy for children, beginning with its development in the late 1960s when it became "an educational practice and a topic of academic scholarship." The study of philosophy for children has taken on great relevance and come to play an innovative role in a range of areas of educational research and practice: curriculum; educational theory; moral, social, and political philosophy; and discourse and literary theory. Gregory traces the movement from its origins in the work of Matthew Lipman (1923–2010), Gareth B. Matthews (1929–2011), and Ann Margaret Sharp (1942–2010). In this chapter, he underlines the movement's major accomplishments—in critical thinking, ethics education, and democratic education—as well as its principal critiques and challenges. He goes on to analyze Shaun Gallagher's (1992) heuristic of four hermeneutical schools: conservative, critical, radical, and moderate. In this chapter, the reader will learn about the whole range of current trends in the theory and practice of philosophy for children, including diverging approaches that signify deep differences with regard to the meanings of philosophy, childhood, and education, as well as disparate educational agendas. Gregory's contribution is not merely a historical account of the role of philosophy for children as an important field of study but an insightful look at how we interpret childhood today beyond a historical perspective.

Agata Bielik-Robson has picked up a song by Pink Floyd, "Another Brick in the Wall, Part 2," as a part of the title of her contribution: Chapter 7, "'Teachers, Leave Them Kids Alone!': Derrida, Agamben, and the Late Modern Crisis of Pedagogical Narrative." In this chapter, the reader will find two very different philosophies of education, each emerging from the thought of one of the two great rivals of late modernity: Jacques Derrida and Giorgio Agamben. By placing them on the larger map of contemporary humanities, Bielik-Robson presents Derrida's deconstruction as the last and most sophisticated variant of the Kantian Enlightenment and Agamben's critical form of messianism as a rejection of Enlightenment pedagogy, grounded in the teachings of Jean-Jacques Rousseau. Bielik-Robson interprets this debate as an abstract mirror of the concrete social processes that nowadays affect our attitude to education in general, by putting in doubt its very purposefulness. The terms that appear in Pink Floyd's song, "Another Brick in the Wall, Part 2," signal that the popular culture of late modernity leans toward Rousseau's primacy of the natural life-world against the alienated artifice of educated culture, a tendency that Derrida attempts to counteract while Agamben endorses.

One of the most original aspects of her chapter is the use of the "Judaic great intangible principle of *torat hayim*," mentioned by Derrida as a crucial dimension for the understanding of life and its transmissibility, taking life to a different symbolic level. As Bielik-Robson states:

> Teaching and learning—the dialogue between the child and the adult—are the integral element of *torat hayim*, the Jewish-Derridean pedagogy of life that could not "live on" without the didactic supplement, transmitting the "principle of life" through the symbolic medium of culture.
>
> Derrida's *torat hayim* is thus simultaneously a *principle* of life, a *tradition* of life, and the *instruction* of life. (Chapter 7, this volume)

In her conclusion, Bielik-Robson aims at a new philosophy of education as "closer to life," an ongoing, always imperfect combination of living and learning to live that has to be an inner part of pedagogy in postmodern times, including "devices of education and culture into the living process itself, not only not reducing the possibility of happiness but, on the contrary, augmenting the vital pleasure of the self-affirmed life."

How does one enact an ethical relation of learning decolonial governance with Indigenous peoples in the pursuit of conceptual clarity in the principles of such governance? In Chapter 8, on "Decolonization, Indigenous Peoples, and Philosophy of Education," Troy Richardson (Saponi/Tuscarora) makes an exercise of conceptual clarification. In his chapter, he defends philosophy of education as a critical intellectual endeavor directed at educational and broader social, economic, or political injustices, among them the problem of dispossession of Indigenous peoples. The author explores and formulates some questions on decolonial governance and political transfer from the perspective of philosophy of education. He differentiates Indigenous decolonial collectives and several foundational topics, including autonomy and Indigenous philosophies for decolonial governance. Critical questions on the inclusion of such philosophies in broader social contexts as well as the complex entanglements with colonial law are also taken up through the work of Spivak and Turner. In his contribution, the philosophical concept of dispossession is at the center of the discussion.

Richardson's account of the issue poses "questions on education for social relations in a novel and more robust sense," but at the same time "resituates questions on the relation between governance and neoliberalism from the point of view of Indigenous peoples." As the author states, "A philosophy of education attentive to dispossession in decolonizing contexts seeks out sites from which this philosophy is enacted to be in dialogue about the principles for plenitude and sociopolitical relations." Richardson highlights a shift in contemporary philosophy of education away from normalizing precarity (and justifying dispossession) and toward enacting plenitude as a way to bear on social, land, and water relations.

What is liberal education for those who want it to continue to make a real difference to societies today? How did the seven liberal arts morph into the very diverse contemporary curricula? Can we understand the historical change in liberal education to be a response to alterations in education's dominant idea? What is the liberal-free idea in education? In Chapter 9, "Liberal Education and Its Existential Meaning," René V. Arcilla examines these questions. Far from adopting a merely scholarly tone, he uses an example from real life: a woman whose son is taking courses on "Humanities." What is the point of completing these courses?

Arcilla's distinctive inquiry elucidates how the crystallization of liberal education in the Middle Ages as *artes liberales* presupposed a certain understanding of freedom. He also explains why this understanding no longer suits contemporary democratic society. The core of his work, though, is the third section, where he defines the experience of a kind of informal, "existential education" outside of schools, where what is at stake is actually a related idea of freedom. This point is particularly revealing of the author's overall perspective. He defines "mortification" as an existential category to understand to what extent liberal arts contribute to education. Mortification is "based simply on the fact that mortal beings like ourselves are bound to respond to the questionable meaning of our lives." Arcilla suggests seeking out "the sacred thing for which one is willing to die," stating that such a quest corresponds to the essential search for a purpose in life.

The author makes us think about the limits of our own existence and our hope of finding a purpose. Liberal education allows us to understand how to exercise the Aristotelian freedom suggested by the Greek term for school, *skholé*: time released from the contemporary imperative to produce and consume that makes it so hard for people to truly dwell in the world.

A NOTE TO THE READER

Before starting the volume, I kindly ask the reader to identify some relevant questions of interest in the field. This orientation will lead spontaneously to one chapter or another. Reading will bring you to the very first beginning, where contemporary philosophy of education blossoms at last, in a variety of surprising and clever ways: one of every contribution taking part in this book.

In any case, the reader must not think this is the end. It just happens to be another speculative and tenacious experiment with time, a contemporary, awkward look at what was thought to be the well-established (but disjointed) educational philosophy landscape, focusing and not focusing at the same time to see something else, to think differently.

Has this Introduction succeeded in describing what is at stake in the philosophy of education today? Might the reader come to a conclusion after reading over the volume. As a playful final exercise, listen to what David Foster Wallace (2005: 8) said in his commencement address, in which I have replaced his words "This is water, This is water!" with those at the heart of this volume:

> It is about simple awareness—awareness of what is so real and essential, so hidden in plain sight all around us, that we have to keep reminding ourselves, over and over: *"This is Philosophy of Education, this is Philosophy of Education."*

REFERENCES

Primary sources

Agamben, Giorgio (2009), "What Is the Contemporary?," in Giorgio Agamben (ed.), *What Is an Apparatus? and Other Essays*, trans. David Kishik and Stefan Pedatella, 39–56, Stanford, CA: Stanford University Press.

Barkhust, David and Paul Fairfield, eds. (2016), *Education and Conversation: Exploring Oakeshott's Legacy*, London: Bloomsbury.

Blumenberg, Hans (2010), *Paradigms for a Metaphorology*, Ithaca, NY: Cornell University Press.

Dewey, John (1997), *How We Think*, New York: Dover Publications.

Foster Wallace, David (2005), *This Is Water*. Available online: http://www.metastatic. org/text/This%20is%20Water.pdf.

Gadamer, Hans-Georg (2001), "Introduction," in Hans-Georg Gadamer (ed.), *Truth and Method*, London: Bloomsbury.

Gearon, Liam and Emma Williams (2018), "Why Is the Relationship Between Philosophy and Literature of Significance for the Philosophy of Education?," *Journal of Philosophy of Education*, 52 (4): 579–92.

Hansen, David T. (2001), *Exploring the Moral Heart of Teaching*, New York: Teachers College Press.

Nabokov, Vladimir (2019), *Insomniac Dreams: Experiments with Time by Vladimir Nabokov*, Princeton, NJ: Princeton University Press.

Nietzsche, Friedrich Wilhelm (1974), *The Gay Science: With a Prelude in German Rhymes and an Appendix of Songs*, Vol. 985, London: Vintage.

Secondary sources

Hansen, David T. (2011), *The Teacher and the World: A Study of Cosmopolitanism As Education*, New York: Routledge.

Heller, Erich (1958), *The Ironic German: A Study of Thomas Mann*, London: Butler and Tanner.

Laverty, Megan Jane and Maughn Rollins Gregory (2017), "Pragmatism and the Unlearning of Learnification," *Childhood and Philosophy*, 13 (28): 521–36.

Levinas, Emanuel (1941/1987), *Time and the Other (and additional Essays)*, trans. Richard Cohen, Pittsburgh: Duquesne University Press.

Milner, Jean-Claude (2012), *Malaise dans la peinture: À propos de La mort de Marat*, Paris: Ophrys.

Mintz, Avi (2018), "The Use and Abuse of the History of Educational Philosophy," in Natasha Levinson (ed.), *Philosophy of Education*, 406–13, Urbana, IL: Philosophy of Education Society.

Nancy, Jean-Luc (1996), "The Deleuzian Fold of Thought," in P. Patton (ed.), *Deleuze: A Critical Reader*, 107–13, Oxford: Blackwell.

Réboul, Olivier (1989), *La Philosophie de l'Éducation*, Paris: Presses Universitaires de France.

Touraine, Alain (1997), *Pourrons-nous vivre ensemble? Égaux et différents*, Paris: Fayard.

Woolf, Virginia (1927), *To the Lighthouse*, London: Penguin.

CHAPTER ONE

Education, Pluralism, and the Dynamics of Difference

CHRIS HIGGINS

INTRODUCTION

There is a remarkable irony in our frequent discussions of education and pluralism: they are neither fully educational nor particularly pluralistic.[1] Our focus has narrowed to the question of how schooling must evolve to deal with problems of cultural difference. This is an undeniably complex and pressing issue. How can schools become more inclusive and equitable to redress historic exclusions and bias, to cope with shifting demographics, or to prepare students for life in the global village? Indeed, is it even possible to retrofit an institution designed for nationalism and cultural assimilation, social sorting and workforce development, with genuine affordances for undoing the structures of oppression and combating the resurgence of xenophobia? To notice our myopia is not to deny the importance of the object under our magnifying glass. Nonetheless, when we equate education with schooling and reduce pluralism to intergroup difference, something crucial gets lost: far from being a special problem of schooling, *difference is the very catalyst of education in all of its forms*. It is the aim of this programmatic chapter to substantiate this claim, re-clearing the overgrown paths leading out into this wider territory so that we can think more pluralistically about pluralism and more dynamically about education.

EDUCATION IN AN ERA OF SCHOLASTICISM

If someone told us that the terms "pizza" and "round things" were synonymous, we would find this very odd. Have you never seen square pizzas, we might ask, or frisbees? And yet it has become natural for us to equate education and schooling when it is the case neither that only schools educate nor that schools only educate. Schools are one among myriad formative influences and arguably not the most important. Family, religion, friendship, media, work, the built environment, and other informal educational forces likely shape us in more fundamental and lasting ways. The claim that schools only educate is equally suspect. As David Labaree (2008) observes, we have "educationalized" a dizzying array of social problems, burdening the schools with an ever-growing list of competing mandates. We ask schools to interrupt prejudice and rectify past discrimination; distribute educational and economic opportunities on the basis of merit; provide the private sector with the employees they need; shape the economy of the future; ensure social mobility in the face of widening income equality; enhance international economic competitiveness; counter food insecurity; strengthen herd immunity; foster sexual responsibility; advance safe driving; cultivate healthy eating; promote recycling; and so on. Even if the schools only had to deal with the subset of these social problems with a genuine educational dimension, they would be schizophrenic. But the fact is that in feeding and vaccinating, sorting and credentialing, and just plain keeping the kids off the streets, the business of the school extends well beyond education into the spheres of human resources, policing, food service, and health care.

Indeed, this suggests not only that schools do more than educate but that they inevitably miseducate. While a definitive proof of this proposition would require a settled understanding of what it means to be an educated person, it is not hard to mount a *prima facie* case as follows. Given its core task of social sorting, intensified by the advent of high-stakes testing, contemporary schooling has become a ruthless process of selection for a highly particular skill set: the ability to recall information and manipulate verbal and mathematical symbol systems under intense time pressure and threat of failure. Even while debates about the exact nature of the educated person continue, we can agree that this is not an institution designed to educate well even the intellect alone, let alone the whole person.

If schooling is a strange mix of the educative, the non-educative, and the mis-educative, why are we so prone to mistake it for the whole of education? John Dewey foresaw this strange state of affairs over a century ago, opening *Democracy and Education* (1916) with a warning about our growing scholastic bias. Though the project of mass compulsory schooling was still gearing up— for example, in the United States fewer than 60 percent of the school-aged population attended school in 1910 (Snyder 1993, table 2, p. 14)—Dewey could already see us forgetting just what a recent and peculiar educational invention this was. Kieran Egan offers this nice, defamiliarizing description: "The young of each country became captives within specially designed buildings, sitting more or less docilely in age sets, available for whatever the state or influential interest groups wanted to try" (2008: 6–7). Both Egan and Dewey acknowledge that this new educational modality has powerful affordances. What worries them is our amnesia about its contingency and its limitations. When it comes to schooling, we are like the proverbial person who, having found that hammers are useful for driving nails, starts trying to hammer everything. To counter this tendency, Dewey (1916: ch. 1) reminds us that social life itself is the great educator and that, regardless of their other functions, all institutions shape our dispositions, making them educative in this broad sense. "The measure of the worth of any social institution," he writes, "is its effect in enlarging and improving experience" (p. 6). If this notion now seems strange to us, Dewey points out, our ancestors would have found it "preposterous to seek out a place where nothing but learning was going on in order that one might learn" (p. 7). However, once we had created an institution that only educates (or so it seemed) we began to leap illogically to the conclusion that only schools educate. This has led us, Dewey suggests, to neglect the educative work of other institutions and to become muddled in our understanding of learning. We have come to overvalue what we are "aware of having learned ... by a specific job of learning" and to devalue "what [we] unconsciously know because [we] have absorbed it in the formation of [our] characters by intercourse with others" (p. 9).

This scholastic myopia limits our understanding of educational pluralism, for it is only when we recall the great domains of informal education—culture, language, the inner life, and history—that certain core dynamics of educative difference come into view. In what follows, I explore these dynamics, drawing on Michael Oakeshott, Mikhail Bakhtin, Sigmund Freud, and Hans-Georg Gadamer. However, we must first free ourselves from another form of myopia. What narrows our vision is not only the reduction of education to schooling but our strangely monolithic view of pluralism.

PLURALISM IN AN AGE OF IDENTITY POLITICS

At first glance, our discussions of difference might seem less reductive than our assumptions about education. After all, with the turn toward identity politics, we have learned to locate inequality and oppression along multiple axes of difference including race and religion, language and culture, gender and sexuality, and ability status. These are sites where differences are transmuted into hierarchies, where some identities are treated as the rule and others as the exception, where some ways of being are lionized and others marginalized, pathologized, or criminalized. While the critical work of exposing the

dynamics of power and privilege along each of these axes is undeniably rich
and important, the turn toward identity has also meant a turn away from other
important aspects of difference. Contemporary discussions typically reduce
difference to intergroup difference, and even here identity politics appears to
have a troubling blind spot around issues of class.

There is no logical reason why class analyses cannot be conjoined with those
focused on race, gender, sexuality, and so on. Indeed, it is just this that the
concept of intersectionality demands: that privilege and oppression occur in
varying degrees at the intersections of the vectors of power/difference. Consider
the intersectional politics of language and class in the United States. The
hegemony of English means that, even in a country that is home to 40 million
native Spanish speakers, speaking Spanish is treated variously as an annoyance,
an inability to speak English, a lack of intelligence or culture, or a subversion of
"Americanness." To understand which discourses come into play, and to what
degree, we must consider other facets of identity. For example, adding class to
our analysis explains why, when both are speaking Spanish, the working-class
immigrant encounters more virulent prejudice than the wealthy expat.

However, there is a difference between factoring social class into our
calculations of privilege and making political economy our starting point.
Identitarians are not wrong, for example, to note that what working-class
people say is often discounted because of how they say it. The worry is that
their ambition only extends as far as rectifying this indignity. In their utopia,
working-class speech is no longer deemed inferior to that of the rich and highly
schooled, but we are not actually emancipated from plutocracy, alienated labor,
and our soul- and planet-destroying cycles of commodity bulimia. The capitalist
is happy to celebrate working-class speech if it will help stimulate new appetites
for another round of overconsumption.

Thus, it is not only class that looks different from identitarian and Marxian
perspectives. A growing chorus of scholars has begun to suggest that identity
politics itself looks like a mixed blessing through the lens of political economy.
Without denying the persistence of unacceptable discrimination on the basis
of race, gender, sexuality, and so on, such critics argue that identity serves a
reactionary role in our contemporary politics. We can distinguish weak and
strong versions of this argument. The weak argument is agnostic about the
progressive potential of identity. It claims only that identity politics has been
pressed into ideological service in this late phase of capitalism, distracting us
from and legitimating economic inequality (e.g., on legitimation, see Benn
Michaels 2016: 212). David Blacker (2019) finds it telling how happily academic
and financial institutions structured to preserve our economic caste system have
embraced identity and diversity talk. Behind the rhetoric, Blacker sees "virtue-
signaling" (p. 92) and "trough jostling" (p. 90), as stressed elites maneuver to
increase their proximity to the flow of capital:

> The glaring lack of concern with economic class among the identity crowd has led only to a "diversity bureaucracy" which is, as bureaucrats typically are, far more concerned with self-perpetuation rather than the achievement of any external aims—whatever the official rhetoric ... : simply get in position above all else, in part by ensuring that previous position holders "check their privilege," i.e., relinquish their reserved trough positions. (pp. 89–90)

In some contexts, identitarians do speak truth to power; in others, they are simply solidifying power by speaking about "speaking truth to power."

Against this weak argument, identitarians could retort that virtually anything can be leveraged for power and profit. After all, at this very moment Amazon. com is doing a brisk business in books about commodification, exploitation, carbon emissions, and the death of small businesses. Here is where the strong argument comes in, proposing that identity politics is actively ideological, constituting "the left-wing of neoliberalism" (Reed 2015; building on Benn Michaels 2016: 75, 101, 109, and *passim*). For Adolph Reed Jr. (2015), far from being passively conscripted, the new politics of identity is "the expression and active agency of a political order and moral economy in which capitalist market forces are treated as unassailable nature." Paradoxically, though it stresses group membership, identity politics can be seen as undermining collective agency by subscribing to the "radical individualism that virtually everything else in our society encourages" (Lilla 2017: 87). Consider that, once we map intersectionality finely enough, what we find at each node is remarkably akin to that supposedly discredited modern fiction, the distinctive individual (since no one else occupies this exact locus of cross-cutting subject positions). But it is not only that the subjects of identity politics happen to be distinct: they seem to be actively bent on drawing ever finer, invidious distinctions. Thus, Blacker points to the "raging sanctimony" of the new call-out culture (2019: 230n12), and Mark Lilla derides the turn to identity as a "pseudo politics of self-regard," as "narcissism with attitude" (2017: 10, 95). Blacker offers an interesting analysis of this endless splintering (2019: see esp. ch. 3). Instead of devoting itself to the construction of a new, livable social imaginary, the contemporary Left dissipates its energy in a perverse form of perfectionism. Beneath the egalitarian drive for inclusion, Blacker finds a second hidden motor of identity politics: the need for ever new moral rejects, excluded paradoxically for their failures to include, for their lack of the "moral-perceptual apparatus" characteristic of the now more clearly defined elect (p. 131).

To claim that identity politics in its current form actively or passively vitiates class politics is not to argue that one cannot work simultaneously for racial and economic justice. We need only recall that the architect of the civil rights movement was also the man behind the "poor people's campaign." For Dr. Martin Luther King Jr., social justice was a unified battle against the "giant triplets of racism, materialism, and militarism" (King 1967, quoted in Laurent 2018: 26). Still, the fact remains that the ascendance of identity politics in educational discourse has been mirrored by a decline in class analyses. Liston and Murray observe that, over the last twenty-five years,

> Neo-Marxist examinations of public schooling have diminished … Agency and empowerment, not structural constraints and reproductive correspondences, have become the overarching concerns. Today talk of oppression rarely highlights class inequities but instead underscores a list of very real injustices, including gendered, sexual, racial, and other cultural ills. (2015: 225)

Thus, while a two-fisted approach might seem both possible and desirable (see, e.g., McCarthy 1988), the fact remains that we have tended to let go of the "correspondence hypothesis" (Bowles and Gintis 1976/2011: ch. 5) to pick up the "invisible backpack" (McIntosh 1989).

However, let us assume that we need not choose between the lenses of identity politics and political economy. With this stipulation, we arrive at something like a complete view of intergroup differences. As noted, educational pluralism is typically understood as a call to deal with the problems of power and privilege surrounding such differences. Every educational initiative can be shown to rely on an idea of the educated person, and every image of the educated person can be unmasked for its partiality. "The educated person," it turns out, has been until recently actually the educated man (Martin 1981); or more specifically, the gentleman (e.g., Newman 1891/1996: 83). It is these false universals that underwrite acts of exclusion, marginalization, and assimilation. The pluralistic ideal in education could, then, be stated in this way: it is time to make the common school truly common.

FROM DIVISIVE SCHOOLING TO DEEP PLURALISM

The common school ideal has two facets. First is the idea of a common level of provision. Regardless of the color of your skin, the wealth of your parents, the language you speak at home, the god you worship, and so on, you should have access to schools of comparable quality to those available elsewhere. Notice, though, that one could theoretically satisfy this criterion with a system in which each school enrolls a homogeneous demographic. In the real world, "separate but equal" is dangerous doublespeak. Since Brown v. Board (1954),[2] we have recognized that separation is experienced as subordination in a structurally racist society (for a defense of separation in the name of social justice, see Merry 2013; Merry and New 2014, 2016). However, let us imagine a society with homogeneous schools that has nonetheless outgrown racism. Imagine further that they employ an army of perfectly perceptive school inspectors constantly making the rounds to ensure that all of their schools boast equally strong faculties, substantive curricula, rich extracurriculars, supportive communities, pleasing architecture, and so on. Even in this alternative universe, where genuinely equal separate schools offer a common level of educational provision to students from all sectors of society, something crucial is still missing.

This brings us to the second facet of the common school ideal, which flows from the need to find common ground in a pluralistic, democratic society. The common school works against the fracturing of society into races, creeds, and classes. It is a place where we learn together across differences. That this ideal has been hard to realize is an understatement. Consider the example of the United States. The episodes of outright exclusion that litter our history are only the most obvious failures. Genuine inclusion must be expansive. Students should be invited to join not a predefined collective identity but a collective process, one in which a new sense of "we" only emerges over time. By contrast, many gestures of inclusion are assimilative, offering subaltern students access at the impossible price of renouncing central aspects of their identities. In the meantime, separation continues in thinly veiled forms. Residential segregation has largely picked up where *de jure* segregation left off. In schools that do manage to enroll a diverse student body, separation reappears in the form of curricular tracking, which maps with depressing predictability onto race (see, e.g., Welner 2001) and class (see, e.g., Lucas 1999).

The first problem of common or democratic schooling, then, is the basic one of actually creating plural educational spaces in the face of segregation, assimilation, and stratification. Were we able to bring diverse students together in a common space, though, we would immediately face a second problem. While proximity to difference may be a necessary condition for pluralism, it is hardly a sufficient one. It is true that pluralism is sometimes used in a flat, descriptive sense, noting that members of a given community or polity differ in their backgrounds and beliefs without saying anything about how they relate across such differences. However, this would count as pluralist even societies whose intergroup relations are ruled by obliviousness, fear, and hatred. This suggests that pluralism is not simply a fact about difference but a stance toward it. The concept has a moral core: the commitment to engage productively across difference.

Some have misunderstood Gordon Allport's famous "contact hypothesis" to mean that mere contact is enough, such that simply growing up going to school together might short-circuit the tendency to see social others as strange and threatening. However, Allport was clear that the quality of contact matters, and research has borne out that proximity intensifies prejudice under inauspicious conditions (see, e.g., Enos 2017). Allport found four conditions under which contact is more likely to erode stereotypes and generate positive ties: equal status, common goals, cooperative effort, and institutional support (1954/1979: 262, 281) (while debates continue about whether these are necessary or facilitative conditions, the broad outlines of Allport's hypothesis have been confirmed; see Paluck, Green, and Green 2019; Pettigrew and Tropp 2006). Given the fact that schooling is inherently competitive (see, e.g., Labaree 2012) and tends to amplify rather than interrupt social status hierarchies (see, e.g., Lareau 2003), it is difficult to see how sheer proximity in school settings would be productive. It appears, then, that there are at least two significant problems of educational pluralism: first, getting the interlocutors into the same room; then, getting them to engage each other in a productive way. But what is this productive way?

Here we confront a third problem of pluralism. For each subculture has its preferred modes of interpersonal engagement, which embody its distinctive ideas about why we should value the other, about what counts as evidence and what leads to error, about when views must be amended and how horizons might be expanded. The first-order political question is easy. Which of our sects and subcultures should get to decide how we ought to live together? All of us should have a say. But this immediately raises a much more challenging, second-order question: whose culture controls the conversation? We can distinguish two broad strategies for responding to this difficulty: a minimalist and a maximalist approach.

Minimalists such as John Rawls and Jürgen Habermas propose to conduct intercultural dialogue not on the basis of any one culture's traditions of talk but rather on universal norms implied by the very fact of public dialogue. I call it "minimalist" because it asks participants to leave their comprehensive conceptions of the good life at the door, as it were, adopting a standpoint of "public reason" (Rawls 2005: lecture VI and part four) or "the public use of reason" (Habermas 1995). In a pluralistic democracy, Rawls explains, "citizens realize that they cannot reach agreement on the basis of their irreconcilable comprehensive doctrines" and therefore must proffer only the kind of reasons that could carry weight when addressing other "citizens as citizens" (2005: 441). While the minimalist view has been rightly faulted for its implausibility, the deeper problem concerns the very desirability of the ideal.

Consider Nancy Fraser's (1992) well-known critique of Habermas's conception of the public sphere. While Habermas himself admits that "the full utopian potential of the bourgeois conception of the public sphere was never realized in practice," he wants to maintain the regulative ideal that "it is possible for interlocutors in a public sphere to bracket status differentials and to deliberate 'as if' they were social equals" (Fraser 1992: 113, 117). Fraser counters that in any "actually existing democracy" this as-if mentality "works to the advantage of dominant groups" (*passim*, p. 120). Progressive politics requires us instead to "*unbracket* inequalities in the sense of explicitly thematizing them" (p. 120, emphasis in original). Habermas was not wrong to see in eighteenth-century British coffeehouses, French *salons*, and German *Tischgesellschaften* (table societies) the opening of a third, public space that is neither private nor governmental. However, as Fraser shows, the exclusion of women and the working class was not a bug but a feature of these civic spaces, which served as a "training ground ... of a stratum of bourgeois men who were ... preparing to assert their fitness to govern" (p. 114). The emerging culture of "rational" and "manly" talk, along with the new distinctions between private and public, were used to "displace ... the plebeian strata it aspired to rule" and to reinforce "new gender norms enjoining feminine domesticity" (p. 114). Thus, the search for a thin, universal mode of engagement fails to solve the "whose culture?" problem. It disguises rather than eliminates the power dynamics that force the subaltern to play the discursive game of the dominant. The minimalist approach proves untenable.

At this point, the third problem of pluralism appears intractable. Pluralists value talking across differences about what matters and why, but these differences extend to the ways we talk about views and values. Thus, pluralism entails meta-pluralism, a valuing of different perspectives about how to talk together across differences. How then to proceed? If we push on, we trade pluralism for pseudo-dialogue; if we halt the dialogue, our pluralism collapses into indifferentism. This is where what I called the "maximalist" alternative comes in. For maximalists, the key point is that comprehensive conceptions of the good contain not only impediments to but also resources for productive engagement across difference. On this view, Habermas was not wrong to think that powerful affordances for productive pluralism emerged in the provincial coffeehouse culture of eighteenth-century Europe. Nor were his critics wrong to expose the partiality in these forms of engagement. However, the antidote is not to create a finer mesh to strain such contingent cultural residues from a purified public reason but to seek an expanded vision drawing on the cultural resources embedded in marginalized traditions. For example, Fraser points to the "feminist subaltern counterpublic" (p. 123; cf. pp. 115–16) spaces in which women have worked out what publicity means in relation to domesticity, rejecting the either-or that had rejected them. This is not a thin universalism of procedures but a thick, syncretic universalism-in-progress, or as William Connolly calls it, "deep pluralism" (for a critique of syncretism, see Rescher 1993: 90–5). For the deep pluralist, "to participate in the public realm does not ... require you to leave your faith at home in the interests of secular reason (or one of its surrogates)" (Connolly 2005: 64). Rather, deep pluralism makes use of each tradition's "awareness of rupture or mystery" (p. 64) or the "fugitive element of care, hospitality, or love for difference simmering in most faiths" (p. 65) or "other ingredients ... that counsel generosity to others" (p. 64).

Thus, the project of the common school is, if we take it seriously, one of immense difficulty. It is a struggle even to bring diverse students together in a common space. Transforming mere proximity into productive engagement represents a further challenge, one made all the more complex by the deep pluralist commitment to problematize and negotiate the terms of that engagement. Given its importance and difficulty, it is unsurprising that this project has garnered most of our attention. However, if our task is to understand the relation of education and pluralism as a whole, we must not stop here. We have shown something of the limits and affordances of identity politics for understanding intergroup difference. And we have investigated the varieties of pluralism itself from mere fact to engaged stance and from pseudo-dialogue to deep pluralism. Does this not capture in full the problem of educational pluralism? That it does not should be obvious from our earlier discussion exposing the false equation of education and schooling. What becomes clear as we lift our gaze beyond schools is that, internally variegated though it may be, intergroup difference is but one dimension of difference. To perceive this diversity within the concept of difference itself, we must turn our attention to the major modes of informal educational experience—cultural, linguistic, intrapersonal, and historical—where novel forms of difference occasion our growth. We begin with culture.

INVITATIONS: OAKESHOTT ON THE CONVERSATION OF CULTURE

We have already considered culture as an axis of intergroup difference. In a common school, students arrive with views of themselves and the world informed by their diverse cultures. This sets two tasks for educators: (1) supporting intercultural dialogues that expand horizons and combat xenophobia; and (2) teaching in culturally relevant ways. The latter task is necessary because students arrive at school with varying degrees of familiarity with the substance and logic of school subjects. Some students have the dumb luck of being born into families whose home cultures overlap significantly with school culture, absorbing from a young age academically useful jargon (e.g., "ironic"; "conic"; "Bubonic"; "tectonic"; "Napoleonic"; "supersonic" …) and discursive habits ("I disagree with the premise of that argument …"). For many others, such school talk represents a formidable foreign language. Culturally relevant (or culturally responsive) pedagogy builds bridges between home and school cultures to ensure that students from marginalized groups need neither (1) expend on merely reaching the curriculum the energy that majoritarian students can immediately devote to mastering it nor (2) sacrifice their competence or confidence to form this second, scholastic habitus. Notice, though, how this assumes a particular conception of culture. Cultures are collective ways of being in the world, organic wholes distinguished by their characteristic sets of norms, beliefs, attitudes, and practices. Each culture represents the familiar to those who inhabit it and the strange to outsiders. We swim along in our taken-for-grantedness until we encounter another culture and a rival way of organizing the world. There is undeniable intuitive appeal in such a model. The only problem is that it glosses over the most interesting aspects of cultural experience. To see why, let us turn to the philosopher of cultural, political, and educational experience, Michael Oakeshott.

In education, the term "culture" has become a kind of semantic Rorschach test. For some, it connotes the supposed elevation and refinement of certain, approved forms of cultural production. For others, it connotes what everybody already possesses, what unites us with those in our subgroup and differentiates us from those in other groups. The term becomes mainly diagnostic: are you a ranker or a leveler? Oakeshott rejects both of these positions as alternate versions of the same taxidermy theory of culture. If the rankers encase culture in a museum display box and the levelers enclose it in a group identity, both construe culture as something settled, homogenous, and sealed off. Oakeshott's alternative view of culture as dynamic, open-ended, conversational encounter is worth quoting at length:

> Human self-understanding is, then, inseparable from learning to participate in what is called a "culture." It is useful to have a word which stands for the whole of what an associated set of human beings have created for themselves ... but we must not be misled by it. A culture is not a doctrine or a set of consistent teachings [but] ... a continuity of feelings, perceptions, ideas, engagements, attitudes and so forth, pulling in different directions, often critical of one another and contingently related to one another so as to compose ... what I shall call a conversational encounter. Ours, for example, accommodates not only the lyre of Apollo but also the pipes of Pan, the call of the wild; not only the poet but also the physicist; not only the majestic metropolis of Augustinian theology but also the "greenwood" of Franciscan Christianity. A culture comprises unfinished intellectual and emotional journeyings, expeditions now abandoned but known to us in the tattered maps left behind by the explorers; it is composed of lighthearted adventures, of relationships invented and explored in exploit or in drama, of myths and stories and poems expressing fragments of human self-understanding, of gods worshipped, of responses to the mutability of the world and of encounters with death. And it reaches us, as it reached generations before ours, neither as long-ago terminated specimens of human adventure, nor as an accumulation of human achievements we are called upon to accept, but as a manifold of invitations to look, to listen and to reflect. (1975/1989: 28–9)

Notice first that Oakeshott, despite his donnish, hortatory tone, does hold a version of intercultural pluralism. He does reveal some chauvinism: Oakeshott is clearly impressed by the Greco-Roman, Judeo-Christian tradition, which he presumptuously refers to as "ours." And simply acknowledging the existence of multiple cultures is no great accomplishment if one goes on to assert that one's own group has alone discovered true Culture amidst these sundry folkways. To the contrary, though, Oakeshott stresses that every culture is but the contingent creation of some "associated set of human beings."

What distinguishes Oakeshott's view, however, is not this external pluralism but his rich evocation of the pluralism within each culture. If the singular, indefinite pronoun in the phrase "a culture" helpfully highlights the first form of pluralism, it tends to hide the second. While it can be useful to have such an umbrella term, Oakeshott observes, it misleads us into thinking that we have some singular, uniform thing in our sights, say, "Western culture," when in truth each culture is itself internally plural, and on multiple levels. A culture, for Oakeshott, is not a uniform doctrine, but it is also not a great debate, as if we agreed on what to dispute and how to discuss it. The internal dynamics of cultures are too complicated to plot along one axis. Cultures are, if you will, both heteroglot and polydox, a layering of rival languages, modes of imagining and describing, within each of which we find conflicting positions. This is why Oakeshott's prose is so full of lists. He is constantly on guard lest our abstractions dull our perception of this internal variegation. Do we look to the ancient world or the Christian tradition when thinking about what it means to lead a good life? If we seek *eudaimonia* then we must wrestle with the further tension between Apollo and Pan. If we seek piety, then we must weigh the merits of Augustine and St. Francis. There are tensions within tensions, and Oakeshott is just getting started. Shall we seek to know the world through the eyes of the poet or those of the physicist? Is the human condition captured best through myths about gods worshipped, dramas about impermanence, lighthearted tales, meditations about death? The point and counterpoint of the cultural conversation occurs in each of our characteristic modes, in our "feelings, perceptions, ideas, engagements, attitudes." Even when Oakeshott seems ready to collect this multilevel multiplicity into one phrase, "a manifold of invitations," he quickly adds another list, noting that some of these invitations are to look, others to listen, and still others to reflect.

In this way, Oakeshott provides a corrective to the default view that we exist in a monological state until we seek out a cross-cultural encounter. The life of culture is itself conversational. Indeed, our tendency to locate difference in the space between cultures may be a way of shielding ourselves from this internal complexity, these collisions so close to home. If this reveals Oakeshott's distance from the identitarian levelers, what about his relation to the other form of taxidermy? Since Oakeshott sees culture as a drama of ideas, shall we count him among the rankers with their "great-books"? On this point, Oakeshott is quite clear. A culture offers not "terminated specimens" but "unfinished journeyings," not perfected works but "tattered maps" revealing "fragments of human self-understanding," not "human achievements we are called upon to accept" but invitations to go further. Oakeshott would probably not mind our calling certain books "great" as long as we were to add that in every cultural inheritance we find not only "the substantial" but also "the somewhat flimsy," not only "the magnificent" but also "the commonplace" (Oakeshott 1975/1989: 29). Culture is not a curated collection of "eternal verities" under glass for which you can buy a timed ticket but "a contingent flow of intellectual and emotional adventures" in which we are already caught up. Culture is a drama of ideas, but we are not spectators, and we are surely not only applauding.

Nor are a culture's ideas arranged in a grand dialectic. Oakeshottian conversation is more like a polyvocal fugue. In a debate, a single discursive logic is unfolded into two poles as claim and counterclaim. By contrast, conversation is guided not by a single (dia)logic but by an ethos, by virtues that enable participants to pursue with conviviality and endure with grace a continual upsetting of norms. Conversation is like setting the table with two places, putting the napkin on your lap, saying grace, and picking up your fork, only to watch your companion pick up two spoons, turn the table on its side, and start drumming a rhythm. Conversation includes not only rejoinders but also "disjoinders" that entirely reframe the issue at hand. Among the virtues needed to endure such gestalt shifts, Oakeshott identifies a disposition that integrates seriousness and playfulness:

> Without the seriousness the conversation would lack impetus. But in its participation in the conversation, each voice learns to be playful, learns to understand itself conversationally and to recognize itself as a voice among voices. As with children, who are great conversationalists, the playfulness is serious and the seriousness is only play. (1959/1991: 493)

First, we must not misunderstand this reference to children. Where the conventional view contrasts childlike whimsy and adult gravity, Oakeshott sees children as role models precisely because they resist this false dichotomy. For Oakeshott, (serious) playfulness is an excellence in the art of conversation. It is the virtue of "conversability," the disposition toward "acknowledgement and accommodation" of other voices (Oakeshott 1959/1991: 492; 1962/1991: 187).

If the delicate dance of polyvocality is sustained by this special form of humility, it is undermined by a species of pride. "Each voice," Oakeshott writes, "is prone to *superbia*, that is, an exclusive concern with its own utterance, which may result in its identifying the conversation with itself" (1959/1991: 492). This vice is especially pernicious because it leads us to mistake a form of monologue for real conversation without realizing what we have lost. Consider, for example, the dominant voice in the contemporary scene: advertising. Within this single register, we find what appears to be a quite capacious conversation between rival modes of imagining. One advert extols sport and fitness; another draws on images of family life; a third features meditative repose. It is not until we check out, as it were, that we come to realize that all of the adverts were selling the same life, a life of consumption. For the "conversation to be appropriated by one or two voices" (pp. 493–4), Oakeshott explains, is "insidious" because the "established monopoly" immediately covers its own tracks. The excluded voices are "convicted in advance of irrelevance" (p. 494) and may only "gain entrance by imitating the voices of the monopolists" (p. 494). Though this only affords "a hearing for a counterfeit utterance" (p. 494), it sustains the fiction that the conversation continues.

Following Oakeshott, we have derived the first of four important correctives to the default view that equates educational pluralism with the challenges of intergroup difference in formal education. Culture is itself a scene of education, and not only on the model of socialization into a supposedly monolithic set of beliefs and attitudes. Even a single culture is alive with differences. It is defined by the tensions between its competing languages of self-understanding, its rival "images of approval and disapproval," its incommensurable answers to the great question of liberal learning—what is truly worth wanting to have, to do, to become? (Oakeshott 1959/1991: 501). Of course, we have contrived myriad ways to tamp down these tensions and reduce complexity. Indeed, our scholasticism may be read precisely as one of these strategies. We equate education with schooling and devote our schools to what Oakeshott calls "instrumental" learning (1975/1989: 25–7). Oakeshott never denies the interest or importance of the instrumental arts, of learning how to get what we already happened to have learned to want. And perhaps this gives schools more than enough to do. But we must create some spaces where human beings can finally take up the question of liberal learning, this uncanny question constantly begged by instrumentalism. Perhaps if we learn to see the school as but one specialized educational tool and to see intergroup variation as but one important vector of difference, culture itself can be that space. To tune into the conversation that is culture is to embark on one of the most dynamic of educational quests, an education in which difference appears not as a problem but as its very occasion.

TONGUES: BAKHTIN ON THE POLYPHONY OF LANGUAGE

To capture the internal plurality of culture, Oakeshott uses the metaphor of voices in conversation. But what exactly are these "voices"? Oakeshott is not entirely precise on this point. As we saw, he describes them as "modes of imagining" and as "languages" or "idioms" of "self-understanding." Oakeshott gives us a further clue when he writes that "each voice is a reflection of a human activity" (1959/1991: 491), by which he means that practices disclose particular worlds and develop traditions for describing them. Imagine, for example, how a set of sand dunes appears and matters to a poet, a scientist, and a developer. How many of these perceptual-evaluative traditions exist? Again, Oakeshott is hard to pin down, explaining that there is "no fixed number to the voices which engage in this conversation" because "within each mode of utterance further modulation is discernible" (p. 491). However, in his various enumerations we find five main voices: history, poetry, philosophy, science, and practical experience. The resemblance of this picture of culture to a university catalog is worrisome. However, if Oakeshott has to plead guilty to intellectualism, he would vehemently deny the related charge of formalism. He rejects the very idea of generic "thinking skills," insisting that, "A culture is not a set of abstract aptitudes; it is composed of substantive expressions of thought, emotion, belief, opinion, approval and disapproval, of moral and intellectual discriminations, of inquiries and investigations" (Oakeshott 1975/1989: 32). Ultimately, what Oakeshott proposes is a hybrid view: "Each voice is at once a manner of speaking and a determinate utterance" (1959/1991: 492).

Rich as this idea of languages of self-understanding may be, it is ultimately just a metaphor for Oakeshott. For Mikhail Bakhtin, to whom we now turn, there is nothing metaphorical about the way in which the life of language embodies "socio-ideological" diversity. This is not to deny the affinities between their views. For example, like Oakeshott, Bakhtin holds a "praxial" conception of value, seeing norms as embedded in languages that are themselves grounded in determinate modes of activity. Thus, Bakhtin looks to "the language of the lawyer, the doctor, the politician, the public education teacher, and so forth," noting how "these languages differ from each other not only in vocabularies" but also "involve specific forms for manifesting intentions, forms for making conceptualization and evaluation concrete" (1934–5/1981: 289).

On the other hand, Bakhtin would likely see in Oakeshott an example of the view of language that he seeks to overcome, observing that,

> Philosophy of language, linguistics and stylistics ... only know two poles in the life of language ... : on the one hand, the system of a unitary language, and on the other the individual speaking in his language. (p. 269)

In fact, Oakeshott does explicitly contrast his "languages" of self-understanding with languages in the "commonplace sense," which he understands as "organizations of grammatical and syntactical rules" (1975/1989: 37). By contrast, "there are no 'neutral' words and forms" for Bakhtin (1934–5/1981: 293). The linguistic and the axiological are fully intertwined; every phrase is "entangled ... [with] value judgments," "shot through with intentions and accents" (pp. 276, 293).

We can develop the contrast further by seeing how each situates the individual learner in language and culture. For Oakeshott, we all begin on an island: "each of us is born in a corner of the earth and at a particular moment in historic time, lapped round with locality" (1975/1989: 24). Whether we are from Paris or Provincetown, the twelfth century or the twenty-first, our early formation is insular. We are reared in our local culture's particular "language of appetite," its ideas about what is worth wanting and its traditions of securing those ends. If we are lucky, we will also receive, and take up, an invitation to liberal learning, exposing ourselves to a wider range of ends and to the threatening but unavoidable question of what is worth wanting. Returning to his island metaphor, Oakeshott describes the liberal learner as one who "lets go a mooring and puts out to sea on a self-chosen but largely unforeseen course" (p. 23).

Bakhtin's world is all ocean. We are at sea from the beginning. All consciousness is "language consciousness" taking shape "in a contradictory and multi-languaged world" (1934–5/1981: 274, 275). He is referring not to the obvious diversity of natural languages but to the often overlooked "speech diversity within language," attacking the very "myth of a language that presumes to be completely unified" (1940/1981: 68). Every language, he insists, "is stratified not only into linguistic dialects in the strict sense of the word ... but also ... into languages that are socio-ideological: languages of social groups, 'professional' and 'generic' languages, languages of generations and so forth" (1934–5/1981: 271). Though these sociolinguistic discourses differ in type and scope, they all represent "specific points of view on the world, forms for conceptualizing the world in words, specific world views, each characterized by its own objects, meanings and values" (p. 291). Bakhtin sees language as not only stratified (descriptively plural) but as dynamically "heteroglossic." Each discourse is aware of the others—and especially of authoritative discourse—and is defined by that awareness. A discourse expresses its angle on the world precisely through its inflections of other discourses; its meaning is located outside itself, in the context of other (hetero) discourses.

Furthermore, this matrix of interlocking, other-aware discourses is always shifting. Bakhtin identifies two main forces driving this dynamism, one "centripetal" and one "centrifugal": "alongside verbal-ideological centralization and unification, the uninterrupted processes of decentralization and disunification go forward" (p. 271). These twin forces are locked in a dialectical dance. There is a push to establish "a firm, stable linguistic nucleus" (p. 271). Then there is a heteroglossic pull, a generative multiplication of discourses through inflection and quotation as the social world is populated with ever new intentions, perspectives, and group formations. The centripetal force then reacts to "the pressure of growing heteroglossia" (p. 270) preaching "correct language" (p. 270) and "mutual understanding" (p. 271). Reacting in turn, the centrifugal force sprouts new, explicitly parodic forms, "aimed sharply and polemically against the official languages of the day" (p. 273). Bakhtin celebrates these "lower," serio-comic genres, the "heteroglossia of the clown" (p. 273), the laughter of the carnivalesque, the satirical removal of "royal robes and pompous academic gowns" (1965/1984: 198). In this way, Bakhtin revives the shopworn notions of "ideology" and "class struggle." Power consolidates by locking up meaning "in the dungeon of a single context" (1934–5/1981: 274); laughter "liberates from fanaticism and pedantry, from fear and intimidation, from ... the single meaning, the single level" (1965/1984: 123). Politics proceeds not as a grand war between abstract "classes" but through this intricate, everyday linguistic dance as each utterance reveals itself to be "a contradiction-ridden, tension-filled unity of two embattled tendencies in the life of language" (1934–5/1981: 272).

It is within this verbal-ideological flux that we come to form our own intentions, our own sense of where we stand. As Bakhtin puts it, "consciousness must actively orient itself amidst heteroglossia, it must move in and occupy a position for itself" (p. 295). "It is not after all," Bakhtin interjects at one point, "out of a dictionary that a speaker gets his words!" (p. 294). Rather, we find our words already existing

> in other people's contexts, serving other people's intentions: it is from there that one must take the word, and make it one's own. And not all words for just anyone submit equally easily to this appropriation, to this seizure and transformation into private property: many words stubbornly resist, others remain alien, sound foreign in the mouth ... ; it is as if they put themselves in quotation marks against the will of the speaker. (pp. 293–4)

This challenges the standard logic of multiculturalism according to which we begin from the taken-for-grantedness of our own language and culture, finding difference in the alien ideas and language of another culture or subculture. For Bakhtin, we find difference in the very founding of ourselves. The language we need to define ourselves already "lies on the borderline between oneself and the other" (p. 293). To articulate our intentions, we reach for words that are already "populated—overpopulated—with the intentions of others" (p. 294). An authentic voice, if that is what we are after, is not a starting point but the result of "a difficult and complicated process" of "expropriating," of extracting a workable vocabulary out of "other people's mouths" (p. 294).

Bakhtin also greatly enriches our conception of dialogue. We commonly think of dialogue as a special kind of interaction between two or more speakers. Each speaker has their discursive moves, style, and assumptions, which then confront the discourse of an other. Once utterances are traded back and forth, we have a dialogue. What Bakhtin shows, however, is that dialogue is always already underway as soon as anyone begins to speak:

The living utterance, having taken meaning and shape at a particular historical moment in a socially specific environment, cannot fail to brush up against thousands of living dialogic threads, woven by socio-ideological consciousness around the given object of an utterance; it cannot fail to become an active participant in social dialogue. After all, the utterance arises out of this dialogue as a continuation of it and as a rejoinder to it—it does not approach the object from the sidelines. (pp. 276–7)

On closer inspection, a seeming monologue reveals rich veins of "internal dialogization" (279–85). Even our soliloquies prove to be rejoinders. Indeed, this "dialogism of the word" is not only backward- but also forward-looking since "every word is directed toward an *answer* and cannot escape the profound influence of the answering word that it anticipates" (p. 280). Dialogue is difficult because it is not only a back-and-forth but because it is a back-and-forth of rival back-and-forths.

Thus, we arrive at the second of our four correctives to the reductive view of educational pluralism. Language is not primarily a tool for sharing our identities and communicating our points of view with those who differ. We form ourselves in language, a fabric always already stretched taut by the tensions of difference, whose very warp and woof is the interplay of value, position, and perspective. Each of us is composed from the beginning as a dialogue with difference. If we find our own voice outside of us, in the mouths of others, we also find the other inside of ourselves. Thus, we turn now from Bakhtin and social polyphony to Sigmund Freud and the uncanny sphere of intrapersonal difference.

INTENTIONS: FREUD ON THE LAYERS OF THE INNER LIFE

At one point, Bakhtin (1934–5/1981: 288) boldly, if indirectly, likens himself to Copernicus, describing as "Ptolemaic" the conception of language he seeks to displace. The analogy is imperfect since Bakhtin proposes not a new center but a decentered linguistic universe. Bakhtin's theory better embodies the later "Copernican principle," cautioning us against any assumption of a special vantage. In the words of Carl Sagan, "we live on a mote of dust circling a humdrum star in the remotest corner of an obscure galaxy" (1980/2013: 16). It has taken hundreds of years to acclimate to this cosmological humility. Bakhtin's theory is unsettling in its own way. The proposition that we are shaped by language becomes harder to swallow when we add the fact of heteroglossia. In Bakhtin's mirror, we appear as creatures of social contestation whose very consciousness lies not deep within but outside, refracted in the language of others. It is not only language that is decentered: it is us.

Interestingly, Freud liked to employ the same analogy to capture what is unsettling about psychoanalysis, viewing modern history as a series of "great humiliations of our naïve self-love" (*große Kränkungen ihrer naiven Eigenliebe*) (1917/1991b: 294). First came Copernicus' cosmological "destruction of this narcissistic illusion" that we are the universe's defining center (Freud 1917/1955: 140). Then, Darwin dealt another "severe blow to human self-love" by tearing "down the barrier that had been arrogantly set up between men and beasts" (Freud 1925/1961: 221). Thus "humbled in [our] external relations," psychoanalysis comes along to challenge even the idea that we are "sovereign in [our] own souls" (*Der Mensch, ob auch draußen erniedrigt, fühlt sich souverän in seiner eigenen Seele*) (Freud 1917/1991a; cf. Freud 1917/1955: 141; 1920: 21). The discovery of the unconscious, Freud contends, constitutes "the third and most wounding blow" to "human megalomania" because it goes "to demonstrate to each of us that 'I' am not even master in my own home, but remain dependent on mere scraps of information about the unconscious happenings of my innerlife" (*welche dem Ich nachweisen will, daß es nicht einmal Herr ist im eigenen Hause, sondern auf kärgliche Nachrichten angewiesen bleibt von dem, was unbewußt in seinem Seelenleben vorgeht*) (1917/1991b: 295; cf. 1917/1963: 285).

If Freud is famous for one thing, it is his trio of concepts: the ego, the id, and the superego. It therefore comes as some surprise to learn that these are actually not Freud's concepts but inventions of James Strachey, the editor and (supervising) translator for the self-proclaimed "Standard Edition" of Freud's works in English. Freud consciously chose "simple pronouns" to name these three main "provinces ... of the soul" because he wanted his terminology to resonate with "expressions used by normal persons," such as, "*it* came to me in a flash" (Freud 1926/1991: 221; for this translation and a discussion of Strachey's choice of "psyche" over "soul" see Bettelheim 1983: 60, §X). He named them *das Ich* (the I), *das Es* (the It), and *das Über-Ich* (the Over-I) (on the translation of these terms, see Bettelheim 1983: §VIII). If Freud's capitalization and use of definite articles partly estranges these commonest of words, Strachey's Latin neologisms utterly sever the link with the everyday. And this was no accident. The Standard Edition was shaped by the desire to legitimize psychoanalysis in the Anglo-American, mid-century medical world. "The agenda ... is clear," John Reddick observes, "and not a little pernicious: Freud's writing is to be presented not as a hot and sweaty struggle with intractable and often crazily daring ideas, but as a cut-and-dried corpus of unchallengeable dogma" (2003: xxxiii). It is as if his "mercurial ... style, ... sometimes combative, sometimes diffident, sometimes solemn, sometimes mischievous" were "fed ... through a kind of voice-synthesizer to make him sound like a droning academic" (p. xxxiii).

The distortion is not simply stylistic, as if Strachey had merely draped a lab coat over Freud's belle-lettristic German. Here form and substance are inseparable. Without denying that Freud himself was conflicted about the scientific status of psychoanalysis, the fact is that he chose a genre, the humane essay, with an existential mode-of-address. The essay, to adapt a remark of Ezra Pound, is written by those who have "taken the risk of printing the results of their own personal inspection," asking the reader, have you yet "made your own survey" (1934/1960: 40)? In hailing the reader as a fellow searcher, the essay is closer to epistolary writing than to the voiceless research report, written for everyone and no one. Recall the crucial dative in Freud's remark quoted above about the discovery of the unconscious. Freud is not filing some general report about the non-mastery of *das Ich* but "wants to demonstrate [this] *to* each 'I'" (*dem Ich nachweisen will*).

It is just this crucial dimension of recognition that the Standard Edition threatens to erase. The "I" is precisely that part of me recognized as such, the part of me from which I consciously speak and act. "To mistranslate *Ich* as 'ego' is to transform it," Bruno Bettelheim argues, "into jargon that no longer conveys the personal commitment we make when we say 'I' or 'me'" (1983: 53). Recognition also comes into play in relation to *das Es*. Psychoanalysis seeks to help the "I" learn to recognize the phenomena that are located outside the capital, as it were, but not off the map of the self. In this way, psychoanalysis rejects both a voluntarist humanism (my actions flow from my will, the independence of which is vouchsafed by my capacity for critical reflection) and a structuralist anti-humanism (subjectivity is an effect of language, history, culture, ideology; critical distance and agency are illusory). Do my actions flow from my conscious intentions or from an external force? Psychoanalysis rejects this question, pointing to a third, uncanny option. My actions do flow from inside but not from my conscious will. There are parts of me that I do not yet recognize as me, intentions that "I" cannot yet intend. For now, I can only speak about them, as something impersonal and foreign, as "It." Like Strachey's "id," Freud's *das Es* is impersonal, but there is an important difference. Recall Freud's homely example, "*it* came to me in a flash." While the "it" signals the narrator's inability to recognize himself in the idea (image, impulse, memory, etc.) arriving in this flash, Freud offers the phrase as a whole to us so that we can recognize our *act* of disavowal. He positions us in the "I," confronting the uncanny stranger at our door. By contrast, Strachey positions us externally, looking in at three psychical agencies, objects of our distanced, scientific gaze. The Standard Edition dignifies our disavowal. This runs directly counter to Freud's effort to coax the "I" into an intersubjective dialogue with the archaic and the repressed. The aim of psychoanalysis is to befriend these internal strangers, learning to speak from this new widened perspective, as "I." As Freud famously puts it, "Wo Es war, soll Ich werden" (Where it was, there

I shall become) (1933/1991: 85; for this translation and a discussion, see Lear 1990: 168–77).

What are these unintegrated, archaic layers of mental life, and how do we learn to befriend them? We can begin to answer these questions by considering a brief but rich clinical vignette from psychoanalyst and essayist Adam Phillips. Phillips was treating a twelve-year-old girl for "what turned out to be an array of symptoms that she had managed to organize into a school phobia" (1993: p. 79). He offers this summary of how the girl's family history led to her current circumstances:

> At the age of ten, having nursed a sense of neglect in the family, which she perceived as two groups, the parents and "the girls," her two elder sisters, both leaving her out, she asked her parents if she could go to boarding school. This had been an unconscious test of their devotion to her; she was dismayed to find herself, within three months of the request, in a public school three hundred miles from home. (p. 79)

We already have our first glimpse of the unconscious at work. To understand a plan, you need to understand the intention. If all intentions are conscious, then the girl's plan is clear. Her intention was to escape from this family that has cast her as the odd one out; her plan was to strike out on her own. However, the analytic dialogue surfaces an unconscious intention that helps to make better, fuller sense of her boarding school proposal (helping to explain, for example, the dismay she felt when her parents took her up on it). What she wanted was a less lonely position in the family, not to leave her family. Her plan for escaping neglect was to enact it so clearly that her parents would have to notice her deep sense of abandonment.

To understand the next part of Phillips's clinical koan, we need first to recall the importance of consistency in psychotherapy. To form an efficacious "therapeutic alliance," the analysand must be able to tolerate the frightening experience of dependence. Such a risk requires trust, and developing trust requires consistency. So, for example, analysts treat holiday breaks (or any disruption to the schedule) with explicitness and care, flagging them in advance and making space before and after to process what the disruption stirs up. An example will bring the point home and give us a further feel for unconscious dynamics. Imagine that a therapist arrives late to a session, explaining that there was a delay on the train. This sets the analysand's mind running in two directions at once. Consciously, he thinks, "well, that could happen to anyone." Thinking otherwise would contradict his self-image as rational and fair. But the analysand *is* thinking otherwise. Unconsciously, he feels dropped, as if ten minutes were ten meters. Or he feels that he must have driven the analyst away, as if he were driving the train. The example demonstrates two ways in which "the unconscious" means more than "unavailable for conscious inspection."

First, some of our intentions are actively disowned. If the analysand in our example cannot bear to acknowledge his dependence on the analyst or cannot square his feelings with his ideal of forgiveness, he will disown his impulse to berate the analyst for his lateness. Second, the unconscious is home not only to disowned thoughts but to an entirely different mode of thinking. We glimpse this in the strange logic of our dreams. In the waking dreamwork, minutes become meters, and one can be waiting at the station even while one drives the train.

Returning to our clinical vignette, Phillips recalls that after settling in to working together the girl took to therapy "with some vigor" (p. 79). She was fully engaged, with one curious exception. When holidays approached, and Phillips went over dates and made "comments to prepare her," she treated it "like a hiatus in the conversation." "I felt quite suddenly," Phillips reports, "as though I was talking in her sleep" (p. 80). This pattern of dissociation continued until, one day, the girl arrived for the session before a holiday carrying an atlas. Phillips, whose practice is in London, explains:

> I had told her, and had been telling her for some time, that I was going to America. In what sense she had heard this I had no way of knowing. But in this session she went straight to the table and traced maps of America and Britain ... and said to me, "While you're *there* [pointing to America] I'll be *here* [pointing to Britain] making the tea. I said, "That's amazing! *T* is the difference between here and there": and she grinned and said, "So I'll be making the difference." (p. 80, emphasis and interpolations in original)

For the first time, an impending holiday did not trigger a dissociative spell. She is able to tolerate a separation from Phillips enough to acknowledge it, but only on the condition that she is able to understand the gap between them, the difference between here and there, as one that she herself is making.

If this seems strange, Phillips explains, it is not because the girl is acting oddly but rather because we have distanced ourselves from the all-too-human, archaic mode of minding she reveals. What is actually strange is our conscious theory of obstacles. Our habitual contrasting of aims and obstacles only makes sense if aims arise from within and then obstacles are imposed from without. As Phillips points out, though, "it is impossible to imagine desire without obstacles" (p. 83). This "inevitable twinning of obstacle and desire" (p. 83) means that, against the logical objections of conscious cogitation, there is a rich fluidity between the two concepts. Strange as it seems to the rational planner in us, we do not just encounter obstacles, we construct them as part of making sense of what we want. Even stranger, we construct them as links, as ways of holding on to what matters. Each of us marks the way with things construed as "in the way," developing a distinctive "vocabulary of impediments" (p. 82), an "unconscious mnemonics of desire" (p. 83).

This enables us to see our young patient as learning simultaneously to love Phillips—which is to say, to feel loving gratitude for his reliable responsiveness, or what Winnicott (see, e.g., 1971/1991: 10, 71, 139) famously called "good-enough" care—and to tolerate losing him. She accomplishes this double action by equipping herself with a strange tool: an obstacle-link. And yet she cannot quite avow this archaic concept. Instead of thinking, "*I* am holding on to this therapist on whom I have come to depend by creating between us a gap that is under my control," *it* just slips out of her mouth as an unintended pun (about "there," "here," and making the tea). After all, the girl is well aware that Phillips is the one leaving, the one creating the gap between them. Rationality dictates that a whole ocean, not a manageable cup of tea, separates the United Kingdom and the United States. Somehow, though, the girl is ready to avow the intention embedded in the pun, making room for this conceptual deep-sea creature, this cunning "kenning" that Phillips can be closer as she sees him off across an ocean than when she has him right in front of her at arm's length. What enables this profound recognition?

It is Freud's great contribution to have believed in what he stumbled upon, a special type of conversation that hedges against our powerful urge to discount, or even to pass over without notice, the illogical and unlovely, the archaic and the disowned. Analyst and analysand create together a space for paying free-floating attention (diffuse, relaxed, nonjudgmental alertness) to the thoughts, feelings, and actions that come into the room with no clear provenance in the "I." Phillips and his patient together found a language with room in it for the uncanny intention she authored to build this bridge that took Phillips all of the way across the Atlantic to keep him near. *Wo Es war, soll Ich Werden.*

Thus, with Freud's help, we have identified a third corrective to the default view of educational pluralism. The interpersonal is a great source of difference, a great catalyst of our edification. But another deep encounter with difference lies much closer to home if we are willing to apprentice ourselves to noticing the layers of the inner life, the intrusions of the unconscious, the intentions that we almost know how to intend. The goal of this process is nothing short of learning to live honestly and vibrantly, of becoming something more than the bank-clerk ego that greets those who come our way and keeps the books clean. Freud (1905/1953: 267; 1916/1957: 311; 1917/1963: 450) himself described this process as a kind of education-after-schooling, a *Nach-erziehung*. And what occasions this great "after education" is difference, a difference at the core of our being.

OCCASIONS: GADAMER ON THE DYNAMICS OF HISTORY

Each of the scenes of (informal) education we have considered so far—culture, language, and the inner life—is of great interest to the leading figure in philosophical hermeneutics, Hans-Georg Gadamer. One of the first orders of business in Gadamer's (1960/2004: 8–16) signature work, *Truth and Method*, is to rehabilitate the concept of *Bildung*. Meaning either "culture" or "education" in ordinary use, the specialized concept refers to their interaction. Specifically, on the Hegelian reading of *Bildung* favored by Gadamer, education involves a twofold mediation: individual self-formation (*bilden*: to form) is mediated by cultural images (*Bilden*), texts, and ideals; cultural re-formation is mediated by the particular ways in which individuals come into their own (cf. Good and Garrison 2010: 44). This idea has obvious overlaps with Oakeshott's idea of culture as edifying conversation (as pointed out, e.g., by Rorty 1979: pt. 3). The resonances between Gadamer and Bakhtin are equally apparent. Both consider language central to human experience, viewing language in terms of concrete discourse, living dialogue, and addressivity (see, e.g., Gadamer 1960/2004: 454, 484, 553). Like Bakhtin, Gadamer (1960/2004: 459; cf. 1979/2007: 335) rejects the idea that language is a mere tool at our disposal, asserting that it is "more correct to say that language speaks us, rather than that we speak it." It is "in language," Gadamer writes, that "the order and structure of our experience itself is originally formed and constantly changed" (1960/2004: 453). Gadamer's relation to Freud is more ambivalent. While holding a rather dim view of psychotherapeutic dialogue (see, e.g., Gadamer 1977/2007a: 70; cf. 1960/2004: 387), he does credit Freud for exposing the limits of self-reflection, helping us abandon the epistemological conceit that the mind's transparent access to itself enables diagnosis and correction of the mind's clouded apprehension of the world (Gadamer 1977/2007b: 272; 1979/2007: 334; 1981/2007: 167). In any case, the inner life is of cardinal importance to Gadamer. While he views human beings as outward-facing, turned toward the other in dialogue, Gadamer is keenly interested in "the dialogue of the soul with itself" (p. 408).

Whether we are interpreting "the contents ... of tradition," caught up in "the play of language itself," or engaged in inward *dianoia*, Gadamer (1960/2004: 484) finds the same logic of educative experience at work. One grows more *gebildet* through cycles of alienation and return. We encounter a Thou inhabiting a horizon "alien enough to effect the necessary separation of ourselves from ourselves, 'but [containing] at the same time all the exit points and threads ... for finding oneself again'," only now with an enriched self-understanding.[3] However, if Gadamer echoes our three previously considered expansions of pluralism, central to his work is a fourth great wellspring of difference: history.

In everyday usage, "history" is something one has, or studies, or writes, but such expressions overstate our autonomy from and control over history. As Gadamer puts it,

> History does not belong to us, we belong to it. Long before we understand
> ourselves through the process of self-examination, we understand ourselves
> in a self-evident way in the family, society, and state in which we live ...
> That is why the prejudices of the individual, far more than his judgments,
> constitute the historical reality of his being. (1960/2004: 278, emphasis
> removed)

This is part of Gadamer's critique of modern epistemology. But notice that,
at first blush, we children of the Enlightenment might heartily agree: "All the
more reason to get on with self-examination!" For Gadamer seems simply
to remind us that, as denizens of Plato's famous cave (*Republic* 514a–520a),
we grant self-evident reality to mere shadows of playthings and self-evident
importance to "praises and prizes" (*Republic* 516c) for fluency in shadow-speak.
It is critical reflection and science that enables us to dispel these illusions, escape
this cave of convention, and apprehend reality. To this, Gadamer replies that
the Enlightenment is itself a tradition shaping our prejudgments, including our
reflexive "prejudice against prejudice itself" (1960/2004: 273). We moderns,
Gadamer explains, have mistaken a part of prejudice for the whole:

> Prejudices are not necessarily unjustified and erroneous, so that they
> inevitably distort the truth. In fact, the historicity of our existence entails that
> prejudices, in the literal sense of the word, constitute the initial directedness
> of our whole ability to experience. Prejudices are biases of our openness to
> the world. They are simply conditions whereby we experience something—
> whereby what we encounter says something to us. (1966/1976: 9)

If this phrase, "biases of our openness to the world," sounds paradoxical, it
is because we think of mind as either open or closed, like a camera with or
without its lens cap. But we do not passively absorb the light of reality. We
reach out to the world with our prejudgments and with the specific questions
these enable. Let us return to the earlier example of the naturalist, developer,
and poet each encountering the "same" sand dunes. The naturalist asks whether
the dunes are intact or eroded; the developer questions their buildability; and
the poet wonders, say, whether the sand piper—"finical, awkward/in a state
of controlled panic"; "looking for something, something, something"—is "a
student of Blake" who divines the whole world in a grain of sand (Bishop
1976/1983; referring to Blake 2008). The sand speaks to all three, but each
dialogue engages a different aspect of dune-being. So, wouldn't it be better to
step out of these partial stances and pose a more general question such as "What
is sand?" To this Gadamer replies that we must not mistake the open question
for the floating question. A good question is informed, committed, pointed
(on the structure of questions and pseudo-questions, see Gadamer 1960/2004:
362–79). It is only on the basis of substantive assumptions that one locates

a genuine controversy capable of opening up the phenomena. The novice writer chooses an Olympian theme: "What is human nature?," the author begins ... and then immediately runs out of things to say. One must descend from on-high, crafting a question whose assumptions make it at once richer and more arguable. We anchor our exploration of human nature in a particular problematic arising within a specific philosophical anthropology. Working, for example, within Simone Weil's (1949/2002) account of fundamental human needs, we find ourselves asking more incisive questions: How does Weil defend the claim that modern rootlessness fuels violence and intolerance? Could it not be that nativism itself deforms our ethical relation to the other? Can a pluralist community satisfy this "need for roots"? What sort of politics flows from Weil's account of the soul?

Our situatedness, then, is at once the condition by which the world speaks to us and the guarantee that we are tuned in to only one bandwidth. Becoming aware of such partiality is not impossible, but it is often painful. Imagine our developer slowly opening himself to ecological or poetic cultural currents, gradually learning to see the dunes not as property values but as a fragile, wondrous, living system. In the brochure for "lifelong learning" the story ends here, editing out the harrowing experience of facing your vanities and failures, of confronting the emptiness of your promises, the contingency of your projects, and indeed the mortality of your existence. On Gadamer's view (1960/2004: 350–1; cf. 217), the most profound forms of learning entail suffering. The developer may well feel gratitude for his expanded vision, but he will likely also feel exposed and bereft, flinching at the realization that he may have devoted his life to something he utterly failed to understand.

At least the developer in our example has interlocutors available to help him attempt this powerful if painful form of growth. Our historicity poses an even deeper challenge. If our developer wanted to maintain his original view of the dunes, he would at least have to work to insulate himself from these other currents in the cultural conversation that threaten to redescribe him. But what if, as Heidegger (1954/1977) suggests, we have all become that developer. What if all of modernity is a collective forgetting that there is more to nature than "standing reserve"? This parochialism seems much harder to correct, for it is no longer clear where to turn to "separate ourselves from ourselves" and expand our horizons. With whom can we dialogue to help us realize the limits of our epochal frames?

The answer may seem obvious: voices from the past, whose untimely perspectives are preserved in historically recessed texts and artifacts. However, dialogue across historical horizons is far from simple. The first pitfall is presentism, our tendency to view the past in terms of the present. This can take various forms. We may simply fail to notice the untimely dimensions of the text; we may primitivize the past, treating its differences as if they were failed attempts to get where we are; or we may romanticize, projecting our hopes and anxieties onto the past. In each of these variations, we insulate ourselves from the unsettling confrontation with our contingency and fail to learn how the world hangs together for the historical other.

The obvious cure for this would seem to be historicism, which cautions against precisely this tendency to assimilate past to present. However, as Gadamer convincingly shows, historicism is not as humble and respectful as it appears. To view the historically recessed text as inhabiting an entirely alien world, speaking only to concerns of its moment, amounts to just another form of condescension. Far from downplaying the difference of the text, its foreign sensibility is emphasized, but this comes at the cost of neutralizing its claim to truth. We do not take the text seriously as having something to say to us about the world, instead treating its speech symptomatically, "as a mere expression of life," a product of its age (Gadamer 1960/2004: 296). The past can speak to us neither if we excise its untimeliness nor if we ourselves back out of the dialogue into the position of the historicist who reconstructs the past "in its own terms." It is also possible to view the breakdown of dialogue in reverse terms. We retain a speaking part, but the historical other is downgraded from a partner in a dialogue about a (putatively) common world into a mute object of our own historical knowledge. The word "dialogue" is somewhat misleading since the process requires not two but three characters, not only the interlocutors but also the subject matter that brings them together and draws out their differences. The presentist engages the subject matter but does so monologically, making the historical other into a mere ventriloquist's dummy. The historicist engages the past only to turn it into the subject matter, losing the original subject. What drops out in both approaches is the perspective of the past on the subject matter, a perspective that might have catalyzed our own expansion of horizons.

Though temporality is what occasions these aporias of historical interpretation, it also contains their solution. The dilemma of presentism/historicism relies on a strangely static, spatial conception both of past texts and of present interpreters. We set out, say, to study the *quattrocento* or the "long nineteenth century." We conceive of figures and events, artifacts and texts, as existing in a period separated by a gulf from our own. Our interpretive dilemma then becomes whether to project our ideas onto the past or maintain a researcher's strict separation between the facts of then and the conjectures of now. Gadamer sidesteps this dilemma by exploring, on the one hand, the temporality of the traditionary text itself and, on the other, the temporality of interpretation. Texts are not like isotypes, at their realest at time zero, decaying more and more over time. Texts are built to travel, to realize themselves anew and more fully in the responses of differently situated interlocutors. Temporality is part of the very being of a work of culture (for a more detailed reconstruction of this part of Gadamer's argument, see Higgins and Burbules 2012: 373–4).

Similarly, we misunderstand interpretation if we view it in static, spatial terms. Gadamer remedies this misconception by recalling the concept of the hermeneutic circle. We build our understanding of the whole from our observation of its parts. At the same time, we need a gestalt to pick out the parts of something as parts. This means that understanding is not a linear process, as if we were collecting data until we can induce a correct generalization. Understanding follows a circular pattern. For example, we notice a couple of comments by our new acquaintance, remarks about things that cause her anxiety. A tentative generalization forms that she is an anxious person. With this frame in hand, though, we start noticing new aspects of her behavior, such as the way her eyes smile when she says certain things. These new particulars lead us to revise our generalization in turn. She now strikes us not so much as personally anxious but rather as someone keyed in to the inevitable nerviness of social situations. This new generalization leads us to notice even further details we had overlooked, aspects of the way she carries herself and the timing of what she says. And, again, our gestalt shifts: she now strikes us as someone who is actually quite comfortable in her skin and performs her anxious-seeming antics to help others relax. In other words, seeing is always "seeing as," a fitting of phenomena into given frames. If interpretation occurred all at once, this would mean that we cannot understand the other except as a screen onto which we project our own assumptions. But over time, we can make greater contact with the otherness of the other by listening to how the answers to our interpretive queries show us something about the limitations of our questions. It is this patient reframing, these endless trips around the hermeneutic circle, that drop out in the sterile debate between presentism and historicism with its false dilemma between indulging or bracketing our prejudices. "Our own prejudice is properly brought into play," Gadamer writes, "by being put at risk" (1960/2004: 299).

In this way, Gadamer not only reminds us of a fourth neglected dimension of educational pluralism, historicity, but helps us to clarify a more general point. Assimilation is only one strategy for mitigating this risk. Exoticism is simply a less obvious means to the same end. In claiming to be able to measure in advance the gulf between us, I still indulge my knowingness. And I protect myself from actually coming into contact with the surprising differences I might discover by risking my prejudices in unpredictable trips around the hermeneutic circle. This suggests that the reductions we have identified—narrowing education to schooling, pluralism to tolerance, and difference to identity politics—may serve a defensive function. For each of the dimensions of difference we have sought to recover—those internal to one's culture, language, self, or history— entail messy, uncanny encounters not with a predefined, distant other but with differences all too close to home.

CONCLUSION

On our default understanding, educational pluralism concerns the problems of schooling in a multicultural society. While seeking to do justice to the complexity and importance of these problems, I have also sought in this programmatic chapter to sketch the contours of a fuller and more dynamic vision of educational pluralism. I have argued that modern scholasticism, identity politics, and simplifications in our understanding of pluralism itself have together blinded us to rich dimensions of difference, all of the key agencies of informal education, and crucial insights about pluralistic engagement. What also comes into view is that difference only constitutes a problem for education under special conditions. In lived life, as we navigate the conversation of culture, the polyphony of discourse, the layers of the inner life, and the occasions of history, difference is no mere problem but education's great catalyst.

NOTES

1   Thanks to Anna Pagès for thinking of me for this topic and for feedback on multiple drafts. I am also grateful to Jennifer Burns, Walter Feinberg, and David T. Hansen for their comments on the chapter. Thanks also to Kirsten Welch for her editorial attention to the manuscript. Discussing pluralism with Emily Wenneborg helped me clarify my version of "deep pluralism." This chapter was completed with support of the Lynch School of Education and Human Development at Boston College.

2   Brown v. Board of Education of Topeka, 347 U.S. 483 (1954).

3   This is Gadamer (1960/2004: 12), quoting from Hegel (1809/2003: 321–2). However, I have discovered that Gadamer made two errors here, both uncorrected by his translators (cf. Gadamer 1960/2010: 19): (1) he fails to attribute the phrase "die uns von uns trennt" (separate ourselves from ourselves) to Hegel; (2) he misreads "Anfangspunkte" (beginning points) as "Ausgangspunkte" (exit points).

REFERENCES

Allport, Gordon (1954/1979), *The Nature of Prejudice*, 25th anniversary edn., Cambridge, MA: Perseus.

Bakhtin, Mikhail (1934–5/1981), "Discourse in the Novel," trans. Caryl Emerson and Michael Holquist, in Michael Holquist (ed.), *The Dialogic Imagination: Four Essays*, 259–422, Austin: University of Texas Press.

Bakhtin, Mikhail (1940/1981), "From the Prehistory of Novelistic Discourse," trans. Caryl Emerson and Michael Holquist, in Michael Holquist (ed.), *The Dialogic Imagination: Four Essays*, 41–83, Austin: University of Texas Press.

Bakhtin, Mikhail (1965/1984), *Rabelais and His World*, trans. Hélène Iswolsky, Bloomington: Indiana University Press.

Benn Michaels, Walter (2016), *The Trouble with Diversity: How We Learned to Love Identity and Ignore Inequality*, 10th anniversary edn., New York: Picador.

Bettelheim, Bruno (1983), *Freud and Man's Soul*, New York: Knopf.

Bishop, Elizabeth (1976/1983), "Sandpiper," in *The Complete Poems, 1927–1979*, 131, New York: Farrar, Straus and Giroux.

Blacker, David (2019), *What's Left of the World: Education, Identity and the Post-Work Political Imagination*, Winchester: Zero Books.

Blake, William (2008), "Auguries of Innocence," in David V. Erdman (ed.), *The Complete Poetry and Prose of William Blake*, 490–3, Berkeley: University of California Press.

Bowles, Herbert and Samuel Gintis (1976/2011), *Schooling in Capitalist America: Educational Reform and the Contradictions of Economic Life*, Chicago: Haymarket Books.

Connolly, William (2005), *Pluralism*, Durham, NC: Duke University Press.

Dewey, John (1916), *Democracy and Education: An Introduction to the Philosophy of Education*, New York: Macmillan.

Egan, Kieran (2008), *The Future of Education: Reimagining Our Schools from the Ground Up*, New Haven, CT: Yale University Press.

Enos, Ryan D. (2017), *The Space Between Us: Social Geography and Politics*, Cambridge: Cambridge University Press.

Fraser, Nancy (1992), "Rethinking the Public Sphere: A Contribution to the Critique of Actually Existing Democracy," in Craig Calhoun (ed.), *Habermas and the Public Sphere*, 109–42, Cambridge, MA: MIT Press.

Freud, Sigmund (1905/1953), "On Psychotherapy," trans. James Strachey, in James Strachey (ed.), *The Standard Edition of the Complete Psychological Works of Sigmund Freud, Vol. 7: (1901–1905): A Case of Hysteria, Three Essays on Sexuality and Other Works*, 255–68, London: The Hogarth Press.

Freud, Sigmund (1916/1957), "Some Character-Types Met with in Psycho-Analytic Work," trans. James Strachey, in James Strachey (ed.), *The Standard Edition of the Complete Psychological Works of Sigmund Freud, Vol. 14: (1914–1916): On the History of the Psycho- Analytic Movement, Papers on Metapsychology and Other Works*, 309–33, London: The Hogarth Press.

Freud, Sigmund (1917/1955), "A Difficulty in the Path of Psycho-Analysis," trans. James Strachey, in James Strachey (ed.), *The Standard Edition of the Complete Psychological Works of Sigmund Freud, Vol. 17: (1915–17): "An Infantile Neurosis" and Other Works*, 135–44, London: The Hogarth Press.

Freud, Sigmund (1917/1963), "Introductory Lectures on Psycho-analysis," Part III, trans. James Strachey, in James Strachey (ed.), *The Standard Edition of the Complete Psychological Works of Sigmund Freud*, Vol. 16, Part III, London: The Hogarth Press.

Freud, Sigmund (1917/1991a), "Eine Schwierigkeit Der Psychoanalyse," in *Gesammelte Werke: Chronologisch Geordnet, Vol. 12: Werke aus den Jahren 1917–1920*, 3–12, London: Imago Publishing.

Freud, Sigmund (1917/1991b), "Vorlesungen zur Einführung in Die Psychoanalyse," in *Gesammelte Werke: Chronologisch Geordnet*, Vol. 11, London: Imago Publishing.

Freud, Sigmund (1920), "One of the Difficulties of Psycho-Analysis," trans. Joan Riviere, *International Journal of Psycho-Analysis*, 1: 17–23.

Freud, Sigmund (1925/1961), "The Resistances to Psycho-Analysis," trans. James Strachey, in James Strachey (ed.), *The Standard Edition of the Complete Psychological Works of Sigmund Freud, Vol. 19: (1923-1925): The Ego and the Id and Other Works*, 211–24, London: The Hogarth Press.

Freud, Sigmund (1926/1991), "Die Frage der Laienanalyse: Unterredungen mit Einem Unparteiischen," in *Gesammelte Werke: Chronologisch Geordnet*, Vol. 14: *Werke aus den Jahren 1925–1931*, 209–86, London: Imago Publishing.

Freud, Sigmund (1933/1991), "Freud, S. (1933): XXXI: Vorlesung. Die Zerlegung der Psychischen Persönlichkeit," in *Gesammelte Werke: Chronologisch Geordnet*, Vol. 15: *Neue Folge der Vorlesungen zur Einführung in die Psychoanalyse*, 62–86, London: Imago Publishing.

Gadamer, Hans-Georg (1960/2004), *Truth and Method*, trans. Joel Weinsheimer and Donald Marshall, 2nd rev. edn., Continuum Impacts series, New York: Continuum.

Gadamer, Hans-Georg (1960/2010), *Hermeneutik I. Wahrheit und Methode: Grundzüge Einer Philosophischen Hermeneutik*, Tübingen: Mohr Siebeck.

Gadamer, Hans-Georg (1977/2007a), "Classical and Philosophical Hermeneutics." Translated by Richard E. Palmer. In *The Gadamer Reader: A Bouquet of Later Writings*, edited by Richard E. Palmer, 44–71. Evanston, IL: Northwestern University Press.

Gadamer, Hans-Georg (1977/2007b), "Greek Philosophy and Modern Thinking." Translated by Richard E. Palmer. In *The Gadamer Reader: A Bouquet of Later Writings*, edited by Richard E. Palmer, 267–73. Evanston, IL: Northwestern University Press.

Gadamer, Hans-Georg (1981/2007), "Text and Interpretation." Translated by Richard E. Palmer. In *The Gadamer Reader: A Bouquet of Later Writings*, edited by Richard E. Palmer, 166–91. Evanston, IL: Northwestern University Press.

Gadamer, Hans-Georg (1966/1976), "The Universality of the Hermeneutic Problem," trans. David E. Linge, in David E. Linge (ed.), *Philosophical Hermeneutics*, 3–17, Berkeley: University of California Press.

Gadamer, Hans-Georg (1979/2007), "The Heritage of Hegel," trans. Frederick G. Lawrence, in Richard E. Palmer (ed.), *The Gadamer Reader: A Bouquet of Later Writings*, 326–44, Evanston, IL: Northwestern University Press.

Good, James A. and Jim Garrison (2010), "Traces of Hegelian *Bildung* in Dewey's Philosophy," in Paul Fairfield (ed.), *John Dewey and Continental Philosophy*, 44–68, Carbondale: Southern Illinois University Press.

Habermas, Jürgen (1995), "Reconciliation through the Public Use of Reason: Remarks on John Rawls's *Political Liberalism*," *Journal of Philosophy*, 92 (3): 109–31.

Hegel, G.W.F. (1809/2003), "Rede zum Schuljahrabschluß am 29. September 1809," in *Werke II*, Electronic Edition, Vol. 4: *Nürnberger und Heidelberger Schriften*, 312–26, Charlottesville, VA: Intellex Corp.

Heidegger, Martin (1954/1977), "The Question Concerning Technology," trans. William Lovitt, *In The Question Concerning Technology and Other Essays*, 3–35, New York: Harper & Row.

Higgins, Chris and Nicholas C. Burbules (2012), "Teaching and Translation," *Philosophy of Education*, 2011: 369–76.

King, Martin Luther Jr. (1967), "Beyond Vietnam: A Time to Break Silence," Sermon, Riverside Church, New York City, April 4. Available online: https://www.americanrhetoric.com/speeches/mlkatimetobreaksilence.htm.

Labaree, David F. (2008), "The Winning Ways of a Losing Strategy: Educationalizing Social Problems in the United States," *Educational Theory*, 58 (4): 447–60.

Labaree, David F. (2012), *Someone Has to Fail: The Zero-Sum Game of American Schooling*, Cambridge, MA: Harvard University Press.

Lareau, Annette (2003), *Unequal Childhoods: Class, Race, and Family Life*, Berkeley: University of California Press.

Laurent, Sylvie (2018), *King and the Other America: The Poor People's Campaign and the Quest for Economic Equality*, Berkeley: University of California Press.

Lear, Jonathan (1990), *Love and Its Place in Nature: A Philosophical Interpretation of Freudian Analysis*, New York: Farrar, Straus and Giroux.

Lilla, Mark (2017), *The Once and Future Liberal: After Identity Politics*, New York: HarperCollins.

Liston, Daniel P. and Kevin Murray (2015), "Schooling in Capitalism: Navigating the Bleak Pathways of Structural Fate," *Educational Theory*, 65 (3): 245–64.

Lucas, Samuel Roundfield (1999), *Tracking Inequality: Stratification and Mobility in American High Schools*, New York: Teachers College Press.

Martin, Jane Roland (1981), "The Ideal of the Educated Person," *Educational Theory*, 31 (2): 97–109.

McCarthy, Cameron (1988), "Rethinking Liberal and Radical Perspectives on Racial Inequality in Schooling: Making the Case for Nonsynchrony," *Harvard Educational Review*, 58 (3): 265–79.

McIntosh, Peggy (1989), "White Privilege: Unpacking the Invisible Knapsack," *Peace and Freedom*, July/August: 10–12.

Merry, Michael S. (2013), *Equality, Citizenship and Segregation: A Defense of Separation*, New York: Palgrave Macmillan.

Merry, Michael S. and William S. New (2014), "Is Diversity Necessary for Educational Justice?," *Educational Theory*, 64 (3): 205–25.

Merry, Michael S. and William S. New (2016), "Is the Liberal Defense of Public Schools a Fantasy?," *Critical Studies in Education*, 58 (3): 1–17.

Newman, John Henry (1891/1996), *The Idea of the University*, ed. Frank M. Turner (Rethinking the Western Tradition series), New Haven, CT: Yale University Press.

Oakeshott, Michael (1959/1991), "The Voice of Poetry in the Conversation of Mankind," in Timothy Fuller (ed.), *Rationalism in Politics and Other Essays*, 488–541, new and expanded edn., Indianapolis, IN: Liberty Press.

Oakeshott, Michael (1962/1991), "The Study of Politics in a University," in Timothy Fuller (ed.), *Rationalism in Politics and Other Essays*, 184–218, new and expanded edn., Indianapolis, IN: Liberty Press.

Oakeshott, Michael (1975/1989), "A Place of Learning," in Timothy Fuller (ed.), *The Voice of Liberal Learning: Michael Oakeshott on Education*, 17–42, New Haven, CT: Yale University Press.

Paluck, Elizabeth Levy, Seth A. Green, and Donald P. Green (2019), "The Contact Hypothesis Re-evaluated," *Behavioural Public Policy*, 3 (2): 129–58.

Pettigrew, Thomas F. and Linda R. Tropp (2006), "A Meta-Analytic Test of Intergroup Contact Theory," *Journal of Personality and Social Psychology*, 90 (5): 751–83.

Phillips, Adam (1993), "Looking at Obstacles," in *On Kissing, Tickling, and Being Bored: Psychoanalytic Essays on the Unexamined Life*, 68–92, Cambridge, MA: Harvard University Press.

Plato (*c.* 380 BCE/2004), *Republic*, trans. C.D.C. Reeve, 3rd rev. edn., Indianapolis, IN: Hackett.

Pound, Ezra (1934/1960), *The ABC of Reading*, New York: New Directions.

Rawls, John (2005), *Political Liberalism*. Expanded Edition, New York: Columbia University Press.

Reddick, John (2003), "Translator's Preface," in Sigmund Freud (ed.), *Beyond the Pleasure Principle and Other Writings*, trans. John Reddick, xxxi–xxxvi, London: Penguin.

Reed, Adolph, Jr. (2015), "From Jenner to Dolezal: One Trans Good, the Other Not So Much," *Common Dreams*, June 15.

Rescher, Nicholas (1993), *Pluralism: Against the Demand for Consensus*, Oxford: Clarendon Press.

Rorty, Richard (1979), *Philosophy and the Mirror of Nature*, Princeton, NJ: Princeton University Press.

Sagan, Carl (1980/2013), *Cosmos*, New York: Ballantine Books.

Snyder, Thomas D., ed. (1993), "120 Years of American Education: A Statistical Portrait," National Center for Educational Statistics, U.S. Department of Education, https://nces.ed.gov/pubs93/93442.pdf.

Weil, Simone (1949/2002), *The Need for Roots: Prelude to a Declaration of Duties toward Mankind*, trans. Arthur Wills, London: Routledge.

Welner, Kevin G. (2001), *Legal Rights, Local Wrongs: When Community Control Collides with Educational Equity*, Albany: State University of New York Press.

Winnicott, Donald W. (1971/1991), *Playing and Reality*, London: Routledge.

CHAPTER TWO

Feminism within Philosophy of Education

LOVISA BERGDAHL AND ELISABET LANGMANN

[S]he said, "I am woman; and I am seeking for the land of freedom ...
Oh, I am alone! I am utterly alone!"
And Reason, that old man, said to her, "Silence! what do you hear?"
And she listened intently, and she said, "I hear a sound of feet, a thousand
times ten thousand and thousand of thousands, and they beat this way!"
He said, "They are the feet of those that shall follow you." (Schreiner 1891:
76, 81–2)

INTRODUCTION: RECLAIMING CONVERSATIONS

One way of describing feminism is to see it as a living and ongoing conversation
between generations.[1] Along similar lines, Michel Oakeshott defines education
as a process of initiation into an inherited world of meaning and to "the skill
and partnership of this [intergenerational] conversation" (1962/1991: 490). To
this extent, both feminism and education are generational phenomena raising
questions about what should be passed on from one generation to the other and
to what extent the new generation needs to rebel against the old. At the same
time, female to female inheritance has always been problematic in the Western
philosophical tradition in which the legacy passed on from male to male has
been regarded as both (gender) natural and of key importance (Spencer 2007).
To be fully educated as philosophers of education, then, means that we need to

"reclaim a conversation" (Roland Martin 1985) that also includes women/girls and what women/girls represent as part of our common inheritance. Against such observations, and inspired by Hannah Arendt's (1961) hermeneutical approach to history, we argue that the past is never a closed "given" but a multifaceted inheritance that calls for interpretation by every new generation. Hence, the purpose of this chapter is to reclaim some key conversations between and within different generations of feminist philosophers of education with future generations in mind, extending a general invitation to the reader to think and practice feminism within philosophy of education anew.[2]

Why feminist theory matters, or is feminism for everybody?

Despite offering important methodological and theoretical contributions to the field, most scholars inspired by feminist theory are still positioned as strangers in relation to mainstream philosophy of education—as if feminist readings are something one can simply choose (or avoid choosing) to apply as an *external* analysis to an otherwise "gender neutral" field (see, e.g., Leach 1991; Schumann 2016; Thayer-Bacon and Turner 2007). For most writers inspired by feminist theory, however, gender is always already *internal to* educational practice and educational theory in at least two ways: firstly, because educational subjects come in "at least two" sexes (Irigaray 1985); and secondly, because educational languages and practices are never neutral but always already coded in feminine and masculine registers (Butler 1990). Hence, a common feature among feminist philosophers of education is that they offer new insights to educational theory and practice by way of a double movement: to make the case that female and other marginalized human experiences have not yet been included in the mainstream development of the field (a mode of critique); and to show the significance and value of feminist inquiry for the general development of educational theory and practice (a mode of creativity). In this sense, adopting feminist perspectives as a way of *doing* philosophy of education can be seen as a joint effort to redefine the center by looking at the contemporary educational landscape from the margins (Thayer-Bacon and Turner 2007). In addition, feminist engagements with both the *style and content* of an otherwise male-dominated philosophical discourse have generated new ways of defining which issues and questions count and have significance within the field itself (see, e.g., Stone 1995; Thayer-Bacon, Stone, and Sprecher 2013).

Against this background, we suggest, feminist theory and feminist philosophy ought to be of interest to any scholar who is committed to the idea that public education is an education for all and who wants the field of philosophy of education to continue to develop and live on as a scholarly mixed-gender community. Or, in the famous words of bell hooks (2000), "Feminism is for everybody."

The focus of the chapter: The "woman" and the "feminine"

In contemporary feminist debate, and as a response to the emerging postmaterialist and postfeminist movements in gender theory, one of the most crucial questions for education is whether feminism itself and its historical focus on the injustices faced by women *as women* have any relevance today or if it only lends itself to identity politics (Mikkola 2017). Given that much contemporary gender and queer theory problematizes "her" and "she" as central pronouns for feminism and criticizes feminist philosophy for introducing irrelevant, essentialist, or even harmful separations between women and men into theoretical inquiry, a crucial question to ask is what relevance, role, and meaning categories such as "woman/girl" and "feminine/femininity" will have in educational research in the future. Or, to paraphrase Bruno Latour (2005) in this regard, has the concept of "woman" run out of steam within feminist philosophy of education?

To our minds, "woman" is far from an outdated concept, but, as we will show, feminist philosophers of education have gone *from taking the empirical* woman/girl as their main and primary object of analysis *to including educational theory* as an object of study from the perspective of the experiences of gender differences more generally (see, e.g., Leach 1991; Thayer-Bacon and Turner 2007). Hence, the lens through which we will explore the vast body of feminist work in philosophy of education will be through the *inherent instability* of the categories of "woman/girl" and "feminine/femininity" in feminist theory (Riley 1988; see also Gillis, Howie, and Munford 2007). This lens, we suggest, will help us make (provisional) decisions about whom to include as a feminist thinker in the chapter in at least two ways: firstly, by focusing on those scholars within the field who address women, gender, and female experiences as a specific way of doing philosophy of education; and secondly, by recognizing that feminist work is not theoretical work in general but work that is "produced in particular ways, in different times and places" (Ahmed 2000: 97). This suggests, in turn, that what counts as feminism in philosophy of education is not a neutral act but an act that always involves decisions and judgments that are open to dispute.

The structure of the chapter: Three waves of feminism in philosophy of education

While philosophical traditions are often named by their male founders, such as Darwinism, Marxism, and Freudianism, it is not a coincidence that different strands of feminisms are *not* named after individual women (Spencer 2007). Instead, the history of Western feminism is traditionally organized around three waves: the first wave (1848–1949), the second wave (1949–90), and the third wave (1990–present). To call something a "wave," Cathryn Bailey

(1997) argues, implies at least two things: that something belongs to a series of movements, and that this something is *both* similar to *and* different from other events in that series of movements. Inspired by Bailey, we use the well-known image of the wave as a way of clustering the different generations of feminist philosophers of education around different key conversations and themes. The wave is here understood metaphorically as a cyclical movement resisting sharp distinctions and absolute boundaries but, at the same time, without "blurring the differences between [or within] older and younger feminists" (Bailey 1997: 17). Even if there is little consensus about how to characterize the three phases, the wave as metaphor, we suggest, offers a helpful way of mapping and navigating a complex and ever-changing feminist landscape.

The chapter is divided into three parts, each highlighting—although in different degrees—some key themes and conversations in both the different waves of feminism in general and in the field of philosophy of education in particular. In the first part, we show how women's and girls' equal access to education and public life has been central to feminist questions during the first wave but also how, in the field of philosophy of education, women and women's writing were absent while men and men's writing dominated up until the 1950s. In the second part, we focus extensively on the work of the second wave's three "mothers" within feminist educational philosophy—Maxine Greene, Jane Roland Martin, and Nel Noddings—and how their work has

FIGURE 2.1 Women standing. *Source*: Rawpixel.com / Shutterstock.

influenced what counts as mainstream educational philosophy and theory in regards to the questions they address, the concepts they adopt, and the style of writing they develop.

The shift among feminist scholars from the *empirical* woman/girl to *educational theory* comes to the fore especially in the shift between the second and the third parts of the chapter. It comes to the fore not in the sense that the concept "woman" is running out of steam (Latour), but in the sense that one of the most central questions in third-wave feminism seems to be whether or not a focus on the experiences and lives of women *as women* still has a bearing on educational philosophy or if it just reproduces gender stereotypes. Hence, in the third part of the chapter we offer a brief overview of the diverse and multilayered feminist theories of the third wave, suggesting that feminist work in philosophy of education can be clustered around three main conversations: *feminism as recovery*, *feminism as critique*, and *feminism as reconstruction*. By way of conclusion, we sketch out what we see as some of the future crossroads to consider in feminist philosophy of education.

THE FIRST WAVE: RIPPLES ON THE SURFACE

The first wave (1848–1949) formally began in the United States at the Seneca Falls convention in 1848, and it is generally associated with famous suffragettes such as Lucretia Mott, Elizabeth Cady Stanton, Susan B. Anthony, and Sojourner Truth. Even if some historians locate the origins of Western feminist thinking in ancient Greece (e.g., Sappho) or the medieval times (e.g., Hildegard von Bingen), it is not until the late nineteenth century that the efforts for women's equal rights merge into a self-conscious series of movements (Freedman 2003). Mary Wollstonecraft's (1792/1996) *A Vindication of the Rights of Woman* is sometimes also considered to belong to the first wave and Wollstonecraft is, indeed, of particular interest here because of her passionate justification of women's right to education. Women are not by nature inferior to men, she argues; they simply lack education. Hence, common to the different feminist voices in the first wave is the advocating of dignity, intelligence, and the basic human potential of the female sex, viewing women's presence in the public sphere not just as a question of rights (e.g., to vote, to own property, to divorce, and to manage their own bodies) but as a way of improving civil life and political processes for all (Freedman 2003).

At the same time as women were encouraged to join forces and stand next to one another, critical voices were raised among women themselves arguing that the central task of a suffragette is not just to "count women in" but also, and more importantly, to address the daring question, "Who counts as a woman?" (hooks 1981/2015). The suffragette movement was connected to the temperance and abolitionist movements, movements that gave voice to the famous activist

Sojourner Truth, whose rhetorical question, "Ain't I a woman?" sheds light on the situation of black women and how women of color were marginalized within the suffragettes (hooks 1981/2015). In turn, the conservative women of Victorian America were critical of the suffragettes acting in "unladylike" ways (e.g., public speaking, demonstrating, spending periods in jail), something that challenged the traditional femininity of the time and made some suffragettes use conventional expressions of femininity as a deliberate political strategy (Rampton 2015).

Hence, the inherent instability of the categories "woman/girl" and "feminine/ femininity" have been central to feminist activism and theory from the very beginning, giving direction and character to the different voices of feminism in philosophy of education today.

Feminism in philosophy of education

Despite the fact that the first-wave feminists achieved major contributions to the rights of education for women, the field of philosophy of education "has been slow to open its doors to women philosophers and recognize the value and diversity of their work" (Thayer-Bacon and Turner 2007: 298). As is pointed out by Mary Leach (1991), men and masculine values have historically dominated the conversation in the field as recently as the 1950s with only a few exceptions (e.g., Charlotte Perkins Gilman, Jane Addams, Maria Montessori, Ellen Key). Hence, even if the names and work of female educationalists in this wave have been acknowledged and retrieved in the second and third waves (see the sections that follow), the educational implications of first-wave feminism within philosophy of education mostly concern empirical women's and girls' equal access to education and public life (Haddock Seigfried 1996; Roland Martin 1985).

THE SECOND WAVE: THE ESTABLISHMENT OF A RESEARCH FIELD

Inspired by Virginia Woolf's *A Room of One's Own* (1929/2004), second-wave feminism is often said to begin with the publication of Simone de Beauvoir's paradigmatic work *The Second Sex* (1949/1989)—publications as much focused on women's cultural and intellectual emancipation as on women's political rights and inequalities (Friedan 1963). If the 1950s was a decade of discontent because women had drawn back into the private sphere of the family from having been active in the war industries of the Second World War, the 1970s managed to transform this discontent into consciousness-raising movements. At the same time as being strongly intertwined with political and social activist movements such as the Black Power movement or the efforts to end the war in Vietnam, the voices of the second wave (1949–1990s) were increasingly theoretical, drawing mainly on liberal, neo-Marxist, and psychoanalytical theory in their analyses (Freedman 2003). Famous feminist slogans such as "the personal is political" and "women's struggle is a class struggle" all belong to this time period, which was both a time of diverse political feminisms and one of different women's studies programs emerging at the university level as legitimate fields of study together with feminist standpoint theory in research.[3]

A central aspect of the second wave was the political idea that women must gain some distance—"a room of one's own" (Virginia Woolf)—to explore their unique voices and form independent judgments. This search for a specifically female experience and subjectivity led to the development of "women-only spaces" and to the idea that women working together can create dynamic social and intellectual environments. Owing to their biology and/or their historical experiences of oppression and marginalization, women and girls were thought to be better equipped to understand fully the different forms of gender biases characteristic of sexist societies and to find ways to contribute to emancipatory intellectual work and to transformative social change (Freedman 2003). The term "eco-feminism" was coined and the "nature/nurture" debate took form, primarily to capture the sense that women, because of their biological connectedness to nature and the earth, are more inclined toward relational, holistic, and environmental thinking then are men (e.g., Carson 1962/2000).

However, the above tendency within standpoint theory to essentialize women's and girls' experiences was soon criticized. The privileging of female experiences, which became an axiom during this period, was challenged by women outside dominant feminist theorizing. Feminists such as Hazel Carby (1982), bell hooks (1984), and Gayatri Spivak (1987), for example, have all pointed out the historical consolidation of feminism with Euro-Western, white, middle-class interests and values and have been addressing the problems of racism within the feminist movement. Since, however, feminism "makes sense only if the term 'woman' can be somehow (*a priori*) isolated and at least somewhat essentialized" (Leach 1991: 299), central to the second wave feminism is that establishing a positive identity for "women"—sometimes by referring to women's experiences as mothers and primary caregivers—is both explored and criticized during this period (e.g., Rubin 1975).

Pioneer feminist writers in philosophy of education

The voices of the second-wave feminist thinkers in philosophy of education are, in comparison to the first and the third waves, quite easily distinguished. The main reason for this is that the field of philosophy of education itself was in its making during this period, and if, in general, women in the field were few, the feminist voices were even fewer. During the 1970s, however, women-led symposia were introduced, such as the one organized by Maxine

Greene, Barbara Arnstine, and Elizabeth Steiner Maccia at the Philosophy of Education Society conference in 1976 on the topic "education and women liberation" (Leach 1991).[4]

In the following sections, we will focus on three pioneers or "mothers" in feminist philosophy of education: Maxine Greene, Jane Roland Martin, and Nel Noddings. While they all belong to the second wave of feminism, their work also stretches into the third wave, both in terms of their time of publishing and in terms of the questions they are addressing.

Maxine Greene

Being the first woman philosopher hired at Teachers College, Columbia University, in 1963, Maxine Greene (1917–2014) is often regarded as one of the first feminist writers within the field of philosophy of education (Jacobs 1997). During her long and prominent academic career, Greene was confronted with the question of how to make meaning of her professional and personal life despite the many social prejudices that were facing women at the time. As a woman, a secular Jew, and a mother of two children, Greene often found herself excluded from important spheres at the university that were dominated by male, middle-class, and Protestant values. In a society unfriendly to women who wanted to maintain both a family life and a professional life, she was forced to invent her own educational and academic path (Greene 1998, 1978/1995; Greene and Griffiths 2003, Hancook 2001).

These personal experiences, which, according to Greene (1978/1995), were the experiences of many women of her time, have influenced her thinking about freedom and social justice in education. Even if Greene regards herself as a "late blooming feminist," one of the central feminist questions that underpins her influential work in educational philosophy is how to become "wide-awake" as a woman in an educational system governed by masculine values (Greene and Griffiths 2003). Inspired by the female heroine in Kate Chopin's novel *The Awakening* (1899), Greene (1978/1995) was convinced that human beings are able to help each other to "wake up" to a common world and to resist oppression by viewing their own and other people's life histories from different perspectives of perspectives. By affirming the intimate relation between personal liberation and societal liberation, Greene (1988) was carefully situating her work in the tension between positive and negative freedom, between opportunities and constraints, between creativity and critique. Rather than focusing on the many modes of prejudice, exclusion, and inequalities suffered by women in different educational settings, Greene took an affirmative stand, highlighting the creative ways in which individual women have come to understand and conceptualize their lived experiences and invent their own educational paths (Jacobs 1997; Pinar 1998). Even if Greene was personally aware of the limitations that women historically have faced in relation to education, she wanted to encourage both men and women to imagine themselves anew by acting in solidarity and in concert. "Wide-awakedness," Greene argues in *The Dialectics of Freedom* (1988) and in *Releasing the Imagination* (1995), is about having the courage to see and listen to things that you perhaps would not want to see or hear, to take risks and to criticize the status quo, but also about finding ways of coming together to heal, connect, and repair by *collectively* imagining the world otherwise.

Characteristic of Greene's approach to philosophy of education is that philosophical understanding involves rational as well as emotional, ethical, and aesthetic sensibilities. In her own writing, she deliberately draws on a multitude of theoretical and philosophical traditions and includes historical, literary, feminist, and artistic references—both to expand the notion of critical reflection and to look at the lived world from a variety of viewpoints (Ayers and Miller 1997; Pinar 1998). Stressing the liberating potential of the arts and the humanities, Greene (1995) was in search of educational practices that can help teachers and students to resist the technical rationality, thoughtlessness, and carelessness that, according to her, characterize many of the inequalities women and minority groups were facing in education. Inspired by the work of American pragmatists (Dewey, James, Addams) and of existential philosophers (Merleau-Ponty, Heidegger, Sartre, Arendt), Greene was convinced that human beings have the power to cultivate a "freed intelligence" by engaging in transformative teaching practices. In *Teacher as Stranger: Educational Philosophy for the Modern Age* (1973), *Existential Encounters for Teachers* (1967), and *Landscapes of Learning* (1978), Greene encourages teachers to think philosophically about their own work to become self-conscious about the cultural, social, and personal influences that construct their curriculum enactments and ways of being teachers (see also Greene 1965). Greene was strongly committed to the idea of teachers as "initiators of change" (1988: 63), particularly by creating public spaces where personal life experiences can be confirmed and challenged and where both men and women can explore what they want to become through collectively deciding what will be their common world.

Throughout her life's work, Greene was in search of ways of transgressing the "surface reality" (1978: 54) or "mystification" of the world that many of us tend to take for granted as natural or objectively true. She wanted an educational system that could "tear aside the conventional masks ... that hide women's being in the world" (1988: 57) and that can open up educational spaces that welcome a plurality of beings to appear publicly. She also argued for a "pluralist democracy" and a "transformative curriculum" in which traditional (sexist) values, knowledge, and beliefs can be challenged and replaced by more welcoming and including ways of being and knowing in the world. One of the "givens" that needs to be laid bare through education, Greene (1988) suggests, is the mystification of women as in "woman as a natural caregiver" or "woman as a natural love object"—not because these stories are limiting for every woman but because they need to be chosen freely as one of many possible life stories. At the same time, Greene (1978/1995) was convinced that many of the traditional gender roles imprison women's and girls' lived experiences and falsify their sense of themselves. In the essay "The Lived World," she argues for an "intensified awareness of women's own realities" to confront and transform what she saw as superficial gender roles (1978/1995: 22; see also Jacobs 1997). Equality between the sexes, according to Greene, can only be accomplished if we act in community with others and if we pay attention to "our nagging sense that things ought not to be this way" (1973: 49). The purpose of education, then, is to create intersubjective spaces where teachers and students may ask existential questions about the world and their own life histories, spaces in which they can begin to see the world and themselves in a different light. "It remains a matter, for men and women both," Greene writes in the *Dialectic of Freedom*, "to establish a place for freedom in the world of the given—and to do so in concern and with care, so that what is indecent can be transformed and what is unendurable may be overcome" (1988: 86).

As a feminist educational philosopher, Greene highlights the importance of acknowledging the complexities and ambiguities involved in the educational situation for women and for minority groups in patriarchal societies and of the power of critical and aesthetic imagination in educational systems dominated by white, middle-class, masculine values (Jacobs 1997).

Jane Roland Martin

Jane Roland Martin (1929–) is one of the most prolific feminist philosophers of education having written more than ten books and a countless number of articles. Born in 1929 in New York City, the geographical closeness to John Dewey's progressive education made an impact on her life and writing, and her work in philosophy of education opened the door to feminist scholarship in the field (Rice 2015).

One way to summarize Roland Martin's rich academic contribution to the field of philosophy of education is to suggest that it centers around the reclaiming and recovering of the *subject of woman* and the *woman as subject* for and in educational theory and practice. This act of reclaiming and recovery has led her to *reinstating woman/women as both subject and object of education* and to reformulating the conception of "the educated person" for a gendered-sensitive curriculum (Roland Martin 1985, 1994); *retrieving the lost women and girls* in the history of education as well as the meaning of the domestic sphere for both boys and girls and for the benefits of society at large (Roland Martin 1992); and advocating *a gender-sensitive approach to culture* and to the intergenerational transmission of cultural wealth (Roland Martin 2002, 2007, 2011).

Exploring these themes more closely, *Reclaiming a Conversation: The Ideal of the Educated Woman* (1985) and *Changing the Educational Landscape: Philosophy, Women, and Curriculum* (1994) both suggest that when the historic exclusion of women and girls from the educational realm is broken and they are allowed to enter the realm of education, "educational thought itself changes" (Roland Martin 1994: 6). Hence, there is a relationship between educational practice and educational thought, and when the education of women and girls are taken seriously, "our culture's concept of what it means to be an educated subject must be redefined" (p. 6). As a way of bringing women into the educational scene, Roland Martin retrieves "old conversations" with thinkers such as Plato, Rousseau, and Wollstonecraft. She shows, for example, how the education Rousseau prescribes for Emile is profoundly modeled in relation to Sophie's; what we tend to forget when we import Rousseau's (male) model of education focused on the productive forces of society is how education ignores Sophie's education and, hence, the reproductive forces of society (Roland Martin 1994). Thus, when "the ideal of the educated person" is formed in this way, it becomes a narrow ideal modeled only on one sex: "the educated man," a phrase Roland Martin (1981) ascribes to R.S. Peters and whose book of the same title she critiques in her presidential address at the Thirty-Seventh Annual Meeting of the Philosophy of Education Society in Houston, Texas, in 1981. Unfortunately, according to Roland Martin (1994), liberal education is still walking down this narrow path when it more naturally seems to be incorporating traits that are culturally and historically associated with men and public life than the traits associated with women. She makes this argument not to stereotype women/girls and men/boys according to the private/public dichotomy but to highlight very concretely that an education for both sexes would have to include not only the three R's—reading, writing, and 'rithmetic (public needs)—but also the three C's of care, concern, and connection (domestic needs) in the education of both boys and girls (Roland Martin 1985, 1994).

Roland Martin further explores the above thoughts in *The Schoolhome: Rethinking Schools for Changing Families* (1992). In dialogue with what she sees as an enlarged outlook on education in John Dewey's *School and Society* (1989) but also in critique of what she here senses to be gendered splits between school and society, the child and the curriculum, mind and body, reason and emotion, Roland Martin (1992) invents the metaphor of the "schoolhome." Through this metaphor and through a close study of the Italian pedagogue Maria Montessori's text "De Casa Bambini" (which wrongly, she argues, had been translated into *The House of Children*, in English), Roland Martin (1992) removes the barriers between the home and the school and exposes the home's part in the educational enterprise. She sees the "schoolhome" as a second womb: a secure, loving, and nurturing space where girls and boys can be schooled in and through domestic affection.

Like a weave that finally comes together, it is in her later books that Roland Martin (2007, 2011) develops her theory of education: "the theory of education as encounter." In contrast to the commonplace and rather straightforward idea that education involves change on the basis of the individual, Roland Martin (2007, 2011) develops an educational theory where culture is placed alongside the individual and change occurs on the basis of all relations involved. Seeking to flesh out what such transformational encounters might hold, she digs deeper into the meaning of culture and—given the marginalization of women in culture and how this narrows down a culture's ideas and ideals of education—focuses particularly on culture's often unspoken and unarticulated dimensions (Roland Martin 2011).

The "cultural amnesia" in educational philosophy and theory critiqued in Roland Martins's earlier work comes to fruition in what she calls "the cultural wealth perspective" (1992: 126) on education—a way of moving away from the individual, focusing instead on culture and on the idea that individuals are both the subjects and objects of education (Roland Martin 2011). It is in relation to the idea of "cultural wealth" that Roland Martins's sensitivity to intergenerational transmission of culture comes into play, and the question she addresses is how teachers and educators can maximize the transmission of cultural wealth and minimize the transmission of cultural liabilities (Roland Martin 2011). The assumption that the individual is the fundamental educational unit has seldom been challenged, Roland Martin (2002) argues, and by putting culture on an equal footing with the individual, her theory of *education as encounter* introduces a relationality between the individual and a culture where change and transformation occur on both sides.

Nel Noddings

It is probably not an exaggeration to assert that Nel Noddings's pioneering work in feminist ethics indicates a paradigm in philosophy of education. Noddings (1929–) is a mother to ten children and has thirty-nine grandchildren, a biographical note that is central to understanding her life and her work because it has explicitly inspired both her ethics of caring and the relationality between the home and the school (O'Toole 1998). Worth mentioning also is that Noddings served as a high school mathematics teacher for seventeen years before receiving her doctorate in educational philosophy from Stanford University in 1975, a faculty to which she belonged for more than twenty years.

Noddings received worldwide attention with her first sole-authored book published in 1984, *Caring: A Feminine Approach to Ethics and Moral Education*. In this book, she begins to develop her ethics of care, a theory that has been part of her academic reflection throughout her career and has constituted the basis of her feminist contribution to philosophy of education. In developing an ethics of care, Noddings takes her point of departure from a critique of the liberal idea of the individual as an autonomous moral agent, and, based on a feminist ethics, she argues for a relational ontology grounded in the idea that human beings are essentially relational creatures (Noddings 1984). To this ontological relationality she adds a feminine approach to ethics by locating her origins for the ethics of caring in women's experience as mothers (Noddings 1984; Verducci 2018).

As a feminist philosopher of education, Noddings also contributes more generally to feminist perspectives on moral philosophy. For example, she offers a rethinking of evil from the perspective of women, suggesting that traditional descriptions of evil are not only male but also masculine in the sense that they have glorified "traits and opinions that have been genderized in favour of males" and have led to the devaluation and distrust of women (Noddings 1989: 2). After this, a series of books followed that particularly explore the implications of an ethics of care and a feminine approach to ethics for moral education (Noddings 1992, 1995, 2002a, 2003).

Noddings's ethics of care is primarily inspired by Carol Gilligan's famous *In a Different Voice* (1982) but also by Sarah Ruddick's *Maternal Thinking* (1990), emphasizing the societal (de)valuation of maternal practices. Noddings (1984, 2002b) takes her point of departure from the position that traditional moral theories and practices are incomplete because of their marginalization of values, virtues, knowledge, and experiences culturally associated with women and with the domestic sphere of the home. Hence, in response to what she sees as traditionally masculinist moral theories (e.g., Gilligan 1982), Noddings suggests an ethics of care based on a relational ethics and on women's experience as mothers and "natural" caregivers. Doing so breaks moral theory away from both utilitarian (making decisions on the basis of anticipated consequences) and deontological reasoning (principled reasoning, " the law"), an essential maneuver to make since neither of these models can provide a proper understanding of the way women approach ethical questions and concerns (Noddings 1984). "The approach through law and principle is not," she writes, "the approach of the mother. It is the approach of the detached one, of the father" (p. 2).

An ethics of care should be seen as "an inversion of Kantian ethics" that has tried "to solve moral problems completely and universally in abstract and codified schemes," writes Noddings (1999: 37). Even if both men and women can be carers, Noddings refers to women's experience and to women as primary caregivers throughout her work (Noddings 2002b). This position has not come without critique, not least from other feminists who argue that the primacy Noddings gives to women as caregivers and the emphasis she puts on women's experiences encourage roles and ethical positions that have been deeply problematic—even destructive—to women and women's lives (Noddings 1984).

Faithful to her critique of a Kantian deontological ethics, Noddings is reluctant to offer systematic accounts of her ethics of care. Instead, she explores how caring is experienced, and she compels us to settle with a broad and informal phenomenological approach to "what we are like" when we engage in caring encounters (Noddings 2002b: 13). Such an approach comes closer to sympathy (i.e., feeling *with*) than empathy (i.e., *in* feeling) because empathy, she argues, is "peculiarly western and masculine" whereas sympathy captures "the affective state of attention in caring" (p. 14). Another aspect of her ethics of care that is of interest here is the distinction she makes between caring-for and caring-about. What is universal, Noddings (1984) argues, is the desire to be *cared-for,* and it is through the experience of being cared-for that we later learn to *care-about.* As the primary mode of caring, caring-for relates to face-to-face encounters, whereas caring-about is subject and content directed—it directs us to the public realm and the things in the world (Noddings 1984). Hence, caring-for is immediate and direct, and it is only natural that we care more for the suffering children close to us than the suffering children far away. In this sense, caring-about is easier and less challenging, Noddings (1984) initially argues, a position she comes to modify in her later work where she becomes increasingly aware of the role of caring-for as a basis for justice (Noddings 1999, 2002b).

A third aspect that has particular feminist bearing is the idea of "the home" in Noddings's work. Like Roland Martin, she takes the home as the model for

FIGURE 2.2 "The Fearless Girl" statue facing Charging Bull in Lower Manhattan, New York City. *Source*: Rawpixel.com / Shutterstock.

a new orientation in public policy, asking "whether the attitudes and responses characteristic in the best homes can somehow be extended into public policy making" (2002b: 6). Ever since Dewey, she argues, educational philosophy and theory have seen education and schooling merely as a preparation for public life, and little has been done to make sure that school curriculum includes also "serious preparation for home life" as well as for civic life more generally (p. 2). Hence, if young people today are to be educated as whole beings, well prepared for handling matters of the social and relational kind, we need to be "starting at home" (2002b). Starting at home, however, "does not mean that we need to remain there" (p. 6). It simply means that the direction of inquiry in educational philosophy and theory is inverted so that, instead of beginning in an idea of an ideal state, we should work from the bottom-up, beginning in the domestic sphere. "What might we learn," Noddings asks, "if, instead, we start with a description of best homes and then move outward to the larger society?" (p. 1).

THE THIRD WAVE: NAVIGATING A COMPLEX RESEARCH FIELD

The birth year of the third wave of feminism is sometimes said to coincide with the publication of Judith Butler's *Gender Trouble: Feminism and the Subversion of Identity* (1990). The wave is associated with the troubling of the notion of "woman" and "universal womanhood" as a central feminist category, a troubling that, as we have seen, began already during the first and second waves. It might, in fact, be argued that if the *discovery and exploration* of the concept "woman/girl" and "feminine/femininity" were given center stage in the second wave, it is the *troubling* of these same categories that are surfacing here.

Arising as a response to the second wave's sometimes essentialist and narrow definitions of (white, heterosexual, middle-class) feminine experience, this diverse and multilayered wave centers largely on poststructuralist, postcolonial, and intersectional analyses of gender and sexuality (St. Pierre 2000).[5] Feminist voices belonging to this wave often focus on "micro politics" and "embodied practices," on a refusal to think in terms of "either-or," and on negotiating spaces within feminist thought for alternative subjectivities (e.g., Braidotti 1994, 2013; Butler 1993, 2004; Cavarero 2000, 2016; Irigaray 1985, 1990; Kristeva 1995), alternative epistemologies (e.g. Harding 1986; Hekman 1990), and intersections between different categories such as gender, race, class, (dis) ability, and sexual orientation (e.g., Ahmed 2000, 2017; Spivak 1987, 1993; Williams Crenshaw 1991, 2019).

Suffering from a backlash in public discourse during the 1990s (e.g., Faludi 1991), research areas such as feminist studies, gender studies, gay and lesbian studies, and queer studies all have taken form and developed during this time period, and a common point of departure in all these fields is that feminism is a "mode of analysis" rather than a set of political conclusions (St. Pierre 2000). Also, feminist theory has become more nuanced and diversified as black feminists, Indigenous women, third world women, Chicanos, Asians, and others have added their voices to the conversation (Thayer-Bacon and Turner 2007).

However, the third wave also continues and intensifies the internal debates between feminist theorists who claim that there are important differences between the sexes to be considered and negotiated (e.g., feminists drawing on the work of Kristeva, Irigaray, Cavarero, and Spivak) and feminist theorists who argue that there are no inherent differences between the sexes and that both sex and gender are best understood from the perspective of social conditionings (e.g., Butler), of queer phenomenology (e.g., Ahmed), or postmaterialism (e.g., Braidotti). As a result of this internal debate, some scholars within the third wave redefine "feminism" as a project that includes general questions about human rights, anti-racism, environmentalism, queer and LGBT concerns (see, e.g., Gillis, Howie, and Munford 2007), while others refuse to identify as "feminists" and reject the word as outdated, limiting, and/or exclusionary due to its binary logic (e.g., Modelski 1991).

This development suggests, for our purposes of presenting a growing and heterogeneous movement, that the question of who counts as a feminist writer becomes more complex during the third wave since the very object of feminism, that is, "the welfare of women and girls" as well as "the very category of "woman" is being increasingly challenged (Devine and Stewart 2018: 2).

Feminisms in philosophy of education

In the field of philosophy of education, there has been a growing interest in feminist theory and philosophy since the 1990s. One reason for this is that there are more women working within the field than ever before, something that is demonstrated by the growing numbers of female memberships in Philosophy of Education societies and in women having leading positions within the field (Rice 2015). Even if feminist theory still does not belong to mainstream philosophical work, handbooks and encyclopedias in philosophy of education more often include a separate chapter on feminism (e.g., Casale and Windheuser 2018; Greene and Griffiths 2003; Mayo and Stengel 2010; Noddings 2009; Rice 2015; Schumann and Adami 2017), and there are feminist readers in educational philosophy and theory to be consulted (e.g., Stone 1995; Thayer-Bacon, Stone, and Sprecher 2013). In addition, a number of networks, groups, symposia, and special issues have been organized during the years with the overall aim of strengthening the place and significance of feminist theory in the field and of supporting the female academics who are inhabiting it (see, e.g., Devine and Stewart 2018; Griffiths et al. 2015; Schumann and Hållander 2017; Thayer-Bacon and Turner 2007; Todd, Jones, and O'Donnell 2016).

A reminder might be in order here: when the third wave began and Mary Leach wrote her now famous essay "Mothers of In(ter)vention" in honor of the fiftieth anniversary of the Philosophy of Education Society in 1991, she found that, until the 1970s, no more than five women had been taking part in the conference each year (Leach 1991). In addition, as Barbara Thayer-Bacon and Bayle Turner point out, it was still not unusual in the beginning of the 1990s that well renowned research journals in the field "included no articles by women" (2007: 299) at all. Even if the number of women participating in the field has increased over the years, the third wave is still characterized by this ambivalent movement: female representation and women's work have gradually gained ground in philosophy of education, but, as is shown in the following sections, it is still to some extent the case that feminist work is seen as marginal and as dealing with "soft" issues in relation to a male-dominated canon in a traditionally male-dominated field.

Against this background, contemporary feminist work within philosophy of education can, broadly speaking, be clustered around three main conversations which can also be seen as three ways of *doing feminism* within the field: *feminism as recovery*, *feminism as critique*, and *feminism as reconstruction*. Even if such a clustering by no means can do justice to the vast amount of work produced and inspired by feminist theory since the 1990s, we hope that this overview will give a sense of the diversity and creativity that is characterizing feminist work within philosophy of education today.

Feminism as recovery

Philosophers of education inspired by feminist theory have long insisted on the significance of recovering the silenced or lost names and work of women in history more generally and in the history of philosophy of education more specifically. Seen as a question of epistemic injustice (Ficker 2007), the feminist project initiated during the second wave by Roland Martin, Greene, and Noddings highlights this *work of recovery*, emphasizing especially the underrepresentation of women's names and work, as well as the lives and concerns of girls and women, within philosophy of education. By criticizing the historical exclusion of women and girls in the philosophical canon, the aim of the work carried out here is not just to retrieve a lost central inheritance but also to challenge and redefine the center of the philosophical tradition from the margins (Palmer 2001; Thayer-Bacon and Turner 2007).

The "recovery project" (Warren 2009) in philosophy is a contemporary example of a joint feminist effort aiming to retrieve and rediscover the names that have been forgotten and the work of women that has been systematically overlooked, undervalued, and neglected in the Western philosophical tradition. Within philosophy of education, similar projects have helped to illuminate the philosophical and educational significance of the work of female philosophers and educational theorists (Rice 2015). For example, Susan Laird's (2008) study of Mary Wollstonecraft and Charline Haddock Seigfried's (1996) work on Jane Addams have both contributed a "recovery project" within educational philosophy. This new visibility of women philosophers within the field both challenges the traditionally male-dominated philosophical canon and opens up new ways of understanding and practicing the tradition itself (Pagès 2017).

Feminism as critique

Some feminist scholars within philosophy of education have, with the empirical woman in mind, brought to light the structural discrimination against women in academia generally as well as in the philosophy of education research community specifically (Devine and Stewart 2018; Schumann and Hållander 2017; Thayer-Bacon and Turner 2007). For example, *feminism as critique* has put in focus the implicit sexism bias in R.S. Peters's influential work in philosophy of education and consequences of this bias. The consequences, it has been argued, have been bad not only for the women in the research field (and the girls in educational practice) but for the mixed-gendered character of the philosophy of education community more generally (see, e.g., Lees 2012; Roland Martin 1994). Drawing on feminist critique with the empirical woman (and man) in mind, research of this kind has had women's and girl's experiences of structural inequality as one of its main foci, suggesting that their conditions in both schools and in higher education are different than those of their male counterparts.

Feminist critique, however, is also being done in relation to a wide range of issues and in relation to others than those driven by a concern for women and girls (i.e., "the object of feminism"). Feminist philosophy and theory is a relatively established field of knowledge within philosophy of education today, and a range of scholars, both women and men, are using feminist themes and thinkers as *a general mode of critique*. In academic contexts and research experienced as too traditional, mainstream, and tapered, feminism as critique seeks to question, for example, excessively narrow notions of rationality and seemingly undisputed hierarchies between mind/body, reason/emotion, and theory/practice. Claudia Ruitenberg's (2009) work on political theorist Chantal Mouffe, for example, shows the educational potential of affect and the risks involved in a too consensus-oriented (i.e., masculine) approach to dialogue in the classroom, and Michalinos Zembylas's (2010) uses Noddings's ethics of care to criticize a limited notion of justice in citizenship education in regards to immigration. Bringing traditionally feminist themes (i.e., affect, emotions, embodiment) to bear on what is seen as mainstream (Western) philosophical thinking and on neoliberal Western society more generally, feminism as critique challenges the androcentrism and logocentrism in mainstream educational research and questions established patriarchal, male-dominated structures in both schools and academia.

Feminism as reconstruction

Feminism within philosophy of education also comes in the mode of affirmation, that is, in the gesture of offering something to the field that mainstream philosophy does not. At some point, as Rita Felski puts it in *The Limits of Critique*, "critique does not get us any further" (2015: 9). Hence, to ask what comes after critique in what is here called *feminism as reconstruction* is not to say that critique is unnecessary and can be left behind. It is rather to suggest, with Felski in her reference to Bruno Latour, that we can "decline to see [critique] as the be-all and end-all" (p. 9) of philosophical inquiry.

Reconstructive feminist work during the past decades has, generally speaking, put a focus on relational and practical issues and has given special attention to applied fields of knowledge such as ethics and moral theory (Alcoff and Potter 1993; Greene and Griffiths 2003; Leach 1991). Feminist philosophers of education have often understood their work to be contributing to public debates on practical issues or, as Maxine Greene and Morewenna Griffiths have put it, feminist analyses are often focused on "rethinking the 'usual'" (2003: 73), thereby exploring the everyday, situated, and seemingly ordinary educational practices that tend to go unnoticed and unresearched in mainstream philosophy of education. Given this focus, feminism as reconstruction can be used as a way of acknowledging, for example, the situatedness of academic work, exploring what becomes possible in educational research and practice if what is rendered marginalized is given center stage, if the material is rendered valuable, if the personal and private is given political and public significance, and if the not-yet-visible is exposed. Moreover, feminism as reconstruction puts in focus issues that have been regarded by traditionally male philosophy of education (as well as by traditional philosophy) as having a feminine coding, such as the meaning of body, gender, matter, experience, and lived practices, both for understanding the world and educational practice and as ways of doing philosophy of education (Greene and Griffiths 2003).

Relationality as content matter is worth particular mention here. For example, Sharon Todd's work on sexual difference (Irigaray 1985) is used to rethink the idea of cosmopolitan education (Todd 2009) as well as a more gender-sensitive curriculum (Todd 2015), and Amy Shuffleton's (2015) work on father and daughter relations shows how social reconfigurations of "new fatherhood" demand a reimagination of relationships that start with the recognition of interdependencies. Drawing on Mary Wollstonecraft's *A Vindication of the Rights of Women* and by expanding the notion of social justice, Morwenna Griffiths (2015) in turn argues for the need of pedagogical techniques that respond to the complexity of educational relations, including relationships between human beings now and in the future, and between the human and the more-than-human world (see also Griffiths 2003).

Some feminist scholars within philosophy of education have moved from the margins toward the "core" of traditional philosophy, that is, epistemology and metaphysics (Alcoff and Potter 1993). Feminist approaches to epistemology generally start in a critique of traditional epistemology, suggesting that, while it tends to come across as objective and neutral, it is, in fact, coded in male and masculine registers (mind/masculine vs. body/feminine) (Thayer-Bacon 2003).

Most feminist scholars working in feminist epistemology have a shared emphasis on *knowledge as relationally constituted* and on the *knower as an embodied and situated subject* (Schumann 2016). While offering a critique of what they see as a too narrow conception of what counts as philosophical work, they also contribute to the development of a broader and more gender-sensitive understanding of central epistemological concepts such as knowledge, rationality, validity, and objectivity. Moreover, feminist epistemologies generally want to challenge and overcome traditional dualisms between mind/body, theory/practice, subject/object, rational/irrational, and relative/absolute to both deconstruct and reconstruct traditional models of epistemology (Schumann 2016; Thayer-Bacon 2003).

While a feminist epistemology must include a notion of a gendered subject to be feminist, there is no common conception of how that subject is constituted. Barbara Thayer-Bacon, for example, argues for a *feminist relational epistemology* that acknowledges women's situated and embodied experiences, while, at the same time, stressing that women "are multiple and heterogeneous, contradictory or incoherent" (2010: 8). Hence, one of the challenges of contemporary feminist epistemology is how to acknowledge the critique of essentialist conceptions of "woman" and "feminine"—categories that historically have privileged white, Western, and heterosexual women and middle-class female experiences—without, at the same time, replacing them with an equally problematic erasure of the very object of feminism (Schumann 2016).

CONCLUSION: WAVES TO COME

To return to some key conversations between and within different generations of feminist philosophers of education with future generations in mind, we have employed the metaphor of the wave as a recurrent image. The wave imagery emphasizes *movement* in a complex and ever-changing feminist landscape and highlights the different *phases* that this thinking has undergone.

Making the landscape even more complex, "a new silhouette is emerging on the horizon and taking the shape of a fourth wave" (Rampton 2015; see also Chamberlain 2016). This fourth wave begins with a focus on social media and how the use of technology affects women's lives and narratives as well as on justice for women in regards to violence and abuse.[6] The generation of feminists now coming of age seems to recognize that we are still facing serious problems because of the way that society is either still male and mono-sexed (Irigaray 1985) or too gender stereotyped (Butler 1990). This brings back to public discourse some of the questions considered by previous generations of feminists, not least the meaning and role of the woman and the feminine.

If moving into the future is not to be characterized by another "cultural amnesia" (Roland Martin 1992) in which the new generation of feminists in philosophy of education loses contact with the work of previous generations, every step forward must be taken in connection with the past and those who have gone before. Which battles were previous generations of feminists in philosophy of education fighting and in response to which historic and academic events? What were their questions, and which of their questions are returning today in, perhaps, new contexts and forms? If Google uses the imagery of standing "on the shoulders of giants" in a vertical gesture when we are making inquiries about the past, the gesture that is inspiring us here is the gesture of holding hands in a horizontal forward-moving line. This is a gesture where the new generation of feminists in the present—both men and women—form a "living chain" that *both* links them to the past *and* reaches for the future.

The emphasizing of this horizontal linking gesture "between the past and the future" *in the present*, to borrow from Hannah Arendt (1961), should be seen as offering a response to the tendency in much contemporary feminist theory and practice—including that within philosophy of education—to be too one-sidedly focused on the future. What might keep feminism in philosophy of education alive for the future, we suggest, is the gesture of being "in link" and "in sync" with those who have invested their life and work in feminism. Hence, what is needed is a new generation of feminist philosophers of education—women and men—that takes previous generations' feminist work to heart, learns from it, and reclaims it for their own times, contexts, and questions.

NOTES

1   We have chosen to use the word "feminism" rather than "feminisms" in the chapter to indicate a common commitment of different feminism strands to "the welfare of women and girls" (Devine and Stewart 2018: 2). We are aware, however, that there is no single feminist voice but rather a plurality of voices with different theoretical orientations, experiences, and histories.

2   We use the term "conversation/s" here to evoke a mental image of communication across times and people. We are well aware that within feminism there are many

disputes and at times outspoken conflicts between different voices and positions, and the choice of term does not have the purpose of covering this up.

3   It is also during this period in time that the feminist theologian at the Jesuit-run Boston College, Mary Daly, encouraged women to leave the church, arguing that since "God is man, therefore man is God." The Christian religion, Daly (1977) argues, is inherently and incurably patriarchal and must therefore be left behind if there is to be any emancipatory change in women's lives.

4   A collection of articles written by feminist philosophers of education belonging to the second wave can be found in *The Feminist Education Reader*, edited by Lynda Stone (1995).

5   According to Julia Kristeva et. al (1981), feminism can be divided into three historical "attitudes" or "generations" but she also stresses "the parallel existence of all three in the same historical time, or even that they be interwoven one with the other" (p. 33, emphasis in originial). This becomes apparent in the third wave, where feminist theorists whose time of writing coincides with the second wave have come to influence much of the work in poststructuralist, postcolonial, intersectional, and postmaterialist feminism.

6   Political movements that have had significance in the fourth wave and have contributed to the current revival of the term "feminism" in public debate, are, for example, the gang rapes in India in 2018, the Bill Cosby allegations, the Weinstein scandal and the subsequent #MeToo movement, the Women's March in Washington in 2017, the Free the Nipple Movement in 2014, and the Women's Wall in Kerala in 2019. Although these movements have gained a lot of attention in the media as well as in public debate, it remains to be seen how much bearing they will actually have on educational theory and practice.

REFERENCES

Primary sources

Ahmed, Sara (2000), *Strange Encounters: Embodied Others in Post-Coloniality*, London: Routledge.

Ahmed, Sara (2017), *Living a Feminist Life*, Durham, NC: Duke University Press.

Beauvoir, Simone de (1949/1989), *The Second Sex*, ed. and trans. H.M. Parshley, New York: Vintage Books.

Braidotti, Rosi (1994), *Nomadic Subjects: Embodiment and Sexual Difference in Contemporary Feminist Theory*, New York: Columbia University Press.

Braidotti, Rosi (2013), *The Posthuman*, Cambridge: Polity Press.

Butler, Judith (1990), *Gender Trouble: Feminism and the Subversion of Identity*, New York: Routledge.

Butler, Judith (1993), *Bodies That Matter: On the Discursive Limits of "Sex,"* New York: Routledge.

Butler, Judith (2004), *Undoing Gender*, New York: Routledge.

Carby, Hazel (1982), "White Woman Listen! Black Feminism and the Boundaries of Sisterhood," in Centre for Contemporary Cultural Studies (ed.), *The Empire Strikes Back: Race and Racism in Seventies Britain*, 212–35, London: Hutchinson.

Carson, Rachel (1962/2000), *Silent Spring*, London: Penguin Books.

Cavarero, Adriana (2000), *Relating Narratives: Storytelling and Selfhood*, London: Routledge.

Cavarero, Adriana (2016), *Inclinations: A Critique of Rectitude*, Stanford, CA: Stanford University Press.

Daly, Mary (1977), *Beyond God the Father: Toward a Philosophy of Women's Liberation*, Boston: Beacon Press.

Faludi, Susan (1991), *Backlash: The Undeclared War Against American Women*, New York: Crown.

Ficker, Miranda (2007), *Epistemic Injustice: Power and the Ethics of Knowing*, Oxford: Oxford University Press.

Friedan, Betty (1963), *The Feminine Mystique*, New York: Norton.

Gilligan, Carol (1982), *In a Different Voice: Psychological Theory and Women's Development*, Cambridge, MA: Harvard University Press.

Greene, Maxine (1965), *The Public School and the Private Vision: The Search for America in Education and Literature*, New York: Random House.

Greene, Maxine (1967), *Existential Encounters for Teachers*, New York: Random House.

Greene, Maxine (1973), *Teacher As Stranger: Educational Philosophy for the Modern Age*, Belmont, CA: Wadsworth.

Greene, Maxine (1978), *Landscapes of Learning*, New York: Teachers College Press.

Greene, Maxine (1978/1995), "The Lived World," in Lynda Stone (ed.), *The Education Feminism Reader*, 17–25, New York: Routledge.

Greene, Maxine (1988), *The Dialectic of Freedom*, New York: Teachers College Press.

Greene, Maxine (1995), *Releasing the Imagination: Essays on Education, the Arts, and Social Change*, San Francisco: Jossey-Bass.

Greene, Maxine (1998), "An Autobiographical Remembrance," in William Pinar (ed.), *The Passionate Mind of Maxine Greene: "I am not yet,"* 9–12, London: Falmer.

Greene, Maxine and Morwenna Griffiths (2003), "Feminism, Philosophy, and Education: Imagining Public Spaces," in Nigel Blake, Paul Smeyers, Richard D. Smith, and Paul Standish (eds.), *The Blackwell Guide to the Philosophy of Education*, 73–92, Oxford: Blackwell Publishing.

Harding, Sandra (1986), *The Science Question in Feminism*, Ithaca, NY: Cornell University Press.

Hekman, Susan J. (1990), *Gender and Knowledge: Elements of a Postmodern Feminism*, Cambridge: Polity Press.

hooks, bell (1984), *Feminist Theory: From Margin to Center*, Boston: South End Press.

hooks, bell (1981/2015), *Ain't I a Woman: Black Women and Feminism*, New York: Routledge.

hooks, bell (2000), *Feminism Is for Everybody: Passionate Politics*, Cambridge: South End Press.

Irigaray, Luce (1985), *This Sex Which Is Not One*, Ithaca, NY: Cornell University Press.

Irigaray, Luce (1990), *Je, tu, nous: Towards a Culture of Difference*, London: Routledge.

Kristeva, Julia, Jardine, Alice, and Blake, Harry (1981), "Women's Time," *Signs*, 7 (1):13–35.

Noddings, Nel (1984), *Caring: A Feminine Approach to Ethics and Moral Education*, Berkeley: University of California Press.

Noddings, Nel (1989), *Women and Evil*, Berkeley: University of California Press.

Noddings, Nel (1992), *The Challenge to Care in Schools: An Alternative Approach to Education*, New York: Teachers College Press.

Noddings, Nel (1995), *Educating for Intelligent Belief or Unbelief*, New York: Teachers College Press.

Noddings, Nel (1999), "Two Concepts of Caring," Philosophy of Education Archive. Available online: https://educationjournal.web.illinois.edu/archive/index.php/pes/article/view/2024.pdf.

Noddings, Nel (2002a), *Educating Moral People: A Caring Alternative to Character Education*, New York: Teachers College Press.

Noddings, Nel (2002b), *Starting at Home: Caring and Social Policy*, Berkeley: University of California Press.

Noddings, Nel (2003), *Happiness and Education*, Cambridge: Cambridge University Press.

Noddings, Nel (2009), "Feminist Philosophy and Education," in Harvey Siegel (ed.), *The Oxford Handbook of Philosophy of Education*, 508–23, Oxford: Oxford University Press.

Roland Martin, Jane (1981), "The Ideal of the Educated Person," *Educational Theory*, 31 (2): 97–109.

Roland Martin, Jane (1985), *Reclaiming a Conversation: The Ideal of the Educated Woman*, New Haven, CT: Yale University Press.

Roland Martin, Jane (1992), *The Schoolhome: Rethinking Schools for Changing Families*, Cambridge, MA: Harvard University Press.

Roland Martin, Jane (1994), *Changing the Educational Landscape: Philosophy, Women, and Curriculum*, New York: Routledge.

Roland Martin, Jane (2002), *Cultural Miseducation: In Search of a Democratic Solution*, New York: Teachers College Press.

Roland Martin, Jane (2007), *Educational Metamorphoses: Philosophical Reflections on Identity and Culture*, Lanham, MD: Rowman & Littlefield.

Roland Martin, Jane (2011), *Education Reconfigured: Culture, Encounter, and Change*, New York: Routledge.

Rubin, Gayle (1975), "The Traffic in Women: Notes on the 'Political Economy' of Sex," in Rayna R. Reiter (ed.), *Toward an Anthropology of Women*, New York: Monthly Review Press.

Ruddick, Sarah (1990), *Maternal Thinking: Towards a Politics of Peace*, London: Women's Press.

Schreiner, Olive (1891), *Dreams, Second Edition*, London: T. Fisher Unwin.

Spivak, Gayatri Chakravorty (1987), *In Other Worlds: Essays in Cultural Politics*, London: Methuen.

Spivak, Gayatri Chakravorty (1993), *Outside In the Teaching Machine*, London: Routledge.

Williams Crenshaw, Kimberlé (1991), "Mapping the Margins: Intersectionality, Identity Politics, and Violence Against Women of Color," *Stanford Law Review*, 43 (6): 1241–99.

Williams Crenshaw, Kimberlé (2019), *Seeing Race Again: Countering Colorblindness Across the Disciplines*, Oakland: University of California Press.

Wollstonecraft, Mary (1792/1996), *A Vindication of the Rights of Woman*, London: Dover Thrift Editions.

Woolf, Virginia (1929/2004), *A Room of One's Own*, London: Penguin Books.

Secondary sources

Alcoff, Linda and Elisabeth Potter (1993), *Feminist Epistemologies*, New York: Routledge.

Arendt, Hannah (1961), *Between Past and Future: Six Exercises in Political Thought*,
New York: Viking Press.

Ayers, William and Janet L. Miller, eds. (1997), *A Light in Dark Times: Maxine Greene
and the Unfinished Conversation*, New York: Teachers College Press.

Baily, Cathryn (1997), "Making Waves and Drawing Lines: The Politics of Defining
the Vicissitudes of Feminism," *Hypatia*, 12 (3): 17–28.

Casale, Rita and Jeanette Windheuser (2018), "Feminism," in Paul Smeyers (ed.),
International Handbook of Philosophy of Education, 703–26, London: Sage.

Chamberlain, Prudence (2016), "Affective temporality: towards a fourth wave," *Gender
and Education*, 28(3): 458–64.

Devine, Nesta and Georgina Stewart (2018), "Women, Philosophy, and Education,"
Educational Philosophy and Theory, 51 (7): 681–3.

Felski, Rita (2015), *The Limits of Critique*, Chicago, IL: University of Chicago Press.

Freedman, Estelle (2003), *No Turning Back: The History of Feminism and the Future of
Women*, New York: Ballantine Books.

Gillis, Stacy, Gillian Howie, and Rebecca Munford, eds. (2007), *Third Wave Feminism:
A Critical Exploration*, London: Palgrave Macmillan.

Griffiths, Morwenna (2003), *Action for Social Justice in Education: Fairly Different*,
Philadelphia: Open University Press.

Griffiths, Morwenna (2015), "Educational Relationships: Rousseau, Wollstonecraft and
Social Justice," in Morwenna Griffiths, Marit Honerød Hoveid, Sharon Todd, and
Christine Winter (eds.), *Re-Imagining Relationships in Education: Ethics, Politics
and Practices* (Journal of Philosophy of Education Book Series), 179–96, Oxford:
Wiley-Blackwell.

Griffiths, Morwenna, Marit Honerød Hoveid, Sharon Todd, and Christine Winter,
eds. (2015), *Re-Imagining Relationships in Education: Ethics, Politics and Practices*
(Journal of Philosophy of Education Book Series), Oxford: Wiley-Blackwell.

Haddock Seigfried, Charlene (1996), *Pragmatism and Feminism: Reweaving the Social
Fabric*, Chicago: University of Chicago Press.

Hancook, Markie (2001), *Exclusions & Awakenings: The Life of Maxine Greene*,
Hancook Productions. Available online: https://www.hancockproductions.com/
maxine-greene/"

Jacobs, Mary Ellen (1997), "Living Dangerously: Toward a Poetics of Women's Lived
Experiences," in William Ayers and Janet L. Miller (eds.), *A Light in Dark Times:
Maxine Greene and the Unfinished Conversation*, 180–9, New York: Teachers
College Press.

Laird, Susan (2008), *Mary Wollstonecraft: Philosophical Mother of Coeducation*,
New York: Continuum.

Latour, Bruno (2005), "Why Has Critique Run Out of Steam? From Matters of Fact to
Matters of Concern," *Critical Inquiry*, 30 (2): 225–48.

Leach, Mary (1991), "Mothers of In(ter)vention: Women's Writing in Philosophy of
Education," *Educational Theory*, 41 (3): 287–300.

Lees, Helen E. (2012), "Is R.S. Peters' Way of Mentioning Women in His Texts
Detrimental to Philosophy of Education? Some Considerations and Questions,"
Ethics and Education, 7 (3): 291–302.

Mayo, Cris and Barbara Stengel (2010), "Compelled to Challenge: Feminists in the
Wide World of Philosophy of Education," in Richard Bailey, David Carr, Robin
Barrow, and Christine McCarthy (eds.), *Sage Handbook of Philosophy of Education*,
151–66, Thousand Oaks, CA: Sage.

Mikkola, Mari (2017), "Gender Essentialism and Anti-Essentialism," in Ann Garry, Serene J. Khader, and Alison Stone (eds.), *The Routledge Companion to Feminist Philosophy*, 168–79, New York: Routledge.

Modleski, Tania (1991), *Feminism Without Women: Culture and Criticism in a "Postfeminism Age,"* New York: Routledge.

Oakeshott, Michael (1962/1991), *Rationalism in Politics and Other Essays*, Indianapolis, IN: Liberty Fund.

O'Toole, K. (1998), "What Matters to Nel Noddings and Why," Stanford Online Report. Available online: https://news.stanford.edu/news/1998/february4/noddings.html.

Pagès, Anna (2017), "Revisiting Tradition: Feminist Perspectives in Philosophy of Education," in *Newsletter of the Philosophy of Education Society of Great Britain*. Available Online: https://drive.google.com/file/d/0Bx0pZ_or3ewJczYwRXpYaDdEWTA/view.

Palmer, Joy A. (2001), *Fifty Major Thinkers on Education: From Confucius to Dewey*, London: Routledge.

Pinar, William, ed. (1998), *The Passionate Mind of Maxine Greene: "I am not yet,"* London: Falmer.

Rampton, Martha (2015), "Four Waves of Feminism," Pacific University Oregon, 2018. Available online: https://www.pacificu.edu/about/media/four-waves-feminism.

Rawls, John. 2005. *Political Liberalism*. Expanded Edition. New York: Columbia University Press.

Rice, Suzanne (2015), "Feminism and Philosophy of Education," in M.A. Peters (ed.), *Encyclopedia of Educational Philosophy and Theory*, Singapore: Springer Science and Business Media.

Riley, Denise (1988), *"Am I That Name?": Feminism and the Category of "Women" in History*, Minnesota: University of Minnesota Press.

Ruitenberg, C.W. (2009), "Educating Political Adversaries: Chantal Mouffe and Radical Democratic Citizenship Education," *Studies in Philosophy and Education*, 28 (3): 269–81.

Schumann, Claudia (2016), "Knowledge for a Common World? On the Place of Feminist Epistemology in Philosophy of Education," *Education Silences*, 6 (10): 1–13.

Schumann, Claudia and Rebecca Adami (2017), "Feminist Philosophy and Education," in Bryan Warnick (ed.), *Philosophy: Education*, 100–19, Farmington Hills, MI: Macmillan Reference USA.

Schumann, Claudia and Marie Hållander (2017), "Shifting Feminist Politics in Education: Contemporary Philosophical Perspectives," *Studier i Pædagogisk Filosofi*, 6 (1): 1–4.

Shuffleton, Amy (2015), "'New Fatherhood' and the Politics of Dependency," in Morwenna Griffiths, Marit Honerød Hoveid, Sharon Todd, and Christine Winter (eds.), *Re-Imagining Relationships in Education: Ethics, Politics and Practices* (Journal of Philosophy of Education Book Series), 38–55, Oxford: Wiley-Blackwell.

Spencer, Jane (2007), "Afterword: Feminist Waves," in Stacy Gillis, Gillian Howie, and Rebecca Munford (eds.), *Third Wave Feminism: A Critical Exploration*, 298–303, London: Palgrave Macmillan.

St. Pierre, Elizabeth Adams (2000), "Poststructural Feminism in Education: An Overview," *International Journal of Qualitative Studies in Education*, 13 (5): 477–515.

Stone, Lynda, ed. (1995), *The Education Feminism Reader*, New York: Routledge.

Thayer-Bacon, Barbara (2003), *Relational "(E)pistemologies,"* New York: Peter Lang Publishers.

Thayer-Bacon, Barbara (2010), "A Pragmatist and Feminist Relational (E)pistemology," *European Journal of Pragmatism and American Philosophy*, 2 (1): 133–54.

Thayer-Bacon, Barbara, Lynda Stone, and Katharine M. Sprecher, eds. (2013), *Education Feminism: Classic and Contemporary Readings*, New York: State University of New York Press.

Thayer-Bacon, Barbara. J. and Gayle Turner (2007), "What Feminist Inquiry Contributes to Philosophy and Philosophy of Education? A Symposium," *Educational Theory*, 57 (3): 297–306.

Todd, Sharon (2009), *Toward an Imperfect Education: Facing Humanity, Rethinking Cosmopolitanism*, New York: Paradigm Publishers.

Todd, Sharon (2015), "Between Body and Spirit: The Liminality of Pedagogical Relationships," in Morwenna Griffiths, Marit Honerød Hoveid, Sharon Todd, and Christine Winter (eds.), *Re-Imagining Relationships in Education: Ethics, Politics and Practices* (Journal of Philosophy of Education Book Series), 56–72, Oxford: Wiley-Blackwell.

Todd, Sharon, Rachel Jones, and Aislinn O'Donnell (2016), "Shifting Education's Philosophical Imaginaries: Relations, Affects, Bodies, Materialities," *Gender and Education*, 28 (2): 187–94.

Verducci, Susan (2018), "Noddings: A Voice from the Present and Past," in Paul Smeyers (ed.), *International Handbook of Philosophy of Education*, 305–12, Cham: Springer.

Warren, Karen J. (2009), *An Unconventional History of Western Philosophy. Conversations Between Men and Women Philosophers*, New York: Rowman & Littlefield.

Zembylas, Michalinos (2010), "The Ethic of Care in Globalized Societies: Implications for Citizenship Education," *Ethics and Education*, 5 (3): 233–45.

CHAPTER THREE

Analytic Philosophy of Education

CHRISTOPHER MARTIN

"All teaching is indoctrination." "Critical thinking means questioning the status quo." "Education is about preparation for the economy." Statements of this kind are common currency in public discourse about education. But how seriously should we take them? People generally see indoctrination as an unethical act. But if all teaching is indoctrination this means that we should conclude that teaching is always morally wrong. Critical thinking is commonly cited as a key educational goal. But if critical thinking amounts to simply questioning authority, it's fair to say that teachers shouldn't focus too much on promoting critical thought—as almost any parent will tell you, children are well disposed to question authority. Education makes an undeniable contribution to human capital. But if education means the same thing as preparation for working life, there is no principled reason why we should not focus all our curricular efforts on job training to the exclusion of all other activities.

This is all to say that terms such as "indoctrination," "critical thinking," and "education" play an important role in educational thought and action. However, if these concepts are misconceived or misunderstood, our thoughts and actions are likely to be *mis*guided. How so? Consider a very basic example: I think that the meaning of the term "hot" is equivalent to "not cold." You caution me that the stove is hot. But this doesn't really convey your intended warning. I think you mean that the stove is "not cold." The meaning that I attach to the concept does not make it absolutely clear to me that touching the stove would be harmful.

Similar problems arise for concepts that have special relevance in educational contexts. Consider the above claim that critical thinking is the same as challenging dominant beliefs or authoritative assumptions. Are they really the same? Imagine a person who always demands answers for why some state of affairs exists no matter the situation: at work, in politics, at home. However, imagine further that they have no interest in assessing the answers they are given in response to their demands. They do not care if those answers are good or bad. They just want to challenge. We would hesitate to label such a person a critical thinker. But why? To begin with, when we describe someone as a "critical *thinker*," we have in mind something more than a disposition to challenge. We are referring to the disposition to *think* critically (Siegel 1999). It means that we care that the reasons we have for believing X or Y are *good* reasons. Therefore, being clear on the concept of critical thinking surely matters for educational thought and action. If teachers operate on the assumption that "critical thinking" is the same as "questioning authority," they will likely be missing something essential in their efforts to instill critical thinking in students.

The importance of being clear on our educational concepts is a key focus for philosophers of education working in the analytic tradition. Analytic philosophers have prized, and continue to prize, argumentative clarity, logic, and the analysis of concepts to enrich our understanding of the nature, aims, and practice of education. In this chapter, I provide an introductory overview of the analytic tradition of philosophy of education. I will, in the main, be discussing the *early* influence of the modern analytic approach on the philosophy of education. This early iteration made a significant impact on educational theory, policy, and practice throughout the 1960s, 1970s, and 1980s. It did so by proffering groundbreaking analysis of a range of educational problems. And while the analytic approach lives on through its engagement with a wide variety of educational topics, this early iteration is, I believe, distinctive by virtue of (1) its focus on the meaning of everyday educational concepts and (2) its claim to the value of education as a distinct epistemic and moral enterprise.

In the first section, I outline the analytic movement in philosophy and its influence on the philosophical analysis of education. In the second, I summarize the work of the analytic tradition by focusing on two major contributors, R.S. Peters and Israel Scheffler. In the third section, I address the analysis of two concepts (autonomy and indoctrination) to show how the analytic tradition was converging on a substantive picture of education's value. In the fourth section, I offer an overview of scholarly criticism of the early analytic tradition. I then conclude with some brief comments on the early analytic tradition's potential contribution to future scholarship in the philosophy of education.

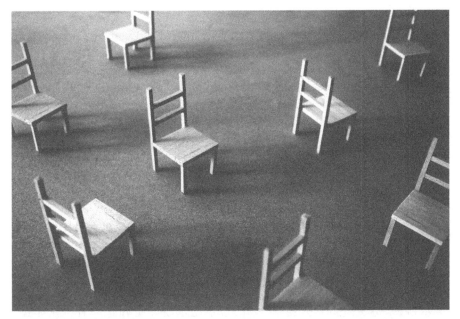

FIGURE 3.1 Many wooden chairs in chaotic disposition. *Source*: francescoch / iStock Photo.

INTELLECTUAL FOUNDATIONS OF THE ANALYTIC TRADITION

Philosophers of education laboring under the analytic approach were influenced, in particular,[1] by the "ordinary language philosophy" variant advanced by Gilbert Ryle and J.L. Austin.[2] Ordinary language philosophy takes the view that philosophical problems arise when terms acquire meanings that rest on a distorted, or selective, uptake of the ordinary meaning(s) that people attach to those terms. Such distortions can arise when scholars assign a highly technical or specific meaning to a commonly used term, when these common terms are explicitly defined in a way that captures only part of their implicitly held meaning, or when we altogether misunderstand the nature of the term itself. (See Ryle's famous account of "categorical mistakes" as an example of the latter.) The task of the philosopher, therefore, is to map out the meaning of key terms and concepts (*conceptual analysis*) so that their usage does not lead to further misunderstandings or misconceptions about the domain to which those terms or concepts are applied.

Analytic philosophers of *education* analyze concepts just like general analytic philosophers, but they do so within the educational context. For example, consider the philosopher Israel Scheffler's (1965) analysis of the concepts of "knowing" and "knowledge." The term "know" has an important function in everyday discourse. But it can have various meanings depending on the context.

Someone says, "I know that a marathon is 42.2 km." There are two conditions attached to this particular use of the term "know." First, knowing refers to the belief that a marathon is 42.2 km. But what if someone said, "I know that a marathon is the same distance as a half-marathon?" This is also a belief, but we wouldn't say that the person espousing this belief "knows." Why? Because it makes little sense to claim to know things that are not true. Therefore, "knowing" refers to a state or act of believing that has as its object something that is also *true*.

"Knowing," understood as having a true belief, is wholly sufficient for getting on in life. I know the score of the football game. I know what time the meeting starts. I know when the project deadline is. In many contexts we attribute "knowing" to a person who has a belief that is also true. However, Scheffler (like numerous other philosophers) identifies cases in which a person holds a true belief while being unable to give good reasons supporting that belief. Consider a person who believes that ice is solid water. This person has a true belief. They know. But we press them to explain why they believe this to be true. They are unable to provide any reasons supporting their belief. We would be unlikely to attribute to them real *knowledge*, in a strong or robust sense, regardless of the fact that their belief is true. This is because when we say that someone knows in the strong sense of the term we have in mind a person who has a belief (B) that is true (T) and that they have *good reasons* for holding that belief (i.e., a justification condition, or J). We can therefore, Scheffler claims, discern at least two senses of "knowing," one weak and one strong. Conceptual analysis enables us to specify the conditions necessary and sufficient for either sense (weak knowing, TB; strong knowing, JTB).

There are contexts where the distinction between strong and weak knowing makes a real difference. Education is one such context. Arguably, a teacher is responsible for transmitting knowledge to students, helping them come to "know." The distinction between strong and weak knowing seems germane here. Should teachers aim for the more demanding, strong knowing? Or is weak knowing sufficient? Is the answer generalizable across all teaching, or does it depend on what is being taught?

The analytic approach pioneered a move away from intellectual traditions that understood philosophy of education as a personal plan for a good life[3] or as an exegetical study of the history of educational ideas (Cuypers and Martin 2014: 8–18). By contrast, it advances a grounded, modest approach focused on educational practice, policy, and aims. To continue the example of "knowing," many teachers see (part of) the task of teaching as transmitting knowledge to future generations. Students should come to know what is already known. But what exactly does it mean to "know"? Given what "knowing" means, what are the methods appropriate for knowledge's "transmission"? If we are teaching for knowing in the strong sense perhaps some methods will be permissible, some necessary, and some entirely inappropriate.

MAJOR REPRESENTATIVES

The contributions of philosophers of education working in the analytic tradition are many and diverse.[4] In what follows, I focus on some of the major initiators of the analytic influence on the philosophy of education: the so-called "London line" led by Professor R.S. Peters and Paul Hirst at the Institution of Education, London, and the work of Israel Scheffler at Harvard University.[5]

R.S. PETERS ON THE CONCEPT OF EDUCATION

The most influential contribution of the London line of analytic philosophy of education has been R.S. Peters's conceptual analysis of "education." In works such as *Education As Initiation* (1963) and *Ethics and Education* (1966), Peters argued that the term "education" denotes a distinctive kind of value, the value of developing the mind for its own sake. On his view, talking about the value of education in terms of economic, political, or other outcomes external to education conflates what education *is* with its possible (contingent) effects or consequences. For example,

> [e]conomic and sociological descriptions of education can be misleading, if taken out of context [because] they are made from the point of view of a spectator pointing to the "function" or effects of education in a social or economic system. They are not descriptions of it from the point of view of someone engaged in that enterprise. (Peters 1963/2009: 60)

We value, for good reasons, the educational system's role in widening social mobility. However, this role does not capture the value of education understood apart from that system. Here is what I mean: it might be true that in an advanced economy a person who is employed in a full-time job has likely received a valid qualification through the education system. However, it is not necessarily the case that such a person is educated. Our "educated person" may have gotten their qualification through a degree mill or by cheating on every examination. They may have been hired because of personal connections as opposed to merit. They may not have developed, acquired, or internalized any of the characteristic features we have in mind when we claim that someone is educated.

What is it, then, that presumably sets the educated person apart from the merely credentialed? The way forward, argues Peters, is through conceptual analysis. Just as we can specify the conditions necessary for "knowing," we can specify the conditions necessary for being "educated." First, Peters argues that education is part of a broader category of terms expressing the idea of betterment. "Betterment" terms, as we might call them, refer to processes that involve taking something or someone through a process that leads to some sort of improvement. The term "reform" is an example of a betterment term. It would be odd, thinks Peters, to say that we reformed someone for the worse. It would be more accurate to claim that we tried to reform someone but failed. This points to a one general feature of education: just as it would be a contradiction to say that someone had been reformed for the worse, so too would it be a contradiction to say that someone had been educated but that the change was not desirable (Peters 1963/2009). Education, in its most basic sense, means betterment. Second, betterment terms do not point to a specific aim or objective (Peters 1967). We reform people by "improving" them, relative to where they begin, and this can involve a variety of interventions. Education, then, understood a betterment term, stipulates no specific "aim." Education is a *process* (p. 15). Third, we can distinguish between "education" and other betterment terms (such as "reform"). Therefore, education must refer to a process *distinct* from other betterment processes (Peters 1963/2009, 1967).

What is the nature of this distinctive process? Peters homes in on the various uses of the term "education" to specify what we think counts as betterment from an educational point of view. He claims, for example, that it would not be right to describe a person who is an expert in a narrow particular area of study, but knows nothing of what falls outside of that area, as an educated person. This suggests that educational processes should broaden our cognitive or intellectual perspective. The educated person understands many things, not just one thing.

Peters sets out three conditions that are individually necessary and jointly sufficient for a process to be educational:

1. Education involves the transmission of something worthwhile, the engagement with which leaves a person better off.
2. Education involves betterment of the person through activities that broaden their intellectual/cognitive perspective through exposure to a range of knowledge forms.
3. Education involves initiating the person into knowledge forms in such a way that (i) the person ascertains the "reasons why" of what they come to know within each form (what Scheffler would call "strong knowing"), (ii) the person understands the values and standards of justification/evidence that define each form of knowledge, and (iii) the person cares about, for their own sake, the values and standards of justification/evidence that define those forms of knowledge.

For example, someone coming out of a successful educational process will have increased their capacity to know the world from different points of view.

Peters combined these three conditions into the idea of "education as initiation." The term "initiation" is drawn from the philosopher Michael Oakeshott (2001), who believed that becoming human requires engagement with, and participation in, historical "conversations" through which the humanity has strived to understand itself. Peters (1963/2009) found the term "initiation" helpful because it discouraged thinking of education as a singular method or aim. On Peters's account, however, "*education* as initiation" refers to a specific process that is focused on the development of mind and is structured by the three conditions outlined above.

PAUL HIRST ON THE NATURE OF KNOWLEDGE

Peters takes education to refer to the development of the mind. As we saw in the previous section, "forms of knowledge" play a special role in this development. But what are forms of knowledge, and why are they essential to such development? The London line's answer can be largely attributed to Paul Hirst's (1965) "forms of knowledge" thesis. This thesis attempted to recover, or understand, the value of what was traditionally known as "liberal education." Broadly speaking, a liberal education refers to the freeing of one's mind through exposure to different kinds of knowledge and through intellectual activity motivated by a love of knowledge and truth. For example, detectives can apply psychological and sociological principles to solve crime. Their ability to examine a mystery from different cognitive/intellectual points of view supplies sufficient evidence for them to solve the case. But they see such knowledge and understanding merely as a means to the end of solving crime (think Thomas Magnum). A liberally educated person can also do this. However, they *also* value science, art, and other forms of knowledge because they simply value knowledge (think Sherlock Holmes, or Magnum's mentor, Higgins).

Liberal education has had a long and esteemed tradition but has often been reserved only for society's elite members. However, during the time Hirst was writing, liberal democracies were undertaking a massive postwar economic expansion. Educational opportunities, such as higher education, were being extended to groups who would otherwise never have had access to them. This expansion raised questions about the value of education. Is a liberal education valuable for everyone, or should the masses focus on vocational learning and skill development? Is the idea of liberating the mind through knowledge a universal educational ideal, or is it simply a cultural construct favored by the West? Hirst's "forms of knowledge" thesis aims to answer these questions.

Hirst maintained that knowledge can be logically divided into various forms. These forms are conventionally, though not necessarily, associated with disciplines (science, history, philosophy). The forms of knowledge are distinguished, in part, by public standards or criteria by which claims to knowledge within each form can be justified. For example, a *true* scientific claim (a claim about the material world) will look different from a *sound* moral claim (a claim about how one ought to act). Each form will also be home to distinctive concepts, standards of evidence, methods of discovery, and so on that have evolved over time to better capture knowledge and understanding specific to each form. For example, scientific discourse makes use of concepts such as evidence and replication, while moral discourse is built on concepts such as justification, character, responsibility, and obligation. While these concepts are sometimes analogous (compare "evidence" and "justification"), their meaning does not fully translate across the forms. For example, we cannot "prove" moral claims in a laboratory. We cannot "obligate" empirical claims to be true. Such uses make no *logical* sense.

Hirst argues that the forms of knowledge are of fundamental educational importance: being *forms* of knowledge, they structure our experience of the world as thinking, rational, cognitive beings. Initiation into such forms is essential to the free pursuit of a good life. To begin with, the forms increase our capacity to deal practically with a complex world. Scientific knowledge can be applied to increase our standard of living. Understanding principles of aesthetics can help us design more pleasant living spaces. But for Hirst, forms of knowledge are valuable for a more fundamental reason. Like Peters, he claims that forms of knowledge enable individuals to make reasoned judgments in the specific domains to which each form is linked. Morality enables us to discern right from wrong, science, true from false, aesthetics, beautiful from ugly. The need to make reasoned judgments is not reserved for elites; rather, anyone striving to live a good and happy life will need to make such judgments. As Hirst puts it, "the determination of the good life is ... to be itself the pursuit of a particular form of rational knowledge, that in which what ought to be done is justified by the giving of reasons" and where the good life consists in "the freeing of human conduct from wrong" (1965: 43).

ISRAEL SCHEFFLER ON RATIONALITY AS AN EDUCATIONAL IDEAL

The influence of analytic philosophy on education in the North American context was largely brought about through the work of Israel Scheffler. Scheffler introduced insights from analytic epistemology to bear on education in his *Conditions of Knowledge* (1965) and *Reason and Teaching* (1973). His conceptual analysis of "knowing" has already been explored in the first section of this chapter, and in what follows I elaborate on the implications of this work for teaching and the aims of education.

It is often common to run together the ideas of "teaching" and "learning." But for Scheffler there are important differences between the two terms. Consider the use of the term "learning." I can say, "I learned how the movie ends." Nothing in this statement requires us to think that I set out to learn the ending. It could have been spoiled for me. Further, we can think of instances where we learn but do not really come to *know*, at least in the strong sense. I may have learned that the stock market has crashed but be unable to offer any reasons why I believe this claim.

Unlike learning, the idea of teaching involves the concepts of intentionality and success (Scheffler 1965: 10). When we are teaching, we are trying to achieve something, to bring about some specific state of affairs. What does this state of affairs look like? What does it mean to have taught someone successfully? Scheffler is worth quoting in detail on this matter:

> What distinguishes teaching [from learning] ... is its special connection with rational explanation and critical dialogue: with the enterprise of giving honest reasons and welcoming radical questions. The person engaged in teaching does not merely want to bring about belief, but to bring it about through the exercise of free rational judgement by the student. This is what distinguishes teaching from propaganda or debating, for example. In teaching, the teacher is revealing his reasons for the beliefs he wants to transmit and is thus, in effect, submitting his own judgment to the critical scrutiny and evaluation of the student; he is fully engaged in the dialogue by which he hopes to teach, and is thus risking his own beliefs, in lesser or greater degree, as he teaches. (1965: 12)

Educators who rely on a weaker sense of "knowing that" will fail to meet this aim because their efforts will be focused squarely on transmitting true beliefs without "rational explanation and critical dialogue." Embedded in the concept of teaching, therefore, is rationality—the capacity to seek out, assess, and give reasons in all spheres of life—as a central aim of teaching (see Scheffler 1965, 1973/2014). In fact, Scheffler argues that, even if teachers are focused on the cultivation of habits through nonrational methods such as training and rehearsal, they ought still to offer reasons "justifying the valuations which are implicit in the teaching of these propensities, habits, traits and attainments" (1965: 107). For example, the teacher ought not to shape students in the interest of bringing about some other economic or social goals. This, because to do so is to treat the student as a mere means to that further end or goal and, as such, disrespects the student in their own developing capacity to set their own reasoned ends or goals.

A NOTE ON CONCEPTUAL ANALYSIS AND JUSTIFICATION

Analytic philosophers see clarification as a means to *justification*, not as an end in itself. The early analytic approach was not only interested in precise descriptions of educational concepts but in the values that inform the use of such concepts. To teach means to bring about a state in the learner that is (presumably) desirable. But do we have good reasons for thinking that this state *is* desirable? Answering this question means going beyond problems of conceptual clarification to questions of justification.

For example, both Hirst and Peters make use of a transcendental form of argument to justify the value of their conception of education. This way of justifying values is largely indebted to the Enlightenment philosopher Immanuel Kant. A transcendental justification is an argument that demonstrates that a certain condition, principle, or value is necessary for some practice or experience to be at all possible. Following this route, Hirst and Peters argue that anyone who strives to make good judgments must necessarily presuppose an education involving an initiation into forms of knowledge, for such an initiation is necessary for the very possibility of making such judgments (Hirst 1965: 41–2; Peters 1966: 162–5). This presupposition is unavoidable. Consider the person who asks, skeptically, "Why should I bother trying to understand history?" or "Why is education desirable?" or "What's the point of all this math?" Common to all these questions is a demand for rational knowledge— for *good reasons*—and, consequently, the questioner is committing himself to the value of rational knowledge in the very attempt to deny its value. In other words, for someone to ask for a justification for the value of education is to ask for reasons, and to ask for reasons presupposes that one has the capacity to understand and assess those reasons in terms of objective criteria (i.e., to be initiated sufficiently into the forms of knowledge).[6] On this view, Hirst's and Peters's conception of education is not fundamentally desirable for the reason that it will lead to some other good; rather, education is necessary if one is to pursue any good at all, for without education one is unlikely to ever really *know* what is good.

Like Hirst and Peters, Scheffler's analytic project also has a justificatory element. Getting clear on the proper manner of teaching and its relationship to epistemic conditions of rationality helps us to discern the moral foundations of teaching. Why, for example, should teachers concern themselves with promoting rationality in their students in the first place?[7] For Scheffler, these moral foundations are justified in Kantian terms: the principle that all of humanity (students included!) ought to be treated as ends in themselves and not merely as means. In his *On Human Potential*, for example, Scheffler argues that

> Kant's view of society, as a kingdom of ends within which free and rational beings would acknowledge such mutuality of freedom and incorporate one another's aims, where not immoral, into their own ... still seem to us to point the way in defining a goal for education in a global society of many cultures destined to share a shrinking work ... Human dignity is to be recognized and prized across whatever diversities divide us, and respect for persons takes primary place among the values we espouse in thinking about education and society. (1985: 39)

Kant argued that each person has intrinsic moral value simply by virtue of their capacity as rational moral agents, agents capable of setting and pursuing ends and checking their pursuit of such ends when morally required to do so. It is a matter of moral "respect for persons" that the teacher teaches so that students can understand, assess, and be moved by reasons. This includes the right of the student to exercise their own reason and to critically question what is taught.[8] Rationality as an aim of education both facilities and recognizes the basic dignity of the student as a rational and responsible human being. It is an epistemic aim of education justified *as* an epistemic aim on (primarily) moral grounds.

OTHER KEY CONCEPTS/THEMES

Peters, Hirst, and Scheffler set the stage for further analytic work in areas such as moral education, religious education, the education of the emotions, and critical thinking. It would be impossible to do justice to the full range of these contributions. In what follows, I focus on the analytic treatment of two educational concepts (autonomy and indoctrination) to illustrate some other features of the early analytic tradition.

Dearden on education for personal autonomy

Robert Dearden's account of "autonomy" is a good example of how early analytic philosophy of education not only described but argued *for* the distinctive meaning of educational concepts. Dearden observes that "autonomy" has a number of different meanings. It can mean independence from another political power (political autonomy). It can mean that a person does the right thing for its own sake as opposed to peer pressure or fear of punishment (moral autonomy). It can mean self-control. But what, exactly, does it mean to *educate* for autonomy? As Dearden puts it:

> A difficulty, however, in attempting a fuller characterization of personal autonomy is to know what it would be to have succeeded in such an attempt, since there is no clear guidance to be gained here from something called "ordinary usage." On the contrary, what one is doing is attempting to formulate a concept of something often still rather vague and inchoate, but nevertheless implicit in a variety of educational innovations and changes. The appropriate check on any suggested analysis would therefore seem to be in asking whether the analysis offered is indeed what people are implicitly making their aim, or one of their aims in education. (2010: 336–7)

In other words, autonomy can have distinctive meanings in different contexts, and we need to be careful not to import these meanings uncritically into the *educational* context. For example, if we were to assume that education should aim for autonomy in the political sense of the term, it could be taken to mean that students should be free to act independently of the authority of the teacher. To be sure, there are some circumstances where this would be a desirable goal for the educator, but it does not seem to capture fully what educators have in view when they promote the autonomy of students. Dearden proposes an educationally specific conception of autonomy, one that reflects the cognitive focus of teaching. On this view, education should aim for students to acquire some degree of independence of *thought*:

> [A] person is "autonomous" to the degree that what he thinks and does cannot be explained without reference to his own activity of mind. (Dearden 2010: 336–7)

For Dearden, being autonomous means that our beliefs and our actions are motivated by reasons in whatever sphere of life we are engaged in. It applies to our lives as citizens, as moral agents, and as individuals trying to live the best life we can. Accordingly, education for autonomy is an education for *personal* autonomy (p. 343).

Dearden's conception of personal autonomy can be brought to bear, critically, on educational terms and practices that try, but fail, to capture fully the same ideal. The idea that students should have more freedom in the classroom is appealing, in part because it is in rough alignment with autonomy's emphasis on independence and freedom of the mind. However, appropriate constraints on freedom may be needed to promote the conditions necessary for autonomy (Dearden 2010: 335–6). If students are too busy doing whatever they want and are not encouraged to reflect critically on the reasons for their wants, to take a very basic example, the teacher may well be neglecting their autonomy. Similarly, some progressive educators argue that students should be allowed to choose what to learn in accordance with their personal interests. Yet Dearden claims that an education for personal autonomy requires the acquisition of basic forms of knowledge and understanding (akin to Hirst's forms of knowledge) (p. 343). This is all to say that the autonomy-minded educator can get behind student freedom, but only as a means to a more basic value: the development of students capable and willing to act and judge on the basis of their own cognitive efforts.

Dearden's work on personal autonomy launched an ongoing and influential debate about the conditions of autonomy and the educational processes appropriate to its realization. Some have argued that Dearden's conception is too cognitively demanding—that it places too strong an emphasis on rationality and reason-giving and consequently overstates the value of "activity of mind" for different domains of life (Callan 1988: 30–1). One prominent alternative, for example, is the idea that autonomy has less to do with the maximization of rationality and intellect and more to do with conditions necessary for living well in free societies, such as a capacity for self-determination and access to a meaningful range of options in life (Raz 1986; J. White 1990).[9] Regardless of these refinements, Dearden's initial efforts to clarify the nature and conditions of personal autonomy continue to play an important role in helping educators think through the nature of their work in societies that value freedom and openness.

Snook on education and indoctrination

While much focus of early analytic work was on the clarification of different educational concepts, equally important is how these concepts relate to one another within a broader picture of the values and purposes of education. What did this picture look like? Rationality, knowledge, understanding, justification, critical thinking: these concepts are the common currency of education, according to the analytic paradigm. They converge on the idea that education is, fundamentally, about the development of a person's mind. The goal of this process is a free, liberated mind empowered to pursue their own path in life aided by an understanding of the rational principles or standards necessary for making good judgments regarding many aspects of human experience.[10]

The framework that holds these educational concepts together is the liberal moral and political values of the Enlightenment: values of individual freedom, social cooperation, and moral respect for persons. As Peters once put it, "in the teaching situation this general respect for persons is overlaid with an awareness that one is confronted with *developing* centres of consciousness" (1966: 59). The latent moral meanings in terms such as "know" and "teach" are (arguably) derived from this general obligation.[11] The modern analytic project therefore sharpened not only the epistemological but also the moral dimensions of education.

To be sure, teachers can try, but fail, to have their students come to know. But this is not necessarily a moral failure. It may be a failure of circumstance. The teachers might not have had enough resources to carry out their work. The students may have been underprepared. What, then, does it mean to fail, *morally*, in the educational domain? By a moral failure, I mean actions that contradict the moral foundations of education and teaching. Analytic philosophers saw indoctrination as a term well situated to capture such a moral failure. While many analytic philosophers advanced competing accounts of the concept of indoctrination (Flew 1966; J. White 1972; Wilson 1964), I.A. Snook's (1970, 2010) account is arguably the high-water mark. Snook aimed to account for the conditions that can distinguish between cases of indoctrination in the morally problematic sense and cases that look like indoctrination but are morally appropriate. This distinction is more difficult to capture than it may at first seem. As Snook points out, the distinction can be too general, in which case the account labels actions that are unavoidable or practically necessary for teaching as indoctrinatory, or it can be too narrow, in which case it permits the teacher to undertake actions that are intuitively indoctrinatory and morally impermissible. For example, if you are committed to rationality as an educational aim, it might seem that *any* use of "nonrational methods" to impart beliefs or skills is indoctrinatory (where "nonrational" means memorization, reward or punishment, and so on). But then we realize that young children *have* to acquire some behaviors (e.g., "don't hit your classmates") or rote facts (e.g., "2 × 2 = 4") without the teacher appealing to the student's reason. Therefore, the concept of indoctrination needs to distinguish between cases in which the use of nonrational methods is morally wrong and cases in which it is necessary or unavoidable (see Snook 1970: 97–9).

Snook argues that a person indoctrinates P (a proposition or set of propositions) if they teach with the intention that the pupil or pupils believe P regardless of the evidence (p. 100). Note that this conception handles cases where nonrational methods are necessary. In the case of 2 × 2 = 4, the belief in question is unlikely to be of the kind in which the weighing of evidence is involved, and so drilling math tables is not like having someone believe *regardless of the evidence*. There is no evidence "against" math tables that the would-be indoctrinator could prevent the student from entertaining. Snook's conception of indoctrination can also handle classroom rules. One can inculcate norms of behavior without intending those norms be held in such a way that they cannot be revised in new situations or in light of new evidence.

For Snook, indoctrination could be summarized as the intention to bring about "undesirable states of mind of a specified sort" (p. 107): a dogmatic, unquestioning, nonrational mind. It is, in a sense, education's dark mirror. We can therefore view Snook's analysis as a contribution to the broader picture of education that began to form as the analytic tradition progressed.[12] A better understanding of the nature and conditions of indoctrination throws the analytic picture into sharper relief.

CRITICISM OF THE EARLY ANALYTIC PHILOSOPHY OF EDUCATION

While the analytic tradition comprised many and diverse contributions, we can identify two main features:

1. An *approach* or *method* characterized by argumentative rigor, justification, and the analysis of key educational concepts.
2. A family of *substantive* conceptions of education understood as a distinctive epistemic and moral enterprise concerned with the promotion of knowledge, understanding, rationality, and mind.

The influence of this tradition—both as a philosophical approach to educational problems and as a conception of education—began to wane through the early

1980s and onwards. There are a few contingent reasons for this decline, some of which are institutional (Colgan 2018).[13] Resurging interest in the thought of John Dewey in North American Schools of Education has surely also been a factor (Waks 2008). But some of this decline can be attributable to scholarly criticisms directed at the tradition itself. What I lay out next is not a systematic account of all the general intellectual trends that motivated those criticisms; rather, I reconstruct some specific claims raised against the analytic tradition.[14]

The analysis of a concept's meaning cannot be generalized

Some scholars criticized the value of conceptual analysis. Consider: the use of a word means something different at different historical periods, places, languages, and cultures. This must mean that the conceptual analysis of terms such as "education" do not disclose any kind of essential meaning. Rather, it simply reveals the dominant values of the culture within which the term is used. To say someone is "educated" in 1960s London means something different than when the same claim is made in ancient Greece (Dray 1973). As a result, it is unlikely that conceptual analysis can lead to any objective truths about the nature, scope, and value of education. Of course, for this criticism to have real bite, we would need to forget that the aim of conceptual analysis is to get a clearer sense of the conditions, values, or goals that people *have in mind* when they use terms. How generalizable or objective those conditions are across different educational contexts is a question of justification, which as I have stressed throughout this chapter, is an equally important feature of the analytic project.

The analytic account of the value of education is too narrow

Others argued that the substantive commitments of the analytic tradition assumed too narrow a view of education and its value.[15] First, the scholarly consensus appears to be that epistemic conceptions of education, especially the Hirst–Peters variety, failed to capture (or unfairly discount) our intuitive sense that there are non-epistemic features of becoming an educated person that are valued by teachers, students, and society. For example, the analytic tradition struggled to justify the value of *physical* education. This has been taken by some to indicate that epistemic conceptions are unable to capture fully the nature of educational value (Carr 1997; McNamee 1998; Reid 1996). Liberal education, arguably the animating ideal behind the Hirst–Peters paradigm in particular, was criticized for its neglect of vocational education (Pring 1995). John White (1990) cogently argues that the epistemic conceptions overvalued knowledge and understanding at the expense of other goods that ought to have pride of place in a school curriculum. Feminist critics also weighed in, with philosophers such as Jane Roland Martin (1981) arguing that Peters's conception of education neglects the role of education in equipping all citizens to engage in what she terms society's "reproductive processes," which include "the rearing of children to more or less maturity and associated activities such as tending the sick, taking care of family needs, and running a household" (1985: 6). These criticisms did not so much reject the analytic picture of education but sought to expand, through careful argumentation, the range of possibilities of what is educationally worthwhile.

Analytic philosophy ignores the political dimension

Analytic philosophy also faced the charge that, by virtue of its narrowness, it neglected the political dimension of education. Is this true? While it might be that case that early analytic work emphasized the epistemic and moral dimensions of education, it would be a mistake to claim that the political dimension was altogether ignored. Examples of politically engaged work include Patricia White's (1983/2010) *Beyond Domination*, which articulated a conception of political education appropriate for liberal democratic society. R.S Peters's later writings also began to shift to questions about the relationship between the concept of education and democracy (Peters 1979). Scheffler's "Moral Education and the Democratic Ideal" (collected in *Reason and Teaching*) was originally published in 1971. Finally, analytic philosophers applied their insights to contemporary debates on educational policy and practice. Notable, for example, was their critical engagement with the child-centered and growth-centered theories of education that began to gain influence in policy circles of the day as evinced by the UK's Plowden Report (see Peters 1969/2012).

Nonetheless, the analytic picture of education rested on liberal/Enlightenment moral and political foundations that were being challenged on a variety of fronts. Some critics, such as those working within a Marxian framework, argued that liberalism was a thoroughly unjust regime. On their view, a "politically liberal" philosophy of education was an uncritical ideology that functioned to reinforce the school's role in capitalist oppression (Sarup 1978/2013).

Early analytic philosophers were writing in a postwar era of massive social change. It was a time in which a booming economy and changing social roles gave rise to an education system that was rapidly democratizing and expanding to a mass audience. Perhaps a more serious problem for the analytic tradition, then, is that it had a blind spot for educational problems of growing concern for the average citizen, problems such as the fair distribution or educational resources/opportunities and the nature and limits of state authority over educational institutions. Accordingly, it is plausible to attribute some of the tradition's decline to a paucity of explicit attention to its own political foundations, including the alleged shortcomings of these foundations in the face of pressing social problems to which education (and more specifically, schooling) was increasingly tasked with addressing. One unfortunate consequence of this neglect is that the early analytic tradition was outmaneuvered and some of its key ideas, such as the idea that knowledge has value for its own sake, were successfully repositioned as elitist interests out of touch with the real needs of liberal democratic citizens.

CONTEMPORARY INFLUENCE AND FUTURE DIRECTIONS

The idea of analytic philosophy of education being the torchbearer of a distinctive and singular conception (or singular family of conceptions) of education has faded. Yet these conceptions continue to inform the broader picture of educational value, policy, and practice. Scheffler's account of teaching and rationality as an aim of education has endured. Harvey Siegel (1988/2013, 1997/2013, 2017), for example, has continued the Schefflerian project of incorporating insights from general epistemology into an educational perspective, writing extensively on the nature and scope of critical thinking as a fundamental educational aim. His work has also demonstrated how education can bear on the claims of general epistemology (Siegel 2005). Recent years have also seen something of a critical reassessment of the Peters–Hirst paradigm (Cuypers 2012; Martin 2014). The persistence of these themes suggests that, while the early analytic tradition may not stand on its own as a final account of what education *is*, it has arguably succeeded in identifying some of its enduring, core features.

As for the analytic *approach*? This is harder to pin down. The term "analytic philosophy" has broadened considerably to include many substantive views and traditions. For example, the analytic approach in education has experienced a degree of resurgence through work derived from analytic political philosophy, taking its cue from John Rawls. This wave has contributed to a growing literature on the relationship between liberalism, justice, and education (Brighouse 2006; Callan 1997). This, and a diverse range of other analytically informed work, has arguably eclipsed the scholarly influence of the conceptual analysis tradition.

What does this mean for the earlier tradition, with its emphasis on conditions of educational value, forms of knowledge, and the development of intellectual autonomy? There is currently a renewed interest in epistemic conceptions of education (see Carter and Pritchard 2017; Kotzee 2018). Included here are efforts to more precisely map the relationship between epistemic value and social and political justice (Fricker 2013). While the problem of justice in education has (rightly) focused on the fair distribution of resources and the role of schooling in promoting fair socioeconomic equality of opportunity, this new work raises important questions about the value of knowledge and understanding, and the implications of such value for educational institutions. It may well be, as Carr (2012) has suggested, that the philosophical wheel is coming "full circle," bringing the epistemic dimension of education back to the fore. This raises the possibility of a turn back to work from the conceptual analysis era.

Forecasting is tricky business and likely to err. Even so, the analytic approach will always have the potential to add precision, where called for, to the thought and action of educational scholars and practitioners. The language of education is always undergoing change. New concepts arise to capture new values and social conditions. In our time, terms like "ways of knowing," "diversity," "mindfulness," "safe space," and "inclusion" have increasingly come to define contemporary thought and action in the educational context. Their overarching influence on contemporary educational thought warrants sustained investigation of their use(s). The analytic tradition is well positioned to address these and other conceptual schemes that are bound to arise to the future. As R.S. Peters put it, "[e]ducation is different from social work, psychiatry, and real estate. Everything is what it is and not some other thing" (1963/2009: 60). We shouldn't take Peters to mean that education should never change. Rather, education is— at least in some respects—home to *distinctive* values and purposes. It is this distinctiveness that needs to be preserved. One way to do so is to insist on being clear about what we mean when we talk about education, and why.

NOTES

1 The general influence comes from Wittgenstein. However, as Standish (2018) notes, Wittgenstein was taken up in a more "intellectualized" form by analytic philosophers of education that were focused on questions of rational justification and conceptual clarification.
2 It is important to note that the term "ordinary language philosophy" is misleading as a full description of the activities and aims of analytic philosophy of education. While analytic philosophers are focused on the meanings and uses of words, they conceive of this focus as a means to developing clearer (and better justified) arguments about the philosophical (moral, political, epistemic, aesthetic) dimensions of education. For more on common misconceptions about analytic philosophy of education, see White and White (2001).
3 However, see Elliott's (1986) reconstruction of what he alleges to be an unexamined conception of the good life underlying the British analytic tradition.
4 In addition to primary sources, there are many works that have sought to revisit or reassess the analytic project through some of its main contributors. These include *R.S. Peters* (Cuypers and Martin 2014), *Reason and Education: Essays in Honor of Israel Scheffler* (Siegel 2012), *Beyond Liberal Education: Essays in Honour of Paul Hirst* (Barrow and White 2013), and *Education, Values and Mind: Essays for R.S. Peters* (Cooper 2010). Readers are also encouraged to seek out the special issue of the journal "Special Issue: Philosophy of Education in the Perspective of R.S. Peters" Edited by David Aspin (2013) *Educational Philosophy and Theory*, 45:2 and Gingell (2013).
5 There are, of course, important precursors to these thinkers, such as C.D. Hardie and D.J. O'Connor (Siegel and Phillips 2018).

6   This only skims the surface of the role of transcendental argumentation in the London line of analytic philosophy. R.S. Peters's "transcendental-pragmatic" version of the argument is especially worth noting, given its influence on contemporary theories of practical reason (Peters 1966). For more on Peters's theory of justification, see Martin (2009).

7   See Siegel (1995) for a transcendental answer to this question.

8   The fact that knowledge is fallible—subject to correction and revision—provides an epistemological reason for why what is taught should be open to question (Hare 1997: 94).

9   Autonomy was later taken up as part of a broader political philosophical analysis of the nature and scope of education in the liberal state. For a comprehensive overview of much of this literature, see Shinkel (2009). Note that in lockstep with the later decline in the analytic tradition of philosophy of education mainstream critiques of the liberal political values that warranted personal autonomy as an educational aim. See John White's (2003) account of how these critiques impacted on the philosophy of education.

10 It is important to note, however, that ideas about the development of mind were not always framed in rationalist terms. See William Hare's (1993) work on the intellectual virtue of open-mindedness, work that anticipated the recent ascendance in the contemporary literature on intellectual virtues and education.

11 That said, it would be uncharitable to claim the analytic tradition pursued the individualistic conception of the liberal person that was the focus of much criticism in the political philosophy of the 1980s and 1990s. Early analytic philosophers had a keen sense of the extent to which, and ways in which, the educated person is not an individual "all the way down" but is part of a shared moral and epistemological community. It is plausible to think that the educational focus of their work—on questions of cultivation, social cooperation, learning to respect others and so on—mitigated the excess individualism that allegedly pervaded much of the liberal political theory of the same era.

12 Like autonomy, the concept of indoctrination has continued to generate philosophical interest. For example, the concept of indoctrination has been used to assess the extent to which, and ways in which, moral education is (or is not) necessarily indoctrinatory (Copp 2016). Others have considered the further respects in which indoctrination is wrongful or harmful in ways more detailed than "an undesirable state of mind" (Callan and Arena 2009). Still others have critiqued the idea that "intention" is necessary for indoctrination to occur (Peterson 2007; Taylor 2017).

13 For a detailed account of the shifting fortunes of analytic philosophy, as well as an overview of its major contributions, see Carr (1994).

14 For example, the ascendance of postmodern/poststructural theory undermined the epistemological foundations on which the analytic picture of education rests. However, this development has had a wide-reaching effect on many disciplines, and my focus is on criticisms that could plausibly be seen as specific to the analytic philosophy of education.

15 How justified these criticisms are is a separate issue. We can and should distinguish between criticisms of an intellectual tradition as it is received and understood (and perhaps stereotyped) and what the members of that tradition understand it to be. For example, in contrast to the idea that the analytic tradition was too narrow, consider Scheffler on the education of teachers: "Justification is not ... simply a matter of minimal necessity. It is rather, a matter of desirability, and a thing may

be desirable not because it is something we could not do without, but because it transforms and enhances the quality of what we do and how we live. If a justification is needed for the teacher's scholarly and theoretical sophistication regarding his work, it is not that, lacking it he cannot manage to teach, but that having it, the quality of his effort and role is likely to be enhanced. It is a maximal rather than a minimal interpretation of the teacher's work that is thus relevant to a philosophical assessment of his education" (2012: 104). There is more than adequate textual evidence to support the idea that, however misconceived, the aim of the analytic approach was to apply conceptual analysis and rational justification to sharpen and *expand* our sense of what is educationally worthwhile.

REFERENCES

Primary sources

Dearden, R.F. (2010), "Autonomy and Education," in R.F. Dearden, Paul H. Hirst, and Richard S. Peters (eds.), *Education and the Development of Reason*, 58–85, London: Routledge.

Hirst, Paul H. (1965), "Liberal Education and the Nature of Knowledge," *Philosophical Analysis and Education*, 2: 113–40.

Peters, Richard S. (1963/2009), "Education As Initiation," in R.D. Archambault (ed.), *Philosophical Analysis and Education*, 59–75, London: Routledge & Kegan Paul.

Peters, Richard S. (1966), *Ethics and Education*, London: George Allen & Unwin.

Peters, Richard S. (1967), "Aims of Education: A Conceptual Inquiry," in Richard S. Peters (ed.), *The Philosophy of Education*, 11–29, Oxford: Oxford University Press.

Peters, Richard S. (1979), "Democratic Values and Educational Aims," *Teachers College Record*, 80 (3): 463–82.

Peters, Richard S., ed. (1969/2012), *Perspectives on Plowden* (Routledge Library Editions: Education), London: Routledge.

Scheffler, Israel (1965), *Conditions of Knowledge: An Introduction to Epistemology and Education*, Chicago: Scott, Foresman and Company.

Scheffler, Israel (1973/2014), *Reason and Teaching* (Routledge Revivals), London: Routledge.

Scheffler, Israel (1985), *Of Human Potential: An Essay in the Philosophy of Education*, New York: Routledge & Kegan Paul.

Scheffler, Israel (2012), "University Scholarship and the Education of Teachers (1973)," *Schools: Studies in Education*, 9 (1): 101–12.

Snook, Ivan A. (1970), "The Concept of Indoctrination," *Studies in Philosophy and Education*, 7 (2): 65–108.

Snook, Ivan A. (2010), *Concepts of Indoctrination: Philosophical Essays* (International Library of the Philosophy of Education, Vol. 20), London: Routledge.

Secondary sources

Barrow, Robin and P. White (2013), *Beyond Liberal Education: Essays in Honour of Paul H Hirst*, London: Routledge.

Brighouse, Harry (2006), *On Education*, London: Routledge.

Callan, E. (1988). *Autonomy and schooling*. McGill-Queen 39;s Press-MQUP.

Callan, Eamonn (1997), *Creating Citizens: Political Education and Liberal Democracy*, Oxford: Clarendon Press.

Callan, Eamonn and Dylan Arena (2009), "Indoctrination," in Harvey Siegel (ed.),
  Oxford Handbook of Philosophy of Education, Oxford, Oxford University Press.
Carr, David (1994), "The Philosophy of Education," *Philosophical Books*, 35(1): 1–9.
Carr, David (1997), "Physical Education and Value Diversity: A Response to Andrew
  Reid," *European Physical Education Review*, 3 (2): 195–205.
Carr, David (2012), "Curriculum and the Value of Knowledge," in Harvey Siegel (ed.),
  The Oxford Handbook of Philosophy of Education, Oxford: Oxford University Press.
Carter, Adam J. and Duncan H. Pritchard (2017), "Epistemic Situationism, Epistemic
  Dependence, and the Epistemology of Education," in M. Alfano and A. Fairweather
  (eds.), 168-90, *Epistemic Situationism*, Oxford: Oxford University Press.
Colgan, Andrew D. (2018), "The Examination of the Decline of Philosophy of
  Education with Institutional Theory: A Focus on the Last Three Decades,"
  Philosophical Inquiry in Education, 25 (1): 66–87.
Cooper, David (2010), *Education, Values and Mind: Essays for RS Peters* (International
  Library of the Philosophy of Education, Vol. 6), London: Routledge.
Copp, David (2016), "Moral Education Versus Indoctrination," *Theory and Research
  in Education*, 14 (2): 149–67.
Cuypers, Stefaan E. (2012), "RS Peters' 'The Justification of Education' Revisited,"
  Ethics and Education, 7 (1): 3–17.
Cuypers, Stefaan E. and Christopher Martin (2014), *R.S. Peters* (Continuum Library of
  Educational Thought, Vol. 18), London: Bloomsbury.
Dray, William (1973), "Commentary," in Richard S. Peters (ed.), *Philosophy of
  Education*, 34–9, Oxford: Oxford University Press.
Elliott, R.K. (1986), "Richard Peters: A Philosopher in the Older Style," in David
  E. Cooper (ed.), *Education, Values and Mind: Essays for RS Peters*, 41–68, London:
  Routledge.
Flew, Antony (1966), "What Is Indoctrination?," *Studies in Philosophy and Education*,
  4 (3): 281–306.
Fricker, Miranda (2013), "Epistemic Justice As a Condition of Political Freedom?,"
  Synthese, 190 (7): 1317–32.
Gingell, John, ed. (2013), *Education and the Common Good: Essays in Honor of Robin
  Barrow*, London: Routledge.
Hare, William (1993), *Open-Mindedness and Education*, Kingston and Montreal:
  McGill-Queen's University Press.
Hare, William (1997), "Reason in Teaching: Scheffler's Philosophy of Education
  'A Maximum of Vision and a Minimum of Mystery'," in *Reason and Education*,
  89–101, Dordrecht: Springer.
Kotzee, Ben (2018), "Applied Epistemology of Education," in David Coady and James
  Chase (eds.), *The Routledge Handbook of Applied Epistemology*, 211–30, New
  York: Routledge.
Martin, Christopher (2014), *Education in a Post-Metaphysical World: Rethinking
  Educational Policy and Practice through Jürgen Habermas' Discourse Morality*,
  London: Bloomsbury.
Oakeshott, Michael (2001), *The Voice of Liberal Learning*, Indianapolis, IN: Liberty
  Fund.
Peterson, Barbara A. (2007), "Holding Teachers Accountable for Indoctrination:
  A Reexamination of I. A. Snook's Notion of 'Intent'," *Philosophy of Education
  Archive*: 298–305.
Pring, Richard (1995), *Closing the Gap: Liberal Education and Vocational Preparation*,
  London: Hodder & Stoughton.

Reid, Andrew (1996), "The Concept of Physical Education in Current Curriculum and Assessment Policy in Scotland," *European Physical Education Review*, 2: 7–18.

Roland Martin, Jane (1981), "The Ideal of the Educated Person," *Educational Theory*, 31 (2): 97–109.

Roland Martin, Jane (1987), *Reclaiming a Conversation: The Ideal of the Educated Woman*, New Haven, CT: Yale University Press.

Sarup, Madan (1978/2013), "The Rejection of Liberal Philosophy of Education," in Madan Sarup *Marxism and Education: A Study of Phenomenological and Marxist Approaches to Education* (Routledge Library Editions: Education), London: Routledge.

Schinkel, Anders (2010), "Compulsory Autonomy-Promoting Education," *Educational Theory*, 60 (1): 97–116.

Siegel, Harvey (1995), "Why Should Educators Care about Argumentation?," *Informal Logic*, 17 (2): 159–76.

Siegel, Harvey (1999). *What (good) are thinking dispositions?*. Educational Theory, 49(2), 207–21.

Siegel, Harvey (2005), "Truth, Thinking, Testimony and Trust: Alvin Goldman on Epistemology and Education," *Philosophy and Phenomenological Research*, 71 (2): 345–66.

Siegel, Harvey (2013a), *Educating Reason*, London: Routledge.

Siegel, Harvey (2013b), *Rationality Redeemed?: Further Dialogues on an Educational Ideal*, London: Routledge.

Siegel, Harvey (2017), *Education's Epistemology: Rationality, Diversity, and Critical Thinking*, Oxford: Oxford University Press.

Siegel, Harvey, ed. (2012), *Reason and Education: Essays in Honor of Israel Scheffler*, Springer Science & Business Media.

Siegel, Harvey and D.C. Phillips (2018), "Philosophy of Education," *Stanford Encyclopedia of Philosophy*. Available online: https://plato.stanford.edu/entries/education-philosophy/.

Standish, Paul (2018), "Wittgenstein's Impact on the Philosophy of Education," *Philosophical Investigations*, 41 (2), 223–40.

Taylor, Rebecca M. (2017), "Indoctrination and Social Context: A System-Based Approach to Identifying the Threat of Indoctrination and the Responsibilities of Educators," *Journal of Philosophy of Education*, 51 (1): 38–58.

Waks, Leonard (2008), "Introduction," in Leonard Waks (ed.), *Leaders in Philosophy of Education: Intellectual Self-Portraits*, Rotterdam: Sense Publishers.

White, John (1972), "Indoctrination and intentions," in I.A. Snook (ed.), *Concept of Indoctrination*, Lancashire: RKP.

White, John (1990), *Education and the Good Life: Beyond the National Curriculum*: London: Kogan Page.

White, John (2003), "Five Critical Stances Towards Liberal Philosophy of Education in Britain," *Journal of Philosophy of Education*, 37 (1): 147–84.

White, John and Patricia White (2001), "Analytic Philosophy of Education and Children's Rights," in Frieda Heyting, Dieter Lenzen, and John White (eds.), *Methods in Philosophy of Education*, 13–29, London: Routledge.

White, Patricia (1983/2010), *Beyond Domination: An Essay in the Political Philosophy of Education* (International Library of the Philosophy of Education, Vol. 23), London: Routledge.

Wilson, John (1964), "Education and indoctrination," in T.B. Hollins (ed.), *The Aims of Education*, 24–46, Manchester: Manchester University Press.

CHAPTER FOUR

A Philosophy of Hope: Paulo Freire and Critical Pedagogy

PETER ROBERTS

INTRODUCTION

Of all the different domains of educational study, few are more diverse, complex, and contested than critical pedagogy. Critical pedagogy is a multidisciplinary field of inquiry, informed and shaped by a wide range of intellectual traditions and theoretical perspectives. Critical pedagogues can, for example, be humanists, existentialists, Marxists, socialists, feminists, postmodernists, or postcolonialists, or various combinations thereof. There is neither a universally accepted "definition" of critical pedagogy nor an agreed account of exactly how the field has progressed and developed. There are, nonetheless, some key ideas at the heart of work in this domain. Critical pedagogues, for all their differences, share a commitment to social justice, democratic struggle, and the value of questioning and critique. They seek to allow the voices of those who have been marginalized to be heard. They stand opposed to authoritarianism and to discrimination in all its forms. Critical pedagogy is concerned with identifying, analyzing, and transforming oppressive structures, practices, and relations, even if there may be considerable debate over how oppression and transformation are best understood. Critical pedagogues are also united in the view that education is a political process, underpinned by an implied or explicit set of assumptions, values, and ideals. Many who work in the field point to both limits to and possibilities for the role of education as a force of social change. Education, they argue, can play a part in reinforcing existing inequalities, but it can also be crucial in contesting and addressing those inequalities.

Before turning to the main focus of this chapter, a brief comment on the constituent elements of the term "critical pedagogy" is in order. The "critical" element of critical pedagogy does not refer to the mere act of *criticizing* (though that can be part of it) or to *criticism* of the literary kind (though literature too might be addressed by some critical pedagogues). Critical pedagogy, in its many different forms, is also usually distinguished from "critical thinking" as espoused by some analytic philosophers. Critical pedagogy implies a willingness to examine and engage not just texts, ideas, or arguments but also hierarchies of power and privilege in economic, political, and cultural systems and institutions (Apple 1999; Darder, Torres, and Baltodano 2017; Kincheloe 2007, 2008a; McLaren 1989; Steinberg 2007). Critical engagement with contemporary developments in policy—for example, under globalization and neoliberalism—is also common (Giroux 2006, 2008; Kumar 2016; Leistyna 2007; Nikolakaki 2012). Critical pedagogy focuses not just on theorizing and discussing but also on resistance, and, in some cases, on revolution (Giroux 1983; McLaren 2000). The "pedagogy" aspect of critical pedagogy is likewise at odds with some common interpretations of this term. Pedagogy for critical pedagogues is not simply "teaching methods." Indeed, scholars working in this field are often sharply critical of the obsession with methods in teaching (Aronowitz 2012; Macedo 1997). Methods need to be appropriate to *contexts* (Kincheloe 2008a; Roberts 1996c). Thus, for critical pedagogues, knowing *how* to teach also involves knowing *why* one is teaching. Knowledge is a contested domain, with not merely the question of truth but also matters of justice at stake (cf. Kincheloe 2008b). A critical pedagogue always needs to ask: What do I stand for, and why? With whom am I working? Under what circumstances? Seen in this light, pedagogy can be conceived as the theory and practice of teaching, as enacted in specific situations, with particular groups, pursuing given ends, with both constraints and opportunities for worthwhile educational change.

Critical pedagogy's eclectic nature is reflected in both its philosophical heritage and its links with other domains of study. With its emphasis on change and transformation, it builds on the tradition of progressive education established by John Dewey, W.E.B. DuBois, Carter G. Woodson, Myles Horton, Herbert Kohl, Jonathan Kozol, Maxine Greene, Samuel Bowles and Herbert Gintis, Martin Carnoy, and others, and on the writings of radical critics of institutional life such as Ivan Illich (Darder, Baltodano, and Torres 2017: 3–5). Antonio Gramsci's ideas on hegemony and organic intellectuals and the critical theory of the Frankfurt School, as represented by thinkers such as Max Horkheimer, Theodor Adorno, Herbert Marcuse, and Jürgen Habermas, have also exerted a formative influence (Giroux 1983, 1988;

Kellner et al. 2009; Kincheloe 2008a; Mayo 1999; Morrow and Torres 2002; Peters, Lankshear, and Olssen 2003). Among more contemporary scholars, Joe Kincheloe, himself a leader in the field, names the following as key figures: Stanley Aronowitz, Henry Giroux, Michael Apple, bell hooks, Donaldo Macedo, Peter McLaren, Ira Shor, Jesus "Pato" Gomez, Ramon Flecha, Deborah Britzman, Philip Wexler, Patti Lather, Antonia Darder, John Willinsky, Shirley Steinberg, and Ana Cruz (Kincheloe 2008a: 75–103). There are also close connections between critical pedagogy and other related bodies of work such as those devoted to critical literacy (Lankshear and McLaren 1993; Wallowitz 2008), critical media studies (Hammer and Kellner 2009; Kellner 1995, 2003), aesthetics and arts education (Lewis 2012), ecopedagogy (Kahn 2010), and critical whiteness studies (Rodriguez and Villaverde 2000).

There is one notable omission from the key thinkers mentioned thus far: Paulo Freire, arguably the most important figure of all in the development of critical pedagogy as a field of study. Born in 1921 in Recife, Brazil, Freire first gained international acclaim in the early 1970s with the publication of his classic text *Pedagogy of the Oppressed* (Freire 1972b). The developer of a highly successful, critical approach to adult literacy, Freire was exiled from his home country when the military seized power in 1964, taking up residence in Chile and later Switzerland, where he continued to refine and extend his educational ideas. In high demand as a speaker and consultant for educational programs the world over, Freire was able to return permanently to Brazil in 1980. Having established his name with his early books, *Education: The Practice of Freedom* (Freire 1976), *Pedagogy of the Oppressed* (Freire 1972b), and *Cultural Action for Freedom* (Freire 1972a), Freire was relatively "quiet" as a writer from the mid-1970s to the mid-1980s before gaining a strong scholarly second wind from 1987 onwards. In the last decade of his life, he authored many books on pedagogy, literacy, and politics, several of which were composed via dialogues with others (Escobar et al. 1994; Freire and Faundez 1989; Freire and Macedo 1987; Freire and Shor 1987; Horton and Freire 1990), others of which reflected on his service as Secretary for Education in the municipality of Sao Paulo (Freire 1993), his previous publications (Freire 1994), and his early educational experiences (Freire 1996). In his later books he paid particular attention to the work of teachers (Freire 1998c) and to the ethical, political, and educational challenges posed by neoliberalism (Freire 1997, 1998a, b, 2004, 2007). He died in 1997.

Freire has been called the "father" of critical pedagogy (Kirylo 2013: 49–52), the "quintessential teacher and learner" (Wink 2011: 101), and "the most influential educational philosopher in the development of critical pedagogical thought and practice" (Darder, Torres, and Baltodano 2017: 5). Rather than trying to do justice to the entire field of critical pedagogy—a difficult if not impossible task given the space available—this chapter will focus on Freire and

FIGURE 4.1 Flying bird in the sky reflected in the glass facade of the building. *Source*: Olga_Gavrilova / iStock Photo.

two other scholars who have acknowledged their profound debt to him: Ira Shor and bell hooks. Among the many critical pedagogues who draw heavily on Freire in their work, Shor and hooks are particularly noteworthy for their strong focus on teaching. In their publications and in their pedagogical practice, they have extended and applied Freirean ideas in novel ways. Both are based in the United States, but the problems addressed in their books resonate with concerns expressed by critical educators across the globe. Freire, Shor, and hooks have, collectively, produced an extensive body of published work that continues to speak to the dilemmas and struggles faced by teachers, in both formal and informal educational settings, on a daily basis. The first part of this chapter provides an overview of Freire's educational philosophy, while the second concentrates on Shor and hooks. The chapter concludes with brief reflections on the meaning and significance of hope in Freirean theory and on the possibilities for critical pedagogy in the future.

PAULO FREIRE: PHILOSOPHY, PEDAGOGY, PRACTICE

Paulo Freire occupies an important place in the history of philosophy of education, not just in terms of his theoretical contributions but also for his legacy as an educational practitioner. His ideas emerged from his extensive involvement with adult education in Brazil, Chile, and other countries. His understanding of philosophy, in turn, played a significant role in shaping his educational practice. Freire is an eclectic thinker, with an educational philosophy shaped by multiple intellectual traditions, including liberalism, Marxism, critical theory, existentialism, phenomenology, radical Catholicism, and postmodernism (Mackie 1980; Mayo 1999; Morrow and Torres 2002; Roberts 2000; Schugurensky 2012; Webster 2016). He adopts a dialectical approach to understanding reality, informed by his reading of Hegel and Marx, among others (Freire 1972a, b, 1985; McLaren 2000; Torres 1994). He focuses on the dynamic, ever-changing, interactive relation between the material world and the inner world of subjective experience. He accepts the Hegelian principles of all things being in motion and of contradictions giving rise to change, but he is at one with Marx in wanting to apply these ideas to social phenomena. As conscious beings, we have the capacity to reflect on the world and to respond to the content of our reflection through action. ("World" in Freire's philosophy includes both the realm of nature and socially constructed reality.) At the same time, the world, as it were, "acts back" on us, shaping patterns of thought. Our ideas, feelings, and attitudes are also influenced by our relationships with others, and by the institutions, workplaces, and social spaces we inhabit. We are conditioned but not determined by what the world brings to us (Freire 1996, 1997, 1998a). This is not a linear process; rather, there is a constant intersecting and intertwining of inner and external worlds. From a Freirean point of view, reality never "sits still"; there is always a need for further reflection and action. Humans are unique not only in the extent to which and ways in which they can reflect but also in their sense of temporality and historical perspective (Freire 1976). As humans, we can place the events of today in the broader context of past experience and also imagine how the world might be in the future. We act not just on the basis of instinct but with purpose and deliberation, even if there may be substantial variations in the way this occurs.

Freire's epistemology builds on his conception of the nature of reality. Faced with a world that is constantly changing, it follows for Freire that we can never know completely or finally or absolutely. We come to know through our interaction with others and the world, and this is a necessarily ongoing process. Knowledge for Freire is not something that is "given" to us; we have to seek to know, throughout our lives. What can seem certain at one moment in time may, through further reflection in the light of subsequent observation, interaction, or experience, seem less certain, perhaps even utterly misguided, at another moment in time. Consistent with a recognition of knowledge as fluid, contestable, and subject to change, Freire encourages the development of key epistemological virtues (Freire 1985, 1996, 1998a, 1998b). In seeking to know, he says, we should adopt an open-minded stance, being ever-ready to listen, to watch, and to learn. Knowers are curious beings; they want to ask questions, to investigate, to explore (Freire and Faundez 1989). Knowing demands rigor and care. Seeking to know is an intellectual process, but it is also more than this. Freire speaks of knowing with his whole body. Knowing is both passionate and rigorous, both disciplined and creative (Roberts 2005). Knowers are restless beings, always with more work to do. While Freire cautions against being too certain of our certainties, this does not mean that we cannot draw meaningful distinctions between different ways of understanding the world. Freire is not a relativist, in either epistemological or ethical terms; he would have been quite happy to say that some ideas, some ways of interacting with others, some ways of living in the world, are better than others.

At the heart of Freire's ethic is the notion of humanization (Freire 1972b). Humanization means becoming more fully human: more completely what we already are, and were meant to be, as human beings. Freire calls this an ontological vocation. Humanization is, however, also an historical vocation, for realizing the ideal of becoming more fully human entails acting, with others, in the world, as temporal and reflective beings. We become more fully human through engaging in praxis: critical, dialogical, transformative reflection and action (Freire 1972b; Mayo 2004; Roberts 2000). The concept of praxis has ancient origins, dating back, in the West, at least as far as the ancient Greeks, but Freire's interpretation and application of this term can be distinguished from other accounts by its political and social elements. Freire's particular interest is in reflective action that transforms unjust social conditions (Darder 2002; Rozas Gomez 2007; Torres 2014). For Freire, we engage in praxis not on a solitary basis but in solidarity with others. We do so, moreover, not just as rational actors but as emotional beings. From a Freirean point of view, Descartes's declaration "I think, therefore I am" needs to be replaced with another maxim: "We think, and feel, and act, in dialogue with others; therefore we are." Just as knowledge and knowing are necessarily incomplete for Freire, so too is the process of becoming more fully human. We remain unfinished beings, always in the making, always in a state of formation or becoming (Freire 1996, 1998a). Freire acknowledges that while humanization may be the ideal, dehumanization is a reality. Dehumanization can be witnessed in the impediments placed in the paths of others seeking to become more fully human. These may be imposed by structures, policies, attitudes, or practices. Dehumanization may be evident at the largest global scale (e.g., in the experience of widespread poverty, malnutrition, and disease, or in the violence of warfare), but it can also be present in the smallest moments of daily life (e.g., in "throwaway" comments with racist or sexist overtones).

In Freirean theory, liberation and oppression are the concrete manifestations of humanization and dehumanization, respectively. Freire's acknowledgment that dehumanization is a reality does not mean that he accepts its existence as inevitable; on the contrary, his work is built upon the idea that oppression, as the lived expression and experience of dehumanization, can be resisted and addressed. Freire saw oppression as a key epochal theme in the twentieth century and liberation as a key task (Freire 1972b, 1976, 1994). Liberation for Freire includes both the process of struggling against oppression and the development of key human virtues. Foremost among these virtues is love, a concept that is always present, directly or indirectly, in Freire's work (Darder 2002; Fraser 1997). Freire did not downplay the significance of romantic love, but in his philosophical, pedagogical, and political work, his principal concern is with what can be called "active" love (Roberts and Saeverot 2018). Love for Freire is a form of deep care and commitment. Freire speaks of loving those with whom we work, the subjects we study, and the very idea of life itself (Freire 1994, 1996, 1997; Freire and Shor 1987; Horton and Freire 1990). In our relations with others, love springs from a recognition of the other as a fellow thinking, feeling, willing being—a being who may experience sorrow as well as joy, frustration as well as success. In the act of study, love is evident in the attention paid to what we are reading, in the agony and exhilaration we experience as we try to grasp ideas, and in the persistence we display in constantly seeking to know. Freire also stresses the importance of hope (Freire 1972b, 1994). This was especially important in the dire situations with which he was dealing as an adult educator. For Freire, despair does not cancel out hope; it gives it its very reason for being (Chen 2016; Roberts 2016). Hope from a Freirean perspective is not blind optimism (Rossatto 2005); it is grounded in a sober analysis of the conditions of the present and a realistic understanding of what is possible in the future. Other virtues that form part of Freire's account of liberation include trust, faith, and critical thinking. Liberation, as Freire sees it, is never given; it is earned, through struggle. Liberation is not merely an individual matter; it is a social process. And, in keeping with the unfinished nature of being human, liberation is never complete. It is not an endpoint, at which one can declare, "Finally, I am now liberated"; rather, the work of liberation continues throughout life as fresh challenges arise and new actions are taken.

Freire's educational theory builds on these underlying philosophical ideas. Many educationists are aware of his distinction between "banking" education and "problem-posing" education (Freire 1972b), though some of the points Freire makes in drawing that distinction are often lost when there is a reliance on secondhand accounts of his work. In *Pedagogy of the Oppressed*, Freire argues that education has suffered from a kind of narration sickness, with teachers who are expected to pass on knowledge in a monological fashion to passive students. Content under this approach is "banked" into the minds of passive students, who receive the teacher's knowledge as a gift. This account has led some to believe that Freire was against "teacher talk" or even against the very idea of teaching. Some have adopted the label "facilitator," preferring this over what is assumed to be the more directive term "teacher." This reading

of Freire has been repeatedly contradicted in Freire's own later writings and
in the work of other interpreters of his thought (Freire 1987, 1996, 1998c;
Freire and Shor 1987; Horton and Freire 1990; Mayo 1999; Roberts 1996d;
Schugurensky 2012; Tan 2018a, b). The key feature of banking education is its
oppressive nature. This is evident in the suppression of questions and of critical
thought in the banking system. Under banking education, students are treated
not as thinking, feeling, active beings but as pawns in a larger game where
power is exercised to maintain existing inequalities and injustices. Teachers
talking is not in itself the problem; the problem from a Freirean perspective
lies in the denial of the possibility of continuing and extending the conversation
started by the teacher in collaboration with the students. Freire's opposition
is to authoritarian education, and banking education is an example of this.
Being authoritarian is, however, not the same as exercising authority or being
an authority in a subject area, both of which are necessary in good teaching as
Freire conceives of this (Freire and Shor 1987). Freire is against an "anything
goes" approach to pedagogy and makes it plain that he is a teacher and not
merely a facilitator (Freire and Macedo 1995). This stance has to do with his
characterization of teaching as an extraordinarily demanding commitment with
important responsibilities, one of which is the obligation to uphold a sense of
structure and direction in an educational setting (Freire 1998a, c; Freire and
Shor 1987).

    Problem-posing education begins from the assumption that humans are
active, curious, inquiring beings, who can ask questions and pose problems in
relation to themselves and the world they encounter (Freire 1972b). Sometimes
called "liberating" or "authentic" education, problem-posing education builds
on the knowledge and experience students bring with them to an educational
environment. Importantly, for Freire, problem-posing education does not simply
affirm the views expressed by students; it fosters critical reflection upon those
ideas. Respect for differences among students is vital, but so is the principle of
being open to having one's existing understanding of the world challenged.
Teachers and students in a problem-posing classroom are both involved in the
process of deepening and extending understanding and of creating knowledge,
but this does not mean they are the same as each other. Both teachers and
students have obligations to their subject area and to other participants in the
educational process, but their roles are not identical. Problem-posing education
emphasizes the fostering of dialogue as a key pedagogical principle, but this
is not aimless chatter. Educational dialogue, for Freire, while keeping open
opportunities for the unexpected to happen, should have a definite sense of
purpose. Freirean dialogue is rigorous and serious (Freire and Shor 1987). This
does not mean it needs to be entirely lacking in humor or that it should be dull
and pedantic. On the contrary, Freire believes that in a structured, purposeful
educational conversation, participants will be both passionate and thoughtful,

with varied contributions from personalities of many different types. Some participants, Freire recognizes, will be more exuberant than others; some will display a quiet earnestness. But regardless of differences, all participants— including the teacher—share a commitment to the subject matter, to each other, and to the ideal of humanization. One other point must be stressed in capturing what Freire means by problem-posing education: this is not problem-*solving* education. Freire prefers the former term for at least two reasons. First, in many of the places where he worked as an educator, the problems faced by students were not of a kind that lent themselves to easy or rapid or straightforward "solutions." Second, the act of posing problems—of reflecting, clarifying, asking questions, and investigating, and then of doing so again as new problems arise—is as significant as any answers generated by the investigative process (Roberts 2000, 2010).

Freire's ideas emerged from, and found expression in, the adult literacy and extension programs with which he was involved in Brazil and Chile (Freire 1972a, 1976). His approach to adult literacy education was based on the understanding that reading and writing can play a role in reinforcing and resisting the status quo. Freire started with the existential realities of the literacy learners, finding out as much as possible about their hopes and dreams, their work experiences, their living situations, their expectations of themselves and others. He found that many participants had a fatalistic attitude toward the world, attributing their circumstances to "God's will" or destiny. This mode of understanding, he argued, was no accident: it served the dominant interests of landowners and urban corporate and political elites in Brazil at that time. Beginning with words drawn from the world of the learners—e.g., favela (slum)—Freire and his coworkers encouraged participants, in dialogue with others, to reflect on not only their own situation but also their relations with others, and their distinctiveness as beings of culture and history. New words were quickly generated, and the adult learners moved from seeing themselves as passive recipients of the teacher's knowledge to active participants in the educational process. In his later work, Freire built on these early observations and experiences, theorizing literacy at greater length (Escobar et al. 1994; Freire 1985, 1996; Freire and Macedo 1987; Freire and Shor 1987). He developed a notion of critical literacy that focused on the linking of "word" with "world," the importance of both challenging and being challenged by a text, and the need for both breadth and depth in university reading (Roberts 1996a). He spoke of wrestling with texts while loving them, of the joys of reading, and of the beauty of the written word (Freire 1996; Freire and Shor 1987).

In his literacy work, and in his educational theory more generally, Freire became widely known for his espousal of "conscientization" (Freire 1972a, b, 1976, 1985). Often misinterpreted as "consciousness raising," conscientization for Freire implies the cultivation of one's conscience and the emergence of a deeper, more critical and rigorous understanding of the society in which one lives (Liu 2014; Roberts 1996c). Conscientization forms part of Freire's broader understanding of education as a non-neutral, political process (Freire 1985, 1987, 1997, 1998b, 2004, 2007). The political nature of education is evident at multiple levels, from the global to the local. International testing regimes such as the Program for International Student Assessment (PISA) process can exercise considerable sway over educational policies at a national level. The priorities determined by politicians have an important bearing on what is taught, how, and to whom in schools and other educational institutions. The politics of education will also be evident in the physical layout of a classroom (this may, for example, inhibit or enable discussion), the assessment system that is adopted and applied, the pedagogical methods that are employed, the reading matter that is recommended, and the attitudes, assumptions, and ideals teachers and students bring with them to an educational setting. Freire's point is that no teacher can avoid being "political"; the key is to be as honest and rigorous as possible in understanding, revealing, and negotiating the politics of educational life. For Freire, teaching is a necessarily interventionist activity (Roberts 1996b, 1999, 2003). Intervention in this context is not the same as imposition. A Freirean teacher must always respect the right of students to disagree and must seek to listen carefully

FIGURE 4.2 Silhouette of birds flying and a broken chain in front of a beautiful mountain sunset background. Photograph by Boonyachoat / iStock Photo.

to what all have to say, avoiding the temptation to thrust their own views on others (Escobar et al. 1994). Teaching can be tremendously powerful in transforming human lives, but it always carries risks and uncertainties (Freire 1998a, c; Freire and Shor 1987). Knowing how to work constructively with those risks, rather than allowing them to become debilitating and obstructive, is one of the hallmarks of liberating education. Freire was highly critical of banking education, but he was a consistent advocate for committed teachers, arguing for the need for better salaries and conditions right up to his last writings (Freire 1998c).

CRITICAL, ENGAGED TEACHING: THE WORK OF IRA SHOR AND BELL HOOKS

Ira Shor is one of the most innovative and important interpreters of Freire's work. He and Freire formed a close friendship and coauthored a key text together (Freire and Shor 1987). Shor has published books on American cultural history (Shor 1986) and critical literacy (Shor and Pari 1999), but his principal focus is teaching. His first major work, *Critical Teaching and Everyday Life* (Shor 1980) has been particularly influential. Subsequent volumes with a pedagogical focus—*Empowering Education* (Shor 1992) and *When Students Have Power* (Shor 1996)—have built on the foundation laid by *Critical Teaching and Everyday Life*, with detailed explorations of the pitfalls and rewards that await progressive and democratic teachers. Shor has also played a pivotal role in bringing together other scholars with an interest in Freire's work, editing one of the first collections devoted to the practical application of Freirean ideas in classroom settings (Shor 1987).

Shor, like Freire, emphasizes the political nature of education (Shor 1980, 1992, 1993, 1996). Politics is not, as Shor puts it, an "aspect" of teaching or learning; rather, education *is* politics. Politics, Shor argues, "resides in the discourse of the classroom, in the way teachers and students talk to each other, in the questions and statements from teachers about the themes being studied, in the freedom students feel when questioning the curriculum, in the silences typically surrounding unorthodox questions and issues in traditional classrooms" (Shor 1993: 27). Shor also highlights the politics at work in discriminatory attitudes toward the use of nonstandard English in educational institutions and in the marginalization of the arts in schools, particularly within poorer neighborhoods. Inequities in the funding of schools and their undemocratic administration can also be seen as political matters, worthy of critical interrogation (pp. 27–8). Shor proposes a model of critical consciousness that has four qualities: "power awareness," "critical literacy," "desocialization," and "self-organization" (pp. 32–3). His approach focuses on understanding how power is exercised by dominant groups, knowing how regressive patterns of thought (e.g., sexism, racism, classism, homophobia) can become embedded in consciousness, building the analytical habits necessary to provide an in-depth critical reading of the world, and developing an awareness that change is possible.

In the classroom, Shor's critical pedagogy focuses on identifying problems and themes to be addressed dialogically and democratically. He sees participation as a "door to empowerment" (Shor 1992: 17). In his classes, students are encouraged to place problems that may appear to be local and specific in their broader social, cultural, economic, and historical contexts. Students will often begin with the everyday, with what is most familiar, analyzing that in great detail, before moving outwards to establishing connections between the object of study and wider structures and practices, both nationally and globally. For American students, the starting point may be something as apparently simple as a hamburger, which, when subjected to critical investigation, reveals itself to be representative of some of the most troubling features of life in their society. A hamburger, when problematized in the manner recommended by Shor, can lead to productive discussion of work, relationships, and even the meaning and purpose of life. Students engage in description, diagnosis, and reconstruction (Shor 1980: 157). Classic texts such as Shakespeare's plays need not be seen as lifeless relics from the past; with appropriate prompts and questions from the teacher, they can be brought back to life in the contemporary classroom. *Henry V*, for example, can be linked with questions relating to law, power, and war that remain as relevant today as they were in Shakespeare's time (Shor 1992: 152–5).

Shor notes that, having become accustomed to antidemocratic classrooms, students can at first be reluctant to take up a more active role in the educational process. Mired in testing cultures, students want teachers to provide them with answers. For Shor, pedagogy should be grounded in the issues and controversies that structure the present. Thus, with the culture wars in full swing (Shor 1986), words like "liberal" and "conservative" can form the starting point for critical discussion (Shor 1992: 91). Other themes such as "utopia" can have application in a variety of educational contexts, at different moments in history (Shor 1980; see also Roberts and Freeman-Moir 2013). When power is exercised by students in a democratic classroom, the results will not always be comfortable for teachers, as Shor found out through his own experience (Shor 1996). Students can, when granted genuine opportunities to determine how and what is taught and to develop their analytical abilities, turn their critical gaze back on the teacher. Teachers may find themselves having to renegotiate their own roles in relation to practices such as grading, radically disrupting the usual formal institutional expectations. Teachers have to be careful not to promise more than they can deliver, and they must be prepared to live with the "discomforts of democracy" (Shor 1996: 82, 150).

The range of themes and topics addressed by bell hooks, the writing voice of Gloria Watkins (hooks 1994b), is impressively diverse. hooks is well known for her contributions to scholarship on race and feminism and for bringing the experiences and voices of black women to the fore in critical conversations in these areas (hooks 1982, 1984, 1989, 1993a, 1995). She has been a powerful critic of racism in American culture and society (hooks 1992, 1994a, 1995) and has also addressed questions of class (hooks 1996, 2000), sex, gender, and masculinity (hooks 1990, 1996, 2004), and place (hooks 2009). Attention here will be limited to hooks's views on teaching. For hooks, teaching is a transgressive form of action with the power to subvert and question structures of authority. Teaching should foster critical thinking of a nonconformist kind. It should, hooks argues, be unsettling and exciting. Education may sometimes be painful, but teachers should not be afraid to speak of pleasure in the classroom. Teaching entails the acknowledgment of all who are present in a pedagogical situation and a valuing of the contribution that each participant can make. Radical pedagogy from hooks's point of view is a collective effort, and the classroom is a communal space. There is a performative aspect to teaching, though not in the traditional sense of creating a spectacle; rather, the focus is on serving as a catalyst for engagement. To teach demands a commitment to reciprocity, to the involvement of participants in the performance being enacted. Good teachers seek to know the students with whom they work, responding to them as unique human beings. The possibility of mutual recognition must always be present, even if there may be constraints on the full realization of such an ideal in given circumstances. Teaching that "respects and cares for the souls of our students" is, for hooks, a sacred vocation, and in university environments, "[t]he classroom remains the most radical space of possibility in the academy" (1994b: 12–13).

Speaking against the "assembly-line approach to learning," hooks argues for an engaged pedagogy that emphasizes active participation by students in an environment of mutual recognition (1994b: 13). She acknowledges her debt to not just Paulo Freire but also Thich Nhat Hanh, a Buddhist monk from Vietnam whose work has also been highly influential. hooks embraces Freire's notion of conscientization, interpreting this as "critical awareness and engagement" (p. 14). She encourages critical thinking as a "way of approaching ideas that aims to understand core, underlying truths, not simply that superficial truth that may be most obviously visible" (hooks 2010: 9). She admires Freire's open-mindedness and his willingness to accept—indeed, encourage—constructive critique of his work (hooks 1994b: 54–6). From Thich Nhat Hanh's linking of learning with spiritual practice, hooks adopts a holistic view of education: one where teachers and students regard each other as "whole" human beings who seek not just the knowledge found in books but also knowledge of how to live in the world (pp. 15–16). From both thinkers, hooks takes the position that reflection must be combined with action. The kind of engaged pedagogy hooks advocates is, she suggests, "more demanding than conventional critical or feminist pedagogy" (p. 15). It is a radical approach to education that has a focus on social transformation but also on personal well-being, requiring teachers to attend to themselves as well as the students with whom they work. Teachers, hooks maintains, need to undergo a process of self-actualization. Thich Nhat Hanh's linking of teaching with healing is important here. Teachers first needs to "heal" themselves to be able to best attend to the task of helping others. The academic world tends to stress the role of the intellect, but "care of the soul" (p. 16) is also needed.

For hooks, traditionally strict boundaries between public and private spheres need to be challenged. Teachers and students in the academy can become unbalanced and "emotionally unstable" (p. 16). They may want liberating education but resist the idea that the classroom can provide any meaningful therapy in their own lives. hooks, like Freire, insists that students cannot be forced to accept the teacher's views; transgressive pedagogy demands that the freedom of the students be respected and that they take responsibility for their own decisions (p. 19). If students are expected to share and confess in the engaged classroom, the same should be true for teachers. This can be threatening, and learning to be vulnerable can be a challenge for many teachers in higher education. Engaged pedagogy is a risky endeavor, but taking up this challenge opens up new ways of knowing for both students and teachers. Building a sense of community helps in overcoming a preoccupation with safety in the classroom, for then the risks are shared, and all who participate are bound by a "common good" (p. 40). These pedagogical principles are particularly relevant in classrooms where themes such as racism, sexism, and colonialism are addressed. Conflict, hooks argues, need not be a source of despair; instead, there is a sense of solidarity when diversity, dissent, and the pursuit of truth are welcomed. Transgressive, engaged pedagogy is not easy; it demands "struggle and sacrifice," but if this has a sense of purpose and conviction, and if such experiences are shared with others, change is possible (p. 33).

Hooks argues that teaching can take place not just in formal institutional environments but also in homes, churches, bookstores, and other settings. Her concept of teaching includes everything from talking with young children to engaging critically with dominant public narratives. In hooks's account, education can take place in the smallest, most intimate moments of engagement between two or more people but is also needed on a much larger scale. hooks calls for "mass-based political movements" that will foster a commitment to democracy and justice among citizens (hooks 2003: xiii). She acknowledges the genuine progress that has been made by progressive educators, while also drawing attention to the powerful conservative backlash against programs such as women's studies and ethnic studies. In the United States, an ideology of "imperialist white-supremacist capitalist patriarchy" has been perpetuated, aided by the media, and free speech and dissent have, following the events of 9/11, been undermined (p. 11). Those killed in the 9/11 tragedy were an embodiment of "the world's diversity," but their deaths, instead of providing the impetus to cherish diversity and difference, have prompted rage, intolerance, distortions and simplifications, confusion, and a sense of hopelessness (p. 12). Teachers have an important role to play in contesting these trends, but they need to care for themselves if they are to serve others effectively. As hooks sees it, all teachers in professional settings, at any level in the education system, need to take a break from their work at some stage in their careers. Teaching for hooks is a form of service to others, a commitment that is devalued (p. 83). Like Freire, hooks sees teaching as an act of love (pp. 127–37). Love for hooks fosters greater openness and honesty in teaching and allows teachers to understand their students better. Love does not make teachers less objective; it simply makes them more sensitive and responsive to those with whom they work. Teaching in this way, hooks admits, is very taxing. Given its extraordinary demands, teaching is a vocation that lends itself readily to burnout. Teaching in other, less formal settings, employing a range of pedagogical styles, can provide the sustenance that is necessary for renewal—for regaining the sense of joy that should be a crucial element of education (pp. 14, 43).

CONCLUSION: A PHILOSOPHY OF HOPE

In his final years, Freire remained politically and intellectually restless. He was particularly concerned with the encroachment of neoliberal ideas into almost every area of social and economic life (Freire 1994, 1997, 1998a, 2004, 2007). He spoke scathingly of the ethics of the market, contrasting the attitudes and ideas implicit in neoliberalism with the humanizing ideals that had always underpinned his work. Freire saw in neoliberalism a revival of the fatalism that had been dominant among some groups in Brazil during his earlier adult literacy efforts. Neoliberals take it as given that societies should be organized along capitalist lines and that individuals are motivated by self-interest in their decisions and actions. Freire was open in declaring his support for democratic socialism, but he was also always willing to put his views to the test in the company of others. Neoliberals, he felt, were too certain of their certainties; they believe that their way is the only possible way. The dampening down of questions pertaining to the fundamental building blocks of contemporary society and the propensity to denigrate alternatives (or to ignore them altogether) struck Freire as particularly pernicious aspects of the neoliberal consciousness he saw unfolding in the last two decades of the twentieth century. Freire stood opposed to neoliberalism on almost every level. Ontologically, the idea of a utility-maximizing, competitive individual consumer as the starting point for a discussion of humankind was repugnant to him. Epistemologically, the notion of construing knowledge as a commodity to be bought and sold like other goods in a marketplace was worlds away from his conception of what it meant to know. Ethically and politically, the favoring of "free" trade, with minimal regulation, by individuals and corporations seeking to maximize their advantage over others, was, for Freire, an affront to the possibility of dialogue, care for others, and collective responsibility for the planet. In educational terms, the prospect of reducing teaching and learning to a system of inputs and outputs designed to enhance efficiency, performance, and economic growth was horrific.

The emergence of neoliberalism as the dominant paradigm for economic and social activity was, however, not just a cause for despair; for Freire, it reinforced the need for hope. Neoliberalism, Freire argued, is utterly dehumanizing, but it is our response to it that matters. Freire could see that, under neoliberalism, inequalities would widen and our views of what counts as education, knowledge, and being human would become steadily narrower. He would have been deeply saddened to see, over recent years, the rise of populist and authoritarian politics in Brazil, the United States, and Europe. In some cases, leaders have been elected on the basis of political rhetoric that is deliberately divisive, anti-intellectual, and often openly sexist and racist. These trends will do much to destroy moves toward greater inclusiveness made by progressive governments in the past, and in education there will be an ever more entrenched focus on narrowly defined, measurable objectives with direct economic value. But it is precisely the desperation created by such policies and practices that gives hope, as an educational virtue, its meaning and significance in our time. Hope is a virtue that cannot be adequately understood purely in abstract terms; it must be lived, and constantly reinvented, as human beings negotiate the changing demands of social, cultural, and economic life. If these points are accepted, critical pedagogy becomes more essential than ever. Encouraging students to ask difficult questions about the way they are expected to live in today's world, deliberately setting up opportunities to explore alternative modes of social organization, and exhibiting qualities that run counter to the spirit of the times (selflessness, humility, openness, and a willingness to listen) can provide hope that change is possible. Hope for Freire, and for Shor and hooks, is neither simply given from one person to another nor generated in a purely individual or internal manner. Instead, it arises from the interaction between two or more people, in dialogue with each other, with a respect for difference that also does not deny what is shared in common. Hope makes most sense not when all is well, when life appears to free and easy, but when situations demand more of us. Thus conceived, hope becomes a profoundly important educational virtue, and a cornerstone of critical pedagogy, providing both the means and the reason for principled, reflective resistance and transformative social change.

Paulo Freire, Ira Shor, and bell hooks have all made lasting contributions to the development of critical pedagogy as a field of study. Collectively and individually, they offer something unique and worthwhile to the broader conversations that make up the history of philosophy of education in the West. Their written work is distinguished by a clarity that is sometimes lacking in educational theory; their ideas are conveyed in a manner that is lucid, direct, and practical. Across these thinkers, there is an abiding interest in the links and tensions between theory and practice in the pedagogical realm. All three have developed and tested their ideas in the company of the students with whom they have worked. For Freire, Shor, and hooks, teaching is a political activity requiring love, care, and commitment. Teachers, they argue, need to have an understanding of what they stand for, of what they value and why. At the same time, they caution, teachers must avoid imposing their truths, their ideals, on students. Teaching should, they suggest, foster a love of learning, respect for others, and a sense of community. Education, they show, is a lifelong process that demands much of all who commit to it. Humanizing, engaging, critical education is often uncomfortable, sometimes disruptive and destabilizing, and always rigorous.

Critical pedagogy prompts us to examine ourselves and the world in a fresh light. In this sense, it has an inherently "subversive" character. Those who feel threatened by this will often recoil from the challenges posed by critical scholars and teachers, sometimes responding with anger or defensiveness. But such responses can themselves have educative value, if gently probed and explored. Critical pedagogy may also, in increasingly instrumentalist times, be dismissed as "irrelevant." Some may claim that it has no place in contemporary teacher education, suggesting that the focus should be on the more immediate practical demands of the profession. Yet, as the work of Freire, Shor, and hooks demonstrates, critical educational theory can be profoundly practical in its orientation, and the activity of teaching is always underpinned by implied theories of what it means to be a human, of the nature of reality, of what we should favor and why, and of how we should interact and live with others. It could be argued that the biggest "threat" to critical pedagogy comes, as it were, from within— in the form of theoretical infighting among scholars of differing philosophical and political persuasions. Yet the history of the field has demonstrated that it has a certain resilience that can withstand—indeed, welcome—critique from both within and without. In the future, it is likely that critical pedagogues will continue to reach out to scholars in other areas, drawing, for example, more heavily on Eastern and indigenous traditions of thought as the field continues to evolve and grow. Critical pedagogy, like all domains of educational study, has its flaws, frictions, and fragilities. But its ongoing importance, in some form, seems difficult to deny. Critical pedagogy can enable students to deepen and extend their understanding of social injustices and provide a platform on which to build a narrative of gritty, realistic, grounded hope, whatever the defining economic, social, and cultural features of a given epoch may be.

REFERENCES

Primary sources

Freire, Paulo (1972a), *Cultural Action for Freedom*, Harmondsworth: Penguin.
Freire, Paulo (1972b), *Pedagogy of the Oppressed*, Harmondsworth: Penguin.
Freire, Paulo (1976), *Education: The Practice of Freedom*, London: Writers and Readers.
Freire, Paulo (1985), *The Politics of Education*, London: Macmillan.
Freire, Paulo (1987), "Letter to North-American Teachers," in Ira Shor (ed.), *Freire for the Classroom*, 211–14, Portsmouth, NH: Boynton/Cook.
Freire, Paulo (1993), *Pedagogy of the City*, New York: Continuum.
Freire, Paulo (1994), *Pedagogy of Hope*, New York: Continuum.
Freire, Paulo (1996), *Letters to Cristina: Reflections on my Life and Work*, London: Routledge.
Freire, Paulo (1997), *Pedagogy of the Heart*, New York: Continuum.
Freire, Paulo (1998a), *Pedagogy of Freedom: Ethics, Democracy, and Civic Courage*, Lanham, MD: Rowman & Littlefield.
Freire, Paulo (1998b), *Politics and Education*, Los Angeles: UCLA Latin American Center Publications.
Freire, Paulo (1998c), *Teachers As Cultural Workers: Letters to Those Who Dare Teach*, Boulder, CO: Westview Press.
Freire, Paulo (2004), *Pedagogy of Indignation*, Boulder, CO: Paradigm Publishers.
Freire, Paulo (2007), *Daring to Dream*, Boulder, CO: Paradigm Publishers.
Freire, Paulo and Antonio Faundez (1989), *Learning to Question: A Pedagogy of Liberation*, Geneva: World Council of Churches.
Freire, Paulo, Ana Maria Araújo Freire, and Walter Ferreira de Oliviera (2014), *Pedagogy of Solidarity*, Walnut Cove, CA: Left Coast Press.
Freire, Paulo and Donaldo Macedo (1987), *Literacy: Reading the Word and the World*, London: Routledge.
Freire, Paulo and Donaldo Macedo (1995), "A Dialogue: Culture, Language, and Race," *Harvard Educational Review*, 65 (3): 377–402.
Freire, Paulo and Ira Shor (1987), *A Pedagogy for Liberation*, London: Macmillan.
hooks, bell (1982), *Ain't I a Woman: Black Women and Feminism*, London: Pluto Press.
hooks, bell (1984), *Feminist Theory from Margin to Center*, Boston: South End Press.
hooks, bell (1989), *Talking Back: Thinking Feminist, Thinking Black*, Boston: South End Press.
hooks, bell (1990), *Yearning: Race, Gender, and Cultural Politics*, Boston: South End Press.
hooks, bell (1992), *Black Looks: Race and Representation*, Boston: South End Press.
hooks, bell (1993a), "bell hooks Speaking About Paulo Freire: The Man, the Work," in Peter McLaren and Peter Leonard (eds.), *Paulo Freire: A Critical Encounter*, 146–54, London: Routledge.
hooks, bell (1993b), *Sisters of the Yam: Black Women and Self-Recovery*, Boston: South End Press.

hooks, bell (1994a), *Outlaw Culture: Resisting Representations*, New York: Routledge.
hooks, bell (1994b), *Teaching to Transgress: Education as a Practice of Freedom*, New York: Routledge.
hooks, bell (1995), *Killing Rage: Ending Racism*, New York: Holt.
hooks, bell (1996), *Reel to Reel: Race, Sex, and Class at the Movies*, New York: Routledge.
hooks, bell (2000), *Where We Stand: Class Matters*, New York: Routledge.
hooks, bell (2003), *Teaching Community: A Pedagogy of Hope*, New York: Routledge.
hooks, bell (2004), *We Real Cool: Black Men and Masculinity*, New York: Routledge.
hooks, bell (2009), *Belonging: A Culture of Place*, New York: Routledge.
hooks, bell (2010), *Teaching Critical Thinking: Practical Wisdom*, New York: Routledge.
Horton, Myles and Paulo Freire (1990), *We Make the Road by Walking: Conversations on Education and Social Change*, Philadelphia: Temple University Press.
Shor, Ira (1980), *Critical Teaching and Everyday Life*, Boston: South End Press.
Shor, Ira (1986), *Culture Wars: School and Society in the Conservative Restoration 1969–1984*, Boston: Routledge & Kegan Paul.
Shor, Ira (1992), *Empowering Education*, Chicago: Chicago University Press.
Shor, Ira (1993), "Education Is Politics: Paulo Freire's Critical Pedagogy," in Peter McLaren and Peter Leonard (eds.), *Paulo Freire: A Critical Encounter*, 25–35, London: Routledge.
Shor, Ira (1996), *When Students Have Power: Negotiating Authority in a Critical Pedagogy*, Chicago: University of Chicago Press.
Shor, Ira, ed. (1987), *Freire for the Classroom*, Portsmouth, NH: Boynton/Cook.
Shor, Ira and Caroline Pari, eds. (1999), *Critical Literacy in Action: Writing, Words, Changing Worlds*, Portsmouth, NH: Heinemann.

Secondary sources

Apple, Michael W. (1999), *Power, Meaning, and Identity: Essays in Critical Educational Studies*, New York: Peter Lang.
Aronowitz, Stanley (2012), "Paulo Freire's Radical Democratic Humanism: The Fetish of Method," in Maria Nikolakaki (ed.), *Critical Pedagogy in the New Dark Ages: Challenges and Possibilities*, 257–74, New York: Peter Lang.
Chen, Rosa H. (2016), "Freire and a Pedagogy of Suffering: A Moral Ontology," in Michael A. Peters (ed.), *Encyclopedia of Educational Philosophy and Theory*, Singapore: Springer.
Darder, Antonia (2002), *Reinventing Paulo Freire: A Pedagogy of Love*, Boulder, CO: Westview Press.
Darder, Antonia, Rodolfo D. Torres, and Marta Boltodano, eds. (2017), *The Critical Pedagogy Reader*, 3rd edn., New York: Routledge.
Escobar, M., A.L. Fernandez, G. Guevara-Niebla, with Paulo Freire (1994), *Paulo Freire on Higher Education: A Dialogue at the National University of Mexico*, Albany: State University of New York Press.
Fraser, James W. (1997), "Love and History in the Work of Paulo Freire," in Paulo Freire, James W. Fraser, Donaldo Macedo, Tanya McKinnon, and William T. Stokes (eds.), *Mentoring the Mentor: A Critical Dialogue with Paulo Freire*, 175–99, New York: Peter Lang.

Giroux, Henry A. (1983), *Theory and Resistance in Education: A Pedagogy for the Opposition*, South Hadley, MA: Bergin & Garvey.

Giroux, Henry A. (1988), *Teachers As Intellectuals: Toward a Critical Pedagogy of Learning*, Granby, MA: Bergin & Garvey.

Giroux, Henry A. (1997), *Pedagogy and the Politics of Hope: Theory, Culture, and Schooling—A Critical Reader*, Boulder, CO: Westview Press.

Giroux, Henry A. (2006), *America on the Edge: Henry Giroux on Politics, Culture, and Education*, New York: Palgrave Macmillan.

Giroux, Henry A. (2008), *Against the Terror of Neoliberalism: Politics Beyond the Age of Greed*, Boulder, CO: Paradigm Publishers.

Hammer, Rhonda and Douglas Kellner, eds. (2009), *Media/Cultural Studies: Critical Approaches*, New York: Peter Lang.

Kahn, Richard (2010), *Critical Pedagogy, Ecoliteracy, and Planetary Crisis*, New York: Peter Lang.

Kellner, Douglas (1995), *Media Culture: Cultural Studies, Identity, and Politics Between the Modern and the Postmodern*, New York: Routledge.

Kellner, Douglas (2003), *Media Spectacle*, New York: Routledge.

Kellner, Douglas, Tyson Lewis, Clayton Pierce, and K. Daniel Cho, eds. (2009), *Marcuse's Challenge to Education*, Lanham, MD: Rowman & Littlefield.

Kincheloe, Joe L. (2007), "Critical Pedagogy in the Twenty-First Century: Evolution for Survival," in Peter McLaren and Joe Kincheloe (eds.), *Critical Pedagogy: Where Are We Now?*, 9–42, New York: Peter Lang.

Kincheloe, Joe L. (2008a), *Critical Pedagogy Primer*, 2nd edn., New York: Peter Lang.

Kincheloe, Joe L. (2008b), *Knowledge and Critical Pedagogy*, Dordrecht: Springer.

Kirylo, James D. (2011), *Paulo Freire: The Man from Recife*, New York: Peter Lang.

Kirylo, James D., ed. (2013), *A Critical Pedagogy of Resistance*, Rotterdam: Sense Publishers.

Kumar, Ravi, ed. (2016), *Neoliberalism, Critical Pedagogy and Education*, New York: Routledge.

Leistyna, Pepi (2007), "Neoliberal Non-Sense," in Peter McLaren and Joe Kincheloe (eds.), *Critical Pedagogy: Where Are We Now?*, 97–123, New York: Peter Lang.

Lewis, Tyson E. (2012), *The Aesthetics of Education: Theatre, Curiosity, and Politics in the Work of Jacques Rancière and Paulo Freire*, New York: Continuum.

Liu, Keqi (2014), *Conscientization and the Cultivation of Conscience*, New York: Peter Lang.

Macedo, Donaldo (1997), "An Anti-Method Pedagogy: A Freirian Perspective," in Paulo Freire, James W. Fraser, Donaldo Macedo, Tanya McKinnon, and William T. Stokes (eds.), *Mentoring the Mentor: A Critical Dialogue with Paulo Freire*, 1–9, New York: Peter Lang.

Mackie, Robert (1980), "Contributions to the Thought of Paulo Freire," in Roberts Mackie (ed.), *Literacy and Revolution: The Pedagogy of Paulo Freire*, 93–119, London: Pluto Press.

Mayo, Peter (1999), *Gramsci, Freire and Adult Education: Possibilities for Transformative Action*, London: Zed Books.

Mayo, Peter (2004), *Liberating Praxis: Paulo Freire's Legacy for Radical Education and Politics*, New York: Praeger.

McLaren, Peter (1989), *Life in Schools: An Introduction to Critical Pedagogy in the Foundations of Education*, New York: Longman.

McLaren, Peter (1997), *Revolutionary Multiculturalism: Pedagogies of Dissent for the New Millennium*, Boulder, CO: Westview Press.

McLaren, Peter (2000), *Che Guevara, Paulo Freire, and the Pedagogy of Revolution*, Lanham, MD: Rowman & Littlefield.

Morrow, R.A. and Carlos A. Torres (2002), *Reading Freire and Habermas: Critical Pedagogy and Transformative Social Change*, New York: Teachers College Press.

Nikolakaki, Maria, ed. (2012), *Critical Pedagogy in the New Dark Ages: Challenges and Possibilities*, New York: Peter Lang.

Peters, Michael, Colin Lankshear, and Mark Olssen, eds. (2003), *Critical Theory and the Human Condition: Founders and Praxis*, New York: Peter Lang.

Roberts, Peter (1996a), "Critical Literacy, Breadth of Perspective, and Universities: Applying Insights from Freire," *Studies in Higher Education*, 21 (2): 149–63.

Roberts, Peter (1996b), "Defending Freirean Intervention," *Educational Theory*, 46 (3): 335–52.

Roberts, Peter (1996c), "Rethinking Conscientisation," *Journal of Philosophy of Education*, 30 (2): 179–96.

Roberts, Peter (1996d), "Structure, Direction and Rigour in Liberating Education," *Oxford Review of Education*, 22 (3): 295–316.

Roberts, Peter (1999), "A Dilemma for Critical Educators?," *Journal of Moral Education*, 28 (1): 19–30.

Roberts, Peter (2000), *Education, Literacy, and Humanization: Exploring the Work of Paulo Freire*, Westport, CT: Bergin and Garvey.

Roberts, Peter (2003), "Epistemology, Ethics, and Education: Addressing Dilemmas of Difference in the Work of Paulo Freire," *Studies in Philosophy and Education*, 22 (2): 157–73.

Roberts, Peter (2005), "Freire and Dostoevsky: Uncertainty, Dialogue and Transformation," *Journal of Transformative Education*, 3 (1): 126–39.

Roberts, Peter (2010), *Paulo Freire in the 21st Century: Education, Dialogue and Transformation*, Boulder, CO: Paradigm Publishers.

Roberts, Peter (2016), *Happiness, Hope, and Despair: Rethinking the Role of Education*, New York: Peter Lang.

Roberts, Peter and John Freeman-Moir (2013), *Better Worlds: Education, Art, and Utopia*, Lanham, MD: Lexington Books.

Roberts, Peter and Herner Saeverot (2018), *Education and the Limits of Reason: Reading Dostoevsky, Tolstoy and Nabokov*, New York: Routledge.

Rodriguez, Nelson M. and Leila E. Villaverde, eds. (2000), *Dismantling White Privilege: Pedagogy, Politics, and Whiteness*, New York: Peter Lang.

Rossatto, C. (2005), *Engaging Paulo Freire's Pedagogy of Possibility: From Blind to Transformative Optimism*, Lanham, MD: Rowman & Littlefield.

Rozas Gomez, Claudia (2007), "The Possibility of Justice: The Work of Paulo Freire and Difference," *Studies in Philosophy and Education*, 26: 561–70.

Schugurensky, Daniel (2012), *Paulo Freire*, London: Continuum.

Steinberg, Shirley R. (2007), "Preface," in Peter McLaren and Joe Kincheloe (eds.), *Critical Pedagogy: Where Are We Now?*, ix–x, New York: Peter Lang.

Tan, Charlene (2018a), "To Be More Fully Human: Freire and Confucius," *Oxford Review of Education*, 44 (4): 370–82.

Tan, Charlene (2018b), "Wither Teacher-Directed Learning? Freirean and Confucian Insights," *The Educational Forum*, 82 (4): 461–74.

Torres, Carlos A. (1994), "Education and the Archeology of Consciousness: Freire and
    Hegel," *Educational Theory*, 44 (4): 429–45.
Torres, Carlos A. (2014), *First Freire: Early Writings in Social Justice Education*,
    New York: Teachers College Press.
Wallowitz, Laraine, ed. (2008), *Critical Literacy and Resistance: Teaching for Social
    Justice Across the Secondary Curriculum*, New York: Peter Lang.
Webster, Scott (2016), "The Existential Individual *Alone* Within Freire's Socio-Political
    Solidarity," in Michael A. Peters (ed.), *Encyclopedia of Educational Philosophy and
    Theory*, Singapore: Springer.
Wink, Joan (2011), *Critical Pedagogy: Notes from the Real World*, 4th edn., Boston:
    Pearson.

CHAPTER FIVE

The Changing Landscapes of Anarchism and Education

ROBERT H. HAWORTH

ANARCHISM AS A CREATIVE FOREFRONT

I was introduced to anarchism through the punk and hardcore scene of the 1980s and 1990s. As a sixth grader in public school, I wore combat boots, ripped-up jeans, and, along with other band logos, an anarchist symbol pin: a capital "A" with a circle around it. At the time, I understood anarchism to mean "no government" and "against all authority." That was enough for me. It validated my questioning of school, society, and the people in charge of my education. As I got older, my curiosity in anarchism continued because it helped me analyze power and challenge the political and economic policies of Ronald Reagan and Margaret Thatcher, which I understood to be destructive to many people's lives.

When I became an activist and academic, I began exploring the political and philosophical ways anarchists have created educational spaces. From info-shops to political actions using consensus-building models, anarchism was always at the creative forefront of these spaces. Individuals needed to teach and learn anarchist morals and values for organizing and relationship building. These educational examples implicitly and explicitly used anarchist ways of organizing and provided activists and community members valuable tools for how they might teach, learn, share knowledge, and, ultimately, live differently in the world. In other words, anarchist ideas and their educational experiments enable us to see what is possible as we strive to develop a more mutual, cooperative, and just society.

Anarchism has had a long history of contesting authoritarian and hierarchical structures and capitalist relationships. At the same time, anarchists not only desire a stateless and anticapitalist society based on individual freedom but also aspire to live cooperatively and in solidarity with others. To be sure, as Judith Suissa (2006) shows, many who are dismissive of anarchist beliefs view the orientation as both politically and economically naïve, falling on the side of utopian thinking. For many, it is difficult to think of a society outside the boundaries of state and vertical structures. However, anarchism's theoretical fluidity and its refusal to create or follow deterministic "blue prints" (Graeber 2013) continues to influence philosophers, political theorists, and various areas of research, including education. In this chapter, I portray anarchist philosophy of education and what it can look like in practice. I address tensions in anarchist practice between the concrete promotion of particular values and the view that any such conduct may be coercive. Suissa highlights one of the major dilemmas anarchists struggle with regarding education:

> [E]ither the education in question is to be completely non-coercive and avoid the transmission of any substantive set of values, in which case it is hard to see how such an education could be regarded as furthering the desired social change; or it is to involve the explicit transmission of a substantive curriculum regarding the desired social order—in which case it would appear to undermine the libertarian ideal. (2006: 17)

I will argue throughout this chapter that anarchists have taken creative pathways to teaching and learning that are not only unconventional but also dispute traditional teacher–student relationships and educational spaces. Over time, anarchists have also developed these spaces using a variety of philosophies ranging from positivist thinking to more contemporary poststructuralist ideas. Jesse Cohn argues that "anarchists are theoretical magpies, and yet express caution in how they integrate and interpret complex relationships among different ideologies" (2007: 97). From an educational standpoint, Cohn's arguments are important to highlight because they enable anarchists to incorporate different and sometimes competing philosophies of how knowledge is constructed. Therefore, teaching and learning become complex and more situated where knowledge is constructed within individuals' different lived experiences (Conway 2013).

For the purpose of this chapter, I will explore not only some of anarchism's historical critiques of education but also, just as importantly, the role education has played within anarchist thinking and its connections to the communities anarchists would like to create. In addition, I will consider contemporary philosophical shifts in anarchist thought.

ANARCHISM AND THE STATE: EARLY EDUCATIONAL CRITIQUES

Anarchism views the state, capitalistic relationships, and hierarchical structures as oppressive to individuals. Anarchists have a deep skepticism of the operations of the state (Bakunin 1882) because it functions hierarchically, with power centralized and situated at the top. Historically, anarchists have been critical of state institutions because they have perpetuated authoritarian, and at times violent, practices toward citizens. Correspondingly, anarchists view the functioning of schools as an influential arm of the state. William Godwin's *An Enquiry Concerning Political Justice* (1793) argued against a national education system. Godwin believed a state-run education would promote obedience to those in power instead of encouraging individual freedom. A national education system tends toward what Godwin saw as "permanence" as opposed to exploration, creativity, and experimentation. In his view, a national education would require a particular obedience to what knowledge is constructed and how that knowledge is taught. According to Chappell, "Godwin believed that human reason and individuality were antithetical to a state-controlled education system which would serve to bolster the power of the political machinery of the state" (1978: 358). Thus, a national education leaves little to no autonomy for the teachers to explore different pedagogical strategies or question the singular information and curriculum that is used. As Mueller puts it, "rather than develop educational systems that gravitate around the needs of the individual children, children are molded to the goals and expectations of the state educational system" (2012: 27).

Working in the mid-nineteenth century, Russian anarchist Mikhail Bakunin believed that there was an alternative to state-driven educational practices, specifically by creating an education for a postrevolutionary society. At that time, Bakunin argued that education created class divisions in which the bourgeoise were the only people who had access to knowledge, while the proletariat was doomed to a forced ignorance. He advocated for what he termed an "integral education." Charles Fourier coined the term in 1822, but it was reimagined by anarchists throughout the nineteenth and early twentieth centuries in different ways. Nevertheless, the overall goal of "integral education" was that it be emancipatory (Morris 2018). Similar to Fourier's ideas of education, Bakunin's approach also emphasized two major components: intellectual and manual labor. He argued that an integral education would provide individuals the tools to exist harmoniously in a postrevolutionary society, where individuals understood the importance of work and theoretical understanding of social life.

FIGURE 5.1 Organized business confused people on tangled ladders. *Source*: wildpixel / iStock.

By the late nineteenth century, Kropotkin echoed some of Bakunin's ideas on integral education, including its capacity to change society through scientific knowledge fused with manual work. Anarchists wanted to move toward scientific thinking as a way to contest the dogmatic thinking they believed both state-run and religious schools supported. Education could play a crucial role in teaching the young to be self-directed in responding to individual and cooperative needs and would include a reliance on mutual aid (Morris 2018). Anarchist critiques did eventually play a role in "progressive" administrative shifts and reforms in education. Nonetheless, anarchists saw little hope in these reforms for the sorts of dramatic change they envisioned. On the contrary, they perceived a deepening hold by the state and capitalist interests on schooling and thus intensified their efforts to generate alternatives.

EARLY TWENTIETH-CENTURY CRITIQUES OF EDUCATION

In the early twentieth century, industrial capitalism systemically dominated the social, political, and economic landscape, particularly in the United States. Capitalists became invested in how to maintain the deep class divide between the poor, the working class, and the wealthy. From labor organizing to anti-war efforts, the beginning of the twentieth century encompassed class struggles, including critiques of education. By the turn of the century, anarchists had developed strong public criticisms of educational institutions and were interested in exploring how alternatives could be created. For example, Emma Goldman's article in *Mother Earth*, "The Child and Its Enemies" (1906), offered biting critiques of education within the state institution. Goldman highlights how, in her view, "[i]nstructors and teachers, with dead souls, operate with dead values. Quantity is forced to take the place of quality" (p. 3). From a larger institutional perspective, she adds, "The systems of education are being arranged into files, classified and numbered ... [and are] incapable of awakening the spontaneity of character" (p. 2).

Goldman's opposition to many of the traditional educational practices taking place in schools during that time highlights anarchist concerns about the morals and values forced upon children—stripping them of creativity, exploration, and, ultimately, freedom. Her words have haunting historical connections to contemporary issues in education such as standardization and tracking students. Moreover, what I find most important from Goldman's critiques is her notion that schools are incapable of "awakening the spontaneity of character." From a philosophical standpoint, this opens up questions of what role spontaneity plays within the construction of knowledge, but, more importantly, what would an education look like that encourages these types of educational practices?

Traditional educational practices were also criticized by another anarchist, Voltairine de Cleyre. Goldman described de Cleyre as "the poet-rebel" because of de Cleyre's strong and articulate writing skills regarding anarchism, feminism, and critiques of capitalism. In her 1914 article "Modern Education Reform," de Cleyre rearticulated many of Goldman's educational critiques but added an important point of discussion surrounding what she describes as the "statesman." De Cleyre argues, "[the statesman] is not actually interested in the actual work of schools, in the children as persons, but in the producing of a certain type of character to serve subsequent ends" (1914: 322). De Cleyre's description of the statesman can be viewed from multiple avenues. One obvious person she is identifying is the federal and state representative who controls and makes educational policies for the masses. The state needs public education to reproduce certain types of citizens, and, as I highlighted earlier with Godwin's critique, the state demands "permanence." The other, not so explicit, statesman may be seen as the capitalist. In the early twentieth century, industrial capitalists were interested in the education of the character of working-class people, particularly in creating workers who were willing, unawares, to exploit themselves (Spring 2008). Public education could be a tool to manipulate, coerce, and mold individuals into a social, political, and economic system that alienates them from their labor and mutual relationships. From an anarchist point of view, public education was not utilized, as many claimed, as the "great equalizer." Rather, as Goldman contends, education was used to "make children foreign to themselves" (1906: 3). Schools, in essence, were coercive and destructive of children's ability to explore, create, and question the world around them.

In sum, anarchists' critiques of early twentieth-century education were premised on the notion that the state supports homogeneous teaching and learning practices and a strong reinforcement of obedience to specific social, political, and economic structures. More specifically, there are outside forces that are concerned with education and that advocate for creating certain types of citizens who would ultimately learn to support their own oppression. These concerns motivated anarchists to create new experiments in education that would coincide with their beliefs in building a better society.

THE TWENTIETH CENTURY: ANARCHIST EDUCATIONAL EXPERIMENTS

Anarchists had already begun to develop some of their philosophical beliefs based on the thought of Spanish anarchist Francisco Ferrer and the creation of Escola Moderna in Barcelona. Ferrer's rationalist educational perspective intended to encapsulate scientific truth and positivist outcomes reflective of the Enlightenment. His book, *Origins and Ideals of the Modern School* (1912), highlighted a need for developing integral educational spaces and ridding the bookshelves and learning materials of dogmatic thinking. Ferrer saw these educational spaces as what Suissa (2006) characterizes as a microcosm of anarchist society, which would incorporate a specific type of moral agenda that coincided with anarchist beliefs. Ferrer was mindful that a true educational experience could not be neutral. In a large sense, and echoing a previous point, the philosophical tensions between supporting a rational and neutral curriculum and interjecting anarchist beliefs of solidarity into the school continued to be hotly debated among anarchists in Spain and in the United States (Bray and Haworth 2018; Suissa 2006: 81).

RATIONALIST/NATURALIST SCHOOLS IN SPAIN

In 1918, Juan Puig Elias, along with the cooperation of the textile union, created what was called the "Nature School" under the name of *La Farigola*. Nature schools embodied similar pedagogical beliefs and practices as the anarchist experiments such as Escola Moderna. They became quite successful in Barcelona, and communities responded positively to the openness, student-centered focus and caring environment that the schools provided. In many cases, these educational spaces provided refuge later on from the violence that was taking place in Spain during the civil war (1936–9). Teachers were highly respected and worked diligently to create learning environments that were supportive of the anarchist struggle against fascist brutality as well as the students' needs (Ackelsburg 1991: 83).

Other educational sites, including what were called "Ateneus populars" (popular athenaeums), began to emerge throughout Barcelona. Most of these were anarchist-generated, informal educational spaces and functioned more like what Acklesburg (1991) describes as "hangouts" and cultural centers for youth. They provided young people an opportunity to engage in reading radical literature, to have political conversations, and to organize, as well as to watch films and go on excursions to natural areas outside of the city. The Ateneus populars were somewhat influenced by the modern schools. However, it is important to point out that these educational experiments were changed by the political environment of the civil war. The focus was less on trying to develop an education based in rational and positivist outcomes and more on instilling cultural changes in communities and a sense of a political agency for young people who were involved in anarchist struggles.

Ferrer's work has been influential in providing educational groundwork for anarchists to debate and transform. This is evident in how modern schools evolved in the twentieth century. In the various educational experiences occurring in Catalonia today, it is noteworthy how some schools root their philosophies and practices directly in anarchist traditions of thought. What is equally intriguing is how they are working on developing these practices with direction participation by students. This commitment demonstrates a voluntary negotiation within the teacher–student relationship. At the same time, it discloses an attempt to work through long-standing philosophical tensions, touched on above, about cultivating the values both in student autonomy and in anarchism itself geared toward the creation of a more just society.

MODERN SCHOOLS IN THE UNITED STATES

The Modern Schools in the United States, particularly the most famous in Stelton, New Jersey, emerged out of the Ferrer School in New York City. The Ferrer School in New York had characteristics and values similar to the original Escola Moderna in Barcelona. According to Goldman (1906), for example, the school's philosophy was directed toward "drawing out" rather than "driving in," leaving children free to engage subject matter in light of their passions and interests and to play a substantial role in directing their own learning. Although some of the initial practices had a student-centered approach, there were differences in how the school was organized. According to Suissa (2006: 82), the school leaders felt students needed a firsthand experience of justice, equality, and cooperation. Hence, the school worked toward creating an educational space that coincided with how anarchists believed society should be organized, particularly through nonhierarchical, anti-authoritarian, and collective means.

The school moved to New Jersey in 1915, in part because of political tensions brought about by anti-communist sentiments in New York City and in part because some of the school's organizers believed an anarchist colony was needed and felt that young people should have the opportunity to have experiences growing up in the countryside away from the struggles of urban life. Although some of the educational philosophies carried over to the colony in Stelton, by the 1920s pedagogical shifts became apparent, thus moving the school from a focus on revolutionary change to inner-personal transformations.

In 1920, Alexis and Elizabeth Ferm were asked to run the Stelton school. According to Veysey (1978: 134), before the arrival of the Ferms the school was in disarray, with teachers and other caretakers engaging in inconsistent activities. The newcomers made some major changes, including in the environment and the organization of the school, as well as some pedagogical modifications. There was less focus on the intellectual side of integral education. Their pedagogical beliefs were more in line with the self-directed child, which was an integral part of developing the environment and educational spaces that the children at Stelton experienced. Over the next thirty years, the Modern School at Stelton continued but in quite a different orientation than originally envisioned by the Ferrer School in New York. As Suissa argues, "[anarchists] made little systematic attempt to provide a theoretical account of the relationship between child-centered pedagogical practice and their own anarchist goals and values" (2006: 85). Certainly, the conflicting political views of the colony's inhabitants and the different philosophical beliefs about teaching and learning led to some of these inconsistencies. There were continued ideological conflicts within the colony as well as organizational failures that ultimately led to its closure in 1953 (Avrich 1980; Velsey 1978).

After the closing of the Modern School and the Stelton colony, other anarchist-inspired educational experiments continued to emerge across the country. Again, similar issues emerged with regard to tensions between libertarian pedagogical practices and having students develop a sense of anarchist values. Taking up fragments of integral and rationalist education, as did Dewey, Fröbel, and other progressive educational philosophies, never fit neatly into anarchist values and the political demands of anti-authoritarianism and anti-capitalism.

REIMAGINING ANARCHISM AND EDUCATION IN THE MID-TWENTIETH CENTURY

By the 1960s, the civil rights and anti-war movements in the United States made a deep impact on communities around the country. In addition, there were other revolutionary and independence movements happening internationally. On a global level, changes in educational philosophies and practices were being discussed and created in different locales to support some of these major societal transformations. New educational practices continued to play an important role in analyzing and organizing against perceived oppressive structures in society. At the same time, anarchists continued to believe education had the capacity to promote mutual aid, dialogue, and solidarity among people and communities. It became increasingly important for communities to organize themselves as the social safety net of the state began to deteriorate, particularly in urban areas.

In the 1960s and early 1970s, Paulo Freire's work was read and utilized in communities in South America and other parts of the world, particularly in the development of radical literacy practices in rural areas. Considered a founder of critical pedagogy, Freire and his world-renowned book *Pedagogy of the Oppressed* (1972) have influenced both Marxist educators and anarchist pedagogues. His critique of the banking model of education—a notion similar to the image of "pouring" knowledge into students—was key in challenging dominant teaching and learning practices as well as the hierarchical and authoritarian teacher–student relationship. As Mueller highlights,

> The goal of critical pedagogy, then, is to develop an educational practice that can provide the necessary space and non-authoritarian guidance for people to grow into their humanity, gain a critical analytical eye, and develop a compassionate and empathetic worldview that is capable of challenging the hegemonic order. This approach clearly shares much in common with the values of anarchist theorists. (2012: 23)

Freire was not an anarchist. His experiences and beliefs stem from European critical theorists and liberation theology. Although there are some differences within Freirean approaches to education, it is important to note his influence on more contemporary anarchist educators, particularly through his unique pedagogical approaches encompassing dialogue, problem posing, and using local and situated knowledge. As Freire points out, there is an important foundational component of education, and that is "a respect for the autonomy of the student" (1996: 59).

In 1970, Ivan Illich's work *Deschooling Society* also offered important criticisms of state-run education. His arguments have had affinity with anarchist educational thinking. Illich saw compulsory education as a process of consuming knowledge from the dominant society. For example, he saw curriculum as a way to "package" values for students to learn. He argues, "we are all involved in schooling, from both the side of production and that of consumption. We are superstitiously convinced that good learning can and should be produced in us—and that we can produce it in others" (Illich 1970: 48). In his view, the school "indoctrinates the pupil about what is right and what is wrong, not only in school, but also in society at large" (p. 31).

Like Freire, Illich saw current educational practices as oppressive. He did not consider himself an anarchist, but his concept of forming "learning webs" decentralizes educational practices and challenges state-run compulsory schooling. He envisioned people informally connecting with others as a way to share references, share skills, and find others with similar interests. He believed that society needed to develop what he called "new relational structures" so that people would have access to these educational resources (p. 78).

At the end of the day, it is understandable that anarchists have gravitated toward Illich's and Freire's work. Both figures strongly questioned the oppressive impact education can have on the individual and society. However, there are still ideological differences that emerge, particularly in how educational practices function within the larger social order. Gabbard's (2017) critique of critical educators demonstrates some of their analytical shortfalls, particularly in how the state functions to support capitalist expansion and enforcement. Gabbard argues that

> [m]any critical educational theorists have been fantasizing about transforming society for over forty years [but], as long as market institutions maintain their dominance over society, the state will function as one of the principal means for enforcing that dominance, and compulsory schooling will function as one of the primary instruments through which the security state fulfills that mission. (pp. 51–2)

Gabbard's viewpoint represents a view of the ruthlessness of the capitalist order that requires continued theoretical and practical response, as that order evolves under changing conditions such as today's globalization.

PAUL GOODMAN AND "INCIDENTAL EDUCATION"

At the same time that Freire's and Illich's works were being read, Paul Goodman's educational philosophies and critiques were being discussed in the United States. Goodman had interests in literature, the arts, psychotherapy, and anarchism. His overt support of anarchism and critiques of education resonated in many radical circles that were resisting the oppressive structures brought about by racism, sexism, and class disparities in the United States. His anarchist beliefs spoke to many young people who saw institutional structures and cultural practices in society as alienating and conforming to social and political norms. Similar to past anarchist philosophies, Goodman argued that one of the major problems with education is that society demands a type of direct learning, where students are supposed to mimic and follow certain ideological beliefs determined by those in power.

To counter the existing problems within education, Goodman wrote *The Present Moment in Education* (1969) and further refined his ideas in a chapter in his book entitled *New Reformation: Notes of a Neolithic Conservative* (1970). In these works, he elucidates a philosophy of education built around the idea of incidental education. He argues that utilizing direct education as a pedagogical standard in schools has historically harmed children and has only reinforced particular types of teaching and learning that are not natural and are alienating (Goodman 1970). Related to other earlier anarchist educational beliefs, he contended that direct instruction is a form of indoctrination (Goodman 2011: 136). Sixty years earlier, Voltairine de Cleyre highlighted similar problems with education, stating that "political institutions must justify themselves to the young generation. They begin by training childish minds to believe that what they do is to be accepted, not criticized" (1914: 332). It is apparent that the anarchist critiques of traditional and state-driven educational practices remained consistent. Goodman viewed direct education as a one-way process in which information was driven into the student. It was also hierarchical since the child was seen as lacking agency and the ability to engage in mutually educative activity.

As Goodman highlights, many of the progressive educational reforms of the early and mid-twentieth century were a response to educational rigidness. However, he argues that, inevitably in his view, Progressive-era educational reforms were almost "total failures": "Dewey's social conceptions have ended up as technocracy, labor bureaucracy, and suburban conformity" (Goodman 2011: 142). Goodman's criticisms, contested by a range of progressive practitioners, stem predominantly from the Progressive-era education that coincided with industrial and technological changes in society. Goodman argues that "progressive education is a political movement; progressive education emerges when the social problem is breaking out. To put it more positively, an old regime is not adequate to cope with new conditions; new energy is needed" (p. 140). Progressive educational reforms, even with their "good intentions," still reinforced and promoted students' particular relationships to dominant ideological forces. Specifically, Goodman viewed Dewey's reforms as "domesticating" but not fundamentally reforming industrialism by the "learning by doing" process (2010: 94). Goodman believed that the bureaucratic and administrative arm of the Progressive era dominated and coopted specific pedagogical practices. These practices intended to reinforce top-down labor practices and market-driven economic relations.

Goodman also argued that A.S. Neill's more libertarian educational project at Summerhill was a part of the larger progressive educational reform, particularly within the cultural and political changes of the 1960s. Although he applauds the educational practices of Neill's Summerhill School, which challenged compulsory attendance, created more participatory engagement, and encouraged self-governmental practices, Goodman argues that Neill's approach "protects his community a few years too long, both from the oppressive mechanistic world and from adolescent solitude" (2011: 142).

It is not clear how Goodman came to this conclusion, but there seems to be a concern with how students might be isolated from participating in the struggles of the world by only seeing how their educational work plays out in the microcosm of the school environment. Overall, Goodman saw progressive education reforms as a "middle-class gimmick" (p. 141). He wanted radical changes to how young people learned, and he believed that progressive educational reforms had failed to create those emancipatory spaces demanded by students during that time.

Goodman attempted to counter "middle-class gimmick" reforms with some practical answers, especially by promoting what he termed "incidental learning." Incidental learning "is not teaching" (Goodman 1970: 93). Goodman saw a "possibility for every education to be tailor-made according to each youth's developing interest and choice" (p. 101). He believed in creating an educational experience that was less academic and was geared toward vocational learning that would better the community. It can be argued that these proposals coincide with those of earlier historical figures who argued for integral education as well as with some of the experiences at the Modern School (Suissa 2006: 103).

From the standpoint of school choice and the development of tailor-made educational systems, Goodman's ideas can be viewed as a contemporary rallying cry of conservative ideologies and neoliberal policies. Arguments for individualized education have been embraced by current conservative movements to create school choice and to uphold marketplace ideologies, where the consumer pays for an education that allows access to employment opportunities. However, Goodman argued against these marketplace values and privatization in general and opposed the reactionary conservatism behind them. He viewed educational practices of the state as more in line with the social engineering of individuals. Goodman (along with other anarchists) believed that "if the schools were truly voluntary associations, the disorders would never occur or would be immediately quelled by the members who would protect what they love" (2010: 85). Examples of the "disorders" to which he referred are the campus uprisings during the 1960s. So, if educational practices were voluntary and if students had autonomy over their learning, the facilities would be protected by the students as opposed to being "burnt down" (p. 86).

Although mainstream America saw Goodman's proposals as far-fetched, he was able to challenge traditional educational practices and institutions. His ideas were popular with young people during a time when resistance efforts were taking place around the United States (free speech movement, civil rights, and anti-war efforts) and when new ideas, particularly surrounding efforts to contest traditional educational practices, were being discussed and openly embraced.

COLIN WARD: A RESPECT FOR THE LEARNER

By the late 1960s and early 1970s, philosophical discussions concerning anarchism and education were also being explored in the United Kingdom. In 1973, Colin Ward's book *Anarchy in Action* revisited important historical questions regarding anarchism and, more importantly, discussed how anarchists were organizing themselves and constructing new ways of being. In the chapter "Schools No Longer," Ward (similarly to Goodman) describes the role of education in society, arguing, "the social function of education is to perpetuate society: it is the socializing function. Society guarantees its future by rearing its children in its own image" (1973: 79). He believed that anarchists could challenge such educational purposes through different pedagogical practices. Ward suggests that, "the anarchist approach to education is grounded not in a contempt for learning but in a respect for the learner" (p. 84). During this time, the de-schooling movement and free schools had already been established and were expanding in the United Kingdom. Although many were not specifically anarchist, they did provide an alternative to state-run schools.

Ward's writings highlighted significant educational practices taking place internationally. He argued "with some irony," as Suissa puts it, that "there is no such thing as anarchist education. There are just different kinds of educational experiments which anarchists have supported and been involved in" (2006: 77). Ward's work is noteworthy because it embraces the wide range of educational community projects that anarchists supported even though they have not always been explicitly so-named. As Breitbart highlights, "Ward saw the future present in the here and now, and he drew great pleasure from pointing out examples of more humane ways of being in the world wherever and whenever he came across them" (2013: 182).

Ward made explicit connections to what was happening on the ground educationally both in the United Kingdom and in the United States. He and fellow Town & Country Planning Association member Anthony Fyson published a book entitled *Streetwork: The Exploding School* (1973). Because of Ward's work in city planning and his interest in learning outside of the school, the book focused on environmental education and learning within urban landscapes. Ward and Fyson (1973: 5) saw formal and institutionalized educational practices as taking away an individual's ability to educate herself. Like Goodman's work on incidental learning, the authors highlight the importance of the self-directed learner based on informal educational practices, particularly experiences that enable youth to navigate city structures and gain a deeper understanding about issues regarding the environment. Environmental studies, or *Streetwork* pedagogies, encouraged students to live and learn in the field. Learning took place outside of school structures—in libraries, cinemas, offices, and other areas (p. 15). The approach encouraged teachers to become more like what Goodman considered "Athenian pedagogues," where learning took place, in nonauthoritarian ways, throughout the city in shopfronts, clubhouses, and elsewhere.

In 1979, Ward published one of his most renowned books, *The Child in the City*. He continued to advocate for environmental studies, where young people would be able to understand better the complexities of life in urban spaces. As Ward later remarked, "I wanted readers to grasp the importance of the child's surroundings as a source of pleasure and in the skills needed for the mastery of the environment" (Ward, quoted in Harris et al. 2000: vii). Ward believed that children were extremely isolated in cities, lacking well-planned spaces for play and community, but could nonetheless learn empowering ways to navigate their environments. He spoke with great numbers of young people around the world and saw firsthand how they were negotiating situated city spaces. He urged community organizers, educators, parents, and others to remember that children have a "right" to a good city life and that they should work together to bring such a life into being. The anarchist appeal in these educational practices was that, instead of focusing on federal or state institutions to create such changes, local and community organizations would work collectively to create these teaching and learning spaces.

In sum, Ward was interested in the diverse educational experiments with which anarchists could become directly involved and that encouraged an intersection of Goodman's incidental learning, Illich's de-schooling, and a focus on environmental studies. Goodman and Ward demonstrated that anarchist philosophies of education were becoming more complex and were based in a web of theories coming from both historical and contemporary figures as well as in the everyday practices within communities. Theoretical discussions and actions regarding anarchism and education continued to evolve into the closing decades of the twentieth century. This was evident in the educational spaces created by the resistance movements against neoliberal and global capitalist shifts around the world.

CONTEMPORARY DISCUSSIONS: POLITICAL AND PHILOSOPHICAL SHIFTS

In 2000, *Time* magazine published an article entitled "The New Radicals." It focused on youth involved in organizing protests in Seattle and in Washington, DC, against neoliberalism and oppressive relationships brought on by globalization from above. Protesters contested the policies and practices perpetuated by the World Trade Organization and International Monetary Fund as well as the power of multinational corporations. The demonstrations were international in scope, bringing in protesters from all over the world. The protests also featured a broad and diverse array of environmental and labor-rights activist organizations. What the article captured for mainstream readers was a snapshot of how anarchism functioned through a decentralized, consensus-based model of decision-making along with building affinity across different networks of individuals. This organizational process did not happen overnight. Major planning efforts as well as educational work had to take place. The movement became an intersection of historical as well as contemporary thought and action. There were explicit organizing tactics that were influenced by both the anti-nuclear movements of the 1970s and by anarchists in Spain during the 1930s.

At this time, theoretical perspectives were being strategically threaded together to support emerging social movements and their analyses of neoliberalism. Five years before the *Time* article, an Indigenous revolt occurred in Southern Chiapas, Mexico. This "Zapatista Movement" sparked a new struggle against global capitalism and influenced unique ways of thinking about organizing. Although they did not label themselves anarchists, many anarchist groups around the world supported efforts to build autonomous communities to support dignified life and work. The Zapatista belief of not adhering to a specific philosophy or theoretical lens is due to the fact that its Indigenous perspective predates these ideologies (Gahman 2016). This belief is also politically strategic. By not aligning with a particular ideology, the movement broadens support so that different and diverse organizations, both locally and internationally, will not be turned off by political or philosophical labels. Part of the importance of highlighting this movement is that social movements toward the end of the twentieth century and into the twenty-first began to think about and utilize anarchism in different ways, especially by weaving through different theoretical and philosophical lenses. Gahman summarizes this view, writing that

> the Zapatistas are not anarchists. But, in fairness, it does not seem to be because they have anything against anarchists. Rather, it is because the Zapatistas seem to consider all categorical options by modernity to be "traps." In practice, many aspects of their rebellion do indeed appear to be quite anarchist, just as many of their actions seem to be Marxist, communist, feminist, queer, poststructuralist, environmentalist, socialist, postmodernist, liberation theologist, and so forth. (2016: 75)

Gahman's analysis of the Zapatistas shows how the movement added fresh challenges to think more critically about the politics and philosophical perspectives regarding anarchism and the organizing of social movements in general.

The Zapatista movement and its unique political and philosophical perspectives did not develop in isolation. The movement's ability to incorporate some of the more dynamic political theories and philosophers of the West while also focusing on Indigenous knowledge broadened its support internationally. For example, Todd May's influential book *The Political Philosophy of Poststructural Anarchism* (1994) argues that new philosophical and political discussions were needed after the collapse of the Soviet Union and traditional Marxist thinking. May suggests that there are direct philosophical connections between anarchism and the poststructuralist philosophies of the collaborators Giles Deleuze and Felix Guattari, Michel Foucault, and other French philosophers. May analyzes the failures of Marxism in the twentieth century and the need to think about power through a more decentralized lens so that new concepts of anarchism can emerge. He also emphasizes the importance of Deleuze and Guattari's and Foucault's discussions on *micropolitics*. Micropolitics is a way to understand the complexities of how power impacts every facet of life, including education. This argument is a major challenge to deterministic, binary, and zero-sum perspectives on power. Attaching poststructuralism to anarchism opened up new philosophical conversations regarding representation, universality, and human nature in classical anarchism. Poststructural anarchism provided different philosophical tools not only to help construct theories of the new social movements that had been emerging toward the end of the twentieth and early twenty-first century but also to understand better the economic mutations that were occurring under neoliberal and global capitalism.

FIGURE 5.2 Abundance too many toys – little boy steps on toys. Photograph by Nadezhda1906 / iStock Photo.

POST-ANARCHISMS AND EDUCATIONAL LANDSCAPES IN THE TWENTY-FIRST CENTURY

As stressed, in the mid-to-late 1990s, new social movements emerged that were influenced by the creative, political, and philosophical features of anarchism. Graeber (2002) argues that many of the new social movements contesting neoliberal and global capitalist agendas were based on anarchist politics that included organizing tactics and consensus-based decision-making. This perspective was particularly evident in the alter-globalization movements that took place in Seattle, Washington, DC, and parts of Europe in the 2000s. Evren (2011) argues that the alter-globalization movement helped to expand philosophical and political discussions surrounding anarchism and moved it into what many scholars have termed "post-anarchism." Debate continues around the validity of the term as contrasted with classical conceptions of anarchism (Evren 2011). However, there is no doubt that new anarchist scholars and activists have expanded the literature outside of traditional late nineteenth-century and twentieth-century anarchist thinking. Todd May (1994), Saul Newman (2001), Lewis Call (2003), Jonathan Purkis and James Bowen (2004), and many others show how post-anarchist ideas have become a part of academic and activist discourse.

It is no easy task to bring into conversation integral education, the modern schools of the early twentieth century, incidental learning, de-schooling, free schools, and other educational experiments and practices reviewed in this chapter. A current concern in the field has been how to reflect critically on over a century's worth of effort in the name of new and productive directions.

Judith Suissa has provided an important volume to help address this question. In her comprehensive book *Anarchism and Education: A Philosophical Perspective* (2006), she provides a philosophical roadmap for readers to be able to understand anarchist values, how these have historically been debated, and, more importantly, how they play out in different educational spaces. As she points out, many of the criticisms of anarchism are based on its positions on human nature. Those who are skeptical of anarchism traditionally use the argument that anarchists believe that humans are naturally good. Suissa argues that this is a misconception and that anarchists have recognized the complexity of human nature and the social and cultural influences on individual action in society. She deploys the work of Bakunin, Kropotkin, and others to demonstrate that anarchists understand that individuals are not born free and that there are historical, social, and cultural forces that shape humans and their behavior. To combat hyper-individuality and competition, she suggests, anarchists turn to education as a way to support cooperation and mutual aid. As Suissa remarks, anarchists appreciate that "human nature involves both an altruistic and a selfish aspect, and that it is environmental factors that determine which of these aspects will dominate at any given time" (2006: 77). Consequently, "anarchists could clearly not leave processes of education and socialization to pure chance" (p. 77).

As pointed out in the introduction to the chapter, pedagogical practices have been a difficult subject within anarchist circles. Most of the debate questions how children develop and the role of the teacher, especially in attempting to construct a mutual, nonhierarchical, and anti-authoritarian space. Making it clear that weaknesses remain in anarchist accounts of education, Suissa observes that "the very status of the connection between anarchist ideology and non-coercive pedagogy is one which still demands theoretical treatment" (2006: 149).

Anarchist activists and scholars still navigate anarchism's complex and fluid nature, particularly in how it pertains to teaching and learning, the teacher–student relationship, and the morals and values embodied within anarchist beliefs. How is it possible to educate people to live freely and autonomously but, at the same time, to work together in solidarity and for mutual aid? Can anarchists educate for such values while remaining noncoercive? Suissa's work provides a sobering assessment of a lingering romanticism among anarchist activists and scholars regarding educational spaces and historical trends.

CRITICAL PEDAGOGY AND ANARCHISM

It was mentioned that contemporary anarchists have used Freire's work in different and sometimes problematic ways. Since Freire's death in 1997, critical pedagogy has continued to expand within progressive and radical educational circles. Abraham DeLeon (2008) adds an important outlook to contemporary discussions between critical pedagogy and anarchism. In his article, "Oh No, Not the 'A' Word! Proposing an 'Anarchism' for Education," DeLeon challenges critical pedagogues to think further about how anarchism can contribute to their efforts. He urges colleagues to look beyond ideological roots—for critical pedagogy, Marxism, and for anarchism, a more fluid theoretical constellation— and consider mutually supportive ideas and practices. DeLeon acknowledges the important contributions of critical pedagogues in critiquing educational institutions and traditional classroom practices. However, he highlights critical scholars' inability to bring anarchism into the conversation, noting that "although anarchist theory contains a rich history of dissent against institutionalized hierarchies, it remains glaringly absent from the educational literature" (DeLeon 2008: 123).

DeLeon tasks critical pedagogues with rethinking anarchism and, more importantly, argues that educators can use anarchist beliefs of sabotage and direct action. "Anarchist concerns with the State," he writes, and with "their autonomous organizational structures, recognition of the complexities of power, subversion of authority, and direct action better equip radical teachers and educators with tools to combat the assault of neo-liberalism and oppressive capitalist practices" (p. 137). DeLeon's work is important to note because it demonstrates a continued effort to link anarchism with other educational theories. Critical educational theorists still embrace the notion that the state has emancipatory qualities as long as it is not supported by capitalism and ruling class interests. On the other hand, anarchists are still against state institutions and vertical relationships. Therefore, anarchists would argue that replacing one hierarchical structure with another will not lead to a society they would support. Although there are still ongoing debates between critical pedagogues and anarchists, DeLeon's work provides possible philosophical and political affinity between these radical perspectives.

ANARCHISM AND UTOPIAN EDUCATION

Over the past few decades, anarchist educators and activists have been navigating across long-standing academic barriers to link geography, political science, sociology, and other scholarly fields as a way to reimagine education and educational spaces. For example, anarchist geographers have used the work of Jacques Élisée Reclus, Peter Kropotkin, and others to open conversations surrounding the development of nonhierarchical, anti-authoritarian, and mutual learning spaces (Clark and Martin 2013). Another example is the Anarchist Studies Network in the United Kingdom.[1] Although the network is based within the political sciences, it centers upon anarchists' multifaceted history. The "About" section of the Network's website states, "Far from having been anti-intellectual 'primitive rebels', anarchists produced a rich critical discourse on every facet of life and knowledge, from economics to linguistics, from social history to aesthetic theory, from urban planning to ontology—a counter-institutional archive that has barely begun to be investigated."

Although there is resistance to having anarchist studies in academia, there are anarchists who work at universities who understand that there are counter-institutional spaces that can be utilized to further different projects including social movement research, radical artwork, and anarchist pedagogies. At the same time, they work against long-standing views of anarchism as politically utopian if not simply naïve. They recognize how anarchist ideals function as just that: ideals, or directions to take, rather than fully realized accomplishments or realities. Suissa argues, "Anarchist utopia is not an end-state model, but has the commitment to constant experimentation and flux built into it" (2009: 243). She and other writers touch on why the fluidity and constant reflection that anarchism demands lends itself to criticism because of its refusal to subscribe to a means/end or concrete blueprint. For many who believe in scientific, historical materialist, and deterministic analyses, these ideas seem far-fetched and easy to criticize. However, Suissa demonstrates that engaging in less rigid and more complex conversation enables anarchists to regard their work as dynamic, including within the diverse and sometimes tension-filled educational experiments anarchists create. Suissa's point of view is worth quoting in full:

> I would suggest that orientating one's educational endeavors around the aspiration for a better—although never perfect—society may perhaps provide a more motivating starting point than that of educational projects characterized by the concern to formulate comprehensive goals and procedural principles. Education, on this view, is not a means to an end, nor an end itself, but simply one of many arenas of human relationships in which we constantly experiment with our ends, our goals, the means we choose to pursue them and the relationship between them. (2009: 255)

LEARNING FROM ANARCHISM'S EVOLVING EDUCATIONAL LANDSCAPE

The historical and philosophical thoughts on anarchism outlined within this chapter should not be seen as all-inclusive. There have been other anarchists of note who have contributed to educational thinking. What is important to note is that anarchist experiments in education are ongoing. Creative organizing efforts, the ability to imagine new ways of learning and being in the world, and experimenting have inspired many to explore anarchism and education. For example, the volume *Anarchist Pedagogies: Collective Actions, Theories, and Critical Reflections on Education* (Haworth 2012) brought together an interdisciplinary group of scholars and activists to discuss theories and educational experiments ranging from anarchist-inspired *Free Skools* and educating street medics to issues surrounding anarchism in the academy. The book addresses questions such as these: How does learning occur within such collective spaces? Are there philosophical and theoretical frameworks driving the practices? What difficulties and roadblocks have they encountered?

The Occupy Wall Street Movement in New York City (2011) was not explicitly anarchist, but many of its organizing tactics were developed through anarchist theories and practices (Hammond 2015). As Gautney argues, "Occupy Wall Street bore the deep imprint of anarchist praxis in its emphasis on building alternative forms of political and social engagement outside conventional politics and the hegemony of the commodity form" (2017: 221). This feature was also evident in the "horizontal" pedagogical experiments developed through some of the Occupy organizing members, where there were explicit ways in which people and collectives were creating their own ways of teaching and learning (Backer 2019).

Additionally, consider more recent conversations surrounding decolonizing anarchism (Ramnath 2011; White 2004). Decolonizing anarchism calls out anarchism's failure to move beyond Western thinking, the impacts of settler colonialism, and racism. These areas are not absent in anarchist literature but have not been explored in depth. Decolonizing anarchism can challenge current anarchist theories regarding how to organize collectively, how to construct knowledge, how to collaborate in creating educational spaces, and how to engage in pedagogical practices. It has the potential to challenge dominant and deterministic worldviews of what White calls "colonial universalism," where Christian and White perspectives permeate the world "through economic domination, sometimes through cultural imperialism, sometimes through force" (2004: 5). These conversations are crucial to anarchists as they engage in constructing new educational projects and work across different communities.

Shantz and Williams have also contributed to new and important discussions surrounding anarchism and sociology (Shantz 2012; Shantz and Williams 2013). In their book *Anarchy and Society* (2013), they make explicit sociological connections to Goldman, Proudhon, Kropotkin, and other anarchist perspectives and provide some direction on what an anarchist sociology might look like in practice. As they note, "anarchist projects provide a framework for practicing, learning about, and exploring new forms of social relationship" (Shantz and Williams 2013: 3). They envision a "radical praxis" in which there is not only a deeper analysis of the problems and issues facing society but also, more critically, a commitment to developing solutions that would coincide with creating anti-authoritarian, self-determining, and cooperative spaces (p. 5). An anarchist sociology is an important lens for educational researchers because it has potential to develop the critiques of both inside and outside forces that contribute to particular educational practices and how anarchists might transform those practices.

Anarchist geographers have also provided significant contributions to education. Springer, Lopes de Souza, and White's (2016) edited book, *The Radicalization of Pedagogy: Anarchism, Geography, and the Spirit of Revolt*, offers significant connections between anarchist theories, radical geographies, and educational praxis. As the editors remark, "The relevance of pedagogy to both anarchist and geographical praxes stems from its ability to guide a new way of thinking about the world and as an educational space that is able to foster transgression in ways that liberate and empower" (Springer, Lopes de Souza, and White 2016: 12).

In closing, it is encouraging to me to see how the above examples are increasing the political and philosophical conversations, actions, and literature surrounding anarchism and education. Continued exchanges can only help anarchists create more dynamic, ongoing experiments in constructing educational environments. Intentional educational experiments can also provide examples of how we may live and learn in different capacities in direct response to traditional and global capitalist agendas, which continue to permeate contemporary educational landscapes. As Day describes, "these new movements and radical spaces have potential to form educative innovations and creative struggle in and around, as well as, outside of oppressive structures, enabling new forms of subjectivity" (2004: 740). As anarchists continue their efforts, it will be vital to continue to create what Antliff eloquently describes as "site[s] of critical reflection and creative license, where life and learning commingle, giving rise to ways of being that prefigure and realize our ideals on a practical level, as a lived reality" (2012: 326).

NOTE

1   Anarchist Studies Network, "About." Available online: https://anarchiststudies network.org/.

REFERENCES

Primary sources

Avrich, Paul (1980), *The Modern School Movement: Anarchism and Education in the United States*, Princeton, NJ: Princeton University Press.
Bakunin, Mikhail (1869/1986), Integral Education, London: The Anarchist Encyclopaedia c/o Cambridge Free Press.
Cleyre, Voltairine de (1914), "Modern Education Reform," in Voltairine de Cleyre, *Selected Works*, 321–41, New York: Mother Earth Publishing Association.
Ferrer, Francisco (1913), *Origins and Ideals of the Modern School*, London: Watts & Company.
Freire, Paulo (1970), *Pedagogy of the Oppressed*, New York: Continuum Press.
Freire, Paulo (1996), *Pedagogy of Freedom: Ethics, Democracy, and Civic Courage*, New York: Roman & Littlefield.
Godwin, William (1793/2013), *An Enquiry Concerning Political Justice*, Oxford: Oxford University Press.
Goldman, Emma (1906), "The Child and Its Enemies," *Mother Earth*, 1 (2): 7–14.
Goodman, Paul (1970), *New Reformation: Notes of a Neolithic Conservative*, New York: Random House.
Illich, Ivan (1970), *Deschooling Society*, New York: Harper and Row.
Kropotkin, Peter (1880), "An Appeal to the Young," *Le Révolté*, June 25; July 10; August 7, 21.
Kropotkin, Peter (1902), *Mutual Aid: A Factor of Evolution*, London: William Heinemann.
Veysey, Laurence (1978), *The Communal Experience: Anarchist and Mystical Communities in Twentieth-Century America*, Chicago: University of Chicago Press.
Ward, Colin (1973), *Anarchy in Action*, London: Freedom Press.
Ward, Colin (1979), *The Child in the City*, New York: Pantheon.
Ward, Colin and Anthony Fyson (1973), *Streetwork: The Exploding School*, New York: Routledge & Kegan Paul.

Secondary sources

Ackelsburg, Martha (1991), *Free Women of Spain: Anarchism and the Struggle for the Emancipation of Women*, Oakland, CA: AK Press.

Antliff, Allan (2012), "Let the Riots Begin," in Robert Haworth (ed.), *Anarchist Pedagogies: Collective Actions, Theories, and Critical Reflections*, 14–31, Oakland, CA: PM Press.

Backer, Dave (2019), "What Is Horizontal Pedagogy?," *Humanities Commons*. http://dx.doi.org/10.17613/xdnc-9y20.

Bakunin, M. (1882). *God and the State*. Translated by B. Tucker, revised. Dover, Paperback.

Bluestein, Abe (1990), *The Modern School Movement: Historical and Personal Notes on the Ferrer Schools in Spain*, New York: Friends of the Modern School.

Bray, Mark and Robert Haworth, eds. (2018), *Anarchist Education and the Modern School: A Francisco Ferrer Reader*, Oakland, CA: PM Press.

Breitbart, Myrna M. (2013), "Inciting Desire, Ignoring Boundaries and Making Space: Colin Ward's Considerable Contribution to Radical Pedagogy, Planning and Social Change," in Catherine Burke and Ken Jones (eds.), *Childhood and Anarchism: Talking Colin Ward*, 175–85, New York: Routledge.

Chappell, Robert H. (1978), "Anarchy Revisited: An Inquiry into the Public Education Dilemma," *Journal of Libertarian Studies*, 2 (4): 357–72.

Cohn, Jesse (2007), *Anarchism and the Crisis of Representation*, Cranbury, NJ: Associate University Press.

Conway, Paul F., Murphy, Rosaleen and Rutherford, Vanessa. "Re-imagining initial teacher identity and learning study." Final Report (2013): School of Education, University College Cork, 1–120.

Day, Richard J.F. (2004), "From Hegemony to Affinity," *Cultural Studies*, 18 (5): 716–48.

DeLeon, Abraham (2008), "Oh No, Not the 'A' Word! Proposing an 'Anarchism' for Education," *Educational Studies*, 44 (2): 122–41.

Evren, Süreyyya (2011), "Introduction: How New Anarchism Changed the World (of Opposition) After Seattle and Gave Birth to Post-Anarchism," in Duane Rousselle and Süreyyya Evren (eds.), *Postanarchism: A Reader*, 1–22, New York: Pluto Press.

Fremeaux, Isabelle and John Jordan (2012), "Anarchist Pedagogy in Action: Padeia, Escuela Libre," in Robert Haworth (ed.), *Anarchist Pedagogies: Collective Actions, Theories, and Critical Reflections*, 14–31, Oakland, CA: PM Press.

Gabbard, David (2017), "Don't Act, Just Think!," in Robert Haworth and John Elmore (eds.), *Out of the Ruins: The Emergence of Radical Informal Learning Spaces*, 35–55, Oakland, CA: PM Press.

Gahman, Levi (2016), "Zapatismo versus the Neoliberal University: Towards a Pedagogy against Oblivion," in Simon Springer, Marcelo Lopes de Souza, and Richard J. White (eds.), *The Radicalization of Pedagogy: Anarchism, Geography, and the Spirit of Revolt*, 73–100, Lanham, MD: Rowman & Littlefield.

Gautney, Heather (2017), "The Influence of Anarchism in Occupy Wall Street," in Tom Goyens (ed.), *Radical Gotham: Anarchism in New York City from Schwab's Saloon to Occupy Wall Street*, 221–40, Champaign: University of Illinois Press.

Goodman, Paul. (2010). *New reformation: Notes of a neolithic conservative*. Oakland: PM Press.

Graeber, David (2002), "The New Anarchists," *New Left Review*, 13: 61–73.

Graeber, David (2004), *Fragments of an Anarchist Anthropology*, Chicago: Prickly Paradigm Press.

Graeber, David (2013), "A Practical Utopian's Guide to the Coming Collapse," *The Baffler*, April. Available online: https://thebaffler.com/salvos/a-practical-utopians-guide-to-the-coming-collapse.

Haworth, Robert, ed. (2012), *Anarchist Pedagogies: Collective Actions, Theories, and Critical Reflections*, Oakland, CA: PM Press.

Kirn, Walter (2000), "The New Radicals," *Time Magazine*, April 24: 42–6.

May, Todd (1994), *The Political Philosophy of Poststructuralist Anarchism*, University Park: Pennsylvania State University Press.

Morris, Brian (2018), *Kropotkin: The Politics of Community*, Oakland, CA: PM Press.

Mueller, Justin (2012), "Anarchism, the State, and the Role of Education," in Robert Haworth (ed.), *Anarchist Pedagogies: Collective Actions, Theories, and Critical Reflections*, 14–31, Oakland, CA: PM Press.

Murolo, Priscilla and A.B. Chitty (2001), *From the Folks Who Brought You the Weekend: A Short, Illustrated History of Labor in the United States*, New York: New Press.

Newman, Saul (2001), *From Bakunin to Lacan: Anti-Authoritarianism and the Dislocation of Power*, New York: Lexington Books.

Purkis, Jonathan (2004), "Towards an Anarchist Sociology," in Jonathan Purkis and James Bowen (eds.), *Changing Anarchism: Anarchist Theory and Practice in the Global Age*, Manchester: Manchester University Press.

Purkis, Jonathan and James Bowen, eds. (2004), *Changing Anarchism: Anarchist Theory and Practice in the Global Age*, Manchester: Manchester University Press.

Ramnath, Maia (2011), *Decolonizing Anarchism: An Anti-authoritarian History of India's Liberation Struggle*, Oakland, CA: AK Press.

Shantz, Jeffrey (2012), "Spaces of Learning: The Anarchist Free Skool," in Robert Haworth (ed.), *Anarchist Pedagogies: Collective Actions, Theories, and Critical Reflections*, 14–31, Oakland, CA: PM Press.

Shantz, Jeffrey and Dana Williams (2013), *Anarchy and Society: Reflections on Anarchist Sociology*, Boston: Brill.

Shantz, J. (2012). *Against all authority: Anarchism and the literary imagination*. Andrews UK Limited.

Spring J. (2008), Research on Globalization and Education. *Review of Educational Research*, 78 (2):330–63.

Springer, Simon, Marcelo Lopes de Souza, and Richard J. White, eds. (2016), *The Radicalization of Pedagogy: Anarchism, Geography, and the Spirit of Revolt*, Lanham, MD: Rowman & Littlefield.

Suissa, Judith (2006), *Anarchism and Education: A Philosophical Perspective*, New York: Routledge.

Suissa, Judith (2009), "'The Space Now Possible': Anarchist Education as Utopian Hope," in Laurence Davis and Ruth Kinna (eds.), *Anarchism and Utopianism*, 241–59, Manchester: Manchester University Press.

White, Roger (2004), *Postcolonial Anarchism: Essays on Race, Repression, and Culture in Communities of Color, 1999–2004*, Oakland, CA: Jailbreak Press.

CHAPTER SIX

Philosophy for Children and Children's Philosophical Thinking

MAUGHN ROLLINS GREGORY

INTRODUCTION

As Gareth B. Matthews observed, the history of young people's philosophical practice extends back at least to Socrates:

> Beyond finding at least some boys attractive in an erotic way, Socrates, as he is presented by Plato in the early dialogues, is simply at home in the company of children ... Socrates himself seems to have found it entirely appropriate to engage children in philosophical discussion; moreover, he clearly respected children as philosophical discussion partners .... Socratic questioning, we could almost say, began as philosophy for children. (1998: 11–12)

Philosophy education patterned on university courses has been a regular part of secondary education in many parts of the world for centuries (UNESCO 1953). However, it was not until the late 1960s that philosophy with younger children became an educational practice and a topic of academic scholarship. Since then, philosophy for children[1] has become a global, multidisciplinary movement involving innovations in curriculum, pedagogy, educational theory, and teacher education; in moral, social, and political philosophy; and in discourse and literary theory. And it has generated the new academic field of philosophy of childhood.

In this chapter, I will first provide a brief account of the movement's origins in the work of Matthew Lipman (1923–2010), Gareth B. Matthews (1929–2011), and Ann Margaret Sharp (1942–2010). I will recount the movement's major accomplishments—in critical thinking, ethics education, and democratic education—and its principal critiques and challenges. I will then employ Shaun Gallagher's (1992) heuristic of four hermeneutical schools to identify what I take to be divergent trends in philosophy for children theory and practice that signify deep differences in the meanings of philosophy, childhood, and education as well as disparate educational agendas.

THE CHILD AS PHILOSOPHER: GARETH B. MATTHEWS

Matthews became interested in children's philosophical thinking when he started noticing the philosophical richness of his own children's remarks and questions and parallels between some of their storybooks and topics he was teaching at the university. His first essay exploring children's philosophical thinking argued that,

> what philosophers do (in rather disciplined and sustained ways) is much closer than is usually appreciated to what at least some children rather naturally do (albeit fitfully, and without the benefit of sophisticated techniques) … If this impulse is frustrated in school and goes underground until college, that fact may have something to do with society's failure to reward any sustained questioning that cannot be given a "useful" response. (Matthews 1976: 14–15)

The most dramatic and far-reaching implication of Matthews' work on children's philosophical thinking is that children have been seriously misunderstood, underestimated, and disrespected (except by philosophically minded authors of children's books). Matthews (2006) traced this mistreatment of children to Aristotle, for whom the child is essentially a pre-intellectual and pre-moral precursor to the fully realized human adult, and for whom the purpose of education is to be guided into adulthood. Matthews dubbed this the "deficit conception of childhood" and wrote extensive critiques of its perpetuation in Jean Piaget's stage model of cognitive development and in Lawrence Kohlberg's stage model of moral development (Mathews 1980, 1985, 2008, 2017). Matthews drew on his own experience philosophizing with children—as well as that of the university students, schoolteachers, and parents with whom he worked—to argue that children's cognitive and moral development may not occur in predictable stages and that children's thinking is not always immature compared to that of adults. In fact, he observed, it is often more daring, critical, and imaginative than that of most adults, who have typically lost their philosophical curiosity and acumen. Another tactic Matthews used to defend the integrity of children's philosophical thinking was to connect children's questions and ideas to the philosophical canon, as when he demonstrated how seventh graders in a Hebrew day school generated classical rationalist and voluntarist responses to the *Euthyphro* problem (Matthews 2009).

Matthews' critique of deficit concepts of childhood and his defense of children's philosophical acuity were two pillars of his own philosophy of childhood. In 1994, he published the first book in the field, which he described in a 2002 entry for the *Stanford Encyclopedia of Philosophy* as follows:

> [T]he philosophy of childhood takes up philosophically interesting questions about childhood, about conceptions people have of childhood and attitudes they have toward children; about theories of what childhood is, as well as theories of cognitive and moral development; about theories of children's rights, notions concerning the status and significance of child art and child poetry; about claims concerning the history of childhood, as well as comparative studies of childhood in different cultures; and finally about theories concerning the proper place of children in society. (Matthews 2002)

In 2006, Matthews offered a new metaphor to describe his own philosophy of childhood:

> I suggest that we should try to develop a *mirror-image* conception of childhood. ... [W]e can say that the strengths of childhood tend to be the weaknesses of adulthood, and vice versa. Thus children have fresh eyes to see what most of us adults no longer see, curiosity to understand what we take for granted, and minds that detect puzzles, incongruities, and perplexities that we have, most of us, long ago become inured to. We adults, on the other hand, have lots of information, many sophisticated skills, deeper understanding about some matters, and much experience to share about how to negotiate the challenges of life. The point of good parenting and good schooling should be to help our children gain some of our adult advantages without losing as many childhood advantages as most of us adults have already lost. (2006: 14, emphasis in original)

Matthews tirelessly advocated adult–child philosophical dialogue. He argued that even academic philosophers can benefit from the freshness and directness of children's thinking, but that parents and teachers do not need philosophical training to enjoy philosophizing with children. The latter argument he supported by writing reviews of philosophically-oriented children's books in the column "Thinking in Stories" he created for *Thinking: The Journal of Philosophy for Children*.[2] These reviews became the pattern for the curriculum series *Wise Owl: Talking and Thinking about Children's Literature* that Matthews produced for first- through third-grade classrooms.[3] The first packet in the series reassures teachers with the following rhetorical exchange:

FIGURE 6.1 Children discussing philosophical stories. *Source*: Ridofranz / iStock.

> If I don't know anything about Philosophy, or about teaching Critical
> Thinking, will I be able to use Wise Owl?
>   Yes. If you can read and think, if you believe that exploring open-ended
> questions is a legitimate pursuit, if you believe that children can think about
> interesting ideas and if you are willing to explore ideas along with them, then
> you've got all it takes! (Matthews, Carlisle, and Tishman 1987: 2)

Matthews' pioneering work in philosophy in children's literature began a
significant trend within the philosophy for children movement of using picture
books and children's literature to prompt children's philosophical thinking (see
Haynes and Murris 2012; Sprod 1993; Wartenberg 2009).

PHILOSOPHY IN EDUCATION: MATTHEW LIPMAN AND ANN MARGARET SHARP

One of the most distinguishing aspects of the philosophy for children movement
is the intellectual, moral, and political agency it attributes to children and
teenagers. Yet the figure of the child has never been uniformly characterized
in the movement. Lipman regarded children as capable of philosophical
questioning and thinking but was not sanguine about the abilities of parents
and teachers to draw out and support that thinking. For Lipman and Sharp, the

child is only potentially a philosophical agent and grows into becoming such by means of a particular—that is, a philosophical—kind of education.[4] To that end, they aspired not only to make philosophy a regular part of education but also to transform education along the lines of philosophical inquiry (see Kizel 2016c; Lipman 1978, 1985; Sharp 1983).

Lipman was preoccupied with problems of education, prompted by his study of John Dewey, by the politics of administration at Columbia University where he taught, and by the struggles his own mixed-race children faced in public schools.[5] From the early 1960s, as he observed,

> I was alerted to the need for protecting children from types of advertising and propaganda that foreclosed on their freedom of choice rather than opening it up … If I was beginning to think of the dangers of children's minds being open to manipulation, I was also beginning to think that their ability to defend themselves intellectually was definitely something that needed to be and could be strengthened. (Lipman 2008: 103)

The approach Lipman invented to introduce children to philosophy was nothing less than a new literary genre: children's philosophical fiction. Unlike the kind of children's literature with philosophical meaning that Matthews was studying, children's philosophical fiction, as conceived by Lipman, is overtly didactic in a number of ways: it systematically reconstructs key philosophical issues and positions in language accessible by children of various ages; it attempts to help children recognize philosophical dimensions of their own experience; and it models children engaged in philosophical dialogues, with and without adults. Lipman successfully piloted his first novel, *Harry Stottlemeier's Discovery*, in 1970 in a fifth-grade classroom in Montclair, New Jersey, with support from Columbia and the National Endowment for the Humanities. When Columbia ceased to support the project, Lipman moved to Montclair State College in 1972, where he was invited to work on the project more or less full time.

The following year Sharp joined the faculty of Educational Foundations at Montclair and met Lipman at a conference on "Pre-College Philosophy" that he organized there. They cofounded the Institute for the Advancement of Philosophy for Children (IAPC) in 1974. Sharp had taken her EdD at the University of Massachusetts, Amherst, in 1973. Her dissertation, "The Teacher As Liberator: An Analysis of the Philosophy of Education of Friedrich Nietzsche" (1973), paralleled Lipman's attempt to reconstruct the history of philosophy as a resource to aid young people in working out the meaning of their experience, often in resistance to the conservative forces of their own education (see Oliverio 2018). Sharp also recognized children's philosophical inquiry as resonant with the pedagogical creed of Dewey—a philosophical hero she had in common with Lipman (see Gregory and Laverty 2018).

The most lasting and far-reaching legacy of Lipman and Sharp's collaboration was the protocol they developed for children's philosophical practice. In a "community of philosophical inquiry," people with diverse experiences, ideas, and concerns dialogue together around a shared philosophical question, during which they are prompted by a trained facilitator to challenge and build on one another's ideas, offer personal stories, attend to emotions, imagine new possibilities, and self-correct. The participants' dual aim is to form reasonable, meaningful judgments about the matter and to grow in their powers of inquiry—individually and as a community—until the need for outside facilitation eventually disappears. The notion of a classroom community of inquiry following a trajectory from doubt through inquiry and self-correction to belief or judgment was adapted from Charles Peirce, but the Lipman–Sharp protocol was also derived from Socratic method, Dewey's epistemology, logic, and political theory, the social psychology of George Herbert Mead and Lev Vygotsky, and Justus Buchler's theory of judgment and method of classroom discussion (Buchler 1954). In addition, Sharp informed her understanding of the practice with feminist, ecological, and religious literature (see Gregory and Laverty 2018).

ACCOMPLISHMENTS AND CHALLENGES

Lipman and Sharp collaborated for thirty-five years on expanding their pre-college philosophy curriculum, producing theoretical and empirical research to justify the program and guide its development, and disseminating the program locally and internationally. The IAPC curriculum was translated into dozens of languages as affiliate centers appeared around the world. At the same time, Matthews offered workshops on philosophy in children's literature and philosophy of childhood in the United States, Germany, Israel, and Japan. As the notion of children's philosophy spread, philosophers in a number of other countries developed unique approaches (see Gregory, Haynes, and Murris 2017: xxvi–xxvii). Today children and teens practice philosophy in one way or another in schools in over sixty countries (UNESCO 2007). A number of universities offer coursework and degree programs in philosophy for children, and numerous national, regional, and international organizations[6] promote scholarship and professional development in the field. Philosophy for children has been recognized by Martha Nussbaum (2010), Robert J. Sternberg (2003), and Howard Gardner (2006) as central to a genuinely liberal education.

The early success of philosophy for children was due in part to its coincidence with the critical thinking movement in education, in which Lipman was an important figure (Gregory and Laverty 2009; Johnson 1984; Lipman 1988, 1993). Indeed, theorizing the nature and elements of good thinking and what should be involved in its teaching and learning was the primary focus of Lipman's scholarship for most of his life, as epitomized in his major work *Thinking in Education* (2003) and his autobiography, *A Life Teaching Thinking* (2008). Working within the pragmatist tradition, Lipman developed an elaborate taxonomy of kinds of thinking useful for improving lived experience, which he organized into three major categories of critical, creative, and caring thinking. The latter was an innovation he developed collaboratively with Sharp to address thinking informed by values—by evolved senses of what is worthwhile or precious and by the emotions and bodily feelings that signal those values. For Lipman and Sharp, good thinking cannot be reduced to sound argumentation but encompasses a life of wakefulness to beauty, justice, and other kinds of goodness. They believed that philosophy was the discipline uniquely capable of fostering this kind of thinking, the aim of which was not rational belief but "ethical, social, political, and aesthetic judgments ... applied directly to life situations" (Lipman 2003: 279). In fact, the positive effect of doing philosophy on children's cognitive abilities has been the most lauded and the most studied aspect of the program from the beginning, and the studies overwhelmingly verify that effect (Gorard, Siddiqui, and See 2015; Soter et al. 2008; Topping and Trickey 2007a, b).

Another popular though controversial feature of philosophy for children is its emphasis on ethics, which has justified its use as a program of ethics, character, and even religious education (Glaser and Gregory 2017; Gregory and Oliverio 2018; Hannam 2012; Matthews 2009; Shea 2017; Sprod 2001). In philosophy for children, moral maturity is taken to be as much a matter of the understanding as of the will or of disciplined behavior (Matthews 1987). In addition, Lipman and Sharp's community of inquiry involves such ethical practices as deep listening, helping others articulate their ideas, respectfully challenging or criticizing others' ideas, and identifying the inquiry as the work of the group. However, regarding moral and religious education, the same aspects of philosophy for children that recommend it to some condemn it for others. First, the program recognizes that children's daily experience is replete with ethical issues involving, for example, trust, loyalty, honesty, cruelty, friendship, and fairness. Second, the program takes children's ethical experience to be just as ambiguous and precarious as that of adults—that is, infrequently resolvable by the simple application of an ethical or religious rule. Third, the program invites children to think openly about ethical issues, to question social and religious norms, to reconstruct the meaning of ethical concepts, and to work out their own ethical judgments.

A third feature of philosophy for children, which has application to civics education, is the way it instantiates democratic deliberation and power sharing (see Burgh 2018; Lipman 1998; Mizell 2015). Thus, Nussbaum (2010) lauds philosophy for children for its genius in promoting Socratic thinking and democratic dialogue. It is no coincidence, of course, that the classroom community of inquiry proposed by Lipman and Sharp so clearly reflects the pragmatist ideal of democracy as a method of cooperative inquiry undertaken by a group of people brought together by their collective stake in clarifying and dealing with shared problems and opportunities (Burgh, Field, and Freakley 2006; Glaser 2017; Gregory 2004; Lipman 1997; Sharp 1991). In addition, philosophy for children invites young people to explore, challenge, and reconstruct the meaning of political and economic concepts (such as citizenship, democracy, freedom, justice, law, peace, property, punishment, rights, sovereignty, and war) that are typically taken for granted or treated as fixed in the standard curriculum. And though the program has been criticized for construing social issues in strictly discursive terms, there are many instances of classroom philosophy discussions resulting in action projects, including students participating in shared school governance.

Apart from its use in ethics and civics education, philosophy for children is predominantly a self-contained program, offered by a single teacher or a small cohort of teachers and/or visiting philosophers or philosophy students (Gregory 2008). In some schools, philosophy for children has been adapted for programs in gifted (Lipman 1981; Splitter 2007), special needs (Lee 1986; Simon 1979), and adult education (Daniel 1989; Kohan and Wozniak 2009; Lipman 1987; Lipman 1989). However, a number of schools have implemented philosophy sessions in every classroom, at every grade level (Golding, Gurr, and Hinton 2012; Thomas-Williams and Lyle 2012). In addition, numerous arguments have been made for implementing philosophy as a standard school subject (Cam 2006; Splitter 2006) and across school subjects (Knight and Collins 2000; Weinstein 1987). In fact, the practice of philosophy across pre-college school subjects is already extensive, including, among other subjects, mathematics (de la Garza, Slade, and Daniel 2000; N.S. Kennedy 2012), science (Lipman 1988; Moura Ferreira 2012; Sprod 2014), literacy (Jenkinsa and Lyle 2010; Murris 2014; Sprod 1993; Yeazell 1982), environmental education (Gomez and de Puig 2003; Toyoda 2008), the arts (Hamrick 1989; Moore 1994; Santi 2007; Turgeon 2000), and physical education (Daniel 1996). This work includes a variety of philosophical practices including problematizing concepts fundamental to the disciplines (e.g., bias, causation, community, discovery, evidence, health, infinity, life, measurement, model, number, objectivity, person, perspective, theory, and time); noting how the meanings of these concepts differ across subjects; inquiring into the epistemological foundations of the subjects and the aesthetic, ethical, and political dimensions of their applications in the world; and using the subjects as vehicles of conducting original ethical and political inquiry into local issues such as income inequality, pollution, and segregation.

Alongside its successes, philosophy for children has attracted overlapping and conflicting criticisms and roadblocks since its inception (Gregory 2011) from religious and social conservatives who believe that children should not question traditional values, from developmental psychologists who believe certain kinds of thinking are beyond children of certain ages, from philosophers who define their discipline as strictly theoretical and exegetical, from continental philosophers who see it as naïvely rationalist and vulgarly pragmatist, and from social justice theorists who see the program as politically neutral and therefore compliant with race-, class-, and gender-based oppression. In the United States and elsewhere, the program is also beset by the fact that philosophy is not a significant element in the national cultural heritage (in spite of there being notable philosophers throughout US history). That fact abets the deeper and wider—indeed global—problem that education is focused almost entirely on the economic goals of individual preparation for employment and national economic competition and growth (Nussbaum 2010). This problem largely accounts for the related phenomena of the crowded educational curriculum, high-stakes standardized testing, and the undermining of the humanities in lower and higher education in deference to STEM (science, technology, engineering, and mathematics) curriculum.

In spite of these struggles, philosophy for children continues to spread and diversify in almost every part of the world. It constitutes a global network of professors and graduate and undergraduate students in philosophy and education, school teachers and administrators, education policy-makers, publishers, parents, children, and teenagers. At the same time, there is a growing phenomenon of branding, with numerous individuals and organizations advertising unique approaches to philosophizing with children, in the marketplace of academic journals and conferences, contracts with schools, and curriculum sales. The diversity of approaches, aims, materials, and grounding theories of these constituents is, on the one hand, an important strength of the movement, as it provides opportunities for cross-disciplinary and cross-cultural critique and collaboration. On the other hand, it presents several challenges to the movement, including the difficulty of comparing the relative merits of different approaches. In fact, the movement's diversity signifies different understandings of philosophy, childhood, and education, which have become "essentially contested concepts" within the movement.[7] Philosophy for children is no longer unified by an identifiable theory, purpose, pedagogy, method, or curriculum but is now used to further a number of disparate educational agendas. In the next section, I employ Shaun Gallagher's (1992) heuristic of four schools of hermeneutics to help understand these competing agendas.

FOUR HERMENEUTICAL SCHOOLS OF PHILOSOPHY FOR CHILDREN

As Gallagher argues, teaching and learning are essentially interpretive processes. Teaching does not reproduce knowledge in students' minds but attempts to interpret it for them. Learning is not a straightforward appropriation of knowledge or skill but the reconstruction of new and old meanings into new understandings. Gallagher distinguishes four hermeneutical schools or approaches to the work of interpretation, including that of education: conservative, critical, radical, and moderate. Applying these hermeneutical approaches to theory and practice in philosophy for children helps to distinguish important differences in that field in relation to differences in educational agendas. In what follows, I will quote and cite the work of numerous scholars, but I do not mean to suggest that any of them belongs squarely within one of Gallagher's categories. Rather, I intend to demonstrate how those categories can help to interpret certain expressions and practices drawn from various sources in the philosophy for children movement, how they contend against each other, and what is at stake in that contention.

Conservative hermeneutics is the attempt to devise methods of interpretation that uncover and preserve truth or original meaning without distortion or bias. According to this approach, careful reading, thinking, discussion, and other means of interpretation both produce knowledge that is (close to) objectively true and preserve the truth of that knowledge and the meaning of texts and cultural practices over time. Such truth or meaning may be a matter of what the author of a text really meant, what rights are really guaranteed by a country's constitution, what the best science says about climate change, or what a religious text or ritual can tell us about what it means to be human. To be conservative about such truths and meanings is to hope to resist heresy, the degradation of standards, and the disruption of tradition. For conservative hermeneutics, the work of education is the reproduction or transmission of knowledge, values, and skills in ways that preserve their integrity. Conservative hermeneutics motivates attempts to control educational experience so that teachers only teach and students only learn a body of knowledge and skill that is unified and stable. Typically, the work of educating children is understood as simply conveying knowledge, elementary skills, and proper values and behavior, while the work of educating young adults is understood as also teaching methods of distinguishing truth from fallacy and knowledge from opinion.

Gallagher identifies two educational movements that, though often taken to be rivals, are in fact equally consonant with conservative hermeneutics: cultural literacy and critical thinking. The aims of cultural literacy are to make students literate in mathematics, science, history, literature, and the other disciplines and to socialize them into the cultural ways and values of a particular society that are taken to be objective or transcultural. Such literacy leads students to identify with one another as members of a common society, enables them to participate and negotiate their interests in the society as equal members with others, and ensures the continuation of particular bodies of knowledge, political institutions, cultural traditions, and other ideals and ways of life into the future.

One of the aims often purported for philosophy for children is consonant with cultural literacy: that young people appropriate the fundamental questions, ideas, and skills of (Western) philosophy as a resource for understanding the world and managing their own experience. Thus, Sharp (1992) refers to philosophy as part of the "birthright" of every person. This aim derives from the claims that aesthetics, epistemology, ethics, metaphysics, and politics are important dimensions of the meaning of human experience (Gregory 2008),[8] that inquiry into questions arising in each of these subdisciplines is important for understanding and directing our lives, and that (Western) philosophy interprets this meaning in a way that is, in some sense, objective and unbiased. One clear instance of philosophy for children as education for cultural literacy is Matthews' work recommending literature that brings important issues from the history of philosophy to children's attention. Another is the Lipman–Sharp curriculum, designed to "represent central themes from the history of philosophy ... translated into ordinary language" (Lipman 1988: 183). As Lipman explained, "Philosophy for Children does not attempt to invent a narrative version of the history of philosophy ... Instead, it depicts fictional children together engaged in dialogical inquiry with regard to the philosophical puzzlements they find themselves experiencing. In this sense, the novels provide the live children in the classroom with models of thinking children who readily lend themselves to emulation" (1994: 285). As Darryl De Marzio has argued, Lipman's novels not only present the reader with a model of how philosophical thinking works but also perform an "ascetic" function, "in which the reading subject becomes modified and transformed, appropriating that very mode of thinking into their own ... The philosophical text as a technology of the exercise of philosophical thinking ... is the true legacy of Lipman's philosophical novels" (2011: 46).

If cultural literacy is concerned with the reproduction of knowledge and value, critical thinking is concerned with the reproduction of skills. Gallagher's list of such skills will sound familiar to philosophy for children practitioners: "problem solving, evaluating arguments, weighing evidence, generalizing, using criteria, discerning and ranking alternatives, organizing and classifying data, recognizing fallacies, and so forth" (1992: 224). Conservative hermeneutics attributes to these skills a certain status and purpose: the conclusions they yield are taken to be valid, and the knowledge they produce is taken to be objective, at least in the sense of being (even relatively) ideologically neutral and free from bias. As Gallagher explains this view, "In thinking critically about a particular ideology, we operate not only outside of that ideology, but outside of any ideology, in a realm of pure, enlightened reason" (p. 226).

Given the historical coincidence of philosophy for children with the critical thinking movement in education, it is not surprising that some of the former's proponents have described its aims and methods in conservative hermeneutical terms, for instance, claiming that reasoning together in a community of philosophical inquiry is a way of being liberated from prejudice and approaching truth (Gardner 2015; Lipman 2003: 116–19; McCall 1989). True to his pragmatist roots, Lipman insisted that "in the long run, what makes good judgments good is their role in the shaping of *future* experience: they are judgments we can live with, the kind that enrich the lives we have yet to live" (2003: 23, emphasis in original). Nevertheless, his insistence that the kinds of thinking children are invited to practice while doing philosophy makes it more likely that their judgments will be good in this pragmatist sense is consonant with conservative hermeneutics.

Critical hermeneutics approaches interpretation—including teaching and learning—as a method of liberating the interpreter from the racist, sexist, homophobic, capitalist, religiously fanatical, and other kinds of ideologies that commonly distort our thinking, feeling, and behavior and facilitate our participation in oppressive systems of power. This approach derives from Marxist, feminist, critical, and queer theories and from liberation theology, which study oppression to find ways to struggle against it. Critical hermeneutics asserts that the production and consumption of meaning is "always already" distorted by oppressive ideologies, and so to read, write, teach, learn, or otherwise engage in interpretive communication in a noncritical way is to participate in and perpetuate unjust power relationships. The predominance of ideologically distorted meaning in culture and mass media and the social injustices that typify families, schools, workplaces, and public spaces call for suspicion, investigation, interrogation, and disruption to arrive at meaning that is ideology-free, and thereby, at human emancipation. For critical hermeneutics, education is an important mechanism of the reproduction of human oppression, especially along lines of race, class, and gender—a reproduction that utilizes both explicit and hidden curricula. However, it is possible to unmask and disrupt this phenomenon and to use education as a tool of emancipation by practicing "critical" or "social justice pedagogy" in ways that liberate students, teachers, and communities from false consciousness and enable more just, equitable, and ideologically undistorted relationships.

Scholars of philosophy for children are divided about its efficacy as critical pedagogy. Those who see a strong connection argue that the attributes of mutual criticism, inclusion, solidarity, self-regulation, and distributed power make the community of philosophical inquiry an ideal site for recognizing and overcoming ideology. Arie Kizel argues, for instance, that in the community of philosophical inquiry the "hegemonic meta-narrative of the mainstream society makes room for the identity of members of marginalised groups ... based on the recognition of diverse narratives within a web of communal narratives that does not favour the meta-narrative" (2016a: 16). In this regard, some scholars (Lipman 2011; Weber 2008; Weinstein 1991) have related the community of inquiry to Jürgen Habermas' notion of the ideal speech community. Others have argued that philosophy for children can and should directly engage children in social criticism. Thus, Sharp writes:

> Dialogical Inquiry is carried out by students who live and learn in a social environment. To educate children in such dialogical thinking is to plant the seeds of social criticism. Deliberating together about matters of justice, freedom, truth, and other ideals provides the raw material—the skills, dispositions, intellectual virtues, information, and procedures of deliberation—necessary to addressing the indifference toward injustice that is all around us ... [G]ood social criticism ... ought to be the outcome of living the life of the community of philosophical inquiry with one's peers and teachers over an extended period of time in one's formative years. (2009: 202)

Kizel (2015) offers the example that young people can develop "socio-philosophical sensitivity" by means of a philosophical community of inquiry focused on texts that raise themes such as poverty. There are also cases of children's communities of philosophical inquiry moving from dialogue into action in ways that are, at least potentially, politically significant (Kizel 2016b; Macht 2016). In fact, philosophy for children scholarship has contributed substantially to the literature on children's oppression and liberation (D. Kennedy 1998). Many see the program as a means of liberating children within the context of contemporary institutions and power structures by insisting on their inclusion in decision-making processes, by preparing them to think critically and creatively about complex issues involving ethical and political values, and by recognizing their right to many kinds of autonomy previously denied them. For these reasons, many have related philosophy for children to feminist education (Sharp 1994, 1997), social justice education (Glaser 2017), and education for global citizenship (Sharp 2006, 2007).

Philosophy for children has also been related to Paulo Freire's (1970) political analysis of human dialogue and his proposals for liberatory education in that philosophy for children promotes student engagement with genuine problems, replaces teacher monologue with classroom dialogue, and shares power among students and teachers (Accorinti 2002; Contreras and Fuenmayor 2007; Costello and Morehouse 2012). In fact, Freire and Lipman were aware of each other's work, and the two met in 1988 (Lipman 2008: 148). However, other Freirean scholars find philosophy for children politically ineffectual due to the limited role of students and teachers in co-constructing the curriculum and its lack of an explicit component of political critique and action (Kohan 2018). As Fuston (2017) explains, the very notion of what it means to think critically is different for Lipman, who understands it as a process of thinking aimed at reasonableness, and for Freire, who understands it as a process of political struggle aimed at justice.

More fundamentally, some scholars argue that the ubiquity of ideology in education makes it unlikely that philosophical dialogue alone will raise consciousness of oppression and that, because there is no such thing as politically neutral education, philosophy for children is actually complicit with neoliberalism and other oppressive ideologies. Walter O. Kohan laments, for example, that in the Lipman–Sharp curriculum "there are few obvious opportunities that give rise to questioning the ills of Capitalism or the potential clash between Capitalism and Democracy" (2018: 626). Darren Chetty (2018) argues that the way reasonableness is understood and practiced in philosophy for children is susceptible to racist assumptions and attitudes that are never recognized or problematized, resulting in a "gated" community of inquiry. And Gert Biesta (2017) criticizes philosophy for children as an instantiation of "learnification" that situates children as egotistical meaning-makers who learn the thinking skills requisite to adapt themselves to late global capitalism without critiquing it.

Radical hermeneutics suggests that there is no interpretive method for arriving at objective meaning since there is no such meaning to be sought. Every text (lesson, experience, cultural tradition, etc.) to be interpreted is essentially a set of signs held together in complex, dynamic relationships, which does not refer to any stable, underlying meaning such as an author's intent. Because every text is open to a plurality of meanings, the purpose of interpretation is not to constrain that plurality artificially but to play with the signs that constitute the text to achieve fresh insights. However, before such free play becomes possible it is necessary to diffuse the pseudo-authority of the text—its pretense to unity or to being controlled by underlying meaning—by means of deconstructionist techniques. As Paul Ricoeur observed (quoted in Gallagher 1992: 21), this approach employs a "hermeneutics of suspicion" about claims to truth, meaning, or consensus, in contrast to the "hermeneutics of trust" employed by other methods of interpretation. As Gallagher notes, "The hope is not to establish some other version of the world as the proper or correct version, but to show that all versions are contingent and relative" (1992: 11).

Radical hermeneutics critiques education that tries to be "instrumental"—to fit students into the global market economy, to make them good citizens, to use them to continue academic disciplines and cultural traditions into the future, or even to free them from predetermined oppressive ideologies. Instead, it seeks to transform education into an experience of un-learning and un-programmed exploration and play, with constant vigilance against the normalizing or standardizing of anything that might result from that play or of any teaching strategy into a discipline. In Gallagher's words, "the objective would be to keep questions open, to keep students thinking in a critical fashion, to keep the play of heterogeneous meaning alive" (1992: 301).

A radical hermeneutical strand is identifiable in the philosophy for children literature when scholars resist the idea that the aim of philosophical dialogue is to find consensus or to narrow down on the most reasonable conclusions. For example, Berrie Heesen laments that "[t]he partisanship for reason and rationality observed in the philosophy for children movement is exactly the enlightenment rationality criticized by postmodernism. Some of the practitioners of philosophy for children still seem to cling to the view of a rational being and an education for rationality once defended by Kant" (1991: 25). David Kennedy argues that "[e]xtending epistemic privilege to the child involves bracketing adult epistemological norms" (1998: 35).[9] Similarly, he (Kennedy 1995) and Kohan criticize Matthews for proposing "to include children in the rational world of adults without questioning its hegemonic knowledge, values, and practices. This approach tends to legitimate the actual dominant form of rationality and to close off space for any eventual alternative world" (Kohan 1999: 4). Nancy Vansieleghem, citing Mikhail Bakhtin's notion of "monologisation," goes so far as to argue that "[t]he community of inquiry turns the dialogue into an argumentative game," producing a scenario of "totalitarianism and oppression [in which] neither the voice of the self, nor that of the other is heard" (2006: 180).

As an alternative to critical reasoning, Vansieleghem, drawing on Jacques Rancière, proposes a form of dialogue in which one listens without the intent of understanding the other but of discovering new possibilities of meaning for oneself. "[T]he words [of the other] are not meant to communicate or to inform but to experience what we [have] at stake in these words" (Vansieleghem 2006: 188). "To be clear," she explains, "the dialogue fulfils nothing: it cuts, it breaks, ... it presents its unfulfillment" (p. 187). Citing Giorgio Agamben's work on speech and infancy, Igor Jasinski and Tyson Lewis propose, similarly, a practice they call "a community of infancy (as the ... profane alternative to community of inquiry). Such a community is not a community that operates according to predefined rules of logical engagement or standardised assessment protocols but rather is an inoperative community that is defined by letting ends idle" (2016: 540). In a community of infancy, students may be given to "babble" or engage in "glossolalia," forms of speech in which "language appears as a pure potentiality to mean without meaning anything in particular" (p. 542). To cultivate this possibility, Jasinski and Lewis recommend that the teacher resist the urge to "intervene to ensure the movement toward increasingly reasonable speech," and "just listen and let the conversation take its course, delight in the students' brilliantly unreasonable ways of tackling philosophical ideas" (p. 547).

Importantly, although scholars working in the radical hermeneutic tradition use words like "freedom" and "oppression," they are not addressing issues of social justice such as poverty, white supremacy, misogyny, homophobia, or even (ironically) ageism. In fact, radical hermeneutics repudiates the claim that critical hermeneutics can identify a meaning of justice stable enough to form the basis of political critique. Rather, these scholars refer to freedom as release from the oppression of having one's perspectives informed by one's participation in a particular culture and language. Thus, Kohan (2014) describes philosophy as a process of becoming uncultured and unlearned.

Another strand of radical hermeneutics in philosophy for children is the way some scholars have linked it to European scholarship that takes up the concept of childhood in ways not directly related to children. Kohan (2014), for instance, writes of childhood as an experience of nonlinear time characterized by the kind of attention given in play and art making and hopes that philosophy for children will become a medium for this kind of experience. Kennedy writes of how the adult may be transformed by "[a]wakening to the voice of the child" and thereby "becoming conscious of the boundaries of instinct and repression which were a result of his own childhood formation" (1998: 34). Karin Murris (2016) likewise affirms childhood as a form of post-human subjectivity that transgresses the linguistic, representational, and anthropocentric binaries of Western culture. Reflecting on these developments, Kennedy and Balher describe childhood as a signifier without determinate meaning such that "we can no longer speak about anything but a variety of childhoods, all determined by socio-cultural constraints" (2017: xii).

FIGURE 6.2 Discussing a philosophical fairy tale. *Source*: Ridofranz / iStock

Following Gadamer, moderate hermeneutics holds that the work of interpretation is the attempt to reach meaning, truth, or shared understanding in a process that is modeled on conversation or dialogue between the familiar and the strange. Interpretation is the attempt to appropriate the unfamiliar into the familiar with the expectation that both will be transformed. The moderate hermeneutical aim of education is to invite students to expand their horizons of knowledge, skill, and value by confronting and attempting to accommodate novel objects of interpretation with the understanding that this process will necessarily result in the transformation of the teacher's and the student's prior horizons and of the meaning of the object of interpretation. In interpreting a text for their students by relating it to something already familiar to them, teachers necessarily reinterpret the text for themselves and expand its meaning. And to learn something new, the student must make a series of adjustments between familiar context and unfamiliar object until the two fit together.

At least four strands of argument relate philosophy for children to the educational aims of moderate hermeneutics. The first is that the manner in which canonical philosophical issues and positions are introduced to children invites dialogue between the philosophical tradition and children's own lives and experiences. This aim is motivated by the assumptions that philosophical traditions can still give meaning to (young) people's lives and that those traditions must be continually reinterpreted to survive and flourish. For instance, Lipman (1988: 5) wrote of philosophy for children as a way of initiating children into the disciplinary language of philosophy as part of "the conversation of mankind" as conceived by Michael Oakeshott. Glaser and Gregory, however, see the community of philosophical inquiry as a method of making that disciplinary "'vertical conversation' across successive generations of inquirers" intersect with the "'horizontal conversation' among peers who seek to interpret their tradition in light of contemporary vocabularies and concerns" (2017: 182).

A second moderate hermeneutical strand of argument is that philosophy for children is an appropriate approach to religious education that has the dual aim of informing new generations with traditional religious meaning and of allowing that meaning to be reinterpreted by successive generations (Glaser and Gregory 2016; Gregory and Oliverio 2018). A third strand sees the community of inquiry as an ideal mechanism for intercultural dialogue (Camhy 2008). Thus, Glasser (1998) and Sharp (2007) relate the practice to Hannah Arendt's metaphor of "going visiting" into the perspectives of others whose knowledge and interests are different enough from one's own to enable one to question and reconstruct one's own horizons. A fourth strand sees the practice of reasoning in philosophy for children not as a method for uncovering truth or preserving cultural meanings intact but, following Dewey, as a method for collaborative inquiry that facilitates mutual understanding, intelligent experimentation, and democratic consensus:

> Participants come to regard the production of knowledge as contingent, bound up with human interests and activities and therefore always open to revision. Further, students become more tolerant of complexity and ambiguity and recognize that justification for belief is rooted in *human action* ... Ultimately this capacity to judge is based on *communal civic sense* that is necessary for making moral and political judgments. Such judgments are intersubjective and appeal to and require testing against the opinions of other judging persons. (Sharp 1991: 32, emphasis in original)

CONCLUSION

Fifty-odd years since its inception, philosophy for children has deepened and diversified, both theoretically and as a field of practice. Perhaps the only point of agreement among (almost) everyone in the movement is that children's philosophical thinking, variously understood, is necessary for the realization of the intellectual, moral, and political agency the movement attributes to them. Scholars and practitioners today are committed to inflections of philosophy for children that make it compatible with—even essential for—divergent philosophies of education consonant with conservative, moderate, critical, or radical hermeneutics. Clearly, some of these inflections are compatible with others, at least at the level of practice. But theoretically they are difficult to reconcile. Should children be treated as fledgling philosopher-citizens in need of skills training and democratic enculturation or as prophets and agents of cultural deconstruction? Should children be invited to practice philosophy as disciplined, open-ended inquiry into the meaning of experience, as an exercise in political consciousness raising, or as an incursion against Enlightenment rationality? Such disagreements are not merely academic. The deep differences they reflect in the meanings of childhood, education, and philosophy are manifest—daily and in nearly every part of the world—in divergent classroom practices, educational policy disputes, and small- and large-scale research studies. In becoming a site for the enactment of such divergent philosophies of education, philosophy for children has also become a necessary site for their study.

NOTES

1   Matthew Lipman coined the phrase "philosophy for children" to refer to both the notion of engaging children and teenagers in philosophical inquiry and (when capitalized) to the program he and Ann Margaret Sharp created for doing so. Today the phrase is used more or less interchangeably with phrases such as "philosophy with children" and "philosophy in schools" to refer to many different programs

and approaches to this work. I will use "philosophy for children" to refer to the movement that includes all such programs and approaches, including professional development and scholarship.

2   The column is now a weblog with a complete archive at https://www.montclair.edu/iapc/thinking-in-stories/.

3   The curriculum was cowritten by Matthews, Amherst Public Schools consultant Shari Tishman, and University of Massachusetts doctoral student Lenore Carlisle Reilly, who is currently Secretary of the College and Assistant Professor of Education at Mount Holyoke College. The curriculum is available at https://www.montclair.edu/iapc/wise-owl/.

4   "The hypothesis would be that, with the help of a specially prepared curriculum and specially trained teachers, children could be induced to engage credibly in creative philosophical behavior" (Lipman 1988: 182).

5   Lipman's first wife, Wynonna Lipman (1923–99), was the first African American woman to be elected to the New Jersey Senate, in 1971. She served for twenty-seven years, making history as the longest-serving member of the state senate.

6   The umbrella network for these organizations is the International Council of Philosophical Inquiry with Children (www.icpic.org), founded in 1985, in Denmark.

7   For W.B. Gallie (1968), essentially contested concepts refer to normative practices that are internally complex. Gregory and Laverty (2018) apply this notion to Philosophy for Children.

8   Matthews (2009) underwrites this claim when he draws parallels between children's questions and insights to those found in the philosophical canon.

9   On the other hand, Kennedy (1994) recognizes that certain logical structures are part of natural language, an important medium of adult–child dialogue.

REFERENCES

Primary sources

Buchler, Justus (1954), "What Is a Discussion?," *Journal of General Education*, 8 (1): 7–17. (Reprinted with edits by Matthew Lipman [1979], *Thinking: The Journal of Philosophy for Children*, 1 [1]: 49–54.)

Lipman, Matthew (1978), "Can Philosophy for Children be the Basis of Educational Redesign?," *The Social Studies*, 69 (6): 253–7.

Lipman, Matthew (1981), "What Is Different about the Education of the Gifted?," *Roeper Review*, 4 (1): 19–20.

Lipman, Matthew (1985), "Philosophical Practice and Educational Reform," *Journal of Thought*, 20 (4): 20–36.

Lipman, Matthew (1987), *Harry Prime*, Montclair, NJ: IAPC.

Lipman, Matthew (1988), *Philosophy Goes to School*, Philadelphia: Temple University Press.

Lipman, Matthew (1989), "The Community of Inquiry in the Teaching of Adults," Address to the Quebec Society for Philosophy, May 15, Montreal, Canada.

Lipman, Matthew (1993), "Philosophy for Children and Critical Thinking," in Matthew Lipman (ed.), *Thinking, Children and Education*, 682–4, Dubuque, IA: Kendall/Hunt Publishing.

Lipman, Matthew (1994), "Do Elementary School Children Need Philosophy?" Kasvatus: *The Finnish Journal of Education*, 3: 281–286.

Lipman, Matthew (1997), "Education for Democracy and Freedom," *Wesleyan Graduate Review*, 1 (1): 32–8.

Lipman, Matthew (1998), "The Contributions of Philosophy to Deliberative Democracy," in David Owens and Ioanna Kucuradi (eds.), *Teaching Philosophy on the Eve of the Twenty First Century*, 6–29, Ankara: International Federation of Philosophical Societies.

Lipman, Matthew (2003), *Thinking in Education*, 2nd edn., New York: Cambridge University Press.

Lipman, Matthew (2008), *A Life Teaching Thinking*, Montclair, NJ: Institute for the Advancement of Philosophy for Children.

Lipman, Matthew (2011), "Philosophy for Children: Some Assumptions and Implications," *Ethics in Progress*, 2 (1): 3–16.

Matthews, Gareth B. (1976), "Philosophy and Children's Literature," *Metaphilosophy*, 7 (1): 7–16.

Matthews, Gareth B. (1980), *Philosophy and the Young Child*, Cambridge, MA: Harvard University Press.

Matthews, Gareth B. (1985), "The Idea of Conceptual Development in Piaget," *Synthese*, 65 (1): 87–97.

Matthews, Gareth B. (1987), "Concept Formation and Moral Development," in J. Russell (ed.), *Philosophical Perspectives on Developmental Psychology*, 175–190, Oxford: Basil Blackwell.

Matthews, Gareth B. (1994), *The Philosophy of Childhood*, Cambridge, MA: Harvard University Press.

Matthews, Gareth B. (1998), "Socrates' Children," in Susan M. Turner and Gareth B. Matthews (eds.), *The Philosopher's Child: Critical Perspectives in the Western Tradition*, 11–18, Rochester, NY: University of Rochester Press.

Matthews, Gareth B. (2002), "Philosophy of Childhood," in Edward N. Zalta (ed.), *The Stanford Encyclopedia of Philosophy*. Available online: https://plato.stanford. edu/archives/fall2002/entries/childhood/02.12.2019.

Matthews, Gareth B. (2006), *A Philosophy of Childhood*, Monograph presented at the Poynter Center Interdisciplinary Fellows Program, "The Ethics and Politics of Childhood," Bloomington: Indiana University Press.

Matthews, Gareth B. (2008) "Getting Beyond the Deficit Conception of Cchildhood: Thinking Philosophically with Children," in Michael Hand and Carrie Winstanley (eds.), *Philosophy in Schools*, 27–40, London: Continuum.

Matthews, Gareth B. (2009), "Holiness," in Eva Marsal, Takara Dobashi, and Barbara Weber (eds.), *Children Philosophize Worldwide: Theoretical and Practical Concepts*, 241–6, New York: Peter Lang.

Matthews, Gareth B. (2017), "Doing Philosophy with Children Rejects Piaget's Assumptions," in Saeed Naji and Rosnani Hashim (eds.), *History, Theory and Practice of Philosophy for Children: International Perspectives*, 53–5, London: Routledge.

Matthews, Gareth B., Lenore Carlisle, and Shari Tishman (1987), "Teacher's Guide: *Albert's Tooth* by Barbara Williams," Littleton, MA: Sundance Publishers & Distributors.

Sharp, Ann Margaret (1983), "Education: A Philosophical Journey," *Formative Spirituality*, 4 (3): 351–66.

Sharp, Ann Margaret (1991), *"The Community of Inquiry: Education for Democracy,"* *Thinking: The Journal of Philosophy for Children*, (2): 31–37.

Sharp, Ann Margaret (1992), "Women, Children, and the Evolution of Philosophy," in Ann Margaret Sharp and Ronald F. Reed (eds.), *Studies in Philosophy for Children: Harry Stottlemeier's Discovery*, 74–87, Philadelphia: Temple University Press.

Sharp, Ann Margaret (2006), "Doing Philosophy in a Global Society," in Daniela G. Camhy and Rainer Born (eds.), *Encouraging Philosophical Thinking: Proceedings of the International Conference on Philosophy for Children. Conceptus – Studien* 17, 9–16, Sankt Augustin: Academia Verlag.

Sharp, Ann Margaret (2007), "Let's Go Visiting: Learning Judgment-Making in a Classroom Community of Inquiry," *Gifted Education International*, 23 (3): 301–12.

Sharp, Ann Margaret (2009), "The Child as Critic," in Eva Marsal, Takara Dobashi, and Barbara Weber (eds.), *Children Philosophize Worldwide*, 201–08, New York: Peter Lang.

Sharp, Ann Margaret, ed. (1994), "Women, Feminism and Philosophy for Children," special double issue of *Thinking: The Journal of Philosophy for Children*, 11 (3–4).

Sharp, Ann Margaret, ed. (1997), "Women, Feminism and Philosophy for Children," special issue of *Thinking: The Journal of Philosophy for Children*, 13 (1).

Secondary sources

Accorinti, Stella (2002), "Matthew Lipman y Paulo Freire: Conceptos para la libertad," *Utopía y Praxis Latinoamericana*, 7 (18): 35–56.

Biesta, Gert J.J. (2017), "Touching the Soul? Exploring an Alternative Outlook for Philosophical Work with Children and Young People," *Childhood and Philosophy*, 13 (28): 415–52.

Burgh, Gilbert (2018), "The Need for Philosophy in Promoting Democracy: A Case for Philosophy in the Curriculum," *Journal of Philosophy in Schools*, 5 (1): 38–58.

Burgh, Gilbert, Terri Field, and Mark Freakley (2006), *Ethics and the Community of Inquiry: Education for Deliberative Democracy*, 2nd edn., Melbourne: Thomson Social Science Press.

Cam, Philip (2006), "Philosophy and the School Curriculum: Some General Remarks," *Critical and Creative Thinking*, 14 (1): 35–51.

Camhy, Daniela G. (2008), "Developing an International Community of Inquiry," *Proceedings of the XXII World Congress of Philosophy*, 27: 15–22.

Chetty, Darren (2018), "Racism As 'Reasonableness': Philosophy for Children and the Gated Community of Inquiry," *Ethics and Education*, 13 (1): 39–54.

Contreras, Reyber Parra and Jesús Medina Fuenmayor (2007), "La comunidad de investigación y la formación de ciudadanos: Consideraciones a partir del pensamiento de Matthew Lipman y Paulo Freire," *Telos*, 9. Available online: http://www.redalyc.org/articulo.oa?id=99314566006.

Costello, Patrick and Richard Morehouse (2012), "Liberation Philosophy and the Development of Communities of Inquiry: A Critical Evaluation," *Analytic Teaching and Philosophical Praxis*, 33 (2): 1–7.

Daniel, Marie-France (1989), "Illiterate Adults and Philosophy for Children," *Analytic Teaching*, 9 (2): 76–82.

Daniel, Marie-France (1996), "Teaching Training in Physical Education: Towards a Rationale for a Socio-constructivist Approach," *Analytic Teaching*, 16 (2): 90–101.

de la Garza, Maria Teresa, Christina Slade, and Marie-France Daniel (2000), "Philosophy of Mathematics in the Classroom," *Analytic Teaching*, 20 (2): 88–104.

De Marzio, Darryl (2011), "What Happens in Philosophical Texts: Matthew Lipman's Theory and Practice of the Philosophical Text as Model," *Childhood and Philosophy*, 7 (13): 29–47.

Freire, Paulo (1970), *Pedagogy of the Oppressed*, New York: Bloomsbury Academic.

Fuston, James (2017), "Toward a Critical Philosophy for Children," *PSU McNair Scholars Online Journal* 11 (1): Article 4, retrieved 16 November 2020 from https://pdxscholar.library.pdx.edu/mcnair/vol11/iss1/4/.

Gallagher, Shaun (1992), *Hermeneutics and Education*, New York: State University of New York Press.

Gallie, W.B. (1968), *Philosophy and the Historical Understanding*, New York: Schocken Books.

Gardner, Howard (2006), *Multiple Intelligences: New Horizons*, New York: Basic Books.

Gardner, Susan T. (2015), "Selling 'The Reason Game'," *Teaching Ethics*, 15 (1): 129–36.

Glaser, Jennifer (1998), "Thinking Together: Arendt's Visiting Imagination and Nussbaum's Judicial Spectatorship as Models for a Community of Inquiry," *Thinking: The Journal of Philosophy for Children*, 14 (1): 17–24.

Glaser, Jennifer (2017), "Social-Political Dimensions of the Community of Philosophical Inquiry in an Age of Globalization," in Maughn Rollins Gregory and Megan Jane Laverty (eds.), *In Community of Inquiry with Ann Margaret Sharp: Childhood, Philosophy and Education*, 217–29, New York: Routledge.

Glaser, Jennifer and Maughn Rollins Gregory (2016), "Education, Identity Construction and Cultural Renewal: The Case of Philosophical Inquiry with Jewish Bible," in Maughn Rollins Gregory, Joanna Haynes, and Karin Murris, (eds.), *The Routledge International Handbook of Philosophy for Children*, 180–8, New York: Taylor & Francis.

Golding, Clinton, David Gurr, and Lynne Hinton (2012), "Leadership for Creating a Thinking School at Buranda State School," *Leading and Managing: Journal of the Australian Council for Educational Leaders*, 18 (1): 91–106.

Gomez, Manuela and Irene de Puig (2003), "Ecodialogo: Environmental Education and Philosophical Dialogue," *Thinking: The Journal of Philosophy for Children*, 16 (4): 37–40.

Gorard, Stephan, Nadia Siddiqui, and Beng Huat See (2015), *Philosophy for Children: Evaluation Report and Executive Summary*, London: Education Endowment Foundation.

Gregory, Maughn Rollins (2004), "Practicing Democracy: Social Intelligence and Philosophical Practice," *International Journal of Applied Philosophy*, 18 (2): 161–74.

Gregory, Maughn Rollins (2008), "Philosophy in Schools: Ideals, Challenges and Opportunities," *Critical and Creative Thinking: The Australasian Journal of Philosophy in Schools*, 16 (1): 5–22.

Gregory, Maughn Rollins (2011), "Philosophy for Children and Its Critics: A Mendham Dialogue," *Journal of Philosophy of Education*, 45 (2): 199–219.

Gregory, Maughn Rollins, Joanna Haynes, and Karin Murris, eds. (2017), *The Routledge International Handbook of Philosophy for Children*, New York: Routledge.

Gregory, Maughn Rollins and Megan Jane Laverty (2009), "Philosophy and Education for Wisdom," in A. Kenkmann (ed.), *Teaching Philosophy*, 155–73, London: Continuum International.

Gregory, Maughn Rollins and Megan Jane Laverty (2018), "Philosophy for Children Founders: Series Introduction," in Maughn Rollins Gregory and Megan Jane Laverty (eds.), *In Community of Inquiry with Ann Margaret Sharp: Childhood, Philosophy and Education*, xiv–xv, New York: Routledge.

Gregory, Maughn Rollins and Stefano Oliverio (2018), "Philosophy for/with Children, Religious Education and Education for Spirituality: Steps Toward a Review of the Literature," in Ellen Duthie, Félix García Moriyón, and Rafael Robles Loro (eds.), *Parecidos de familia: Propuestas actuales en Filosofía para Niños / Family resemblances: Current proposals in Philosophy for Children*, 279–96, Madrid: Anaya.

Hamrick, William S. (1989), "Philosophy for Children and Aesthetic Education," *Journal of Aesthetic Education*, 23 (2): 55.

Hannam, Patricia (2012), "The Community of Philosophical Inquiry in Religious Education in Secular School: Supporting the Task of Building Religious Understanding in the 21st Century," in Marina Santi and Stefano Oliverio (eds.), *Educating for Complex Thinking through Philosophical Inquiry: Models, Advances and Proposals for the New Millennium*, 209–29, Naples: Liguori.

Haynes, Joanna and Karin Murris (2012), *Picturebooks, Pedagogy and Philosophy*, New York: Routledge.

Heesen, Berrie (1991), "Philosophy for Children Under Postmodern Conditions: Four Remarks in Response to Lardner," *Analytic Teaching and Philosophical Praxis*, 12 (2): 23–8.

Jasinski, Igor and Tyson E. Lewis (2016), "Community of Infancy: Suspending the Sovereignty of the Teacher's Voice," *Journal of Philosophy of Education*, 50 (4): 538–53.

Jenkinsa, Philip and Sue Lyle (2010), Enacting Dialogue: The Impact of Promoting Philosophy for Children on the Literate Thinking of Identified Poor Readers, Aged 10," *Language and Education*, 24 (6): 459–472.

Johnson, Tony W. (1984) *Philosophy for Children: An Approach to Critical Thinking*. Bloomington, IN: Phi Delta Kappa Educational Foundation. Retrieved 16 November 2020 from https://files.eric.ed.gov/fulltext/ED242629.pdf

Kennedy, David (1994), "Helping Children Develop the Skills & Dispositions of Critical, Creative & Caring Thinking," *Analytic Teaching*, 15 (1): 3–16.

Kennedy, David (1995), "Review of Gareth Matthews' *The Philosophy of Childhood*," *Thinking: The Journal of Philosophy for Children*, 12 (2): 41–4.

Kennedy, David (1998), "Reconstructing Childhood," *Thinking: The Journal of Philosophy for Children*, 14 (1): 29–37.

Kennedy, Nadia Stoyanova (2012), "Lipman, Dewey, and Philosophical Inquiry in the Mathematics Classroom," *Education and Culture*, 28 (2): 81–94.

Kennedy, David and Brock Balher (2017) Â *Philosophy of Childhood Today: Exploring the Boundaries*. New York: Lexington Books.

Kizel, Arie (2015), "Philosophy with Children, the Poverty Line, and Socio-Philosophic Sensitivity," *Childhood and Philosophy*, 11 (21): 139–62.

Kizel, Arie (2016a), "Enabling Identity: The Challenge of Presenting the Silenced Voices of Repressed Groups in Philosophic Communities of Inquiry," *Journal of Philosophy in Schools*, 3 (1): 16–39.

Kizel, Arie (2016b), "From Laboratory to Praxis: Communities of Philosophical Inquiry as a Model of (and for) Social Activism," *Childhood and Philosophy*, 12 (25): 497–517.

Kizel, Arie (2016c), "Philosophy with Children as an Educational Platform for Self-Determined Learning," *Cogent Education*, 3 (1). https://doi.org/10.1080/2331186X.2016.1244026.

Knight, Sue and Carol Collins (2000), "The Curriculum Transformed: Philosophy Embedded in the Curriculum Areas," *Critical and Creative Thinking*, 8 (1): 8–14.

Kohan, Walter O. (1999), "What Can Philosophy and Children Offer Each Other?," *Thinking: The Journal of Philosophy for Children*, 14 (4): 2–8.

Kohan, Walter O. (2014), *Philosophy and Childhood*, New York: Palgrave.

Kohan, Walter O. (2018), "Paulo Freire and Philosophy for Children: A Critical Dialogue," *Studies in Philosophy and Education*, 37: 615–629.

Kohan, Walter O. and Jason Wozniak (2009), "Philosophy as Spiritual and Political Exercise in an Adult Literacy Course," *Thinking: The Journal of Philosophy for Children*, 19 (4): 17–23.

Lee, Karen J. (1986), "Doing *Mark* in a Juvenile Correctional Facility," *Thinking: The Journal of Philosophy for Children*, 6 (3): 9–16.

Macht, Katrina G. (2016), "Roots and Shoots Remembered: A Qualitative Study of the Influence of Childhood Place-based Experiences on the Lives of Young Adults," EdD dissertation, Montclair State University.

McCall, Catherine C. (1989), "Functions of Training in Philosophy for Children," *Analytic Teaching and Philosophical Praxis*, 10 (2): 15–21.

Mizell, Karen (2015), "Philosophy for Children, Community of Inquiry, and Human Rights Education," *Childhood and Philosophy*, 11 (22): 319–28.

Moore, Ronald (1994), "Aesthetics for Young People: Problems and Prospects," *Journal of Aesthetic Education*, 28 (3): 5–18.

Moura Ferreira, Louise Brandes (2012), "Philosophy for Children in Science Class," *Thinking: The Journal of Philosophy for Children*, 20 (1–2): 73–81.

Murris, Karin (2014), "Philosophy with Children as Part of the Solution to the Early Literacy Education Crisis in South Africa," *European Early Childhood Education Research Journal*, 2014: 1–16.

Murris, Karin (2016) *The Posthuman Child: Educational Transformation Through Philosophy with Picturebooks*. London: Taylor & Francis.

Nussbaum, Martha C. (2010), *Not for Profit: Why Democracy Needs the Humanities*, Princeton, NJ: Princeton University Press.

Oliverio, Stefano (2018), "The Teacher As Liberator: Ann Margaret Sharp Between Philosophy of Education and Teacher Education," in Maughn Rollins Gregory and Megan Jane Laverty (eds.), *In Community of Inquiry with Ann Margaret Sharp: Childhood, Philosophy and Education*, 63–75, New York: Routledge.

Santi, Marina (2007), "How Students Understand Art: A Change in Children through Philosophy," *Childhood and Philosophy*, 3 (5): 19–33.

Simon, Charlann (1979), "Philosophy for Students with Learning Disabilities," *Thinking: The Journal of Philosophy for Children*, 1 (1): 21–33.

Shea, Peter (2017), "Do We Put What Is Precious at Risk through Philosophic Conversation?," in Maughn Rollins Gregory and Megan Jane Laverty (eds.), *In Community of Inquiry with Ann Margaret Sharp: Childhood, Philosophy and Education*, 161–73, New York: Routledge.

Soter, Anna O., Ian A. Wilkinson, P. Karen Murphy, Lucila Rudge, Kristen Reninger, and Margaret Edwards (2008), "What the Discourse Tells Us: Talk and Indicators of High-Level Comprehension," *International Journal of Educational Research*, 47 (6): 372–91.

Splitter, Laurance J. (2006), "Philosophy in a Crowded Curriculum," *Critical and Creative Thinking*, 14 (2): 4–14.

Splitter, Laurance J. (2007), "Delving Ever Deeper: Gifted Students and Philosophy," *Gifted Education International*, 22 (2–3): 207–17.

Sprod, Tim (1993), *Books into Ideas*, Cheltenham, VIC: Hawker Brownlow.

Sprod, Tim (2001), *Philosophical Discussion in Moral Education: The Community of Ethical Inquiry*, Routledge: London.

Sprod, Tim (2014), "Philosophical Inquiry and Critical Thinking in Primary and Secondary Science Education," in Michael R. Matthews (ed.), *International Handbook of Research in History, Philosophy and Science Teaching*, 1531–64, Dordrecht: Springer.

Sternberg, Robert J. (2003), *Wisdom, Intelligence, and Creativity Synthesized*, New York: Cambridge University Press.

Thomas-Williams, Junnine and Sue Lyle (2012)," Dialogic Practice in Primary Schools: How Primary Head Teachers Plan to Embed Philosophy for Children into the Whole School: Education Studies," *Educational Studies*, 38 (1): 1–12.

Topping, K.J. and S. Trickey (2007a), "Collaborative Philosophical Enquiry for School Children: Cognitive Effects at 10–12 Years," *British Journal of Educational Psychology*, 77: 271–88.

Topping, K.J. and S. Trickey (2007b), "Collaborative Philosophical Inquiry for School-Children: Cognitive Gains at 2-Year Follow-up," *British Journal of Educational Psychology*, 77: 787–96.

Toyoda, Mitsuyo (2008), "Applying Philosophy for Children to Workshop-Style Environmental Education," *Proceedings of the Xxii World Congress of Philosophy*, 27: 101–9.

Turgeon, Wendy (2000), "The Mirror of Aesthetic Education: Philosophy Looks at Art and Art at Philosophy," *Thinking: The Journal of Philosophy for Children*, 15 (2): 21–31.

UNESCO (United Nations Educational, Scientific, and Cultural Organization) (1953), *The Teaching of Philosophy: An International Enquiry of UNESCO*, Paris: UNESCO.

UNESCO (United Nations Educational, Scientific, and Cultural Organization) (2007), *Philosophy: A School of Freedom: Teaching Philosophy and Learning to Philosophize: Status and Prospects*, Paris: UNESCO Publishing.

Vansieleghem, Nancy (2006), "Listening to Dialogue," *Studies in Philosophy and Education*, 25: 175–90.

Wartenberg, Thomas E. (2009), *Big Ideas for Little Kids: Teaching Philosophy Through Children's Literature*, Lanham, MD: Rowan & Littlefield Education.

Weber, Barbara (2008), "J. Habermas and the Art of Dialogue: The Practicability of the Ideal Speech Situation," *Analytic Teaching and Philosophical Praxis*, 28 (1): 1–8.

Weinstein, Mark (1987), "Extending Philosophy for Children into the Standard Curriculum," *Analytic Teaching and Philosophical Praxis*, 8 (2): 19–31.

Weinstein, Mark (1991), *Critical Thinking and Education for Democracy* (Resource Publication Series 4, No. 2), Montclair, NJ: Montclair State College Institute for Critical Thinking.

Yeazell, Mary I. (1982), "Improving Reading Comprehension through Philosophy for Children," *Reading Psychology*, 3 (3): 239–46.

CHAPTER SEVEN

"Teachers, Leave Them Kids Alone!": Derrida, Agamben, and the Late Modern Crisis of Pedagogical Narrative

AGATA BIELIK-ROBSON

INTRODUCTION

In this chapter, I focus on two very different philosophies of education, which arise from the thought of the two great rivals of late modernity: Jacques Derrida and Giorgio Agamben. By locating them on the larger map of contemporary humanities, I present Derrida's deconstruction as the last and most sophisticated variant of the Kantian Enlightenment, and Agamben's critical form of messianism as the rejection of Enlightenment pedagogy, which is grounded in the teachings of Jean-Jacques Rousseau.[1]

My aim is to interpret this debate as an abstract mirror of the concrete social processes that nowadays affect our attitude to education in general by putting in doubt its very purposefulness. The title deriving from the well-known song of Pink Floyd's *The Wall*, "Another Brick in the Wall, Part 2," signals that the popular culture of late modernity leans toward Rousseau's primacy

FIGURE 7.1 Berlin Wall. *Source*: NatalyaLucia / iStock.

of the natural life-world against the alienated artifice of educated culture, a tendency that Derrida attempts to counteract but that Agamben endorses. In the conclusion, however, I also suggest a space for their potential collaboration, aiming at a new philosophy of education that is "closer to life."

LIFE AGAINST THE MACHINE: ROUSSEAU VERSUS KANT

The clash between Derrida and Agamben reflects what Jürgen Habermas rightly diagnosed as the "legitimation crisis" of modern Enlightenment: "the incomplete project of modernity," which, questioned from the moment of its inception, fell completely out of grace due to the postmodern critique of "grand narratives" (1985: 3–15). Kant's verdict, with which he concludes his famous essay—"Do we live at present in an enlightened age? The answer is: No, but in an age of enlightenment" (1784/2001: 140)—has indeed been interpreted by the postmodernists as a *sentence*: if, after more than two centuries of molding the social practice of the West, the Enlightenment still did not produce a fully "enlightened age," then the project itself must be inherently flawed and, because of that, abandoned. This is certainly true for Agamben, the follower of Rousseau, for whom the only way out from this incipiently incomplete project is to acknowledge its failure. For Derrida, however, who at least in this context can be seen as the follower of Kant (as well as an ally of Habermas, though not without reservations),[2] the incompleteness of the project of modernity does not necessarily spell a fault or failure; just as Kant saw the enlightened age of "perpetual peace" in terms of regulative idea, Derrida also proposes to accept the forever asymptotic incompleteness of the ideal as a normal condition of deconstruction, which can never rest on laurels and lose its ethical vigilance. Derrida, who believes in the Enlightenment as an ongoing reconstruction of every aspect of social life, a reconstruction based on the education of mankind, refuses to see the future-oriented incompleteness of the task as an excuse to desist from it—which is precisely the move proposed by Agamben, for whom Kant's verdict announces the ultimate doom of the project that, never to be realized in concrete living "here and now," in this manner only proves its infeasibility.

This opposition has a deeper dimension that reveals an even more fundamental difference between Derrida's and Agamben's respective understanding of the *messianic* mission in all its modern/secular avatars, the problem of education included. While for the former the messianic fulfillment is always *deferred* to the future, with the present remaining determined by the task of the ethical de/re/construction of our living conditions, for the latter such *deference* can only mean that our life here and now stays unfulfilled as a "life in deferral" (*Leben im Aufschub*), a term with which Gershom Scholem describes an unhappy existential condition of life still waiting for its redemptive liberation (Scholem 1970: 167). Derrida fully affirms deferral and incompleteness as indelibly part and parcel of the *conditio humana*, where deconstruction, conceived as a grand educational scheme for the whole of mankind, teaches us how to lead a better, though never absolutely fulfilled, life: its ongoing challenge is "learning to live finally" (Derrida 2011).[3] Agamben, on the other hand, speaks in the name of life *hic et nunc*, demanding its instant liberation from any *taught*—externally imposed—cultured forms of life that stifle its original spontaneity. In the end, therefore, the difference boils down to disparate conceptions of what human life is and can be. For Derrida, human life is never pure, simple, or complete in itself: it is *originally prosthetic*, which means that it must prop itself up on the heteronomous element of the law, taught from the outside, to acquire form and survive. For Agamben, on the contrary, human life can be fulfilled in its anarchic simplicity, but only when it dares to reject all the props imposed on it externally by culture and the latter's formatting "anthropological machines." While for the former education forms a necessary *prosthesis* of "learning to live," for the latter it constitutes a dangerously artificial imposition, which makes the child unlearn how to live and plunge into an essentially unhappy "life in deferral." It would thus seem that the issue of education is tightly bound to the problem of life, which, in late modernity's crisis of Enlightenment, became a hotly debated topic. But, why exactly are we talking about this connection?

The answer seems to lie in the deep pattern underlying the development of Western modernity: the dualistic opposition of life rebelling against the machine. In his diagnosis of the late modern crisis of Enlightenment, Habermas brings in a new and rarely discussed factor that he calls a "nostalgia after the *Lebenswelt*": a painful sense of the loss of the everyday life-world, filled with direct experiences and full of "living presence," unmediated by the cold "knowledge of experts." According to Habermas, it is precisely this idealized image of the holistic *Lebenswelt*, in which nonexpert masses could feel at home, which mostly endangers the completion of the project of Enlightenment, based on the fragmenting and alienating practices of modern specialists created by the Western model of higher education. Habermas, therefore, prophesizes the "return of the life-world" in an analogical manner to Kepel's "return of religion," that is, as a *revanche*: a vengeful return of the repressed, which comes back with a destructive and reactionary power (Kepel 1993). And indeed, the major part of what we define nowadays as a populist anti-elitism, aimed against the masters of Enlightenment, is formed by an attitude that can be called a *life-world fundamentalism*: a return to the "basics" of the immediate life and direct communication, which evades any mediation through the specialized "expert knowledge" and its Weberian machine of total rationalization.

But, as I have already indicated, there is a deeper dimension of this conflict, which can be best presented through the confrontation of two philosophical names and two strategies associated with them: Kant versus Rousseau, *maturation versus infantilization*. While, for Kant, the modern subject's only way forward is to exit the state of minority (*Unmündigkeit*) and embark on the path of education leading toward maturity, for Rousseau, the only way is back, toward a mythic lap of nature where mankind lived in the primeval state of infancy, facing only the natural and familiar life-world. The opening definition of Kant's essay states that:

> Enlightenment is man's exit from his self-incurred minority. Minority is the incapacity to use one's intelligence without the guidance of another. Such minority is self-incurred if it is not caused by lack of intelligence, but by lack of determination and courage to use one's intelligence without being guided by another. *Sapere Aude!* "Have the courage to use your own intelligence!" is therefore the motto of the enlightenment. (1784/2001: 135)

In Kant's understanding, the actual historical Enlightenment is nothing but education, and education is the most natural of all processes: just as any human child eventually learns how to walk and stand on its feet without the protection of its parents, so can every man and woman learn how to walk independently about the complex reality of the modern universe, and the only way to start this walking is to use one's reason. For Kant, to walk in this *metaphorical* sense—

not just through the familiar life-world but also through the disenchanted Newtonian universe of modern science and Humean skepticism—is, in fact, not so much a trope as a real continuation of the first educational effort to take a "wandering step."[4] It is, as Hermann Cohen suggested, a kind of a *halakhah* of Enlightenment, where the root *h-l-kh* means "teaching how to walk," a law of reason, which must be taught, but only to let the rational subject walk/reason alone (Cohen 1995: 418). This teaching for autonomy remains valid even if the current state—"the age of enlightenment"—is not yet "the enlightened age"; even if full autonomy is an unattainable ideal, it still remains valid as the regulative notion of maturity.

But this is also where the intended super strong analogy between physical and rational walking breaks down, for while most children reach easily the level of biological maturity that allows them to walk about the surrounding world alone, most of them stay immature and dependent when faced with rational "walking" about the complexity of the modern universe. Yet Kant insists on his parental analogy because the *continuum* between the early-stage weening and the ongoing education of the child is the *only* legitimation of his project of Enlightenment. He thus refuses to see in the mass resistance against the Enlightenment model of education anything but fear and inertia, which are induced in children by their manipulative guardians who, unlike responsible parents, dissuade children from learning to walk alone and prefer them to live in a state of passive dependence:

> Through laziness and cowardice a large part of mankind, even after nature has freed them from alien guidance, gladly remain in minority. It is because of laziness and cowardice that it is so easy for others to usurp the role of guardians. *It is so comfortable to be a minor!* After having made their domestic animals dumb and having carefully prevented these quiet creatures from daring to take any step beyond the lead-strings to which they have fastened them, these guardians then show them the danger which threatens them, should they attempt to walk alone. Now this danger is not really so very great; for they would presumably learn to walk after some stumbling. However, an example of this kind intimidates and frightens people out of all further attempts. (Kant 1784/2001: 135–6)

And indeed, it can be said that the major bulk of today's rejection of the Enlightenment consists in questioning the purpose of maturation in favor of perpetual infancy and the "comforts of being minor," which were strongly advocated for by Rousseau. Contrary to Kant's unfavorable portrait of the dependent childlike condition, Rousseau's *Discourse* brings an alternative view of the child-world of mankind as the golden age of ease, equality, spontaneity, and immediacy, where all the relations are clear to all its participants in the light of the living presence:

Before art had fashioned our manners and taught our passions to speak an affected language, our mores were rustic but natural, and differences in behavior heralded, at first glance, differences of character. At base, human nature was no better, but men found their safety *in the ease with which they saw through each other*, and that advantage, which we no longer value, spared them many vices. (1755/1987: 4, emphasis added)

If Rousseau mistrusts the idea of Enlightenment, which arose in the Parisian salons, it is mostly because it is based on an *abstract* idea of justice. In his suspicious view, the transition from the spontaneous empathy and transparency of neighborly relations to abstract right is a corruption that replaces the natural given by the merely *taught* and, for this reason, never properly internalizes value. Moreover, the plot of Enlightenment, forming a part and parcel of this corruptive grand narrative of modernity, is inherently hypocritical: its true goal is not an education of morals but the protection of property—the original sin and the foundational evil of human civilization. The moment mankind discovers private property—most of all of land—there automatically emerges inequality, where one person becomes dependent on the property of another. Thus, while in the state of nature, the "primeval forest" offered a cornucopia of goods for everybody to sustain herself, the invention of ownership led to the emergence of scarcity and, in this manner, work became indispensable: "equality disappeared, property came into existence, labor became necessary. Vast forests were transformed into smiling fields that had to be watered with men's sweat, and in which slavery and misery were soon seen to germinate and grow with the crops" (Rousseau 1755/1987: 65). The next stage, which only deepened the corruptive fall from the natural state, was the social contract, plotted by the property owners, which Rousseau calls "the profoundest plan that has ever entered the mind of man" and which, according to him, constitutes the gist of the Hobbesian Enlightenment:

"Let us unite," [the rich man] says to [the other rich people], "in order to protect the weak from oppression, restrain the ambitious, and assure everyone of possessing what belongs to him. Let us institute rules of justice and peace to which all will be obliged to conform, which will make special exceptions for no one, and which will in some way compensate for the caprices of fortune by subjecting the strong and the weak to mutual obligations. In short, instead of turning our forces against ourselves, let us gather them into one supreme power that governs us according to wise laws, that protects and defends all the members of the association, repulses common enemies, and maintains us in an eternal concord." (p. 69)

In this manner, the social contract replaces natural compassion with the abstract justice of reciprocal civil obligation, which, being unnatural (plotted, contrived, forced), must be taught (imposed from the outside). Education, therefore, becomes a tool of the manipulative system used to keep the hypocritical arrangement of the "rich and powerful" intact. Here, the Kantian image undergoes a radical reversal: education not only fails to foster a healthy maturation of the human individual by allowing her to exit the state of passive reliance on the mighty guardians but, on the contrary, plunges the subject into an artificial dependence on the privileged beneficiaries of the essentially evil system based on property and inequality. This is not to say that Rousseau is against *any* form of teaching; the slogan "we don't need no education" targets only this specific model of taught abstract values that underlie the liberal social contract. Just as he believes in a revolutionary version of the Enlightenment, which would reestablish honesty, self-sufficiency, and universal sympathy, he also believes in the counter-pedagogy that will revolutionize the educational model: instead of teaching children how to live, as if they did not know it already, it lets them be and leaves them to their own natural devices. Emile, Rousseau's imaginary perfect pupil, thus represents a natural life that learns how to enhance its spontaneous abilities and not how to replace and overwrite them with an abstract code of moral values. And although Rousseau admits that "it is no light undertaking to separate what is original from what is artificial in the present nature of man, and to have a proper understanding of a state which no longer exists, which perhaps never existed, which probably never will exist" (1755/1987: 34), his argument is, in fact, similar to Kant's notion of the regulative ideal, this time, however, relegated not into the future but into the past of infancy. He thus claims that it is nevertheless "necessary to have accurate notions of the natural state in order to judge properly our own present state" (p. 34). Just as Kant judges the unsatisfactory present of the "immature" social relations from the vantage point of the future "age of Enlightenment," of which we can also say that it "probably will never exist"—so does Rousseau judge the "hypocrisy" of the social present from the vantage point of his infantile state of natural humanity.

In late modernity, the Kantian model of pedagogy has undergone the same "legitimation crisis" as the Enlightenment, which immediately resulted in the rising popularity of Rousseau's counter-pedagogy as a *reditus* into the state of *Unmündigkeit*, celebrating the notion of the eternal child. While the Habermasian elite of experts stepped into the role of the Kantian adults, the mass of the profanes, feeling deprived of the power to decide about their lives, assumed the role of wronged minors. The most profound revision of Rousseau's counter-pedagogy, speaking in the name of these minors, has been offered by Giorgio Agamben in his attempt to restore the power of self-rule to human children, which can be regarded as a strong philosophical voice justifying the rise of political populism as the return to the immediacy of the life-world. The question, however, is what went wrong with the Enlightenment that it once again propelled such a strong Rousseauist reaction? Is there any redeeming moment in the rise of today's populism that justifies its attack on the Enlightenment elite? In his essay, Habermas warned against the *Verfremdungseffekt*, the effect of alienation, caused by the "discontinuity on everyday life," which is brought by modernity's "mobility in society and acceleration in history" (1985: 5), far surpassing a capability of individual experience. While the modern processes speed up in a manner of a global turbo-machine, the life-world of individual experience visibly lags behind, never able to live up to the present state of affairs. Life feels threatened by the ever more fragmenting, disenchanting, and alienating thrust of the modern/Enlightenment machine, in which, as Theodor Adorno put it in the epigraph to *Minima Moralia*, "life does not live."

The populist defense of the familiar and understandable life-world of transparency and immediacy, where people "see through each other with ease," against all the highly educated expert aliens comes, therefore, from outside of the Kantian conceptual universe; it is Rousseau's radical vindication of the "lost childhood," colonized and corrupted by an *alien* influence. On Rousseau's account, modern civilization is not, as in Kant, a natural result of human maturation; it is a life-denying and alienating machine that destroys all that is good, that is, all traces of the "living presence." It is precisely this echo of the lost life-world, childlike spontaneous ease, and its simple comforts that returns with a vengeance in Gilles Kepel's mode of *revanche*, in the late modern populist rebellion that demands that "the teachers leave them kids alone." Can the cold, alien, colonizing machine of Enlightenment be jammed? "The only possible answer to this question," says Agamben, is "*human life*, as *ethos*, as ethical way. The search for a *polis* and an *oikia* befitting this void and unpresupposable community is the *infantile* task of future generations" (Agamben 2007a: 11).

Thus, once again, we find *life rising against the machine*. Whenever the modern pendulum swings toward the Weberian machine of total rationalization, the opposite pole, the phantasm of pure life, is inevitably activated and strengthened. For some, this may sound obvious: what can be mobilized in this struggle against the alienating machine if not the anarchic powers of pure life? Yet it must be emphasized that it is a very Christian (as well as post-Christian) trope that invests life with the rebellious potential of subverting the "anthropological machine," together with all the other Hobbesian and Weberian rationalizing *automata* of modernity, and reverting to the innocent *Lebenswelt* of a "simple human life." It is Christian because only Pauline Christianity has developed to perfection the idea of a pure undying life, a life hyper-distilled, super- and quint-essential, completely free of any contaminating elements such as death and the mechanical laws of habit and instinct. This life is infinite in its anarchic freedom to choose what it wants to be, strong enough to shake off any external, imposed, legalistic form. While already Judaism can be regarded as a religion of life, based on the *torat hayim* and the Deuteronomy imperative to "choose life,"[5] it is always, as Derrida incessantly reminds us in his polemics with Agamben, a *real* life: finite, limited, contaminated by death and law, never powerful enough to become fully autarchic and autonomous, and never *simple*.[6] From Derrida's point of view, which, as he himself admits, is determined by the "Judaic great intangible principle of *torat hayim*" (2008: 112), the Christian elaboration of life as a messianic vehicle of redemption bears all the characteristics of what he calls "the phantasm of the unscathed": the salvific investment in the category of life, which is carefully avoided by Christianity's older brother.

Much ink has been spilled on the rivalry between Derrida and Agamben, but perhaps it boils down to this one pretty obvious opposition. On the one hand, Derrida affirms the reality principle of *la vie la mort*,[7] life finite, complex, contaminated by death, law, teaching, and the machine, never fully spontaneous but rather, in the Kantian manner, always "learning to live." On the other hand, Agamben endorses the pleasure principle of life infinite, simple, pure, self-confident in its vitalistic omnipotence, and perfectly self-ruled. In this context, therefore, Agamben would appear as the heir of the phantasmatic Christian notion of life strictly opposed to the "universe of death." This notion immediately translates into his political choice of affirmative biopolitics and its anarchic populism, in which the sacred simplicity of Life rises against the alienating complexity of the Machine. All the characteristic features of his works—the praise of perpetual infancy, belief in magic understood as the priority of the pleasure principle,[8] the affirmation of the natural state as the simplicity of life and the directness of experience in the familiar life-world, and spontaneous self-rule—are intended to deactivate the "anthropological machine" of culture and the associated "phantasms" of "living presence" conjured by the Enlightenment. Derrida, in *Of Grammatology*, was eager to expose in Rousseau these phantasms of the Enlightenment in the hope (apparently in vain) that they will never return to haunt us again. But if they nonetheless persistently come back, it is because the default mode of modernity is set precisely alongside this great Christian divide—life versus machine, nature versus culture, children versus adults, simplicity versus complexity, pleasure versus reality—which manifests itself politically as the perpetual opposition of the romantic/sentimental populism rebelling against the pedagogical elite that enforces the maturational process of civilization.

THE ORIGINARY SUPPLEMENT: DERRIDA

Derrida's deconstruction is an attempt to get beyond this aporetic double bind on all fronts of modern life, the issues of Enlightenment and education included. The notion that allows us to step outside the dualism of Life versus Machine is the "originary supplementarity" or "originary prosthesis," elaborated by Derrida in *On Grammatology* in his deconstructive reading of Rousseau.[9] *Prosthesis* is a machine yet not imposed on pure life to negate it: it is a supplementary machine upon which life is propped to facilitate its survival. While the whole Platonic or Greco-Christian tradition of pure life favors the living presence of voice over the medium of writing, which it then perceives as a merely external machine, Derrida defends *ecriture* as the originary mode of human experience and communication. The abstract law of writing, which constitutes the *grammatological model of education*, is not the Pauline "letter that kills" but, on the contrary, a prosthetic tool always already inscribed in the seemingly most immediate "living presence." In reference to Rousseau's admission on the phantasmatic status of his ideal natural state, Derrida writes:

> *there has never been anything but writing*; there have never been anything but supplements, substitutive significations which could only come forth in a chain of differential references, the "real" supervening, and being added only while taking on meaning from a trace and from an invocation of the supplement, etc. *And thus to infinity*, for we have read, in the text [Rousseau's *Discourse*], that the absolute present, Nature, that which words like "real mother" name, have always already escaped, have never existed; that what opens meaning and language is writing as the *disappearance of natural presence*. (1997: 159, emphasis added)

Although, in *Of Grammatology* the name of Johann Herder appears only twice and in passing, his theory of the emergence of language, published in his *Essay on the Origin of Language* in 1772, constitutes an important polemical foil for Rousseau's essay on the origin of languages (composed earlier but published only posthumously in 1781), which is the main target of Derrida's deconstruction. Both thinkers employ the concept of the supplement but value it differently: Rousseau negatively, as an apostasy and fall from the natural course of things; Herder positively, as the necessary foundation of culture, which alone allows human beings to live and survive. The Herderian school of philosophical anthropology presents man as a *Mangelwesen*, a "deficient being" and "the most orphaned child of nature," who simply cannot live when left to its purely natural devices. Herder famously states that, in the case of human beings, nature appears as "the most cruel stepmother," careless and negligent, and this lack of care must be compensated/supplemented by the artifice of language and culture (Herder 1966: 108). While animals are well taken care of by mother nature and fit their niches perfectly naturally, human beings are condemned to rely on *techne*, artifice, and prosthetic technology from the moment they are born; the original lack of the instincts of survival must be immediately supplemented by the *prosthesis* of cultural artifacts; otherwise, the "deficient creature" will die.

This, in a nutshell, is also Derrida's deconstruction of Rousseau; Derrida exposes Rousseau's phantasms of the "living presence," attempting to restore the spontaneous, direct, and undisturbed relation between human subject and Nature, once again presented as a good and reliable mother. The supplementary moment of *techne*—especially writing—is perceived by Rousseau as an unfortunate accident and a "dangerous supplement," the beginning of the Fall, which is synonymous with the falling from grace of the natural existence *sponte sua et sine lege*. Although Rousseau can never identify convincingly a single moment of the original living presence, directness, spontaneous ease, and plenitude in human life, he nonetheless regards everything else, which is already contaminated by law, mediation, absence, written letter, and death, as deficient and *fallen*, as the lapsarian colonization of the always potentially healthy life by the thanatic alien powers of artifice and *techne*. Derrida, convinced that the idea of a pure absolute life is one of the powerful roots of evil plaguing Western, Greco-Christian thought by setting this thought by default, against any kind of machine,[10] chooses instead the Herderian narrative in which the prosthetic education becomes a necessity of survival, an indispensable moment of *survie* as "learning to live."

Derrida's impact on the theory of education has been well documented, from the introduction of a new method of reading, emphasizing not the dogmatic structure of the text but its moments of vacillation and (in)decision, to the propagation of the "ethics of deconstruction," focusing on plurality of perspectives, which should not be treated as an obstacle but rather a prompt in the infinite conversation of mankind.[11] In this chapter, however, I concentrate on Derrida's *meta-approach*: his defense of education as such. The legitimation crisis of the Enlightenment, which defines the late modern era, is also the time of the most serious educational catastrophe (understood philologically as the "turning point"), which undermines the very value of teaching or cultural transmission in the name of the idealized spontaneity of life forming itself in the autarchic condition of self-rule.[12] Everything Derrida ever wrote speaks against this simple Rousseauian image: education is a necessary *prosthesis*, allowed to "displace," though never fill, the Herderian "originary lack" of human beings, which manifests itself as child's "fear or/and desire" (the two aspects of primordial negativity, which are strictly bound together). The concept of the "dangerous supplement" (obviously, dangerous only from the Rousseauian point of view) appears also in "Plato's Pharmacy," where Derrida finds Plato defending it surreptitiously against his own overt declarations as a necessary *pharmakon*:

> Philosophy consists of offering reassurance to children. That is, if one prefers, of taking them out of childhood, of forgetting about the child, or, inversely, but by the same token, of speaking first and foremost for that little boy within us, of teaching him to speak—to dialogue—by displacing his fear or his desire. (1981: 125)

Derrida may be critical of Plato's antipathy toward writing, which later would become so prominent in Rousseau, but he is not contesting the very idea of education as a dialogue addressing the most vital need in the "little boy within us," anxious about his finitude and insecurities of life. In this very Kantian fragment, echoing Kant's definition of Enlightenment as a pedagogical assistance in taking children out of childhood, Derrida sees philosophical education as a means of achieving maturation that never fully compensates for the lack constituting human beings but merely displaces it. By teaching the child how to speak, read, and write, philosophical education allows it to enter a vast archive of culture as an arsenal of all possible prosthetic strategies for dealing with the originary lack/fear/desire. Enlightenment, therefore, is not an access to knowledge that fills the primordial lacuna; it rather provides access to discursive aids, which supplement the lack with self-reflection.

For Derrida, therefore, the prosthesis of education is not a mechanical foreign body imposed on life but a necessary means of survival belonging to human life itself. Teaching and learning—the dialogue between the child and the adult—are the integral element of *torat hayim*, the Jewish-Derridean pedagogy of life, that could not "live on" without the didactic supplement, transmitting the "principle of life" through the symbolic medium of culture.

Derrida's *torat hayim* is thus simultaneously a *principle* of life, a *tradition* of life, and the *instruction* of life. Human life is never just a natural process; it is always a matter of symbolic transmission, which attempts to *educate children into life*. Life is never simply passed on by the biological fact of birth but must form its own tradition–tradition as symbolic transmissibility—which will format the deficient human being into a living, or rather, in Derridean terms, a *living/ loving* entity, capable of saying a self-reflexive "yes" to its life despite all the anxiety caused by its inherent lack. But the tradition of life—*torat hayim*— means also that the symbolic sphere is never simply cut off from the "vital order," as it is, for instance, in Lacan. It is not based on the contemptuous gesture of rising above animal life but on a sublimatory effort that will continue the elementary instruction to live by taking it to a different symbolic level.[13] On this account, language, as well as all achievements of culture, religion and philosophy included, constitute not the negation of the natural dimension of *zoe* but an *extension* of the tradition of life, or the sublimatory forms of the *education into life* that, according to Derrida, forms the fundamental affirmation of survival. The machine of civilization, created by the educational process, is not an enemy of life, allegedly deadened by its overgrowth: it is a continuation of human life which can affirm its survival only in the prosthetic manner, via the *pharmakon* of the life-saving machines.

For Derrida, therefore, survival is *not* rooted in the Hobbesian paradigm of the natural *conservatio vitae*. For Derrida—just as for the whole Jewish tradition of life, speaking the Herderian idiom *avant la lettre*—survival is never a biological *factum brutum* (which is to be either accepted as a self-evident cornerstone of modern naturalism or rejected as animal and unworthy for the very same reason) but a symbolic object of *torat hayim*, which gains new significance especially after the Holocaust: it is the instruction to live— *again*, as well as *finally*—which deliberately and consciously "chooses life" in an apothropaic gesture against the Shoah. Derrida's claim—"Auschwitz has obsessed everything I have ever been able to think" (1992: 211–12)—has thus to be taken fully seriously. For Derrida, the right definition of the finite life is not the Heideggerian *Sein-zum-Tode* but the *survival*, which has a symbolic tradition behind it. It is a problematic form of life, which must be taught and learnt, the most precious kernel of every education. Hence, Derrida arrives at his figure of "learning to live finally," where the finality of *vivre finalement* refers both to the experience of real finitude and to the desire to grasp the symbolic strategy of coping with it:

> Someone, you or me, comes forward and says: I would like to learn to live finally. Finally but why? To learn to live: a strange watchword. Who would learn? From whom? To teach to live, but to whom? Will we ever know? Will we ever know how to live and first of all what "to learn to live" means? And why "finally" ... By itself, out of context—but a context, always, remains open, thus fallible and insufficient—this watchword forms an almost unintelligible syntagm. Just how far can its idiom be translated moreover? ... A magisterial locution, all the same—or for that very reason. For from the lips of a master this watchword would always say something about violence. It vibrates like an arrow in the course of an irreversible and asymmetrical address, the one that goes most often from father to son, master to disciple, or master to slave ("I'm going to teach you to live") ... *And yet nothing is more necessary than this wisdom*. It is ethics itself: to learn to live-alone, from oneself, by oneself. *Life does not know how to live otherwise*. And does one ever do anything else but learn to live, alone, from oneself, by oneself? This is, therefore, a strange commitment, both impossible and necessary, for *a living being supposed to be alive*: "I would like to learn to live." *It has no sense and cannot have unless it comes to terms with death*. Mine as (well as) that of the other. *Between life and death*, then, this is indeed the place of a sententious injunction that always feigns to speak like the just. (1994: xvi–vii, emphasis added)

This passage, appearing in the Exordium to the *Specters of Marx*, is, in a way, all about education: the very need and, at the same time, aporetic almost-impossibility of learning based on the desire to "learn to live finally." The *torat hayim*, this "intangible Jewish principle," concentrates around the "unintelligible syntagm" or the "magisterial locution" of the injunction to live and choose life well because "life does not know how to live otherwise." Survival is not a spontaneous biological know-how of *conservatio vitae* but a complex symbolic ratio between life and death, which we all must learn ourselves, only helped by the conceptual props of the tradition. The phrase *I-would-like-to-learn-to-live-finally* is a "watchward," a slogan, a shibboleth even, which, for late Derrida, would single out those trying to inscribe themselves into the new Book of Life against the post-Holocaust thinking of death. This life, however, is not pure Life, the new Absolute insinuating itself in the place of divine transcendence; always posed "between life and death," it is a finite singular life, which must cope with its limitation yet does not lose ontological significance because of its limits. This pre-affirmation belongs necessarily to the phenomenon of life understood as the symbolic effort of living-on and not as a biological process that goes on instinctively: *life does not know how to live unless it loves itself.*[14] Education that "takes children out of their childhood"—their inherent incapability to live, marked simultaneously by fear and desire—is thus indelibly part and parcel of human life, which lovingly teaches itself "how to live, finally."[15]

It is no surprise, therefore, that the last words of Derrida were, "Always prefer life and constantly affirm survival" (*Preferez toujours la vie et affirmez sans cesse la survie*) (2007: 244). While the first part of the imperative contains the biblical crypto-quotation—"I set in front of you life and death: choose life!" (Deut. 30:19)—the second appeals to us late modern thinkers to rethink seriously our attitude toward life in its finitude in terms of survival that must be taught, learned, and cherished symbolically. Choose *vie*, yes—but also affirm it as *sur-vie*, "more-life," life educated and enlightened against the phantasmatic Life pure, infinite, and indestructible, *this* life, ordinary, livable, which inescapably ends but does not have to be determined by its end. It is only natural that we all should die, but it is not at all natural that we should want to live. This, for Derrida, is the ground of education as the life-enhancing prosthesis.

AGAMBEN: THE MESSIANISM OF UNEDUCATED LIFE

If Kant's definition of Enlightenment as an exit from the self-inflicted immaturity inspires Derrida's ingenious reinterpretation of the "Judaic principle of *torat hayim*" as an education of/for life, Giorgio Agamben's philosophy locates itself on the opposite pole. *Pace* the Kantian/Derridean idea of human life as complex and aporetic—a living contradiction between body and mind, nature and culture, only to be solved only by the extra effort of education as self-enlightenment—Agamben advocates the idea of a "simply human life": *haplos bios*, pure, undivided, and unproblematic, which could have been lived, in the Pauline manner, full of grace and without care if mankind had not chosen (wrongly, of course) the cruel process of civilization. The famous report from the limbo (the middle realm between salvation and damnation, populated by the souls of unbaptized children) with which Agamben opens his messianic anticipations of the "coming community" gives us a taste of what this simple pure life could look like:

The greatest punishment, the lack of the vision of God, thus turns into a *natural joy*; irremediably lost, they persist without pain in divine abandon. God has not forgotten them, but rather they have always already forgotten God ... Their nullity ... is principally a neutrality with respect to salvation—the most radical objection that has ever been levied against the very idea of redemption. The truly unsavable life is the one in which there is nothing to save ... these beings have left the world of guilt and justice behind them: The light that rains down on them is that irreparable light of the dawn following the *novissima dies* of judgment. But the life that begins on earth after the last day is *simply human life*. (1993: 5–6, emphasis added)

The "simply human life"—"beyond every idea of law" (Agamben 1998: 59)—is, for Agamben, the final messianic achievement, beyond "the world of guilt and justice" as well as beyond God, spirit, or basically everything that the human subject used to assume to give its life a *form*, and beyond any *task*. It just is what it is, *lacking nothing*, a life "in which there is nothing to save," and because of that already fulfilled and completed. Agamben calls this form of life a "whatever being," *quodlibet* from the nominalist scholastics, like an unbaptized child, abandoned from the moment of its birth, with no task or work, and for that reason "naturally joyful." The Christian imperative—"be like children"—thus comes here with a post-Christian twist: "be like *unbaptized* children." The blessed bare life that those unbaptized—non-initiated, non-formatted, and uneducated—infants enjoy, does not have to be infinite to be pure, as in the original Pauline version: it is a *vita nuda*, meaning that it is denuded of all forms external—non-living, ergo, mechanical—to life.

Agamben's thought had been constantly evolving since his first essays on *Infancy and History*, in which he still gives credibility to the Herderian story of *Mangelwesen*, to *Homo Sacer* and beyond, where he departs from what he now calls the modern myth of deficiency, reinforced by the parallel Hobbesian story of the necessary exit of man from the state of nature. In a vein similar to Rousseau's critique of the social contract, Agamben claims that the Hobbesian/Herderian/Kantian founding narratives of modernity, which present human life as lacking from the natural point of view and, because of that, forced to exit the state of nature as a necessary means of survival, merely perpetuate the propaganda of the modern machine of sovereignty. In the perspective of his Franciscan–Rousseanist subversion, Herder's idea of the original negativity/deficiency is yet another pedagogical horror story, designed to keep humans on the leash of the external forms of *bios*, created by the "anthropological machines" of culture. Together, therefore, with Hobbes's phantasm of the evil state of nature, from which humans must escape to survive, the Herderian myth must be firmly rejected and replaced by an *alternative model of anthropogenesis*, this time based on the originally positive naturalness, simplicity, and spontaneous inoperativity. Or, at least, the model must be thoroughly modified, for, while Herder presents the original lack in terms of an immediate danger to preservation of life, Agamben approaches the lack of natural vocation of the human species in a much more playful—deliberately childlike—manner. While, for Herder, the lack translates into *deficiency*, which first makes human animal the most precarious and least cared-for being in nature, called by him a "cruel stepmother," for Agamben, the lack, far from spelling a threat, is rather a chance to maintain the original *inoperativity* in which there is nothing "specific" to do. In "The Work of Man," while discussing the Kojèvian notion of the end of history, he states clearly,

> The *voyou désoeuvré* in Queneau, the *shabbat* of man in Kojève, and the "inoperative community" in Nancy would then be the post historical figure corresponding to the absence of a truly human work. More generally, however, what is at issue in this question is the very nature of man, who appears as *the living being that has no work, that is, the living being that has no specific nature and vocation*. If he were to lack an *ergon* of his own, man would not even have an *energeia*, a being in act that could define his essence: he would be, that is, a *being of pure potentiality*, which no identity and no work could exhaust. (Agamben 2007c: 2)

Unlike the *maturational* anthropogeny, therefore, which operates on the basis of lack and threat (or, as in Derrida, fear and desire), Agamben's relaxed (Heidegger would say *"gelassen"*) version "liberates living human beings from every biological and social destiny and every predetermined task, and renders them available for that peculiar absence of work that we are accustomed to calling 'politics' and 'art'" (2016: 278). When all threats, dangers, and hazards become exposed as fables of black social pedagogy of enlightenment, the human being can finally dare to become what it is and as it is: a *voyou désoeuvré*, a happy rogue of the natural world, or a creature in which nature itself has opted out from the hard work of survival and gone on the Italian Strike. Once the discourse of the original lack becomes neutralized, the need to compensate for it in an extra-natural way also expires. The man-child no longer must assume tasks, works, and the hardships of the maturation process. It is now just pure potentiality, inoperative *whatever*, "as-you-were" relaxed and "as-you-like-it" proud of itself, lacking nothing, always already perfect—and, at the same time, a clear mirror for contemplation.[16] When all criteria of better/cultured life, hierarchies, value judgments, and self-styled educational elites become deactivated, it is also finally possible to affirm the *whateverness* of the simple life, now proudly posed against the civilizational machine in the name of "pure politics." The last post-historical task of the populist-anarchic world politics would thus be to depose the modern apparatus of coercive survival and, once again, open a possibility of life *sicut dei* or "like children"—*without care*.

FIGURE 7.2 Teenager jumping with colorful ink splatter. *Source*: ra2studio / iStock.

This is a "simply human life," finally set free of the last external forms imposed by the Hobbesian sovereignty, Herderian anthropology of lack, and the false Kantian ideal of maturation. Naked life—as it is.

Infancy is Agamben's favorite theme, a liminal zone close to pure life and, because of that, capable of subversion against the imposition of the "anthropological machine." In *Infancy and History*, it is even granted a status of semi-sacral transcendence:

> What Wittgenstein posits, at the end of the *Tractatus*, as the "mystical" limit of language is not a psychic reality located outside or beyond language in some nebulous so called "mystical experience," it is the very transcendental origin of language, nothing other than infancy. The ineffable is, in reality, infancy. (Agamben 2007a: 58)

For Agamben, indeed, "the child is father of the man,"[17] and the constant possibility of virtual regression to the "ineffable" state of infancy, which suspends the validity of the educated forms of life, is a *conditio sine qua non* of human sanity. To go back to the anthropogenic moment allows for a reexamination of the way in which language has been grafted onto the infant's body but also to test a potentiality of a less and less external form-of-life, reducing the alienating moment to the minimum, perhaps even to zero. Thus, in *The Use of Bodies*, in the fragments devoted to the lives of two "infamous" men—Debord and Foucault—Agamben focuses on the phenomenon of the private life as a sphere of blissful indecision, where we can suspend our public identities and play with being neither/nor in the safety of the intimate retreat. The *Highest Poverty*, too, lovingly portrays a retreat in the form of the cloister life of Franciscan brothers, sheltered from the intrusions of external powers; if, as Agamben suggests, those *fratres* call themselves *minores*, it is indeed because they perceive themselves as "minors" or as "children at heart," non-adults who do not possess anything and do not answer to the external institution of the law (Agamben 2013: 111). The play with the perpetual infancy reverses the Kantian-Derridean exodic vector, which urges the child to exit the state of self-inflicted immaturity, and offers a mirror-like advice: education, instead of "taking children out of childhood," should rather dwell in the potentialities of infancy, protecting it from the perfectly symmetrical *self-inflicted maturity*. The less decisive and irreversible the state of adulthood, the better chance for a human being to evolve into a happy *forma-di-vita*, formed and alive simultaneously, that is, not encumbered from the start with too many mechanical props, which may seem to ease the pressure of survival but soon negate the very possibility of life. If, following Adorno, Agamben agrees that, in modernity, "life does not live," it is precisely because all its educational-cultured forms are invested in the Herderian/ Hobbesian implementation of efficient survival and lead to a forgetting of what truly pleasurable living can be. "Man's original home is pleasure," says Agamben in *Infancy and History* (2007a: 115), and education, accordingly, must be devised not within the survivalist exigency but "in the *epoche* of pleasure," that is, in the suspension of the pressing necessities of what Derrida calls *survie*.

EDUCATION CLOSER TO LIFE

Yet the difference between Derrida and Agamben—just as the difference between Kant and Rousseau—is not as absolute as it might seem. Though differing on the issue of nature versus nurture, none of them advocates a philosophy of education as a purely external and heteronomous system of language/forms/values to be forcibly imposed on the childish psyche by the institutions of culture, starting from the severe paternal rule. Neither Kant nor Derrida are Herderian conservatives who perceive the institutional *prosthesis* as the civilizational machine necessarily opposed to life, which, remaining anarchic and unruly, remains a threat to human survival.[18] They rather belong to the Herderian Left, which would like to incorporate the prosthetic devices of education and culture into the living process itself and thus make them an integral part of child's healthy maturation, not only reducing the possibility of happiness but, on the contrary, also augmenting the vital pleasure of the self-affirmed life. In that sense, the Rousseau/Agamben project of finding a "form of life" that is not "fatal to happiness and innocence" (Rousseau 1755/1987: 64) does not have to be read as a protest against education. In its extreme variant, which invests in the phantasmatic image of pure life and was eagerly taken up by populist politics, both Rousseau and Agamben can indeed be interpreted in the light of the anti-Enlightenment slogan: "teachers, leave them kids alone." In their subtler version, however, they offer a helpful correction to the condition of heteronomy, which determines every childhood. The discussion between Kant and Rousseau/Derrida and Agamben, which we could paraphrase in the Nietzschean manner as the debate "on the uses and disadvantaged of education for life," finds a nice conclusion in Luce Irigaray's admonition:

> instead of recognizing that life itself involves transcendence, and of teaching children to transcend themselves, then to a cultivation and a sharing of life, teachers more often than not require them to forget life, to leave life at home and to confine life as such at the level of needs. (2017: 2)

Irigaray's intention is similar to Derrida's: instead of making education an integral part of the continuous maturational process of "learning to live," teachers forget life and confine it to the *oikonomia* of biology, as if it had nothing to do with culture. Uprooted from the living bedrock of all learning, education may then indeed become an "antiquarian burden," which, as Nietzsche famously claimed, can only stifle the child's vitality: "instruction without invigoration" and "knowledge not attended by action" are those twin pedagogical evils that merely exacerbate the alienating moment of all education instead of alleviating it (Nietzsche 1873/1997: 59). Hence Nietzsche's vitalist declaration:

> We want to serve education only to the extent that education serves life: for it is possible to value the education to such a degree that life becomes stunted and degenerate—a phenomenon we are now forced to acknowledge, painful though this may be, in the face of certain striking symptoms of our age. (p. 59)[19]

Prima facie Nietzsche would locate himself on the side of Rousseau and Agamben, speaking in the name of pure life against the deadening machine of education. Yet, in fact, he never questions the "value of studying" (p. 59) as such, but rather "wants to serve education only to the extent that education serves life," which sides him with Derrida's generalized theory of *torat hayim*. Human life may be originally lacking and thus exposed to the "colonial" impact of language and culture, but this does not mean that it loses some uniquely vital part in the process. On the contrary, although living and "learning to live" can never be fully fused to form a perfect *forma di vita*, pedagogy can nonetheless be closer to life, first of all by explaining to the pupil that she needs it *for life*: if she were to be "left alone," she simply would not be able to survive without the cultural *prosthesis*. Life, this *thema regium* of late modernity, simply cannot be forgotten, so it would be wiser to have education on its side.

NOTES

1 Although traditionally Rousseau is regarded as one of the foundational thinkers of the Enlightenment, the late modern developments of his thought emphasize its sentimental/reactionary elements; this is what I will attempt to demonstrate in this chapter.

2 Seeing himself as one of the last defenders of modernity, Habermas has a lasting tendency to regard Derrida as an enemy of Enlightenment reason, a suspicion that he first articulated in *Philosophical Discourse of Modernity*, in the chapter "Beyond the Temporalized Philosophy of Origin: Derrida's Critique of Phonocentrism" (Habermas 1987: 161–84). Derrida, however, was never a straightforward kind of postmodernist; he definitely subscribed to the Enlightenment tradition, yet with a hope to transform it from within and thus "save the honour of reason" (Derrida 2003).

3 One must keep in mind, however, that the adverb "finally" is used by Derrida in an ironic manner: there is never an ultimate lesson of life.

4 This is an allusion to the famous concluding verses of John Milton's *Paradise Lost*, where Adam and Eve, banned from the Paradise of childhood, enter the world "with wandering steps and slow."

5 "I have set before you life and death: choose life" (Deut. 30:19).

6 See Derrida's critique of Agamben's notion of "bare life" in *The Beast and the Sovereign*, his last seminar (Derrida 2009: 92–6).

7 This is the title of one of Derrida's early seminars, only recently published: *La vie la mort: Séminaire (1975–1976)* (2019).

8 "Walter Benjamin once said that a child's first experience of the world is not his realization that 'adults are stronger but rather that they cannot make magic'" (Agamben 2007b: 19).

9 The term "originary prosthesis" or "the prosthesis of origin" appears later in Derrida's career in the essay *Monolingualism*, but its sense is fully consistent, if not synonymous, with the earlier concept of the "originary supplement." In *Monolingualism of the Other*, Derrida describes his own situation as a Franco-Maghrebian Jew who was deprived of his "original language" and thrown into the "language of the other," that is, the French Empire. Yet he does not deplore his predicament; quite to the contrary, he turns it into an exemplary case of the "inalienable alienation," which is a universal truth of every childhood submitted to the education of speech that always belongs to the other: "This is a priori universal truth of an essential alienation in language—which is always of the other—and, by the same token, in all culture" (Derrida 1998: 58).

10 In *Specters of Marx*, Derrida is extremely clear on this point, reminding us that "this absolute evil (which is, is it not, *absolute life, fully present life, the one that does not know death and does not want to hear about it*) can take place" and is indeed constantly resurging, both in theology and philosophy (Derrida 1994: 220, emphasis added).

11 Derrida's reflections on education have given rise to a new academic discipline of which the most representative are Burik (2009), Farahani (2014), Trifonas (2000), and Biesta (2009). Derrida's own two famous texts dealing directly with the problems of higher education are "The Principle of Reason: The University in the Eyes of Its Pupils" (1983) and "University Without Condition" (2002). In the latter essay, in which he passionately defends academic freedom to teach and profess, Derrida defines university as "the place in which nothing is beyond question … Here, then, is what we could call, in order to call upon it, the unconditional university or the university without condition: the principal right to say everything, even if it be under the heading of fiction and the experimentation of knowledge, and the right to say it publicly, to publish it. *This reference to public space will remain the link that affiliates the new Humanities to the age of Enlightenment*" (2002: 205–6, emphasis added).

12 Think here, for instance, about the homeschooling movement as a hostile takeover
    of educational heteronomy by the familial life-world, which, in a Rousseauian
    manner, enhances parental control against the abstract rule of the state.

13 In Lacan's theory, the acquisition of language is a process that violently overwrites
    the "vital order," that is, the biological system of needs of the human animal,
    and creates a symbolic sphere of the subject as a radical negation of life, which
    psychoanalysis calls the "death drive." To turn a child into a speaking subject means
    thus to disappropriate her from her living body and subject her to the linguistic
    law of the Other, here represented by the Name of the Father. Lacan's concept
    of the human subject as always *belonging to the Other* also derives from the
    Herderian narrative of the constitutive lack, but, in contrast to Derrida, he tends
    to overemphasize the othering inherent in the acquisition of language because he
    sticks, in the Rousseauian manner, to the phantasmatic ideal of natural "mineness":
    the immediate bodily reality of the child before she became subjected to the
    colonizing violence of culture. Derrida, on the other hand, deconstructs the ideal of
    "mineness" as a nostalgic side effect of what he calls *alienation without alienation*
    (Derrida 1998: 25). A child's entrance into taught language, which, precisely
    because it is to be appropriated, can never be fully owned. Thus, when Derrida says
    that "all culture is originally colonial" (p. 39), he does not state it purely negatively,
    with a Rousseauist ideal of natural "mineness" in mind. He rather wants to stress
    that, *pace* Lacan, while culture and language always *come* from the other, they do
    not *belong* to the other simply because they cannot be anyone's property: "It is the
    monolanguage of the other. *The of signifies not so much property as provenance*:
    language is for the other, coming from the other, the coming of the other" (p. 68,
    emphasis added).

14 The Derridan "living/loving," which replaces the Heideggerian "living/dying," is
    Derrida's version of *love strong as death*, forming the "intangible principle" of the
    Jewish *torat hayim*: "*Living-loving* ... Life loves itself in the living being, life loves
    itself, period, it loves to live, it loves itself in living for life. This love is its relation to
    itself, its self-intimacy with itself, its inevitable self-intimacy with itself, before any
    other supposed interiority" (2016: 111).

15 This is why, in his essay on Enlightenment, Derrida states, "I would like to situate
    the question of life and of the living being, of life and of death, of life-death, at the
    heart of my remarks" (2003: 15).

16 Agamben offers his own Franciscan-optimistic version of Herderism in *The Idea
    of Prose*, where he praises the potentialities of the imagined "neotenic infant,"
    who, unlike all human children destined to grow, "would hold onto its immaturity
    and helplessness": "in his infantile totipotency [which, non-accidentally, closely
    echoes the Freudian concept of the omnipotence sensed by the foetus], he would
    be ecstatically overwhelmed, cast out of himself, not like other living beings into
    a specific adventure or environment, but for the first time into a *world*. He would
    truly be listening to being. His voice still free from any genetic prescription, and
    having absolutely nothing to say or express, sole animal of his kind, he could, like
    Adam, *name* things in his language" (1995: 96–7). Colby Dickinson, infused with
    the same optimism, comments, "We may not have a specific, unique vocation that
    we are called to ... but the absence of a particular calling is precisely the freedom
    to experience the unlimited potential of what we truly are" (2011: 39) and then
    advocates "embracing our *animality* in contrast to the all-too-familiar (rationally
    constructed) human subject" (p. 146, emphasis added). This, however, is a serious
    non sequitur, which often goes unnoticed by Agamben commentators: If we are "not

like other living beings" from the start, then how can we embrace our animality? How can we regain that which was never there in the first place? There is, however, an answer to that question, with which Agamben himself would probably have agreed: we have never been animals—*yet*. But we can be, provided *we will hold onto our immaturity and helplessness*: our animality lies in the future as the messianic promise, hence the image of a "theriomorphous" Messiah with an animal head, with which Agamben begins his meditation in *The Open* (Agamben 2003: 9).

17 This famous phrase derives from *The Rainbow*, the 1802 poem of William Wordsworth, where he praises the "natural piety" of infancy as opposed to the "universe of death" calculated by the Enlightenment science.

18 Freud seems to come very close to the Herderian Right in *Civilization and Its Discontents*, where he portrays human being as inescapably torn between the destructive powers of *id* and the law-giving institutions of *superego* and praises the civilizational process as offering modern man a chance to become a "prosthetic God," provided he gives up the dream of happiness and pleasure—something against which Agamben protests most strongly (Freud 1930/1962: 39).

19 In the quote, I deliberately substituted "education" for "history," but the overall meaning stays the same.

REFERENCES

Primary sources

Agamben, Giorgio (1993), *The Coming Community*, trans. Michael Hardt, Minneapolis: Minnesota University Press.

Agamben, Giorgio (1995), *The Idea of Prose*, trans. Michael Sillivan and Sam Whitsitt, Albany: State University of New York Press.

Agamben, Giorgio (1998), *Homo sacer: Sovereign Power and Bare Life*, trans. Daniel Heller-Roazen, Stanford, CA: Stanford University Press.

Agamben, Giorgio (2003), *The Open: Man and Animal*, trans. Kevin Attel, Stanford, CA: Stanford University Press.

Agamben, Giorgio (2007a), *Infancy and History: On the Destruction of Experience*, trans. Liz Heron, London: Verso.

Agamben, Giorgio (2007b), *Profanations*, trans. Jeff Fort, New York: Zone Books.

Agamben, Giorgio (2007c), "The Works of Man," in Matthew Calarco and Steven DeCaroli (eds.), *Giorgio Agamben: Sovereignty & Life*, Stanford, CA: Stanford University Press.

Agamben, Giorgio (2013), *The Highest Poverty: Monastic Rules and Form-of-Life*, trans. Adam Kotsko, Stanford, CA: Stanford University Press.

Agamben, Giorgio (2016), *The Use of Bodies: Homo Sacer IV, 2*, trans. Adam Kotsko, Stanford, CA: Stanford University Press.

Derrida, Jacques (1981), *Dissemination*, trans. Barbara Johnson, Chicago: University of Chicago Press.

Derrida, Jacques (1983), "The Principle of Reason: The University in the Eyes of Its Pupils," (coauthored by Catherine Porter and Edward P. Morris Source), *Diacritics*, 13 (3): 2–20.

Derrida, Jacques (1992), "Canons and Metonymies: An Interview with Jacques Derrida," trans. Richard Rand and Amy Wygant, in Richard Rand (ed.), *Logomachia: The Conflict of the Faculties*, 195–219, Lincoln: University of Nebraska Press.

Derrida, Jacques (1994), *Specters of Marx: The State of Debt, the Work of Mourning, and the New International*, trans. Peggy Kamuf, New York: Routledge.

Derrida, Jacques (1997), *Of Grammatology*, trans. Gayatri Chakravorti Spivak, Baltimore: Johns Hopkins University Press.

Derrida, Jacques (1998), *Monolingualism of the Other, or, The Prosthesis of Origin*, trans. Patrick Mensah, Stanford, CA: Stanford University Press.

Derrida, Jacques (2002), "University Without Condition," in Peggy Kamuf (ed.), *Without Alibi*, trans. Peggy Kamuf, 202–37, Stanford, CA: Stanford University Press.

Derrida, Jacques (2003), "The 'World' of the Enlightenment to Come (Exception, Calculation, Sovereignty)," *Research in Phenomenology*, 33: 10–51.

Derrida, Jacques (2007), "Final Words," trans. Gila Walker, in W.J.T. Mitchell and Arnold I. Davidson (eds.), *The Late Derrida*, 244, Chicago: University of Chicago Press.

Derrida, Jacques (2008), *The Animal That Therefore I Am*, trans. David Wills, New York: Fordham University Press.

Derrida, Jacques (2009), *The Beast and the Sovereign*, Vol. 1, trans. Geoffrey Bennington, Chicago: University of Chicago Press.

Derrida, Jacques (2011), *Learning to Live Finally. The Last Interview*, trans. Pascal-Anne Brault, New York: Melville House.

Derrida, Jacques (2016), *The Death Penalty*, Vol. 2, trans. Elizabeth Rotenberg, Chicago: Chicago University Press.

Derrida, Jacques (2019), *La vie la mort: Séminaire (1975–1976)*, Paris: Seuil.

Freud, Sigmund (1930/1962), *Civilisation and Its Discontents*, trans. James Strachey, New York: W.W. Norton & Co.

Herder, Johann Gottfried (1966), *Essay on the Origin of Language*, trans. Alexander Gode, Chicago: University of Chicago Press.

Kant, Immanuel (1784/2001), "Answer to the Question: What Is Enlightenment?," trans. Thomas K. Abbott, in Allen W. Wood (ed.), *Basic Writings of Kant*, 135–41, New York: The Modern Library.

Nietzsche, Friedrich (1873/1997), "On the Uses and Disadvantages of History for Life," in *Untimely Meditations*, trans. R.J. Hollingdale, 57–124, Cambridge: Cambridge University Press.

Rousseau, Jean-Jacques (1755/1987), "Discourse on the Origin of Inequality," in D.A. Cress (ed.), *Basic Political Writings*, trans. D.A. Cress, 25–82, Indianapolis, IN: Hackett Publishing.

Secondary sources

Biesta, Gert (2009), "Witnessing Deconstruction in Education: Why Quasi-Transcendentalism Matters," *Journal of Philosophy of Education*, 43 (3): 391–404.

Burik, Steven (2009), "Opening Philosophy to the World: Derrida and Education in Philosophy," *Educational Theory*, 59 (3) 297–312.

Cohen, Hermann (1995), *Religion of Reason: Out of the Sources of Judaism*, trans. Simon Kaplan, Atlanta, GA: Scholars Press.

Dickinson, Colby (2011), *Agamben and Theology*, New York: T. & T. Clark International.

Farahani, Mohsen Farmahini (2014), "Educational Implications of Philosophical Foundations of Derrida," *Procedia: Social and Behavioral Sciences*, 116: 2494–7.

Habermas, Jürgen (1985) "Modernity: The Incomplete Project," speech delivered in Frankfurt in September 1980, on the occasion of awarding its author with the

Theodor W. Adorno Prize. (Reprinted in Hal Foster [ed.], *Postmodern Culture*,
London: Pluto Classics.)

Habermas, Jürgen (1987), *Philosophical Discourse of Modernity*, trans. Frederick
Lawrence, Cambridge, MA: MIT Press.

Irigaray, Luce (2017), *To Be Born*, Cham: Palgrave Macmillan.

Kepel, Gilles (1993), *"The Revenge of God" The Resurgence of Islam, Christianity,
and Judaism in the Modern World*, trans. Alan Brailey, Pennsylvania: Penn State
University Press.

Scholem, Gershom (1970), *Über einige Grundbegriffe des Judentums*, Frankfurt:
Suhrkamp.

Trifonas, Peter (2000), "Jacques Derrida As a Philosopher of Education," *Educational
Philosophy and Theory*, 32 (3): 271–81.

CHAPTER EIGHT

Decolonization, Indigenous Peoples, and Philosophy of Education

TROY RICHARDSON (SAPONI/TUSCARORA)

INTRODUCTION

The contrasting images of "flag raising" ceremonies and that of "*guerilla* fighters" might be the popular ways many teachers and students interpret decolonization. For the former, the signification would be of a formal event in which a "peaceful transfer" of political authority is made from colonial rule for the establishment of an autonomous country or territory. With the latter, the signification is that of "rebels" struggling against colonial oppression and military forces. If schooling served a role in creating such familiarity with decolonization among teachers or students, it would have most likely occurred through a history curriculum. As a topic of history, decolonization generally takes a periodizing approach, giving specific historical contexts in which former colonies become independent states. Such historical accounts are important for the details relevant to learning some of the social, economic, and cultural forces operating as both colonizing and decolonizing. These images and references are also indicative of the centrality of the question of governance as a project of decolonial thinking.

Philosophy of education is an academic field that formulates a range of questions relevant to interrogating relationships between schooling, education, and society. Some questions can be general (what do schools do?), others very narrow (discussing Locke's epistemology and its legacies for cognition). On the whole, it is an exercise in posing and pursuing questions to elaborate defensible arguments in the service of conceptual clarifications. These clarifications may be further deployed to defend or critique educational policy proposals, inform teacher training, intervene in curricular debates, or be pursued for clarity as its own end. As a critical intellectual endeavor, such clarifications are also directed at educational and broader social, economic, or political injustices. Justice itself is a concept under consistent scrutiny within philosophy of education in relation to race, gender, sexuality, and economic social locations, among others (see Applebaum 2010; Glass 2001, 2013; Hytten 2018; Margonis 2007b; Mayo 2007, 2013; Thompson 1997, 1998).

Thus the opening images of historical ceremonies regarding transfers of political authority as decolonization are philosophically rich for the exploration and formulation of questions on decolonial governance. This has generally not been pursued within philosophy of education but will be considered here as a central question. Moreover, insofar as these images may mark the assertion of political authority by local and Indigenous peoples, questions on the nature of local and knowledges as readily available to philosophy of education—or the differing intellectual collectives writing on decolonization—become crucial. That is, how does one enact an ethical relation of learning decolonial governance with Indigenous peoples in the pursuit of conceptual clarity in the principles of such governance?

FIGURE 8.1 Mata Atlantica – Atlantic Forest in Brazil. *Source*: FG Trade / iStock.

This chapter clarifies and elaborates on these questions in the spirit of solidarities for extending these conversations with Indigenous peoples from the high colonial moment of the geopolitical context of North America. To do so, the sections that follow differentiate Indigenous decolonial collectives and several foundational topics, including autonomy and Indigenous philosophies for decolonial governance. Critical questions on the inclusion of such philosophies in broader social contexts as well as the complex entanglements with colonial law are also taken up through the work of Gayatri Spivak (1999) and Dale Turner (2006). More specifically, the chapter takes up commitments crucial for the conditions of decolonial governance, namely the politicization of everyday life, ethico-political responsibilities toward the particular Indigenous communities being engaged, not obscuring class differences between university-based and rural and Indigenous decolonial projects, learning of Indigenous languages, and Indigenous land reclamations in broader movements based for social interdependencies.

DIFFERENTIATING DECOLONIAL TRAJECTORIES

Contemporary intellectual discussions of decolonization, which include historians, critical theorists, feminist and gender studies scholars, philosophers, and political theorists, among others, perceive the period (roughly 1947–79) as a moment in a longer history of struggle against colonialism and its legacies, but one that has left many elements of decolonization as "unfinished business" (Maldonado-Torres 2012: 205). Notable for philosophy of education, such business includes the topics of epistemology, ontology, power, gender, and sexuality, among others. Latin Americanist decolonial intellectuals such as Lugones (2007), Maldonado-Torres (2007), Mignolo (2000), Quijano (2000, 2007), and Dussel (1985) have been engaged in the elaboration of these topics as essential to the always unfinished business of decolonial emancipatory projects. In such contexts, the normalization of statist discourse in the postcolonial state contributes not to the reformulation of citizen but to the deepening of a rights-bearing subject underpinned by the financialization of everyday life. The latter, as a central aspect of neoliberalism, is a mode of living that instills specific epistemic and ontological commitments. With regard to gender, Maria Lugones (2007) provides examples of the heteropatriarchal power exercised in such ontological commitments as they dehumanize nonbinary expressing persons. Like many in the Latin Americanist discussions of decolonization, Lugones engages with Indigenous peoples, Aymara in particular, as a way toward terminologies and practices apart from the privileged binary gender (rights-generating) system formulated through Eurocentric knowledge formations. In this way, Lugones can be read as expanding the conditions of possibility for moving from categories of gender and sexuality emanating from colonial contexts and their legacies toward decolonial modes of relating to and being with such differences.

Yet Indigenous peoples also participate in a particular intellectual culture of decolonization as "unfinished business" on their own terms and with their own projects. That is, many Indigenous peoples have been and continue to be engaged in maintaining forms of life that adhere to and enact philosophical and intellectual traditions that run parallel and variously intersect with much in contemporary social life. To say this, however, is not to argue that Indigenous peoples are not modern peoples. It is to argue that their "cultural scripts" are seen as worth preserving, with some perhaps more intact than others on particular topics. And yet as Aymara queer youth may be engaged with allies such as Lugones (2010), this must occur according to a multidirectional "answerability" and accountability. Such ethical relation would be stunted by unquestioned admiration of the person as "Aymara example" on the one hand or the reduction of queer indigeneity to an insistence on applying "gay rights" by the other.

Within Indigenous discussions on decolonization there are significant debates on how to be engaged with those outside the daily life of Indigenous communities. Committing to the revitalizing and widespread usages of specific languages, community practices, and broader forms of life within their respective tribal nation experience is central to decolonization for Indigenous peoples within ongoing colonial and neocolonial contexts such as the United States. For some, Indigenous resurgence and nation-building are the central projects for decolonization with regard to governance; the latter efforts of Indigenous peoples may deploy the language of sovereignties, rights, and self-determination insofar as they have to navigate legal systems that have been devised largely to oppress and dispossess.

Indigenous peoples are not monolithic and there are those who operate at the borders of broadly defined Indigenous decolonial projects who may hold a faith in the Eurocentric principles of "justice" and democratic processes as central to relationships of accountability. This faith may nonetheless be kept while simultaneously asserting broader normalizations of Indigenous principles of governance internally and as inspirations for those external to the daily lives of tribal nations. Clearly Indigenous participants in these intellectual discussions of decolonization do not speak in a singular voice regarding governance or a range of other topics. Variations, differences, and creative tensions between a range of positions are to be expected; from robust assertions of a role for Indigenous philosophies in broader cross- and multicultural social relations to a more conservative, Indigenous-centered set of concerns. Nevertheless, one crucial topic that is shared across Indigenous elaborations of decolonization is the attention to lands and waters and critiques of the historical/contemporary strategies of and commitments to Indigenous dispossession. The latter is experienced and formally defined as a settler colonial relation.

Working within and against the contexts of settler colonialism in Canada, Indigenous peoples are not always nor necessarily seeking models for governance exclusive to their particular contexts. Yellow Knife Dine scholar Glen Coulthard elaborates:

> The significant political leverage required to simultaneously block the economic exploitation of our people and homelands while constructing alternatives to capitalism will not be generated through our direct actions and resurgent economies alone. Settler colonization has rendered our populations too small to affect this magnitude of change. This reality demands that we continue to remain open to, if not actively seek out and establish, relations of solidarity and networks of trade and mutual aid with national and transnational communities and organizations that are also struggling against the imposed effects of globalized capital, including other Indigenous nations and national confederacies; urban Indigenous people and organizations; the labor, women's, GBLTQ2S and environmental movements; and of course those racial and ethnic communities that find themselves subject to their own distinct forms of economic, social and cultural marginalization. (2014: 173)

Importantly, Coulthard suggests processual—if uneven and unpredictable—emergent "relations of solidarity" as a minimalist form of shared governance that does not ignore or abandon the current political context. Writing on the asymmetry of the political relationships between Indigenous peoples and nation-states such as Canada, he poses the following questions, returning specific attention to dispossession. "What are the implications of this profound power disparity in our struggles for land and freedom? Does it require that we vacate the field of state negotiations and participation entirely?" He follows with this response: "Of course not. Settler colonialism has rendered us a radical minority in our own homelands, and this necessitates that we continue to engage with the state's legal and political system" (p. 179). He adds that "we begin to shift our attention away from the largely rights based/recognition orientation that has emerged as hegemonic over the last four decades to a resurgent politics of recognition that seeks to practice decolonial, gender-emancipatory, and economically nonexploitative alternative structures of law and sovereign authority grounded on a critical refashioning of the best of indigenous legal and political traditions" (p. 179).

The effort here is to navigate the colonial architecture of legal policies dependent on (colonial) forms of "recognition" as experienced in the present, but to do so while simultaneously enacting the conditions for alternatives as the critical refashioning of the best of Indigenous legal and political traditions. Coulthard (2014) provides a set of principles for modes of Indigenous resurgence that are more and less directed toward governance; those salient to the current discussion include the necessity of direct action, gender justice, and decolonization beyond the nation-state.

Philosophers of education have been highly attentive to the injustices of racism, classism, sexism, homophobia, and broad forms of oppression (see Applebaum 2010; Glass 2001; Haymes 1995; Hytten 2018; Margonis 2007a; Mayo 2007, 2013; Thompson 1997, 1998). As a community of scholars there have been long-standing intellectual commitments to mobilize philosophers and texts—sometimes canonical, sometimes heretical—toward critical observations of social oppressions, injustice, and ecological crises. In this sense, the critical projects within philosophy of education tend to emerge from within a canonical philosophical tradition, yet they can be read as anticolonial and contributing to the conditions of possibilities for decolonial practices—even as scholars themselves may not conceive of their work in terms of decolonization per se.

Frank Margonis is a philosopher of education who has been especially attentive to the role of colonialism in the learning relation. In this way, he has nurtured an explicit trajectory of thought for anticolonial philosophies of education. His critical assessments of central figures within the canon of philosophy of education—notably, Rousseau, Dewey, and Freire—have been juxtaposed with the works of Charles Mills, Miles Horton, and Elizabeth Ellsworth to rethink central concepts and educational practices such as authentic learning, ethics, solidarity, and critical pedagogy (see Margonis 1999, 2007a, b). One of the recurring questions he poses for philosophy of education is: What can students and I become, given who we are? This question is pivotal for educators considering decolonial philosophies as bases for pedagogy. That is, like Ellsworth (1992), Margonis does not assume that a learning relation can emerge without critical assessments of the differences at play in the desire "to learn from each other." Speaking of classroom-based teachers in particular, Margonis writes: "Teachers who believe they can become unified with their students in solidarity, despite the historical chasms created by colonial histories of genocide, enslavement and stolen lands can reach such an optimistic conclusion by substituting abstract and ahistorical metaphors of 'critical consciousness,' 'liberation' and 'love' for the concrete dynamics that transpire amongst themselves and their students" (2007b: 67).

Margonis's thought here can be broadened out in the context of decolonial projects in education to highlight the complexities of any learning relations between Indigenous peoples in academic and popular contexts. With regard to interests in Indigenous knowledge traditions, for example, Margonis would likely highlight romantic and sentimental "patterns at play" such as romantic stereotypes that "operate regardless of whether we know or heed them" (1999: 6). Such patterns would limit the possibility for solidarities and ultimately anticolonial practices as these engrained perceptions anticipate the learning relation that may then be overlain and saturated by an unexamined notion of love, liberation, or decolonial consciousness.

Indeed problems such as these are well captured by feminist philosopher of education Audrey Thompson's characterization of those "spaces of innocence" facilitated by discourses of colorblindness by white teachers and those of white feminists emphasizing the home-space for philosophies and ethics of care. Like Margonis (1999, 2007a, b) and Ellsworth (1992), Thompson (1998) highlights the move to spaces of innocence on the topics of race as a profoundly difficult, often unrecognized obstacle by white participants in the forging of relations of learning and care. Decolonial relations of learning then must be attentive to these challenges and understand them as opportunities to undermine naïve or unintentionally superficial engagements with decolonial projects, specifically those with Indigenous peoples for whom changing the patterns of ongoing territorial dispossession is a central project. "Innocence," writes Thompson "is not only a mythical ideal but a specifically White, social ideal that provides us with no means of understanding or changing the ways in which we fail in our responsibilities to one another" (1998: 530–1).

These philosophers of education are noted for elaborating anticolonial thinking in philosophy of education, to indicate something of the history of the questions on anticolonial/decolonial possibilities as well as those conditions of "who we might become" by learning from minoritized students and their communities striving for and enacting decolonial practices. That is, these philosophers point to anti-racist, anti-sexist, anti-homophobic trajectories in philosophy of education for organizing and clarifying some of the conditions for anticolonial philosophizing. Yet it remains challenging to offer a full throated decolonial philosophy given the obstacles and patterns that would appear to condition the structures of relationality with minoritized, racialized, and dispossessed peoples. Indeed, decolonial projects for *learning from* are in effect conditioned on the voices of those largely excluded from the tradition of philosophy of education itself (see Grosfoguel, Hernandez, and Valesquez 2016).

More recently, Leigh Patel (2014) provides some important elaborations on this point of distinction between the anticolonial and the decolonial for theories and philosophies of education broadly conceived. He writes:

> [The term] anticolonial still allows for locating the hydra-like shape-shifting yet implacable logics of settler colonialism, but does not include in its semantic shape the unmet promises of stripping away colonization, as the term *decolonization* gestures to do. This, in itself, marks anticolonial stances as incomplete, as they don't necessarily address material change. (p. 360)

The relevant issue Patel is addressing here regarding material change is the reclamation of lands and waters by Indigenous peoples and the ways intellectualization of decolonization may avoid discussions of such reclamations: another instance of enacting the "space of innocence." "This [anticolonial] stance," Patel continues, "must be vigilant about the deeply colonial structures of institution, thought, and relationality to reimagine and, falteringly, begin to put into practice ways to be in relation that do not begin and end with ownership" (p. 360). An anticolonial stance against ownership may not be decolonizing as Patel understands the latter. However, it does provide a trajectory that intersects with decolonial thinking as a commitment against ongoing Indigenous dispossession through the policies of settler colonialism in North America. Dei (2018) elaborates on these solidarities from the contexts of African Indigenous in the diaspora as citizens of settler states such as Canada. While "not complicit in the sense of perpetuating colonial violence against Indigenous peoples," Dei writes, citizenship in settler colonial states do "implicate [Black and African Indigenous peoples] in how we own up to our responsibilities and begin to build solidarities to support struggles against white settler violence" (2018: 133).

Owning responsibility for learning decolonial governance is a project that exists at a point of contact between anticolonial and decolonial educational orientations. Both seek to generate the conditions needed in the broad struggle against colonial relations, particularly in terms of practicing collective relationalities of learning from and interdependencies contrary to ownership. Patel (2014) and Dei (2018) call for the bending of practices of solidarities with Indigenous peoples toward autonomous collectivities, which they see as conditions for an elaboration of decolonial governance.

KUXLEJAL, AUTONOMY, AND DECOLONIAL RELATIONALITY IN DIECISIETE DE NOVIEMBRE

Mariana Mora began her engagements with several Zapatista communities in 1996 as a participant in the Encuentro Intercontinental por la Humanidad y contra el Neoliberalismo (Intercontinental Meeting for Humanity and Against Neoliberalism). In 2004, she submitted a proposal for research to a newly refined set of Zapatista protocols, receiving her approval from the municipality of Diecisiete de Noviembre in 2005. Among the women from Diecisiete de Noviembre, Chiapas Mexico, Mora foregrounds Amalia in a discussion of autonomy in governance. Amalia states that autonomy speaks to an ability "to create a new life; it is the struggle for life" (quoted in Mora 2017: 150). In the context of the work of the women's collectives and their role in the larger projects of governance, enacting autonomy is intimately linked to the politicization of everyday life. The everyday acts of autonomy by Amalia, her mother, and the generations since the "uprising" (1994) "demonstrate how [the Tseltal, Tsotsl and Tojolobal (Mayan)] Zapatista women's praxis destabilizes and profoundly alters the category of the Indigenous woman on which central aspects of the

Mexican state rest" (p. 151). The category of "indigenous woman" maintained by the Mexican state is one that reduces Tseltal, Tsotsl, and Tojolobal women to unhygienic, uneducated, and so poverty stricken that they "hold back" the "development" of their families. Begun in the late 1990s, a state entity called Oportunidades reiterated and further embedded this historically racist view into contemporary policies, aggressively targeting Indigenous women throughout the country. Mora describes Oportunidades as a program that "regulates the social reproduction activities of women by providing an economic stimulus in exchange for alterations of their social and cultural habits" (p. 151). Having grown up in Diecisiete de Noviembre after the uprising, Amalia's reflections on Zapatista women's autonomy are specific to such historical policy backdrops and undercut the gendered and racialized views of Indigenous women by the Mexican state. Mora further describes Zapatista women's collectives as they likewise impact broad enactments of autonomy by the Zapatista collective: "From the praxis found in the women's collectives emerges a politicization of everyday life connected to household tasks in such a way that decolonization in autonomy transforms into a collective drive to define the terms of social and biological life" (p. 155).

Decolonization in autonomy for those of Diecisiete de Noviembre and elsewhere emanates from an understanding of this politicization of everyday life as enactment of *kuxlejal*, "reflecting on life existence, as part of the accumulated exercise of the power to be" (Mora 2017: 151). Kuxlejal is a term that can be used in a variety of ways. Though translated reductively into English as "life," the term evokes temporal and locative allusions as in the elements and entities within and upon lands—and the land itself—across the past, present, and future. Mora's translational linkage here to "to be" indicates further something of the reflective processes kuxlejal conjures, that is, being reflective of oneself in relation to the entities of place in previous, present, and future moments. With the latter kuxlejal elaboration in mind, decolonization in autonomy for Amalia and Zapatista of Diecisiete de Noviembre is a drive "to define the terms of social and biological life." As such, the politicization of the everyday is an intimate and relational Mayan, Zapatista governance formulated in significant part by kuxlejal. Mora writes: "Autonomy must be understood as a series of kuxlejal practices that assert control over material and immaterial conditions—land territory, individual and collective bodies, local knowledge of health and care—that renders it possible to establish a collective identity as indigenous people in a timeframe that extends beyond and behind the present" (2017: 161).

Some thinkers of decolonization see the role of Indigenous philosophies in the form of kuxlejal disrupting Western ontologies, offering fertile ways of thinking about sociopolitical arrangements against neoliberalism and statist forms of governance. Other perspectives within decolonial orientations might raise questions on gender and the "home," wondering how kuxlejal speaks to (decolonial) gender relations and heteronormative practices within Diecisiete de Noviembre. Yet others within decolonizing frameworks might raise concerns about the term "praxis" and wonder about the influences of Marxist thought on wider currents of Zapatismo. More specific to Coulthard's (2014) analysis of gender justice and decolonization, the autonomy of the women's collectives actively addresses the multidirectionality of decolonization—externally toward the state, internally regarding "traditional" patterns of gendered labor practices within the domain of Tseltal, Tsotsl, and Tojolobal families and broader Zapatista governing practices. Autonomy emanates from kuxlejal. Thus, considered within Coulthard's gender justice and decolonization principle, it points to a rethinking of the best of Indigenous traditions.

But the ethical, economic, and political relationships between academically based discussions of decolonization and the women of Diecisiete de Noviembre are no more easily aligned than those described by Margonis (1999, 2007b), Thompson (1998), or Ellsworth (1992). The use or assimilation of kuxlejal, for example, can recreate patterns of imperial relation to the Mayan by enabling a financialization of their knowledges through university knowledge production and a lack of commitment to learning the language, compounded by wrenching the term apart from the everyday practices and contexts of the Mayan. The following sections of this chapter proceed by elaborating on the obstacles noted by Margonis (1999, 2007b) and Thompson (1998) by highlighting two critical readings of this specific concern for decolonial pedagogies—the borrowing of Indigenous knowledges and the obscuring of political contexts—by Spivak (1999) and Turner (2006).

CRITICAL REFLECTIONS WITH AMALIA AND MAYAN PHILOSOPHY: CLASS LOCATION AND ETHICO-POLITICAL SINGULARITY

Spivak (1999) has written in many places of the tensions within the theorization of postcolonialism and decolonization. The area I would like to attend to here as a deepening of Margonis's discussion of "patterns at play," has to be situated in her commentaries on a particular culture of postcolonial identity fashioning and class location. "The lines of contact between imperialism and de-colonization," she writes "constitute the most encompassing crises today—the problem of producing plausible stories so business can go on as usual" (Spivak 1999: 340). On one reading, this passage echoes the refrain of creating conditions of possibility in the production of plausible stories, which include those of the most marginalized in contemporary political and economic systems. More critically, Spivak is saying that there is an absorption of decolonial impulses toward the maintenance of "business as usual." With the latter, the complexity of this circulation of the decolonial within the dominant has a crucial participant, the Indigenous intellectual elite, who appear to always have been looked to by the European intellectual class to sharpen certain historical moments of critique—Japan for Barthes, or China for Jameson, for example. In the longer historical contexts of such practices, Spivak notes that an "indigenous" intellectual elite emerges, taking up influential positions and mediating a relation to these knowledges, yet it does so from a certain remove from the practices of those most oppressed. Spivak goes on to argue that deeply engrained scripts for the nonnative researcher/theorist (script of vanguardism) and this Indigenous elite (script of native informant) can too easily obscure the ethico-political commitments to specific persons like Amalia within a pedagogical relation for decolonization. Where such commitments are not realized, Spivak argues they are "ontopology" (1999: 404) (the study of the being of others) through a kind of "anthropologistic contamination" (p. 383): extractive projects, for example, enacted on the women of Diecisiete de Noviembre, which thus enact, in turn, imperial relations.

Elaborating her deconstructive readings between "subject" and "history," Spivak writes that deconstruction is "not [directed] specifically at the identity of the two poles in a binary opposition, but at the hidden ethico-political agenda that drives the differentiation between the two" (p. 332). We can ask: what ethico-political agenda co-constitutes the differentiations between academically based decolonial discussions, and autonomous Tseltal, Tsotsl, and Tojolobal women, and between imperialism/decolonization and subject/history, and how do these critical junctures of learning animate plausible stories for decolonization? For Spivak (1999), the economic difference between elite intellectuals discussing decolonization and autonomous Tseltal, Tsotsl, and Tojolobal speakers provides for the mobilization of ethics as both the commitment to not conflate forms of resistance and decolonial projects and likewise a moment of critique on the financialization of the globe. This critique can be a moment of solidarity to disrupt the getting back to business of such financializations, but it cannot, for Spivak, transplant kuxlejal into the contexts of academic, intellectual elaborations of decolonization as if "resistance" were the same in both instances.

There are at least two cautions then to be taken from Spivak (1999) relevant to some of the dynamics within and across this spectrum of efforts in/for decolonization. One has to do with the obscuring of class difference by theorists in those that they often write about. Writing on the specific moments of the absorption of postcolonial intellectuals into US academic institutions in the 1970s, Spivak remarks: "The aura of identification with those distant objects of oppression, clings to these [postcolonial] informants as, again at best, they identify with the other racial and ethnic minorities in metropolitan space" (1999: 360). At worst, she goes on to say, "they take advantage of the aura and play the native informant uncontaminated by disavowed involvement with the machinery of the production of knowledge" (p. 360). Theorists of decolonization may not always be as attentive to Spivak's concern, ignoring class privilege and how that has been achieved through a participation within the dominant forms of knowledge production. Her similar arguments regarding those who claim "upward class-mobility as resistance," whereby ethnic diversification of the middle class provides for a "destabilization of the metropole," are astute, especially where those intellectuals come to "stand in" as the resisters and the "racial underclass and subaltern South step back into the penumbra" (p. 361).

Finally, the class difference and the context of radical income inequalities similarly highlight, for Spivak, the importance of an attention to rights in both contexts. There are differing contexts and in fact needs for the mobilization of civil rights for rural and Indigenous peoples as distinct from projects to critique the colonial bases of rights frameworks among a decolonial intellectual elite. Coulthard's caveat is relevant here in a similar way. In his view, there is a necessity to continue to engage with the state's legal and political system, and this engagement is generally conceived as rights-based. And as Turner (2006) argues, per the section that follows, it is this entanglement of colonialism as the contemporary situation of rights-based forms of governance that is the most fraught for those who claim projects for decolonization.

TURNER'S CRITIQUES OF DECOLONIAL THEORIZING: THE RELATIONAL ENTANGLEMENTS OF COLONIAL LAW

Turner (2006) takes up a discussion of Indigenous rights, sovereignty, and self-determination within a legal-political context he describes according to "Kymlicka's constraint," named after political philosopher Will Kymlicka. For Turner, Kymlicka's constraint states that

> For better or worse, it is predominately non-Aboriginal judges and politicians who have the ultimate power to protect and enforce Aboriginal rights, and so it is important to find a justification of them that such people can recognize and understand. Aboriginal people have their own understanding of self-government drawn from their own experience, and that is important. But it is also important, politically, to know how non-Aboriginal Canadians— Supreme Court Justices for example—will understand Aboriginal Rights and relate them to their own experiences and interpretations. (2006: 58)

Turner characterizes Kymlicka to be arguing that the principal task for Indigenous peoples is to convince non-Indigenous judges and politicians that their claims for self-determination and self-government are legitimate. For Turner, one of the central issues here is the historical nature of the relation. He writes that the philosophical relationship between indigenous ways of knowing the world and the legal and political discourses of the state has evolved within the ongoing political relationship. That is, the very ways we frame the language of rights, sovereignty and nationalism are also steeped in colonialism; yet like the political relationship, indigenous resistance has weathered these discourses. (p. 95)

Thus, while resistance to the normative language of law, rights, and so on as colonialist is correct, it is no less correct that to use them is to simultaneously continue to claim rights in a dialogue with colonialism. This is the principal reason Turner sees colonialism as "inextricable" from the current moment of Indigenous political life and struggle. Turner is confounded then by those who would claim to enact decolonial "political" projects of nationhood whereby one extracts oneself from the language of rights. This is especially the case where the claimed ability to withdraw or separate from the discourses of rights and Indigenous nationhood are based on notions of tradition. "The politics of nation-hood," Turner writes, "remain a distinctly Eurocentric practice" and a "discourse of the state" (p. 110).

However, Turner insists that what Indigenous peoples mean when they say "nation-hood" is based in oral traditions (p. 26). In this way, he echoes Spivak's concerns, not so much based on the class difference of Indigenous intellectuals but with regards to her discussion of the university location of decolonial intellectual locations as a form of life.

Turner does not write as one committed to a future of a colonial rights-based relationship as a foregone conclusion. Indeed, he calls for the unrelenting dismantling of colonialism by Indigenous intellectuals as "word warriors" who "[make] an investigation of the meaning and praxis of colonialism a central activity of an indigenous intellectual community" (p. 101). "Abolishing colonialism is the goal of many indigenous and non-indigenous peoples," he summarizes; "finding a way to do it is the great dilemma" (p. 109). Thus, Turner's position does not insist on or indeed commit to a rights framework for the future. Instead, one could read Turner as saying that Indigenous governments do not at this time have the alternative of heeding the call from the Indigenous intelligentsia to bypass talk of a right to self-determination. "Most Aboriginal leaders," he argues, "understand that the state's legal and political processes are, in many ways, 'the only game in town'" (p. 111). To be in this latter moment is, for Turner, to operate within Kymlicka's constraint and a dialogue with colonialism. At the same time, this dialogue by Indigenous and non-Indigenous people can provide for the "unpacking of colonialism" through the emerging praxis of a "critical indigenous philosophy" (p. 101). Importantly, Turner is not saying that this *is* in fact the only game in town, or that it will last forever, but rather is a component of the contemporary dialogue. He suggests that changes will happen to all those involved, but where that goes is not knowable. He has a hard time imagining it without it being affected by colonialism, even as the attempt is to dismantle the latter.

Turner (2006) is no less attentive than Spivak to the difficult patterns at play that inform questions of an ethico-politico relation, "cultural difference," and potentials for the appropriation of Indigenous tradition. Unlike Spivak, he does not focus on the economic difference of university-based Indigenous intellectuals. Yet like Spivak, Turner takes seriously the cultural location of university-based Indigenous critics and differentiates between the Indigenous philosopher and the Indigenous intellectual, the latter a "word warrior." Unlike what Spivak's analysis implies, Turner does not locate word warriors within the legacies of native cultural informants and Indigenous elites. For him, the crucial distinction between the Indigenous philosopher and the word warrior is the work they do.

Turner defines an Indigenous philosopher as an individual who is fluent in their native language, has a leadership capacity in the life of the community, and lives in the community attending to the lives of the people. These persons are part of formal and informal governance practices who may or may not identify their roles as "decolonizing." The Indigenous philosopher, Turner emphasizes, is not a university professor, even though he applies a university designation ("philosopher") to these community-based persons. Be that as it may, Indigenous philosophers "are central to the future survival of indigenous communities as distinct peoples because without indigenous philosophies we lose our languages, our ceremonies, and our unique ways of understanding the world" (Turner 2006: 119). As noted, the word warrior engages in the work of academically based disciplines to identify, name, and interrupt neocolonial relations in law, policy, economics, and social practices as these limit native peoples. Both of these communities are, for Turner, necessary for the present contexts of governance for Indigenous peoples.

Turner may be more generous in his consideration of Indigenous intellectuals and can be read as assuming they are participants in the broadest aspects of their communities. In fact, this participation is a necessary condition for the criticality of doing Indigenous philosophy. "The primary responsibility of a word warrior," he argues, "is to be intimately familiar with the legal and political discourses of the state while remaining citizens of indigenous nations" (Turner 2006: 119). "Word warriors," he adds, "retain strong connections to their communities" (p. 117). These word warriors participate in the community of critical Indigenous philosophy to "assert and defend the rights, sovereignty, and nation-hood we believe we possess," and to "defend the position that indigenous philosophies of knowledge are rational and coherent" (p. 116). As noted, Turner does not mean by this that these traditional knowledges are to be *ipso facto* shared with the dominant society. He recasts the issue Spivak names as dissimulation. For Turner, the Indigenous intellectual is not covering over their class or university location or identity. The word warrior is not an Indigenous philosopher, as such, and is thus not in a position to expound on the rich conceptual frameworks for university audiences. A word warrior, according to Turner, does not claim to be an authority on such knowledge in the university setting.

Nonetheless, perhaps circumspect about such a possibility and likewise highly cautious toward broader non-Indigenous audiences, Turner writes that "history has shown us that at least at this time in the relationships [between Indigenous and non-Indigenous], we must keep to ourselves our sacred knowledge as we articulate and understand it from within our own cultures, for it is this knowledge that defines us as indigenous peoples" (2006: 110). Thus, Turner distinguishes himself from those thinkers in decolonial collectives who affirm that Indigenous knowledges can be taught removed from community context and practices and avoid larger, historically engrained stereotypic patterns at play in Indigenous and settler relations.

On the reading offered here, Turner's project for critical Indigenous philosophy is a methodical effort to abolish colonialism and is more akin to a decolonial project than perhaps he would acknowledge. His pragmatism regarding Kymlicka's constraint is an acknowledgment of the current colonial situation but certainly not a normalization of a colonial future. He writes that "It is not enough to simply engage European thought on its own terms; indigenous intellectuals need to critically engage European ideas, methodologies, and theories to show how they have marginalized, distorted, and ignored indigenous

FIGURE 8.2 A bright summer day at Opossum Lake in Pennsylvania. *Source*: JoeBinderPhotography / iStock.

voices" (Turner 2006: 100). Still, Turner unfortunately does not indicate when or upon what criteria he thinks indigenous knowledges on governance and broader intellectual traditions might be promoted in university settings. On this latter point, Turner would not be able to contribute to Coulthard's (2014) decolonizing principle of "beyond the nation-state."

REFLECTIONS ON RELATIONAL ETHICS FOR DECOLONIZING GOVERNANCE WITHIN INDIGENOUS LANDS/WATERS

If a relation of ethico-political singularity is not achievable as a pedagogical one to Amalia through Mora's transcriptions and descriptions, due to what Spivak (1999) calls "anthropological contamination," and if Turner's (2006) caution to the inclusion of Indigenous philosophies is upheld, how can Coulthard's (2014) or Margonis's (2007b) solidarity project find partners for generative projects of decolonial governance within and across these various trajectories? Spivak argues that what "suppresses the possibility of decolonization [is the] financialization of the globe," as the "definitive transnational activity" (1999: 399). Spivak does not obscure the central importance of law and rights, stating that "we must fight to pass laws, and be vigilant that they are implemented" (p. 391). In her view, this movement must occur while mindful that "white supremacist culture wants to claim the entire agency of capitalism—re-coded as the rule of law within a democratic heritage—only for itself" (p. 398).

With Spivak (1999), Turner (2006) is clearly alert to the latter coding of law for white supremacy, even as he is less focused on the transnational flows of finance and its punishing effects of poverty. For Turner (2006), the differentiations between the location and work of the Indigenous philosopher and the word warrior have less to do with economic class differentiation and more to do with their roles in defending the rights of Indigenous peoples to be self-determining according to their own internally defined practices and philosophies. Because this defense of the rights of Indigenous people is mediated with/in colonial structures of law, Turner is left with the assertion that it is and will continue to be relational to that colonial structure. Word warriors labor at the intellectual academic borders of Indigenous and colonial laws. Turner can only bear witness to this ongoing negotiation as a bidirectional structuring that he claims cannot be decolonized. He holds out the possibility of greater influence by Indigenous philosophers for changing the relationship toward justice but argues "the track record for courts recognizing the legitimacy of Aboriginal ways of knowing is not good—in fact it is abysmal" (2006: 111). Here, Turner names another facet of the failure of the ethico-political singularity: the refusal of the law to hear Indigenous peoples. While

Turner would agree with Spivak on the necessity of changing laws, in actual practice justice would continue to be denied within the so-called "rule of law."

Coulthard's (2014) thesis "beyond the nation-state," even as a critique of Turner's limited notion of decolonization (internal to Indigenous communities), provides gestures and a minimal formulation toward this governance of the beyond. Coulthard's Indigenous resurgence "seeks to practice decolonial, gender emancipatory, and economically nonexploitative alternative structures of law and sovereign authority" (2014: 179). The foundation for this practice is again the "critical refashioning of the best of indigenous traditions." Here, too, Coulthard curiously sidesteps the question of the role of Indigenous traditions as a broader social foundation and likewise obscures the pedagogical question inherent to Spivak's ethico-singularity. On ecological knowledge specifically, Spivak comments: "I have no doubt that we must learn to learn from the original practical ecological philosophies of the world" (1999: 383). She adds:

> This learning can only be attempted through the supplementation of collective effort by love. What deserves the name of love is an effort—over which one has no control yet at which one must not strain—which is slow, attention on both sides—how does one win the attention of the subaltern without coercion or crises?—mind-changing on both sides, at the possibility of an unascertainable ethical singularity that is not ever a sustainable condition. The necessary collective efforts are to change laws, relations of production, systems of education, and health care. But without the mind-changing one-on-one responsible contact, nothing will stick. (p. 383)

Coulthard (2014), Spivak (1999), and Turner (2006) do not provide quick, easily formulated ways to situate Amalia and Zapatista in relation to academic elaborations of decolonial theorizing—and, by extension, philosophy of education. To love Amalia as Spivak describes here, to attempt that ethico-political effort of singularity in noncrises moments for changing minds, would be to criticize what Turner identifies in the broader legal and social patterns at play. For Coulthard and Spivak, Turner would likely be seen as overlooking the histories and contemporary actions of those contributing to those conditions that make such a possibility material and concrete. Theorists and philosophers invested in decolonization must take up this effort of a loving relation to Amalia, but not from a space of innocence, naïveté, or intellectual imperialism.

SOCIAL INTERDEPENDENCIES FOR RELATIONAL GOVERNANCE

More generative statements can be made about this relation to elaborate on the conditions of possibility for decolonization from within critical contexts of philosophy of education. An emphasis should be reiterated on the ever-emergent *conditions* that contribute to the possibility of decolonization as a continual striving. Not understood as a linear progression but as an always already occurring process for Indigenous peoples, decolonization is an effort to enact principles of interdependent relationalities of learning from, in contexts of Indigenous reclamations of lands/waters despite settler colonial violences through economics, policies, racisms, and militarization. Judith Butler and Athena Athanasiou (2013) take up these trajectories of decolonial interdependencies in a discussion of the varying, ongoing structures of dispossession. "If a certain kind of political mobilization," they state, "even one against land dispossession, is based on an idea of social interdependency, or on modes of ownership that sometimes seek recourse to sovereignty, this suggests that land reclamations work with and against traditional notions of sovereignty" (Butler and Athanasiou 2013: 28). Social interdependence, not possession by individuals as sovereigns, speaks to the overlapping simultaneity, not linearity, of the conditions of decolonization. More specific to Indigenous peoples, Butler and Athanasiou comment that "reclaiming stolen lands is crucial for many indigenous people's movements, and yet that is something different from defining the subject as one who possesses itself and its object world, and whose relations with others are defined by possession and its instrumentalities" (p. 28).

"Something different relationally," understood as social interdependencies, is an expansive concept for Butler and Athanasiou, alluding to the effort at love, the attempts for observing ethico-political singularity for broader governance principles—perhaps beyond the nation-state. As such, their thinking continues its generative dismantling of possession, negating any too simple reversal from dispossession to possession. "If we talk about responsibility in the context of this idea of the ethical," they continue, "it would be precisely the counter example to moral narcissism. I do not augment myself with my virtuousness when I act responsibly, but I give myself over to the broader sociality that I am" (Butler and Athanasiou 2013: 108). Giving oneself over to a broader sociality—without narcissism, without ontopology, without anthropology—is a fundamental condition for theorizing and facilitating a learning relation for decolonization.

This chapter opened with curricular images of the transfer of political authority from the direct rule of colonies to newly autonomous, self-governing nation-states. Employing a periodizing view of such movement would make invisible the parallel historical and ongoing efforts to enact a decolonial governance that does not end in traditional ownership. Philosophers of education attentive to the possibilities for decolonial learning relations can contribute to such a project by continuing to lay bare those newly emergent obstacles—material and theoretical—that undermine relations of learning to Indigenous peoples. Importantly, such a dialogue can foster multiethnic solidarities for decolonial governance. It can bring attention to practices for autonomy without possession but rather for the reclamation of lands/waters as a culture of socio-natural interdependencies.

REFERENCES

Primary sources

Butler, Judith and Athena Athanasiou (2013), *Dispossession: The Performative in the Political*, Cambridge: Polity Press.
Coulthard, Glen S. (2014), *Red Skins, White Masks*, Minneapolis: University of Minnesota Press.
Dei, George J. Sefa (2018), "'Black Like Me': Reframing Blackness for Decolonial Politics," *Educational Studies*, 54 (2): 117–42.
Ellsworth, Elizabeth (1992), "Why Doesn't this Feel Empowering?," in C. Luke and J. Gore (eds.), *Feminisms and Critical Pedagogy*, 297–324, New York: Routledge.
Jansen, Jan and Jürgen Osterhammel (2017), *Decolonization: A Short History*, Princeton, NJ: Princeton University Press.
Lugones, Maria (2007), "Heterosexualism and the Colonial Modern Gender System," *Hypatia*, 22 (1): 186–209.
Maldonado-Torres, Nelson (2007), "On the Coloniality of Being," *Cultural Studies*, 21 (2): 240–70.
Maldonado-Torres, Nelson (2012), "Epistemology, Ethics and the Time/Space of Decolonization: Perspectives from the Caribbean and the Latino/a Americas," in Ada Maria Isasi-Diaz and Eduardo Mendieta (eds.), *Decolonizing Epistemologies: Latina/o Theology and Philosophy*, 193–206, New York: Fordham University Press.
Margonis, Frank (1999), "The Demise of Authenticity," in S. Tozer (ed.), *Philosophy of Education: 1999*, 99–107, Urbana, IL: Philosophy of Education Society.
Margonis, Frank (2007a), "Reconstructing Pragmatism to Address Racial Injustice," *Journal of Philosophy of Education*, 41 (1): 141–9.
Margonis, Frank (2007b), "A Relational Ethic of Solidarity?," in B. Stengel (ed.), *Philosophy of Education: 2007*, 62–70, Urbana, IL: Philosophy of Education Society.
Mora, Mariana (2017), *Kuxlejal Politics: Indigenous Autonomy, Race and Decolonizing Research in Zapatista Communities*, Austin: University of Texas Press.
Patel, Lisa (2014), "Countering Coloniality in Educational Research: From Ownership to Answerability," *Educational Studies*, 50: 357–77.
Spivak, Gayatri Chakravorty (1999), *A Critique of Postcolonial Reason: Toward a History of the Vanishing Present*, Cambridge, MA: Harvard University Press.
Thompson, Audrey (1997), "For: Anti-Racist Education," *Curriculum Inquiry*, 27 (1): 7–44.
Thompson, Audrey (1998), "Not the Color Purple: Black Feminist Lessons for Educational Caring," *Harvard Educational Review*, 68 (4): 522–54.
Turner, Dale (2006), *This Is Not a Peace Pipe: Towards a Critical Indigenous Philosophy*, Toronto: University of Toronto Press.

Secondary sources

Applebaum, Barbara (2010), *Being White, Being Good: White Complicity, White Moral Responsibility and Social Justice Pedagogy*, Lanham, MD: Lexington Books.
Dussel, Enrique (1985), *Philosophy of Liberation*, Eugene, OR: Wipf & Stock.
Glass, Ronald D. (2001), "On Paulo Freire's Philosophy of Praxis and the Foundations of Liberation Education," *Educational Researcher* 30 (2): 15–25.
Glass, Ronald D. (2013). "Critical hope and struggles for justice: An antidote to despair for antiracism educators," in *Discerning critical hope in educational*

practices, Vivienne Bozalek, Brenda Lebwitz, Ronelle Carolissen and Megan Boler (eds), 123–34. Routledge.

Grosfoguel, Ramón, Roberto Hernandez, and Ernesto Rosen Valesquez (2016), *Decolonizing the Westernized University: Interventions in Philosophy of Education from Within and Without*, Lanham, MD: Lexington Press.

Haymes, S. *Race Culture and the City: A Pedagogy for Black Urban Struggle*, Albany State University of New York.

Hytten, Kathy (2018), "On Building Islands of Decency," *Educational Studies*, 54 (1): 99–108.

Mayo, Cris (2007), "Queering Foundations: Queer and Lesbian, Gay, Bisexual and Transgender Educational Research," *Review of Research in Education*, 31: 78–94.

Mayo, Cris (2013), "Unsettling Relations; Schools, Gay Marriage, and Educating for Sexuality," *Educational Theory*, 63 (5): 543–58.

Mignolo, Walter D. (2000), *Local Histories/Global Designs: Coloniality, Subaltern Knowledges and Border Thinking*, Princeton, NJ: Princeton University Press.

Quijano, Anibal (2000), "Coloniality of Power, Eurocentrism, and Latin America," *Nepantla: Views from the South*, 1 (3): 533–80.

CHAPTER NINE

Liberal Education and Its Existential Meaning

RENÉ V. ARCILLA

INTRODUCTION

What is liberal education? This is of course my overarching topic. Initially, however, I want to imagine the question being asked in a tone opposed to the scholarly. Think of someone who has just received the bill for her son's first college term. Although this working woman is unhappy with how crushing it is, she knew what to expect. What causes her temper to flare is rather the transcript of courses she paid for. Introduction to World Religions, Ancient Greek History, The Foundations of Quantum Physics: these provoke her because they appear to contribute nothing to her struggling child's dream to be an engineer. When she berates him for throwing money away on such whimsical subjects, she is doubly shocked when he explains that he was merely following institutional requirements. "They tell me these classes form my liberal education." "What," the anxiously concerned, beleaguered mother thunders, "is liberal education?"

My examination of liberal education is accordingly framed by this kind of critical doubt, if not incredulity, that many of its stakeholders have today. To be sure, it is impossible to comprehend this education even roughly without some sense of its long, complex history. The practice is above all the deliberate continuation of a tradition. At the same time, this tradition makes sense for us only if it still intimates an attractive future rather than simply getting in the way of what we are trying to do now. Governing my view of liberal education's historical nature, then, is the question of whether it has reached a dead end. In the short space I have, I propose to focus on the idea that originally inspired the practice of liberal education. I want to understand how it once illuminated and affirmed a particular social world and why it no longer seems to some to have a place in ours. If others of us nevertheless find ourselves still drawn to the practice, perhaps we can explain and enhance that appeal by articulating more fully some underappreciated implications of the idea. In other words, perhaps we may discern something deeper in this conception of liberal education that bridges the divide between its original world and our own.

Such an approach loosely resembles the logic of modernism that shaped the fine arts from the end of the nineteenth century until the middle of the twentieth. Critics such as Clement Greenberg and Michael Fried have explained that genres such as easel painting or the lyric poem are liable, when their surrounding society alters, to enter into a state of crisis in which their traditional conventions no longer compel much conviction (Arcilla 2010). For instance, artists and audiences alike may come to hear in a sonnet, or see in a nude, nothing but the formulaic; these forms appear forced and arbitrary. Such disenchantment is not far from that which may be felt by someone listening to a dean pontificate about the "nobility of the liberal arts." The challenge taken up by modernists, then, was that of regenerating their arts by stressing in an innovative way some taken-for-granted feature of their traditional mediums. This is what I would like to do with respect to liberal education.

My inquiry is divided into four sections. In the first, I elucidate how the crystallization of liberal education in the Middle Ages presupposed a certain understanding of human freedom. In the second section, I explain why this understanding no longer suits contemporary democratic society. My third section suggests, however, that many of us experience a kind of informal, "existential education" outside of schools in which what is at stake is actually a related idea of freedom. I conclude in the last section that a revised and renewed liberal education today could serve to provide this existential education to everyone.

A TRADITION OF CULTIVATING FREEDOM

Bruce Kimball (1986, 2010) supplies us with a cogent history of the idea of liberal education and a useful perspective on this idea's origins. Its anchor is the materialization in early medieval literature of references to the *septem artes liberales* (seven liberal arts). We find this, for example, in the *Institutiones* written by Cassiodorus (*c.* 484–*c.* 584). These arts are famously partitioned into the *trivium* of grammar, rhetoric, and logic, on the one hand, and the *quadrivium* of arithmetic, geometry, music, and astronomy, on the other. The first group is mainly concerned with verbal persuasion; the second, with the laws of number and measure. Liberal education is thus understood by the society that first recognized its institutional conventions to be the pursuit of these arts in concert with each other, however this pursuit is conceived and executed in detail. At the start of its tradition, the term designates a certain curriculum of study. As universities and colleges arose, they furnished this curriculum with a home.

Two questions follow that motivate Kimball's account. First, what inspired the curriculum in the first place? In particular, besides the contextual social pressures that surely shaped it, is there some idea that led our ancestors to see the importance and belonging-together of these specific arts? The second question regards the wide distance between this initial conception of liberal education and the kinds of collegiate core classes and course distribution requirements that characterize this education today. How did the seven liberal arts morph into such very diverse contemporary curricula? In addition to being once more a product of institutional and social developments, may we understand this historical change to be a response to alterations in the education's ruling idea?

Kimball's answers boil down to a tale of how the idea of liberal education multiplied into two. Initially, there was a conception of the practice oriented toward what he calls the "*artes liberales* ideal" (1986: 37–8). He traces its lineage back to writers and thinkers of ancient Rome and Greece. It stipulates that the aim of liberal education is to form leaders of society. The way to accomplish this is for educators to identify the virtues that distinguish good character and conduct and to prescribe them to their students. Such virtues have already been informing the society that this young generation and their fellow citizens all support; they are authoritatively portrayed and communicated in a canon of texts. To ensure that the virtues continue to project wide influence, then, special care should be taken to teach these classics to those who are able to understand their ethical meaning and put it constantly and effectively into practice. The pedagogical approach of this teaching is that of passing a set body of knowledge down to students rather than inciting the latter to search for it. As for the question of why we should support a society that is formed in such a way, one ruled by leaders who have been educated in the liberal arts, the answer is that this kind of society is intrinsically good; it is not an instrumental means to some further good.

With an eye in particular to Isocrates, Cicero, and Quintilian, Kimball suggests that this idea of the liberal education project is personified in the figure of the orator. The orator is the teacher of society's privileged elite. Once again, the aim is to encourage and guide those so favored by fortune, those who are likely to step into leadership positions in any case, to become virtuous and effective. And the chief vehicle for doing this is moving words. The orator uses eloquence to drive home to the young the principal terms and modes of understanding of the tradition. In addition to being formed by classical texts, students develop their own verbal capacity to sway their fellow citizens by evoking the wisdom of the community. In the wake of such a recognition of the orator's crucial mission, the medieval architects of the liberal arts' institutionalization assigned capital importance to the *trivium* of arts, which we would today place in the field of the humanities.

Now, Kimball observes that a few centuries later, in the high Middle Ages of the thirteenth and fourteenth centuries, the commanding position of the orator in this education was overthrown. Another figure rose to preeminence: the philosopher. Exemplified by Aristotle, whose writings were rediscovered during this period, this figure stands for the pursuit of truth over all other considerations. As scholastic thinkers such as Peter Abelard, Thomas Aquinas, and John of Salisbury attained prominence in the rising universities, *philosophia* was separated from, and elevated above, the liberal arts; it was furthermore divided into natural, moral, and metaphysical fields. Meanwhile, the arts of logic and mathematics were given new meaning and stature. The concern for moral formation and the development of eloquence became secondary.

Needless to say, this is hardly the last word in the story. The Renaissance revived the prestige of the orator and the *trivium*. In contrast, the Enlightenment that succeeded it affirmed the primacy of the quest for truth for its own sake. As modernity developed further, the philosopher became less emblematic of this search, giving way to the natural scientist, whose accomplishments further elevated the standing of mathematical and empirical study. In general, the broad lines of Kimball's history are more or less set by the time we come to the eighteenth century. The ongoing evolution and changes to liberal education practice, he suggests, may be largely understood as driven by the struggle for dominance within liberal education between the descendants of the orators and those of the philosophers. As I indicated, the orator represents the *artes liberales* ideal. The philosopher pursues the implications of prioritizing the quest for truth. Eventually associated more, in modern popular imagination, with the children of Galileo and Darwin, this figure ends up elaborating an alternative conception of liberal education.

Kimball calls this conception the "liberal-free ideal" (1986: 119–22). It encourages us to free ourselves from dogmatism and develop our critical reason. The way to do this is to cultivate a stance of wary skepticism toward given beliefs. Translated to the political realm, such an attitude encourages the questioning of established authority and conventional wisdom and favors instead a democratic ethic of tolerance and egalitarianism, as well as, J.S. Mill (1859/1978) affirms, the cultivation of individual, potentially groundbreaking experiments in thinking and living.

Kimball argues, then, that liberal education design and practice, from its codification in the early Middle Ages until the present day, develops historically in response to two conflicting inspirations. After the rise of the liberal-free ideal in the eighteenth century, this conflict usually entailed, practically speaking, the favoring of one or the other ideal by a particular university or college at a particular time and place and the accommodation of characteristic features of its competitor in various jury-rigged curricular arrangements. Indeed, it is because neither side, from generation to generation and under differing circumstances, expresses much interest in totally uprooting the other ideal that we may understand this struggle to be one inside a unitary tradition. Most recently, from the second half of the twentieth century until the present, the steady and then precipitous decline of support for the humanities suggests that the liberal-free ideal has achieved complete hegemony.

Obviously, this stick-man sketch of Kimball's history leaves out all the detail and documentation on which its plausibility rests. My point in introducing his work is simply to bring into focus a philosophical question at the heart of the liberal arts tradition. Suppose we grant that the orator epitomized liberal education's original inspiration. Why were the liberal arts not accordingly called the *oratorical arts*? (The *trivium* could have been viewed as primary to the orator's mission, the *quadrivium* as ancillary.) Why were they instead essentially, in name, linked to freedom? Another side of this question becomes clear when we turn to the rival ideal of the philosopher. By calling this ideal "liberal-free" and by emphasizing that it champions freedom from dogmatism, Kimball highlights how much more ambiguous is the freedom nominally at stake in the *artes liberales*. In what sense, exactly, do these arts serve freedom? Finally, we may notice that Kimball's history principally tries to map the

FIGURE 9.1 Large group of students or young people sitting in a circle with copybooks, having discussion together. *Source*: svetikd / iStock.

changing discourse and curricular arrangements inside liberal education. What is left more in shadow is the understanding of what differentiates liberal education from other concurrent educational projects at its borders. How may this understanding, too, rely on a certain idea of freedom and how may shifts in our conception of freedom have something to do with liberal education's fluctuating appeal?

To probe these tightly related issues, I turn, a bit ironically, to Aristotle's *Politics*. This philosopher provides us with an explication of what is at stake in the orator's education. Aristotle remarks that political societies rely not only on laws but also on education for their orderly flourishing and reproduction; both legislation and teaching are key vehicles for habituating citizens to good standards of behavior. Such norms vary somewhat depending on the nature of society. In a democracy, in which all citizens participate in ruling and thus pride themselves on being free from foreign subjection, one of the most insidious threats to social stability is the notion that this freedom amounts to the license to do whatever one wants. When one yields to this notion, one is yanked about by one's happenstance and unthinking appetites and ceases to govern oneself, let alone others, in a well-considered, rational fashion. Accordingly, Aristotle looks to education to check this tendency. Specifically, he considers how it may help democratic citizens understand and cultivate the best use of their free time.

This leisure is famously termed *scholē* and constitutes the root of the idea of school.[1] For Aristotle, it is a defining mark of the free person. At least to some degree, such a character is free from the necessity of having to labor. In contrast, one who has to work is a slave, and, to the extent that one orients one's life toward such a necessity, one leads a life that is slavish.

What it means to educate people to be free in the most constructive sense is therefore first of all to habituate them to scorn and minimize in themselves the slavish. One may need to engage in some labor simply to survive; however, this should not be something to enjoy or take pride in but rather ought to be considered a necessary evil. Part of the reason that a free person seeks to moderate appetite, then, is so that they can protect and hopefully extend their leisure. Once this free time is established, it becomes the stage for one's real actions and life.

So, what should one do in one's *scholē*? As the term suggests to us today, Aristotle argues that we should devote it in part to study. However, not just any education suits it; in particular, he proscribes learning that is primarily concerned with the occupational side of life. Such training and work are servile arts that should be clearly put in the service of our separate, nobler, free life. Nor does Aristotle find much value in recreational activities of play or entertainment: he understands their pleasures to be by nature mostly compensatory relief from the pains of toil. They are forms of relaxation and rest and thus remain tied to the routine of labor. The arts that educate us in our free *scholē* are rather those that both exercise and strengthen our capacities to govern ourselves, build a virtuous character, and attain an enduring happiness. They are intrinsically fulfilling. Furthermore, because humans are by nature social animals, one's self-government entails that one participates in collective self-government. A partial exception to this rule is the philosopher who pursues a contemplative life of self-sufficient withdrawal from politics. However, Aristotle calls such a life "godly"; he acknowledges that humans can achieve it only incompletely and for moments at a time. This suggests that philosophers too have to rely on and be engaged with the rest of the *polis*. The liberal arts that they and their fellow citizens cultivate thus also prepare people for politics.

Freedom *from* slavish worries, freedom *to* participate in political action: according to Aristotle, this is what is at stake in the orator's education of democratic citizens. When some such figure promotes a practice as a liberal art, then, that person is claiming it develops these negative and positive freedoms in us. Jumping to the present, this understanding moreover enables us to distinguish liberal education from two other familiar and prevalent kinds of contemporary education alongside it. One is what Michael Oakeshott calls "school education" (1991: 189–90); today, we might more precisely label it *grammar education*. It consists mainly of teaching children fundamental skills of literacy and numeracy and basic bodies of common knowledge. Pupils are expected to absorb this content whether they wish to or not; their freedom in the matter is scarcely recognized, let alone encouraged. Because of the relatively passive nature of this learning, we may associate this education with our overall socialization: it fosters the adaptation of children to the grammar, in the broadest sense, of the society into which they were born. The other education alongside liberal education is vocational or professional. Unlike grammar education, it does presuppose the initiative of students as its prime motivation. They choose, as responsible adults, to expend money, time, and effort in acquiring the expertise requisite for a specific occupation. This education thus represents a shift in its students from adapting to the world to controlling a part of it. However, as Aristotle would point out, the part that is mastered pertains to the subservient side of our lives. This education may lead us to a living that amply satisfies our necessary needs, but it tells us little about what we might do with our leisure, our free life.

A liberal education is thus distinct from, and does not grow automatically out of, our grammar and professional educations. The former may successfully turn one into a well-adjusted, gregarious, and loyal member of one's society. One may then successfully graduate from the latter education a well-trained, skillful, innovative contributor to this society who is individually and plentifully rewarded. But that society might be an authoritarian and exploitative police state. And this person might well have learned no reason to care.

THE ISSUE OF ELITISM

We may already sense something problematic about this Aristotelian way of thinking. Yet its demise could be fatal for liberal education. To spell out why, I shall focus on two common and familiar complaints about this education today, ones that are likely to incite the kind of anger voiced by the mother in this chapter's opening. When we articulate these concerns, it becomes clear that they especially target the pertinence of the *artes liberales* ideal to our type of democracy. However, I shall also argue that, if we then try to base liberal education instead on the liberal-free ideal, we lose any compelling reason to distinguish the former from grammar and vocational educations. The mother would then be right to demand that her son's college abolish its liberal education requirements.

I turn to complaint number one. However it is exactly phrased, it points to the fact that liberal educators do not evidently even try to offer their students anything of specific, measurable, accountable practical value. They do not advertise that studying Jane Austen's novels will improve your love life, for instance, or that understanding the categorical imperative will land you a job in a top law firm. To be sure, some of them and their advocates hasten to reassure us that this education *is* beneficial nonetheless. They point to the many prosperous careers of its students. Perhaps the data does support a contention of this kind. Still, it cannot conceal the stubborn, customary disinclination on the part of most of these educators to make explicit promises about how their teaching will make a difference. They proffer only the vaguest answers to the question of what makes a class on Sophocles, and its hefty price tag, worth it, answers that in any case can scarcely be verified. We should not be surprised that the mother of our opening pages may find this fishy.

Complaint two is related to the previous one: liberal education is actually elitist and antidemocratic. This grows out of the previous suspicion that it ignores what working people positively want. From here, it is but a small step to identify other needs and interests that this education similarly seems to be brushing aside, whether thoughtlessly or nefariously. Given that its traditional curriculum is mainly composed of works of men, it fails to represent adequately women's experiences. Given that it is Eurocentric, it fails to address the experiences of people living in other parts of the world and in other cultures, except in often derogatorily stereotypic terms. The same holds for issues of sexual orientation. Broadly speaking, the multiculturalist critique of conventional liberal education curricula that emerged in the 1980s and the association of such curricula with high culture as opposed to popular culture are consistent with skepticism that liberal education actually serves anyone beyond the already privileged. No matter how openminded and disputatious liberal education's culture may appear to be, its overarching political orientation seems to be protective of the powerful and the status quo they enforce.

Both of these complaints attack a central principle of the Aristotelian conception of liberal education, namely that what this education aims to cultivate is freedom from slavishness. "Slavishness," to repeat, is concern for fulfilling the demands of necessary labor. As the term indicates, those who are preoccupied with this worry resemble, at least to Aristotle and his fellow ancient Greeks, slaves—that is, the people in their society who really were coercively tasked with these necessities. What enabled someone to be an engaged and equal citizen in the *polis* were the servants he ordered around; they were the condition for him having leisure and acting as a member of the ruling class. For us, of course, this is utterly unacceptable. Our modern democracy prohibits anyone from being reduced to slavery so that someone else can be free. As a consequence, everyone has to take care of their own basic needs. Only the most sheltered and coddled person who delusively refuses to see the unnaturalness and likely injustice of their condition would disdain this concern as "slavish."

At the very least, then, the Aristotelian conception of liberal education goes against the grain of modern democracy. If it was originally meant to foster the development of democratic virtues, it surely seems to hamper that today for us. No wonder, then, we are bound to object to an education that calls insulation from the ordinary condition of folks, not to mention that of various subaltern groups around the world, "freedom." And even when a liberal education curriculum does not do this explicitly, no wonder that, when we are required to take courses that ignore occupational concerns in favor of something "higher," we feel we are being sold an expensive accessory that will not work on the standard equipment most people have outside the ivory tower.

Suppose, then, that we give up once and for all on the *artes liberales* ideal and try to revise and continue the liberal education tradition on the basis of its liberal-free conception. Let us imagine promoting this education as a vehicle for cultivating freedom from dogmatism and freedom to pursue truth. Why might this as well be looked at askance by not only our mother but also our fellow, nonliberal educators? The answer is that the latter surely think that their endeavors too serve this freedom. Neither the grammar-school arithmetic teacher nor the music-business professor would for a moment understand themselves to be dealing in dogma. Along these lines, when we think of the kind of courses in general intellectual skills that typically form part of a student's liberal education requirements, such as classes in "expository writing" or "critical thinking," two things are apt to strike us. First, these sorts of courses may be viewed as straightforward extensions of one's grammar education: they remain concerned with the project of socialization. And secondly, the skills that they feature need not be viewed as existing abstracted from all particular fields of study; rather, they may be cultivated in the context of any number of different fields. Accordingly, why not work on one's writing in response to journalism rather than literature or improve one's critical thinking by examining debates about corporate strategy rather than theology? The main point I am driving at is that, if liberal education becomes entirely about advancing freedom from dogmatism and freedom to seek truth, then it will lose its distinctiveness vis-à-vis grammar and vocational education. Any teacher will feel justifiably entitled to think that they are providing a liberal education. And added to our mother's suspicions will be one that the specific liberal education courses she is required to pay for are simply the spoils of power struggles among a college's faculty and administrators and have little to do with students' genuine welfare.

Indeed, it does not take undue cynicism to wonder if the growing marketization of liberal education programs and colleges today to countries around the world is not facilitated precisely by the vagueness of what this education stands for. What enables a university to accept an enormous "signing gift" from a rich state's rulers after agreeing to open and run a "liberal arts" branch campus in their manifestly undemocratic country is that few universities have any sense that there is anything incongruous in this action. (To be sure, it is conceivable that the rulers are self-denying visionaries who want to lay the groundwork for a democracy to come and that the university leaders are in fact subversive liberators who only accept the money as a cover.) Most treat the "freedom" evoked by liberal education to be a rote and decorative matter, like the presence of classical nymphs and shepherds in a nineteenth-century landscape painting. Who believes it actually means anything? Hence, if this education, like the painting, fetches a good price because its brand provides wealthy consumers with some kitschy cachet, why not take advantage? And when evocations of freedom are no longer in educational fashion, one can easily rename the enterprise—nothing really substantial will be lost.

What is liberal education, then, for those of us who want it still to make a real difference to societies today? How may we find meaning in its idea rather than use its meaninglessness as an opportunity to profit from its simulation? In particular, how may we find a way to square its original inspiration in the Aristotelian idea of freedom with the hard-won, anti-elitist scruples of modern democracy? These questions broach the hope of reaffirming this education's tradition by unearthing new possibilities for us that are latent in its original idea.

My first step in this direction, however, is actually one away from the liberal arts and their institutions. Instead, I follow the lead of Jean-Jacques Rousseau and John Dewey, who critically evaluated formal education practices of their days with respect to how well they accorded with and augmented a prior, informal education that these philosophers claimed we are, largely unconsciously, undergoing (Dewey 1916/1985; Rousseau 1979). Analogously, I want to hypothesize the existence of an education that many of us experience outside of schools or any other institutions, in the "wild." Unsurprisingly, while the experiences that compose it are familiar enough, they are hardly recognized to constitute an "education" since we are so used to automatically equating the term with schooling. Nevertheless, in the next section, I try to explain why these experiences are well described as an "education" and how this view grows out of a roughly Aristotelian sense of freedom. My name for this web of experiences is *existential education.*[2]

THE QUESTION OF MEANING

Let me return to this chapter's opening anecdote and focus on the mother's son. Imagine that he has actually watched quite closely the preceding college career of his older cousin. She was very taken by her liberal education courses and ended up majoring in art history. After graduation, though, she found it hard to engage the interest of employers; she has consequently been bouncing from one temporary, low-paying job to another, struggling to make ends meet. The main reason the young man has decided to major in engineering is that he is determined to avoid this fate.

He knows he cannot assume that his basic needs will be magically taken care of. Hence, this already mature and serious person is ready to invest all his energy in securing for himself and his family healthy, comfortable, and long lives. If and when he encounters in his classes Aristotle's critique of this kind of life as slavish, he will be dubious, to say the least. What could possibly be preferable about his cousin's precarious situation?

If we pursue this question seriously, rather than treating it as rhetorical, we may find that it stirs in us a certain kind of anxiety. Its hook is the concept of *necessary needs.* What exactly makes them necessary? Obviously, they are the ones that must be met if our biological life is to continue. Because everything in our life depends on maintaining our bodies' health, it follows that we would want to prioritize the latter's requirements. Far from being slavish, a life that is devoted to keeping its physical host in good running order, such that we are as free from suffering and illness as much as possible for as long as possible, seems the very paradigm of common sense. Who would want to depart from it?

Yet the project of satisfying these necessary needs is bound to succumb eventually to a stronger necessity. Everyone must die. The more effort and resources we pour into deferring this end, then, the more troubled we are apt to become about our inevitable failure someday. At some point, our investment will be to no avail. In the meantime, we may be haunted by all the things we gave up, and all the roads we did not take, to "make it." Even as we strive to reassure ourselves about our bodies' health, then, we may be unsettling our souls.

This anxiety about mortality may eventually take articulate form as a familiar set of questions: What is the point of prolonging one's life if ultimately all will be lost, including one's memories of pleasures that might as well have never been? What makes living the life one is given at birth worth the troubles it entails, especially all the suffering one experiences and causes in others? What reason is there for addressing one's biological needs and going on, rather than ignoring them and giving up? Does continuing one's life have some sort of meaning? Needless to say, these are classic existential questions. They make sense to virtually everyone. What makes them also the butt of endless jokes is that hardly anyone believes they can be authoritatively resolved. Nevertheless, many of us would admit that we have been at some point struck by them, often when we are struggling with some serious loss that arouses serious doubt. Regardless of whether the questions have conclusive answers, then, they appear unavoidable. Accordingly, my claim that many of us are engaged in an existential education outside of schools is based simply on the fact that mortal beings like ourselves are bound to respond to the questionable meaning of our lives. We may not do this very clearly or methodically, but the clichéd, old-hat quality of the questions testifies that they have already taken up residence in us.

Now, when such questions stress the possibility of understandingly affirming our mortal lives, they are also confirming that we are in a crucial sense free. The fact that we can give up on life as not worth the trouble means that our biological needs are not as necessary as all that. We need not assume that the direction of our lives is predetermined by them. Following the least resistant path to satisfying these needs, as the mother's son understands himself to be doing, is one among several options before a person. Depending on one's understanding of one's life and death, one may pursue a different path. The riddle of existential meaning thus presupposes that those who respond to it are free from even their biological necessities (should they be willing to perish then and there) and free to determine a meaningful life course, however short it may be, for themselves.

What would such a life look like, at least generally, from the outside? I imagine it would be one that is, to be sure, responsive to the demands of self-preservation. Like most of us today, the person concerned would have to take responsibility for making their own living. Moreover, this person would consciously accept that the necessity of doing this is bound to bow in the end to that of death. What truly distinguishes the person's life, then, would be the realization that one does not have to be simply *resigned* to this eventual fate. One can wholeheartedly embrace it. One may decide to die, or to view one's life, from its very commencement, as one long process of dying, willingly and freely rather than defeatedly. And why would one do this? The reason would be that one has found and understood something that one wants to give one's life to— that one wants actively to die for. A good part of the sting of mortality dissipates when it is understood as the condition for a life of meaningful *devotion*.

When I suggest that this way of life, however sketchily I portray it, is the prize of our existential educations, I am claiming that most of us feel its attractive force; we would be glad to adopt some version of it if this were practically feasible. The crucial challenge to this feasibility, of course, is that of finding the sacred thing for which one is willing to die. Since I am not in the guru business, I will be excused if I do not hand it over forthwith. Perhaps we may look for it together, though, in the neighborhood of those experiences that bring us face to face with death in the first place.

Moments of palpable peril, such as when we stand on the threshold of catastrophe or violence: these naturally arouse in us an awareness of mortality. However, I propose to focus on a kind of experience that usually involves much less bodily risk. It does not require that we put ourselves in actual danger of dying. Nevertheless, it evokes death because it is characterized by the felt loss of self-possession. In its grip, for a moment, our whole sense of who we each are is torn away, and this persona's existence is terminated. This is the experience of mortification.

Examples of it may range from the mild to the permanently scarring. Imagine a man at a party blurting out after a few drinks a racist remark. Or, imagine a woman, famous for taking a stand as a politician against abortion, facing her supporters after her own recent, secret abortion has been exposed by the press. Common to these and the like is the experience of suddenly, and shockingly, being deprived of our identities. The politician's may represent a rather anodyne case: she presumably already knew she is not who she tries to seem to be, and she may be quite prepared for the likelihood of her lie collapsing. Nevertheless, a pang of shame may catch her off guard. As for the man, his friends may laugh off the insult ostensibly directed at them. They may reassure him that their self-esteem has not been touched. But the violence of his blush, and his later, mysteriously overwhelming aversion to any company at all, symptomatically indicate that he is no longer able to trust himself.

What triggers these kinds of experiences is the eye of the other, the disbelieving view that someone may take on who we suppose ourselves to be. Most of the time, we steer away from mortification by associating with people like ourselves who are more or less predisposed to collude sympathetically with our self-conceptions, as we do with theirs. On occasion, though, we run into strangers who lack this sympathy mainly because they are not in any historical relationship to us. For the purposes of this elucidation of existential education, then, I define the stranger as someone who mortifyingly dispossesses a person of their own self-possession and self-conception, thus disclosing that this person is really an alien to themselves. The person may in turn play the role of a stranger for someone else.

Suppose, then, that we lived in a world—call it an expanded *polis* or a *cosmopolis*, to invite the Aristotle connection—in which we are all equally strangers to each other. Each person repeatedly brings home to their fellow inhabitants a taste of mortifying death. Each person reminds them of Arthur Rimbaud's insight, *"Je est un autre"* (I is an other) (1973: 202). As upsetting as this may be, if we can check by law any impulse to eliminate each other—hardly the easiest proposition, history and current politics tell us—this world could serve as a stage for our existential educations. Such, at any rate, is my suggestion, motivated by the sense that our actual world is not all that different from this one, roiled as it is by seemingly ineradicable misunderstanding and mistrust of otherness. Instead of mourning the comfort that such mortification destroys, however, I want to take seriously how this world's inhabitants would raise for each other the question of the meaning of this kind of death. In this *cosmopolis*, everyone is in effect asked this question by their neighbor: Is there something for which I would be *willing* to lose my self-possession in the eyes of surrounding strangers? Something for which I may likewise, by extension, be willing to lose my life? More pointedly, could my life with such strangers, our being together in the same predicament, democratically, be precisely what leads me to this sacred thing? Could it be my existential education?[3]

If we allow this line of thinking to take flight in admittedly rather abstract language, it may lead us to a distinctive way of understanding what it means for something to *be*. Consider, first, what makes mortification generally possible. It is our ultimately uncontrollable responsiveness to each other. No matter how composed we may be, the stranger can always surprise. A world of strangers, then, is one that is always reminding each of us that we are *not*, however much we may wish we were, beings who regard things from a safe distance, trying to

FIGURE 9.2 Aristotle, located in Aristotle's park, Stagira, Halkidiki, Greece. *Source:* sneska / iPhoto.

make up our own, autonomous minds about what we each want and how we each shall act. Exposed to each other, we *are responding* to the things, including conceptions of ourselves, which strangers have already communicated to us, provokingly. Indeed, this overarching framework of social responsiveness, Jean-Luc Nancy (2000) suggests, may be understood to be an ontological condition of whatever exists. Accordingly, if something *is* at all, it is in this world framework and is conditioned by it. This means that things are not at bottom objective beings or objects. They *are*—they engage in the activity of being—*socially*.

What follows from this? One consequence is that strangers communicate things to us as a *surprise*. Not only their views of us but also everything they pass on and share disconcerts us, reminds us of how alien our exterior, social being is to our inner self-understanding in this suddenly stranger world. To stress this amazement we may feel at a thing's very being in this framework of social responsiveness, then, I draw attention to the thing's *appearing*. It emerges from out of nowhere, from out of nonbeing. In a framework of objectivity, of course, appearance is understood to be the opposite of truth, and true things are supposed to be already there as such. In our framework, on the contrary, appearing is the truth of the *miraculous*. It reminds us that we live in a world that is fundamentally based not on loss but on an inexplicable surplus: where nothing was, there appears something. If, in contrast to the disenchanted rationalist, we acknowledge that such appearing is enchanting, our mortification, our loss of self-possession, may be accepted by us as something less tragic than comic. We might even affirm it as a condition for gaining access to the immortal miracle.

Now, in this world, once something appears, what does it appear as? Here, again, I want to underscore our constant, unsealable openness to *thaumazein*, a Greek term that Arendt beautifully glosses as "the shocked wonder at the miracle of Being" (1998: 302). Because it may still surprise us, because it is still appearing, the thing the stranger communicates is not yet anything set. It cannot be itself, something finally identifiable. Rather, in our socially responsive world, this thing can only be coming to be. It *is* as an *intimation*.

Having drawn out a bit the ontological dimension of this *cosmopolis*, I can bring matters closer to earth by summarily characterizing the things of our socially responsive world as things *being born*. They appear, breathtakingly, out of nonbeing. And they have not yet taken definitive form. In this sense, they resemble our children, who inspire our wonder and call for our celebration and assistance. We all know how natural it is to devote ourselves to them, even to die for them. What I am suggesting, then, is that, just as the birth of a child can fill its parents' lives with meaning, so the appearing of all sorts of unpredictable things communicated by strangers can inspire us to give our lives to their care. Like the famous duck/rabbit figure, the world of our mortification can flip into the world of our existential education, where, in particular, education is rooted in *ēdūcere*, the experience of being led out. What we would be led out to is the possibility of actively dying for something beyond us being born.

In support of my claim that this education is not *that* unfamiliar, as evidence that many of us, at least, are currently undergoing it, let me note how continuous it is with the socializing process that Dewey (1916/1985) describes in *Democracy and Education*. According to him, we experience a primal, natural education beyond the schools just by virtue of taking part in communication. The latter is the process by which we are formed as rational individuals and by which our community at the same time regenerates itself. What I am doing here may be understood to be simply emphasizing the existential stakes of this Deweyan conception. As we transmit and share experiences, the question of the meaning of our mortal lives becomes increasingly recognizable, and we evoke for each other possible answers. (Not *the* answer.) Furthermore, I find that a conception of communication that stresses our mortification by ever-proliferating kinds of strangers captures the sense that the world is marked by ineliminable difference, a sense more prevalent in our time than in Dewey's. As a counterpart to his hope that we may all be finally gathered into a democratic community with a strong sense of solidarity, I want to hold out the possibility that the very mode of sharing that seems to frustrate such assimilation because it constantly dispossesses us of our individual and collective identities may nevertheless act democratically on us in a way that we all may each affirm. The stranger may awaken us to possibilities of which we have never dreamed. For that reason, our weaker, more vulnerable, and changeable sense of identity and belonging may matter less if we realize that it is precisely these strangers who are our prophets. They intimate what calls for our devotion.

Finally, in preparing to return to the discussion of liberal education, let me also recall that this existential education is predicated on an idea of freedom, one whose Aristotelian kinship may now be more apparent. Revising Aristotle's insistence on a distance from "slavish" labor, we affirm a distance from the biological need that seems to make such labor necessary. And revising his notion that the resulting leisure should be dedicated to political action, we actively support the cosmopolitan world of our mutual responsiveness for the sake of finding in it something being born to die for. Freedom from a meaningless life, freedom to participate in our existential education: these are what the liberal education still coming to be may enhance.

AN EMERGING POSSIBILITY

What is liberal education? For us, it could institutionally embody our collective support for each of our existential educations. Liberal educators would proceed from the premise that thinking mortals are generally responsive not only to the need for self-preservation but also to that for self-giving. We are looking for something to which to devote our lives, meaningfully. When we allow ourselves to pursue this quest, we claim our existential freedom. Analogous to how Aristotelian liberal educators guided their students in the use of their *scholē*, liberal educators today may guide us in the exercise of this freedom.

Another comparison with Aristotle is also illuminating. Just as he did not take into account whether students want to be free, so we may understand that our liberal education does not depend on the desires of students. Admittedly, this may sound counterintuitive: if the whole point is to recognize and cultivate a student's freedom, then why should not one be at liberty to opt out of this education if one feels like it? The reason, recalling our earlier discussion of *scholē*, is that freedom is not at all synonymous with doing what one wants. There is a crucial difference between license and self-government and, more specifically for our purposes, between license and self-giving. To be sure, as students enter into adulthood, they ought to be treated with respect for their responsible autonomy. In concrete terms, this means, among other things, that they should be encouraged to exercise choice in the classes they take. However, in the same way that we do not invite novices to determine which courses communicate the knowledge necessary for brain surgery, so we should realize that there is no educational contradiction in offering elective courses within a curricular framework of liberal education requirements.

Since our discussion has moved to matters of curriculum, this may be a fitting place to consider whether our liberal education, pursuing the tradition established by our medieval precursors, should remain keyed to the initiation of students into certain practices. Are there liberal arts that cultivate existential freedom? In my view, there are, but I do not see that they map onto distinct fields of study or subject matter, such as rhetoric or astronomy. I am not sure how acquiring a certain body of knowledge or know-how, such as historical facts about class struggle in Italy or the skills to evaluate Anselm's proof of God's existence, would, by themselves, make a crucial difference to one's existential education. Conversely, I have no reason to doubt that the study of other topics, such as the emergence of the AIDS virus or black-hole theory, could matter to someone's existential education. Given this uncertainty, then, I shall only very preliminarily suggest that we might try to center liberal education on encouraging and disseminating the practice of two cross-curricular liberal arts.

The first is one of questioning. When teachers question students, they are usually requesting either an action from them—as in, "Johnny, could you please pass me the big scissors?"—or, more significantly, the correct solution to a problem—as in, "Who can tell me how long it would take a beam of light to reach here from Alpha Centauri?" The chief questions of a liberal educator, in contrast, could aim to draw student attention to a problem that can have no authoritative answer. Indeed, the predicament that these questions constantly evoke is that the students, like the rest of us, are not who they think they are and live in a more mysterious world than they realized. Practitioners of this art of "torpedo-fish" questioning, to recollect Socrates' paradigm example in Plato's *Meno* (80a–80b), in effect, but under carefully supportive conditions, mortify us. They deliberately suspend our self-possession and self-conceptions and spur us to acknowledge our primal openness to the unknown.

That such kind of Socratic questioning on the part of liberal educators may not only arouse the experience of *aporia* in students but also provoke the latter to respond with their own words points to a second crucial liberal art: that of conversation. Liberal education turns on the move from mortification to inspiration, from feeling threatened by strangers to feeling appreciatively revitalized by these surprising messengers. In his elegant and insightful writing on this kind of education, Oakeshott emphasizes it is the form and virtues of conversation that enable this turn to take place. Because we are naturally responsive to diverse others, we should more fittingly communicate with them not in tones of "assertion and denial" but in those of "acknowledgment and accommodation" (Oakeshott 1991: 187). Such a mode of exchange cannot be reduced to a debate or an argument; it does not try to prove a point by triumphing over others. Rather, it is an open-ended adventure in thinking with others who are not "disconcerted by the differences or dismayed by the inconclusiveness of it all" (p. 39). When we initiate students into a conversation about questions that concern the mortal meaning of their lives, we are encouraging them to experience their responsiveness to strangers as a good. These people, whether they are teachers, authors, or fellow students, have the power to surprise and inspire us with intimations of the world being born. It is the latter, not information or knowledge, that is ultimately at stake in our exchanges with them.

These liberal arts of Socratic questioning and Oakeshottian conversation may be applied to materials from many different fields of study. Accordingly, a liberal education for us may be distinguished from grammar and vocational education less by its content than by its pedagogy and the freedom it stimulates. Furthermore, these arts evidently combine traits of both the philosophical and the oratorical ideals. An education that cultivates them would be one that reaffirms a tradition that emerged in the Middle Ages in response to an Aristotelian conception of freedom yet that finds in that original inspiration a prior question of existential freedom to which it is newly responsive. It would be a modernist liberal education.

Would it be supported by our mother? To make this question more tractable, I propose to separate it from the financial cost of such support. Admittedly, taking it out of the world of capitalist *realpolitik* and placing it in one of ideal theory dispels most of its actual difficulty. But this maneuver has the virtue of focusing the issue on what is *educationally* good. If price were not the overriding factor, would our mother want this liberal education for her son? In particular, would she continue to worry that it has no practical value or that it is antidemocratic?

Grounds for persuading her otherwise are already clear. Once one realizes that, prior to being a worker in search of comfort and security, one is a human being concerned with one's mortality and what might redeem it, the practical value of educations that are exclusively grammatical or vocational in nature is bound to appear limited. Such educations do not address the challenge of living a meaningful life, one in which we are each personally at stake and thus one that cannot be merely a matter for theoretical speculation. In comparison, liberal education is concerned precisely with what is of ultimate practical value.

As for this education's support of democracy, this point follows from its affirmation that we gain access to this prize precisely through our questioning conversation with strangers, not through any instruction by authorities. Conversation presupposes equal responsiveness and respect among all its participants: everyone has something to say, something that may be epiphanic for someone else. Accordingly, many of the multiculturalist critiques of liberal education curricula and "canons" are quite true to the education's genuine spirit. Indeed, the more that we appreciate the power of its kind of conversation to surprise us and thus evoke the world's appearing, and then to accommodate our various responses to such surprise and thus demonstrate the world's open-endedness, the more we may come to understand ourselves to be less the utilizers than the vehicles of this collective way of being democratic. I already noted that in Aristotle's view a democracy requires the support of both a system of laws and a project of education. Immanuel Kant (1785/1990) encapsulates the former in his conception of a realm of ends in which we are each both law-givers and law-followers. Mikhail Bakhtin captures what it would mean for liberal education to be the very life blood of democracy in his conception of polyphonic dialogue: "It is not a means for revealing ... the already ready-made character of a person; no, in dialogue a person ... becomes for the first time that which he is ... not only for others but for himself as well. To be means to communicate dialogically" (1984: 252).

All of this is still a possibility for us. We can find meaning in renewing the liberal education tradition.

NOTES

1 Associated with *scholē* is also the concept of study; see McClintock (1971) and more recently Lewis (2015), Masschelein (2011), and Ruitenberg (2017).

2 In this, I build on the work of Maxine Greene, who prominently linked education and existentialism; see Greene (1967) and (1973).

3 Incidentally, this revised conception of a *polis* plays off of Hannah Arendt's influential account of the original historical society. In *The Human Condition*, she explains that the original *polis* provided its citizens with a stable stage on which

they could exercise, display, and be admired for their individually distinguishing "greatness" (1998: 192–9). They could attain a kind of immortality in the eyes of others. I am imagining, on the contrary, a *polis* in which its members are all mortified. Perhaps, though, this experience leads in a different way to something immortal.

REFERENCES

Primary sources

Arcilla, René V. (2010), *Mediumism: A Philosophical Reconstruction of Modernism for Existential Learning*, Albany: State University of New York Press.

Arendt, Hannah (1998), *The Human Condition*, Chicago: University of Chicago Press.

Aristotle (2013), *Aristotle's* Politics, trans. Carnes Lord, Chicago: University of Chicago Press.

Bakhtin, Mikhail (1984), *Problems of Dostoevsky's Poetics*, trans. Caryl Emerson, Minneapolis: University of Minnesota Press.

Dewey, John (1916/1985), *Democracy and Education: An Introduction to the Philosophy of Education*, in J.A. Boydston (ed.), *John Dewey, the Middle Works 1899–1924*, Vol. 9: *Democracy and Education 1916*, Carbondale: Southern Illinois University Press.

Kant, Immanuel (1785/1990), *Foundations of the Metaphysics of Morals*, trans. Lewis White Beck, New York: Macmillan.

Kimball, Bruce A. (1986), *Orators and Philosophers: A History of the Idea of Liberal Education*, New York: Teachers College Press.

Mill, John Stuart (1859/1978), *On Liberty*, ed. Elizabeth Rappaport, Indianapolis, IN: Hackett.

Nancy, Jean-Luc (2000), *Being Singular Plural*, trans. Robert D. Richardson and Anne E. O'Byrne, Stanford, CA: Stanford University Press.

Oakeshott, Michael (1989), *The Voice of Liberal Learning: Michael Oakeshott on Education*, ed. Timothy Fuller, New Haven, CT: Yale University Press.

Oakeshott, Michael (1991), *Rationalism in Politics and Other Essays*, Indianapolis, IN: Liberty Press.

Plato (1997), *Meno*, trans. G.M.A. Grube, in *Complete Works*, ed. John M. Cooper, Indianapolis, IN: Hackett.

Rimbaud, Arthur (1973), *Poésies, Une saison en enfer, Illuminations*, ed. Louis Forestier, Paris: Gallimard.

Rousseau, Jean-Jacques (1979), *Emile, or On Education*, trans. Allan Bloom, New York: Basic Books.

Secondary sources

Greene, Maxine (1967), *Existential Encounters for Teachers*, New York: Random House.

Greene, Maxine (1973), *Teacher As Stranger: Educational Philosophy for the Modern Age*, Belmont, CA, Wadsworth Publishing.

Kimball, Bruce A. (2010), *The Liberal Arts Tradition: A Documentary History*, Lanham, MD: University Press of America.

Lewis, Tyson (2015), *On Study: Giorgio Agamben and Educational Potentiality*, New York: Routledge.

Masschelein, Jan (2011), "Experimentum Scholae: The World Once More ... But Not (Yet) Finished," *Studies in Philosophy and Education*, 30 (5): 529–35.

McClintock, Robbie (1971), "Toward a Place for Study in a World of Instruction," *Teachers College Record*, 73 (2): 161–205.

Ruitenberg, Claudia W., ed. (2017), *Reconceptualizing Study in Educational Discourse and Practice*, New York: Routledge.

CONTRIBUTORS

René V. Arcilla is Professor of Philosophy of Education at New York University. He is the author of numerous articles and of the books *For the Love of Perfection: Richard Rorty and Liberal Education* (1995); *Mediumism: A Philosophical Reconstruction of Modernism for Existential Learning* (2010); and *Wim Wenders's Road Movie Philosophy: Education Without Learning* (2020). His scholarly and teaching interests include existentialism, modernism, and liberal education. He has served as President of the Philosophy of Education Society and is currently coeditor of a book series published by Bloomsbury Academic entitled *Philosophies of Education in Art, Cinema, and Literature.*

Lovisa Bergdahl is Associate Professor of General Pedagogy at Södertörn University, Stockholm, Sweden. Her research can be placed in the intersection of humanities-based traditions of scholarship and pedagogic theory, drawing mainly on feminist and postsecular philosophy. She is particularly interested in values education exploring questions around the formative task of schools in pluralistic contexts. Her recent publications include "Educationally Connecting to the Past in Teaching: In Philosophical Perspectives on Teacher Training" in the edited volume by M. Peters (ed.), *Encyclopedia of Teacher Education* (2019); and the article "Pedagogical Postures: A Feminist Search for a Geometry of the Educational Relation" in the journal *Ethics and Education* (2018).

Agata Bielik-Robson is Professor of Jewish Studies at the University of Nottingham and Professor of Philosophy at the Polish Academy of Sciences. She has published articles in Polish, English, German, French, and Russian on philosophical aspects of psychoanalysis, romantic subjectivity, and the philosophy of religion (especially Judaism and its crossings with modern philosophical thought). Her publications include the books *The Saving Lie: Harold Bloom and Deconstruction* (2011), *Judaism in Contemporary Thought: Traces and Influence* (coedited with Adam Lipszyc, 2014), *Philosophical Marranos: Jewish Cryptotheologies of Late Modernity* (2014), and *Another Finitude: Messianic Vitalism and Philosophy* (2019).

Maughn Rollins Gregory is Professor of Educational Foundations at Montclair State University, where he succeeded Matthew Lipman as the director of the Institute for the Advancement of Philosophy for Children in 2001. He publishes and teaches in the areas of philosophy of education, philosophy for children, pragmatism, gender studies, Socratic pedagogy, and contemplative pedagogy.

Robert Haworth teaches at both New Mexico State University and Western New Mexico University. He has published and presented internationally on anarchism, youth culture, informal learning spaces, and critical social studies education. He is the editor of *Anarchist Pedagogies: Collective Actions, Theories and Critical Reflections on Education* (2012) and more recently coedited (with Mark Bray) *Anarchist Education and the Modern School: A Francisco Ferrer Reader* (2018).

Chris Higgins is Associate Professor in the Department of Teaching, Curriculum, and Society in the Boston College Lynch School of Education and Human Development. He has written on the dynamics of the teacher–student relationship; action research and the philosophy of inquiry; ignorance and open-mindedness; humanism and liberal learning; imagination and aesthetic education; practice and vocational formation; and general education and personal integration. His book *The Good Life of Teaching: An Ethics of Professional Practice* (2011) offers one of the first systematic extensions of virtue ethics to questions concerning work and professional identity. His current book project is titled *Essays on Educational Integrity*.

Elisabeth Langmann is Senior Lecturer in Education at Södertörn University, Sweden. She is currently the chair of the Nordic Society for Philosophers of Education. Placing educational practice and social justice at the center of her work, her research is situated within the field of the philosophy and theory of education and is informed primarily by continental philosophy and feminist theory. Her research interest focuses on tolerance, care, hospitality, the complex nature of educational encounters, and on embodied dimensions of teaching and learning. Her recent articles include "Time for Values" (2017) and "Pedagogical Postures" (2018) both coauthored with Lovisa Bergdahl.

Christopher Martin is Associate Professor in the Faculty of Education and Associate Member of the Department of Economics, Philosophy, and Political Science at the University of British Columbia. He is the author of *Education in a Post-Metaphysical World* (2014), *R.S. Peters* (2014, with Stefaan Cuypers), and *Questioning the Classroom* (2016, with Dianne Gereluk, Bruce Maxwell, and Trevor Norris). His research areas include political philosophy and the philosophy of education. He is currently working on a project on the values and aims of higher education in liberal societies.

Anna Pagès was born in Barcelona in 1965. She has been Assistant Professor at Autonomous University of Barcelona and Senior Professor at the Open University of Catalonia (UOC). In 1992, she joined Ramon Llull University where she is a senior researcher in Philosophy of Education. Her field of study includes hermeneutics and education; tradition from a pedagogical perspective; feminist philosophy; and philosophical background from the early twentieth-century progressive school movement. Among other writings she has *published At the Edge of the Past* (2005); *On Oblivion* (2012); and *Dinner with Diotime: A Philosophy of the Feminine* (2017).

Troy Richardson (Saponi/Tuscarora) is Associate Professor in the American Indian and Indigenous Studies Program at Cornell University. As a philosopher of education and scholar in American Indian and Indigenous Studies, his research and teaching center on the intellectual traditions of Indigenous and other minoritized communities. He draws particular attention to the epistemological and ontological dimensions of Indigeneity as it is revealed in literature, visual culture, and nonfiction works by Indigenous peoples. He attends to conceptions of selfhood, ethics, gender, ecology, and power from Indigenous intellectual traditions to chart alternative social and philosophical imaginaries. His scholarship seeks to contribute to philosophical and theoretical discourses developed by Indigenous peoples to advance forms of decolonial education.

Peter Roberts is Professor of Education and Director of the Educational Theory, Policy and Practice Research Hub at the University of Canterbury in New Zealand. His research interests include the ethics and politics of education, literature and education, the pedagogy of Paulo Freire, and tertiary education policy. Among his recent books are *Education and the Limits of Reason: Reading Dostoevsky, Tolstoy and Nabokov* (2018, with Herner Saeverot), *Happiness, Hope, and Despair: Rethinking the Role of Education* (2016), and *Better Worlds: Education, Art, and Utopia* (2013, with John Freeman-Moir).

INDEX